T0305778

Central Banking in the Twentieth Century

Central banks are powerful but poorly understood organisations. In 1900 the Bank of Japan was the only central bank to exist outside Europe but over the past century central banking has proliferated. John Singleton here explains how central banks and the profession of central banking have evolved and spread across the globe during this period. He shows that the central banking world has experienced two revolutions in thinking and practice, the first after the depression of the early 1930s, and the second in response to the high inflation of the 1970s and 1980s. In addition, the central banking profession has changed radically. In 1900 the professional central banker was a specialised type of banker, whereas today he or she must also be a sophisticated economist and a public official. Understanding these changes is essential to explaining the role of central banks during the recent global financial crisis.

JOHN SINGLETON is Reader in History at Sheffield Hallam University. His previous publications include *Innovation and Independence: The Reserve Bank of New Zealand, 1973–2002* (2006).

Central Banking in the Twentieth Century

John Singleton

CAMBRIDGE
UNIVERSITY PRESS

CAMBRIDGE
UNIVERSITY PRESS

University Printing House, Cambridge CB2 8BS, United Kingdom

One Liberty Plaza, 20th Floor, New York, NY 10006, USA

477 Williamstown Road, Port Melbourne, VIC 3207, Australia

314-321, 3rd Floor, Plot 3, Splendor Forum, Jasola District Centre, New Delhi-110025, India

79 Anson Road, #06-04/06, Singapore 079906

Cambridge University Press is part of the University of Cambridge.

It furthers the University's mission by disseminating knowledge in the pursuit of education, learning and research at the highest international levels of excellence.

www.cambridge.org
Information on this title: www.cambridge.org/9780521899093

First published 2011
Reprinted 2012

A catalogue record for this publication is available from the British Library

Library of Congress Cataloging in Publication data
Singleton, John.
  Central banking in the twentieth century / John Singleton.
    p. cm.
  Includes bibliographical references and index.
  ISBN 978-0-521-89909-3
  1. Banks and banking, Central–History. I. Title.
  HG1811.S378 2011
  332.11009′04–dc22
                          2010035572

ISBN 978-0-521-89909-3 Hardback
ISBN 978-1-107-62876-2 Paperback

For Wendy

Contents

viii   Contents

Illustrations

Acknowledgements

I should like to thank a number of people and institutions who offered help of various kinds during the writing of this book. Liz Castle and the staff of the Knowledge Centre at the Reserve Bank of New Zealand provided congenial library facilities and, importantly, somewhere to hide from other calls upon my time. Members of staff at the Bank of England Archive were also very helpful. Mark Casson and his colleagues at the Centre for Institutional Performance, in the Henley Business School, University of Reading, kindly offered a base of operations in the UK during the winter of 2008–9. As part of my stay in Reading, I organised a workshop on central banking, at which the other speakers were Forrest Capie, James Forder, Alexander Mihailov, Catherine Schenk, and Richard Werner, and I thank them for their contributions. Victoria University of Wellington provided a measure of funding during my research leave in the UK. I presented papers arising from this project to seminars or conferences at the LSE, the RBNZ, Queensland University of Technology, and the University of Wolverhampton. I also had a number of interesting conversations on central banking with Muge Adalet, Michael Bordo, Mark Casson, Gary Hawke, Alexander Mihailov, and Michael Reddell. I am grateful to Michael Watson and Chloe Howell of Cambridge University Press for their efforts and to Rob Wilkinson (Out of House Publishing Solutions) and Alison Walker. I apologise to anyone omitted inadvertently from this list.

Abbreviations

BBC	British Broadcasting Corporation
BCCI	Bank of Credit and Commerce International
BCEAO	Banque Centrale des États de l'Afrique de l'Ouest
BdL	Bank deutscher Länder
BEAC	Banque des États de l'Afrique Centrale
BIS	Bank for International Settlements
BNB	Banque Nationale de Belgique
CAMA	Central African Monetary Area
CBA	Commonwealth Bank of Australia
CBBH	Central Bank of Bosnia-Herzegovina
CBC	Central Bank of China
CBM	central bank money
CCC	Competition and Credit Control
CEMLA	Center for Latin American Monetary Studies
CFA	Colonies Françaises d'Afrique
CHIPS	Clearing House Interbank Payments System
CLCB	Committee of London Clearing Bankers
CPI	consumer price index
CPSS	Committee on Payment and Settlement Systems
DCE	domestic credit expansion
DFC	Development Finance Corporation
DM	Deutsche Mark
DNS	deferred net settlement
ECB	European Central Bank
EEA	Exchange Equalization Account
EEC	European Economic Community
EMI	European Monetary Institute
EMS	European Monetary System
EMU	Economic and Monetary Union
EPU	European Payments Union
ERM	Exchange Rate Mechanism
ESCB	European System of Central Banks

ESF	Exchange Stabilization Fund
FFR	federal funds rate
FOMC	Federal Open Market Committee
FRBNY	Federal Reserve Bank of New York
FSA	Financial Services Authority
GAB	General Agreement to Borrow
IBI	Imperial Bank of India
IMF	International Monetary Fund
LMU	Latin Monetary Union
LTCM	Long-Term Capital Management
LZB	Landeszentralbanken
MPC	Monetary Policy Committee
NBFI	non-bank financial institution
NMC	National Monetary Commission
NRA	National Reserve Association
OCA	optimum currency area
OCR	official cash rate
OECD	Organisation for Economic Cooperation and Development
OEEC	Organisation for European Economic Cooperation
PBC	People's Bank of China
PTA	Policy Targets Agreement
RBA	Reserve Bank of Australia
RBC	risk-based capital
RBI	Reserve Bank of India
RBNZ	Reserve Bank of New Zealand
RBS	Royal Bank of Scotland
RFC	Reconstruction Finance Corporation
RTGS	real-time gross settlement
S&L	Savings and Loan
SARB	South African Reserve Bank
SDR	Special Drawing Right
SEACEN	South East Asian Central Bank
SEANZA	South East Asia New Zealand Australia
SMU	Scandinavian Monetary Union
SUMOC	Superintendency of Money and Credit
TARGET	Trans-European Automated Real-time Gross Settlement Express Transfer System
WAMU	West African Monetary Union
YSB	Yokohama Specie Bank

1   A beginner's guide to central banking

> When I went to Washington in 1979, most people thought the Federal
> Reserve was either a bonded bourbon or a branch of the National
> Guard.
>
>   Frederick H. Schultz, Vice-Chairman of the Board of Governors of the
>   Federal Reserve System, 1979–82 (Schultz 2005: 343)

> Central banking is a strange profession little understood by mem-
> bers of the public whose interests it exists to protect, by governments
> with which it shares responsibilities, or by financial institutions whose
> activities it to some degree controls. Those who practise it often feel
> themselves to be members of an international freemasonry, a kind of
> 'mystery' in the medieval sense of a group who possess some exclusive
> knowledge or skill, and indeed there has always been an element of
> mystery … about what central bankers do.
>
>   H. C. (Nugget) Coombs, Governor of the Australian Central Bank
>   1949–68 (Coombs, H. C. 1981: 141)

Most central banks nowadays claim to abide by the principle of transparency, yet the world of central banking retains an element of inscrut-
ability. This partly reflects the nature of the subject. Central banking is
a weightier and more technical business than chicken farming or running a bus company. Though central banking might not be as delicate
as brain surgery, or as complicated as the exploration of space, it is evidently a highly skilled trade. Until transparency became fashionable in
the late twentieth century, central bankers did little to promote a wider
understanding of their role. Shunning the limelight, their rare public statements were notable for brevity and calculated vagueness. Such
reticence was often excused by referring to the (central) banker's duty
to respect client confidentiality.

    The public knew that central banks were important and powerful even
if they did not fully understand them, and this created a problem. As
Dan Brown readers will understand, there is a market for blockbusters
on powerful and esoteric organisations. Some years ago, William Greider
(1987), a journalist, published an 800-page exposé of the Federal Reserve
System entitled *Secrets of the Temple*. Greider argued that the Fed was a

mysterious, capricious, and immensely powerful force in the US economy. More recently, an economic historian, Peter Temin, has remarked upon the curious ability of central banks to alter the behaviour of those who come into contact with them: 'There is a theory of personality that says when in church people act church and I think that the economic analog of that is when in central bank people act central bank' (quoted in Parker 2002: 37–8). At the time of writing, in August 2009, Congressman Ron Paul was campaigning for the more intrusive auditing of the Fed: 'What information are they hiding from the American people?' (Paul 2009b).

By coincidence, *Secrets of the Temple* was published at a time when academic economists and even some central bankers were beginning to show greater interest in matters of transparency and accountability. In an important paper on 'Monetary mystique', Marvin Goodfriend (1986), an economist at the Federal Reserve Bank of Richmond, called for more research into the pros and cons of central bank secrecy. This research programme gathered pace over the following decade. Of course, secrecy had its uses. Central banks conducted many transactions on behalf of governments and needed to obtain the best deal for their clients. In the short run, moreover, central banks could exert a bigger impact on financial markets by taking them by surprise, though this was at the cost of generating uncertainty and mistrust in the long run. Nevertheless, there was a strong case for public policy agencies such as central banks to become more transparent.

By 2000 most central banks were much more open than they had been in 1990, and even expressed pride in this transformation. People in the early twenty-first century had better access to information about central banks and their activities than ever before. In order to understand any type of organisation, however, it is necessary to examine its history. Organisations and their functions and methods evolve over time. Their attitudes and behaviour are moulded by past successes and failures. Central banks today are in many respects very different from central banks one hundred years ago. Telling the history of central banking is an important aspect of the process of demystification. The purpose of this volume is not to unearth conspiracies; rather it is to make the central banking past more transparent by synthesising the work of hundreds of economists, historians, and political scientists, and even the writings of central bankers themselves.

Central bank histories

There is already a substantial literature on the history of central banks. The most useful previous synthesis is provided by Goodhart, Capie, and Schnadt (1994) in a volume marking the tercentenary of the Bank of England. The thickest books on central banking history have been commissioned by central banks themselves. Central banks have a strong corporate culture (Mooij 2005), and sponsoring an institutional history is one way of preserving and celebrating that culture.

The Bank of England was a pioneer, commissioning a two-volume work, totalling 765 pages, on the period from 1694 to 1914, which was published to mark the bank's 250th anniversary in 1944 (Clapham 1944). Further massive instalments appeared in 1976 and 1992 (Sayers 1976; Fforde 1992), and the volume on the 1960s and 1970s is in press. There was a trickle of imitators. For example, a massive history of the Reserve Bank of India (RBI) up to 1951 (Simha 1970), and a briefer history of the Reserve Bank of New Zealand (RBNZ), appeared in the early 1970s (Hawke 1973).

With increased openness in the 1990s, more official histories appeared. Schedvin (1992) published a hefty volume on central banking in Australia up to the mid 1970s. The second enormous volume of the history of the RBI (Balachandran 1998) dealt with the period from 1951 to 1967. A collectively authored history of the Deutsche Bundesbank (1999), running to 836 pages – a typical length for this type of work – came out just as the Bundesbank was being subsumed into the Eurosystem and subordinated to the European Central Bank (ECB). The first volume of Meltzer's (2003) authoritative history of the Fed, covering the years until 1951, was published early in the new century, and weighed in at 800 pages. The Swedish Riksbank marked 350 years of existence with the launch of a historical volume at the Bank of England (Wetterberg 2009), the British being reminded that the Swedes regard the Bank of England as a little sister.

With respect to length and attention to detail, central bank histories merit comparison with official histories of military and naval campaigns. Central bank histories are usually written by external academics but sometimes by retired insiders. Their authors seem to have at least as much freedom to view evidence as do the historians of other institutions in the private or public sectors. Sometimes they might discover that important evidence has been lost or destroyed, but this would also be the case in any other kind of organisation. The possibility that central bank historians have 'gone native' cannot be ruled out. On the other hand, recent central bank histories appear to be more critical of their subjects than were some earlier ones.

Most central banking histories are unforthcoming on the recent past. This could be because recent events are too sensitive to cover. In some cases, though, several volumes will have to be completed in order to bring the story up to the present. And only a conspiracy theorist would regard the slow progress of the Bank of England, RBI, and Fed histories as indicative of Machiavellian intent. There are some exceptions to the rule about coverage of recent times, including the second volume of the history of the RBNZ (Singleton *et al.* 2006), which comments on events up to 2002, including matters that were still topical at the time of publication.

A considerable investment of time and effort is required to read the larger central bank histories. Some may prefer to search for alternative sources of analysis. Biographies and autobiographies of important central bankers (see Chapter 2) appeal to those with a strong interest in the human dimension of central banking. Readers concerned with international comparisons may turn to several excellent volumes on the evolution of central banking, the fall and rise of the concept of central bank independence, the development of policies relating to financial stability, and the growth of central bank cooperation (Goodhart 1988; Holtfrerich, Reis, and Toniolo 1999; De Rosa 2003, Toniolo 2005; Borio, Toniolo, and Clement 2008). They may also find much of value in the collection of historical case studies of central banks edited by Toniolo (1988), and the three-volume set of classic literature edited by Michael Collins (1993).

It would not be practicable here to chronicle the history of each central bank. In fact the purpose of this book is different: it is to identify and assess broad trends in central banking since the early twentieth century. These developments will be illustrated with examples from the major central banks, as well as from some smaller, but no less interesting, institutions, especially those in the British Commonwealth.

Central bank functions

The narrowest definition of a central bank is a bank at which other banks hold deposits and use them for the settlement of interbank payments. However, all central banks have additional functions, several of which are of at least equal importance. Observers have struggled to capture the essence of central banking in one sentence. Hawke (1973) came close when he described a central bank as an organisation that stands 'between governments and banks'. Kisch and Elkin (1932: 67), two of the classic authorities, concluded that a central bank was 'an organ of public policy and not an instrument of private advantage'. Central banks implement (and often help to formulate) public policy towards the banking sector, and in relation to those economic variables that can be influenced through the banking sector.

Economists and central bankers have strained to come up with a satisfactory list of central banking functions. Price (1998), for example, identified five main activities – setting interest rates, supervising commercial banks, managing government debt, running payment systems, and operating a branch network. He used this framework to compare the institutional footprints of European central banks. Bruni (2001) offered a more complicated framework extending to eight policy areas. An older work by M. H. De Kock (1949), a South African central banking authority, devoted separate chapters to the central bank's various roles: (i) the bank of issue; (ii) the government's banker, agent, and adviser; (iii) the custodian of the cash reserves of the commercial banks; (iv) the custodian of the nation's reserves of gold and international currency; (v) the bank of rediscount and lender of last resort; (vi) the bank of central clearance, settlement, and transfer; and (vii) the controller of credit. While this list is more comprehensive than Price's, it is rather quaint in at least two respects. First, De Kock uses the term 'controller of credit', whereas most people today would say 'monetary policy agent'. Secondly, he does not discuss the banking supervision function, which became an important duty of many central banks, especially between the 1970s and 1990s.

Perhaps we should start afresh, and offer our own schedule of central bank activities, bearing in mind that there have been substantial variations, both between countries and within the same country over time (Singleton *et al.* 2006: 5):

1. *Central banks commonly issue legal tender banknotes (and often coins) to meet the requirements of the public.* Sometimes they are also responsible for related activities such as the printing of notes, and their processing and distribution to the banking industry. It is worth pointing out that the right to issue non-interest bearing liabilities in the form of banknotes is a valuable privilege. Banknotes are cheap to manufacture: a Canadian $20 note costs about 6 cents (Bank of Canada 2001). If the central bank is not required to back the face value of the banknotes issued on a one for one basis (if at all) with reserves of precious metal, then there will be an opportunity for earning seigniorage. This type of income is generated when the central bank uses non-interest-bearing notes to purchase securities that do pay interest. Gains from seigniorage typically allow the central bank to support a high level of internal costs (a 'gold plated' institution) while having ample profit left over to share with the government and/or private shareholders.

2. *Central banks implement and may formulate monetary policy.* This aspect of central banking has attracted most interest from

economists and other observers. As a result of their strategic position in the financial sector, central banks can influence monetary and credit conditions, the aggregate level of spending, and, with more or less accuracy, key economic variables such as the rate of inflation and the short run level of output and unemployment. Several tools are available to the central bank. Bindseil (2004) provides a good survey of their history and current use. First, the central bank may adjust the interest rate at which it is prepared to lend money, either on a routine or an emergency basis, to commercial banks and other eligible institutions. The bank rate or discount rate or rediscount rate – the latter is the most accurate term – is in fact a charge equivalent to an interest rate that is imposed when financial institutions offer securities for sale at the central bank's discount window. Second, the central bank may engage in open market operations (OMOs) or the purchase and sale of eligible securities such as commercial bills or Treasury bills. Such transactions may be outright, or there may be an agreement to reverse them after a specified interval, in which case they are called repurchases or repos. Third, the central bank may offer various loan facilities to commercial banks. Fourth, the central bank may employ administrative measures, such as variations in required levels of bank reserves, caps on commercial interest rates, and limits on the permissible level of bank loans. Fifth, it could use moral (per)suasion, backed by the implicit or explicit threat of other action, to influence the behaviour of banks. Whichever technique or mix of techniques is used the central bank aims to influence bank lending and aggregate spending in the economy. Whether monetary policy decisions should be taken by the central bank alone or by the central bank and the government together or by the government alone is one of the biggest questions in central banking.

3. *Central banks carry out banking and agency services for the government, and often manage the public debt.* The central bank is usually the main, though not always the exclusive, supplier of banking services to the government. Settlement of payments between the government and commercial banks normally takes place through accounts at the central bank. When governments wish to borrow, whether domestically or abroad, they often ask the central bank to act on their behalf. Central banks may be requested, or even required, to make loans to the government or other public sector agencies. But there may be strict limits on the amount of credit that the central bank is permitted to extend to the government, either directly or through the purchase of Treasury bills and government securities

on the secondary market. In some cases, such lending is prohibited on the grounds that 'printing money' to assist the government is inflationary.

4. *Central banks act as the custodian of the cash reserves of commercial banks and assist in the settlement of clearance balances between them.* The central bank is a convenient and highly secure location for the reserves of other banks. Commercial banks willingly hold some cash reserves at the central bank. These may be used in the settlement of interbank payments and payments between banks and the government. (Whether or not the authorities compel banks to hold additional reserves at the central bank varies according to the circumstances.) In some countries the central bank also owns and/ or operates some of the payment systems through which payment instructions are exchanged among banks and aggregated in preparation for settlement.

5. *Central banks endeavour to preserve the integrity of the financial system, and in some circumstances act as an emergency lender of last resort and prudential supervisor of banks.* Banking crises can be highly damaging to the economy: they may wipe out deposits and make it difficult for individuals and businesses to obtain new credit (a credit crunch). The failure of systemically important banks may create log jams and havoc in the payment and settlement system. The central bank has a responsibility to uphold the overall stability of the banking system. It may discharge this duty in one or more of several ways: by managing the settlement system, by standing ready to intervene as the lender of last resort to the banking system (and perhaps also to individual banks), and by regulating, monitoring, or supervising individual banks. Central banks may also have a role in the resolution of bank failures and the management of deposit insurance schemes. (Most central bank lending to commercial banks occurs during the conduct of normal business – lender of last resort lending is exceptional.) In some instances, central banks have powers of supervision over the wider financial sector, including finance companies and insurers. Practice varies enormously, as do the views of economists as to which arrangements are most beneficial (Goodhart and Schoenmaker 1995). Nowadays the central bank's oversight of the banking system as a whole is called macroprudential policy. The supervision of individual banks falls within the microprudential sphere. In practice a tidy distinction between these categories often proves elusive. The classic prescription is for the central bank to provide emergency assistance at a penalty interest rate to illiquid but solvent banks. But when a snap

decision is required the solvency of a bank may be hard to determine (Bordo 2002). Ideally, central banks would prefer to provide emergency liquidity to the banking system instead of picking and choosing between individual banks, but this might not be practicable. Governments often insist on a role in the lender of last resort function, either because of the political implications of bank failures or because they are not prepared to allow the central bank to expose the taxpayer (the ultimate lender of last resort) to potentially large losses.

6. *Central banks may carry out government policy on the exchange rate and on custody of the national reserves of international currency and may assist in their management.* Central banks have often been assigned the task of implementing exchange rate policy. This has frequently involved the buying and selling of gold or foreign currencies in order to influence market conditions, resulting in additions to or subtractions from the external reserves, which are held on the balance sheet of the central bank and/or the government. Central banks may also influence the exchange rate by adjusting interest rates, or by operating administrative controls over external transactions.

7. *Central banks may intervene to promote economic development.* Especially in developing economies, central banks have often been given a broad mandate to foster economic development. In the absence of a strong commercial banking sector, the central bank may step in as a substitute and operate its own branch network. (The establishment of a central bank may also give potential new entrants to the banking industry the confidence to proceed.) The central bank sometimes plays a part in the financing of development projects and corporations, and in borrowing externally for the promotion of such activities. Central banking experts in the core countries of North America and western Europe are inclined to overlook these aspects of central banking in other parts of the world.

8. *Central banks advise their governments on economic policy.* Central banks possess considerable expertise on a range of economic and financial matters, and since the 1960s have been in the forefront of economic modelling. Ministers find it useful to be able to supplement advice from treasury officials with counsel from central bankers. As Malcolm Fraser, the Australian prime minister (1975–83) put it, 'there is safety in having advice from different sources. If you get two points of view, you're more likely to make better decisions ... it's just prudent management' (quoted in Weller 1989: 22).

9. *Central banks participate in cooperative international monetary arrangements.* Central banks may cooperate in the management of the

international monetary system and the regulation of the international banking system by exchanging information, by formulating and discussing new policy initiatives, and by making credit available to their peers. Central bankers from different countries have often talked to one another even when their nations were at odds. Since 1930 the main hub for central bank cooperation has been the Bank for International Settlements in Basel.

10. *Other functions.* As an agency with a close relationship to the government, the central bank may be asked to take on additional tasks, such as the provision of banking services to the public, consumer protection (as in the USA), the part ownership of a stock exchange, or the operation of a stock registry (McKinley and Banaian 2005: 51–6).

This is quite a list. The RBNZ, for example, prides itself on being a 'full service' central bank, though it currently has no involvement in the promotion of economic development. In truth, no two central banks are identical. It is worth stressing that a central bank is not absolutely necessary to perform any of the functions described above. Commercial banks and governments could (and often have) issued money under their own names. Monetary policy could be implemented by a department of Treasury. Commercial banks could provide the government with a full range of banking services including the management of the external reserves. Large commercial banks or specialist institutions could hold the reserves of other banks and offer settlement services. Other agencies could promote economic development and tender economic advice to the government. How then can the dominance of central banks be explained? Clearly the advocates of central banking have been able to persuade governments that they can perform some important functions more efficiently and/or securely than other entities. Governments generally do not know much about the technicalities of banking and monetary affairs (though this obviously does not inhibit them from having strong views on policy). Once the central bank has opened for business, it may become the obvious institution to be entrusted (or dumped) with other responsibilities in the banking and monetary arena.

Some important central bank activities are closely interrelated, and this may be a source of difficulty for the external observer. De Kock (1949: 25) explains this accurately, if somewhat wordily:

[A] specific loan operation of a central bank (i.e. in its capacity as a bank of rediscount) might have been caused by a commercial bank requiring more note currency (involving the central bank as the bank of issue) or foreign exchange or gold (involving the central bank as the custodian of the nation's reserves), or having to replenish its cash reserves and clearing balances (involving the central bank as the custodian of the commercial banks and the bank of central clearance) which it could not obtain from any other source owing to general monetary stringency (involving the central bank as lender of last resort); and before effecting the rediscount, the central bank might have raised its discount rate or imposed certain conditions in its capacity as the controller of credit.

Sometimes the functions of the central bank may clash. For example, monetary policy objectives could be compromised if the central bank felt impelled to create a large amount of new liquidity in order to avert a banking crisis. But monetary and financial stability go hand in hand most of the time.

Core and peripheral functions

We would expect some central banking activities to be more important than others. Several long standing functions pertain only tangentially to the essence of central banking. There is no compelling reason why the central bank should be involved in the manufacture of banknotes. McKinley and Banaian (2005: 52–3) list seven core areas of business: monetary policy management; foreign exchange and reserves management; the lender of last resort; the supervision and regulation of commercial banks; the management of payment and settlement systems; currency and coin management; and the fiscal agency. Seven is a large number, and universities make do with teaching and research.

Assessing the overall performance of an organisation with overlapping functions is difficult, but demerging such an organisation could result in a decline in effectiveness. Crucial information flows could be obstructed by new institutional rivalries or simply by reduced contact between former colleagues. During the late 1990s several central banks were stripped of their role in banking supervision, but the experience of the early twenty-first century does not suggest that better outcomes have been achieved in either the macroprudential or the microprudential areas.

The core versus periphery, or 'wide versus narrow bank', debate was considered by the RBNZ in the early 1990s. The RBNZ was responsible for promoting monetary stability and financial stability and efficiency. This mandate was deemed broad enough to embrace several functions, including monetary policy, a limited form of prudential oversight, and the supply (but not production) of banknotes and coins. There was room for debate over the future of other activities, including foreign reserves management, the provision of registry services, and the staffing of the Overseas Investment Commission. The more diversified the central bank, the greater the potential for both economies and diseconomies of scale and scope. On the one hand, the combination of functions could lead to synergies. A wide bank could offer a greater variety of jobs, and therefore attract and retain a better pool of talent. It could also sustain a stronger management team with the capacity to check an errant governor, and resist bullying from the government or large foreign banks. In a small country, there were strong grounds for avoiding the proliferation of policy making agencies. On the other hand, a wide central bank would be more bureaucratic. Higher operating costs would render it more vulnerable to external criticism. Clarity and accountability would be harder to achieve, and peripheral activities could distract management from core tasks. One participant in the debate suggested that the central bank should keep only those functions that met a certain cost benefit hurdle. But the discussion was inconclusive, and the governor, Don Brash, decided that there was no pressing need to abandon non-core activities unless they interfered with core functions or imposed heavy costs (Singleton *et al.* 2006: 243–5).

Perhaps modern central banking boils down to the conduct and formulation of public policy in three broad areas: monetary stability, financial stability, and the integrity of the currency. The relative priority to be assigned to these overarching functions, and the appropriate policies and tools to be employed in their performance, are open to debate.

Broad outline of central bank history

The oldest central banks, the Sveriges Riksbank and the Bank of England, trace their history back to the seventeenth century. They were not at first central banks in anything like the modern sense of the term. Central banking evolved over the eighteenth, nineteenth, and twentieth centuries. Though considerable progress was made during the nineteenth century towards understanding some central bank functions, Palgrave's definitive *Dictionary of Political Economy*, published in 1894, contains no entry for central banking. In the entry on 'banking', the Bank of England is described as 'the centre of banking operations in the United Kingdom', and the provider of important services to the government, especially in times of 'war and difficulty', and to commerce in general (Palgrave 1894: 92). This definition is not very illuminating. By the First World War, however, the term 'central banking' had gained a wide currency, partly because of the lively debate over the creation of a central bank in the USA.

Stanley Fischer (1994) identified four main stages in the development of central banking. In the first, special banks were established in some European countries. For example, the privately owned Bank of England was set up in 1694 to raise loans for the government, and in exchange it was given certain banking privileges. Such banks typically became involved in regulating the note issue; indeed they were known as banks of issue for many years. The second stage, beginning in the nineteenth century, marked the beginning of central banking proper. Leading banks of issue started to place more emphasis on their role as bankers to other banks, and with reluctance accepted some responsibility for preserving systemic banking stability by acting as lenders of last resort. By 1900, most central banks were required to maintain the convertibility of the national currency into gold at a fixed exchange rate. As a result they became responsible for maintaining fixed exchange rates between national currencies. This was the gold standard era.

In the 1930s and 1940s, central banking entered a third stage. National economic policies changed in the aftermath of the depression of the early 1930s and the collapse of the gold standard. Many privately owned central banks were taken into state ownership, while those still in private hands entered into closer – some would say subservient – relationships with their governments. Between the 1940s and the 1970s and 1980s many central banks played a largely subsidiary role in the formulation of monetary policy. Fiscal policy was believed to be more effective in the Keynesian era. Governments now had multiple macroeconomic goals: full employment, rapid economic growth, price stability, and stable exchange rates.

The fourth stage was reached in the late twentieth century. By the 1970s, a reaction was setting in against the Keynesian approach to macroeconomic policy, which critics believed was causing rising inflation and exchange rate instability. Central banks started to regain more autonomy. In the macroeconomic arena, there was a renewed emphasis on monetary policy, and central banks began to focus more single-mindedly on the objective of internal price stability. By the early 1990s, most developed countries had reduced inflation to acceptable levels. Throughout stages three and four, central banks retained the currency function, as well as overall responsibility for the stability of the financial system. Between the 1970s and 1990s, moreover, many central banks became more involved in the prudential supervision of banks, but this function was withdrawn from several of them in the late 1990s. Throughout each of these four stages the development of central banking was closely intertwined with the development of financial markets, institutions, and instruments.

Fischer's summary, which is fleshed out by Goodhart, Capie, and Schnadt (1994), provides an excellent starting point for the student of central banking history. Bruni (2001) combines Fischer's first two stages into the 'classical or archaic' period; this was followed after the collapse of the gold standard by the 'traditional' period of discretionary monetary policy; finally in the 'modern' period the primary consideration was price stability. Most other accounts supplement this sort of approach, in some cases by focusing on a shorter period. Holtfrerich and Reis (1999: 2–5) highlight five developments in central banking since 1918: the abandonment of the imperative of gold convertibility, the growth of prudential supervision of commercial banks, the adoption of OMOs as a key policy instrument, an increased emphasis on domestic macroeconomic objectives, and the fall and rise of central bank independence. Siklos's (2002) study of central banking since the Second World War is broadly consistent with this pattern of development.

An alternative perspective is supplied by Mendzela (2005). He advances a three-period model. In the first age of central banking, routine operational activities, such as currency processing, inter-bank settlement, and government banking, were dominant, and the central bank was administered rather than managed. The second age witnessed increased concentration on policy functions. Fewer but better qualified personnel were needed, while more sophisticated management techniques were used to get the best out of the central bank's resources. Central banks, he suggests, are starting to enter the third age, in which the boundaries between organisations and nations are more permeable and there is a stronger focus on knowledge and the imagination. The timing of the transition between these stages is nebulous, but there is merit in drawing attention to the growth of the policy side relative to the operational side of central banking.

The position taken in this book is that there were two revolutions in the central banking world. The first occurred in the 1930s and 1940s in reaction to the great depression and the Second World War, and the second took place in the 1980s and 1990s in reaction to the great inflation. We cannot rule out further upheavals in the wake of new crises.

Issues in central banking

Several issues are of perennial interest to observers and practitioners of central banking. First, the question of whether central banking is beneficial lurks permanently in the wings. Advocates of free banking argue that there is no need for a central authority to issue or manage the currency, and no role for discretionary monetary policy. They also maintain that the banking system is robust and does not require the oversight or regulation of a central bank or any other public sector agency. (Any perceived instability is the result of inappropriate regulation and meddling.) From this point of view, central banks were set up for self interested reasons including the desire to profit from the sale and exercise of monopoly powers. On a slightly more generous interpretation of history, the establishment of central banks could reflect genuine misunderstanding of the properties of the monetary system. The superiority of the case for central banking, which depends on the core functions discussed earlier, is by no means as clear cut as central bankers would have people believe (Capie and Wood 1991; Dowd 1992; White, L. 1989; Smith 1936). Nevertheless the present book has little to say about free banking; this is not because free banking lacks interest, but rather because the task at hand is to investigate central banking history and not to ask what might have happened in the absence of central banking.

A second concern that is never far from the minds of central banking scholars and practitioners is the appropriate form and level of central bank autonomy or independence. How much autonomy should the state grant the central bank, especially in a democratic society, and how should central bankers be held accountable? Few would question that the central bank should be accountable to someone, but to whom, how, and for what? It is worth noting that the same problem crops up in many areas of public policy, from public sector auditing (Green and Singleton 2009) to the conduct of war. Detailed political direction of the central bank has often been deprecated by economists and central bankers on the grounds that it leads to inferior outcomes. Obtaining a tolerable balance between autonomy and accountability is difficult. These matters were given considerable thought in interwar writing (Kisch and Elkin 1932: ch. 2), and the balance of power between central banks and governments has changed markedly on several occasions during the twentieth century (Toniolo 1988; Stiglitz 1998). No definitive solution is provided by history, a discipline that is more inclined to relativism than is economics. Each era in central banking history has found answers that have met the political and intellectual requirements of the day, but these answers have proved contingent. Circumstances will continue to evolve and future generations are likely to revisit these issues and find new solutions, or even revert to neglected ones.

Third, there has been a lively debate for many decades over the appropriate goal (or goals) of monetary policy. Should the central bank concentrate on trying to maintain the convertibility of the national currency into gold or a strong external currency? Should it give priority to domestic price stability? Should it aim to reduce unemployment and smooth fluctuations in output? Or should it attempt to achieve some combination of these goals? Again the conventional wisdom has fluctuated over the years, with each generation believing that it has arrived at the truth.

Fourth, there is a long-running, and at times confused, debate over whether central banks should make decisions on the basis of rules or discretion. A very simple rule would instruct central bank staff to increase the money supply by 3 per cent per annum. Of course, this is easier said than done, especially if a broad definition of the money supply is used and/or the country has a fixed exchange rate. Though there has been strong support for rules amongst some schools of economics, their advocates have struggled to agree on what actually constitutes a rule, let alone on which rule is best. By contrast, central bankers have usually maintained that policy makers cannot avoid exercising discretion, since the context in which decisions are required is always changing (Simons 1936; Bibow 2004). By the late 1990s, however, a synthesis based on 'constrained discretion' was emerging (Bernanke *et al.* 1999: 6), which recognised that in practice monetary policy involves a mixture of the two approaches.

Fifth, questions have been asked about the motivation and behaviour of central bankers. Some writers in the 1960s and 1970s cast doubt upon the traditional assumption that central bankers were driven by a self-sacrificing public service ethos, portraying them instead as rent seeking bureaucrats (Toma and Toma 1986). The economics of bureaucracy approach seems to have been forgotten by economists working on central banking in the 1980s and 1990s (Forder 2002), but it retains considerable power as a means of qualifying more naive views of motivation. The aims of central bankers, like those of politicians, generals, and bishops, are complex. We should not assume they are disinterested servants of the public, nor should we be ready to assume the worst about them.

Conclusion

Central banks were relatively mysterious organisations for nearly all of the twentieth century. They were also very powerful entities, occupying strategic territory 'between governments and banks'. They were responsible for several important economic policy functions, including the issue of banknotes, the conduct of monetary policy, and the oversight of the financial system. These and other functions had been acquired in several ways: some had been assigned by the state, while others had evolved over time. The objectives and methods of central banks, and the nature of their relations with governments, were revolutionised twice during the twentieth century, first in the 1930s and 1940s, and second in the 1980s and 1990s. The goal of this book is to explain these revolutions. We begin in the next chapter by introducing the central banking profession, and examining the careers of some prominent central bankers.

2   Very boring guys?

Rogoff's [conservative central banker] ... is a splendid illustration of the humorous definition of an economist as someone who sees that something works in practice and asks whether it can also work in theory. Is there any doubt that central banks in general ... have been dominated by quite conservative people?

Alan Blinder (1998: 47)

Felipe Pazos has been replaced as President of the National Bank of Cuba following disagreement with Fidel Castro. He has been replaced by Ernesto Guevara ... Guevara, aged 31, is an Argentine, a communist, and is neither an economist nor a banker ... He has been a prominent leader of the revolutionary movement and may be regarded as a fellow conspirator of Castro ... By this latest move Castro has swept away the last vestige of orthodox authority in the financial field.

(Report on National Bank of Cuba, 1 December 1959, Bank of England Archive, OV162/5)

Che Guevara, whose reign at the National Bank of Cuba was relatively brief (Yaffe 2009), is the most iconic exception to the general rule that central bankers are rather cautious and conservative people. One of the messages of this chapter is that central bankers come in a number of varieties. Some are headstrong, others compliant. Some have strong economic views (whether orthodox or unorthodox), while others are opportunistic. Thus, when Jean-Pierre Roth, chairman of the Swiss National Bank, describes central bankers as 'very boring guys' (quoted in Baker and Singer 2006: 64), he is being rather modest.

Though the spotlight will be on selected chief executives – governors in most cases – it is not implied that other central bankers did not matter. Some governors have been dictators, whereas others have acted as members of a management team. In some instances authority within the central bank has rested not with the governor but with the board of directors or with the government. However, directors, especially part-time directors, have rarely been an obstacle to a determined central bank governor. Central bank chief executives have tended to be

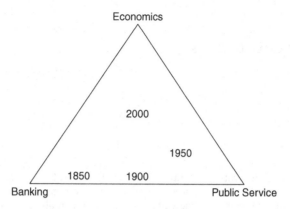

Figure 1 A three-dimensional profession

appointed either by the government or at least with the government's acquiescence. There will also be some discussion of the development of the central banking profession. The modern central banker must think like a banker, a public servant, and an economist, though this has not always been the case.

Central banking: a three-dimensional profession

During the nineteenth century, the central banking profession started to emerge out of the banking profession, as banks of issue took the first tentative steps towards acknowledging their public policy responsibilities (see Figure 1). By the mid twentieth century central bankers were as much public servants as they were bankers. When complimented on his expertise as a banker at a Senate hearing in 1945, Allan Sproul of the Federal Reserve Bank of New York (FRBNY) responded testily: 'I appear here not as a banker ... but as a central banker' (quoted in Ritter 1980: 2). With the growth in the influence of economics and economists in the second half of the twentieth century, the central banking profession experienced a further development (Singleton 2006: 104–5). Sproul himself was a good economist, a discipline that he learnt within the Federal Reserve System, especially from John Williams, his degree being in pomology or fruit growing.

Central bankers in the early twentieth century knew little, if anything, about economics. They were bankers whose customers were commercial banks and related institutions (including discount houses in the UK) and the government. As Einzig (1932: 107–8) put it, the 'conventional' view of central bankers was that they 'should be something between the typical banker and the typical permanent official', and should look as well as act the part, unlike the arty and eccentric Montagu Norman, the long-serving governor of the Bank of England.

Beginning with the financial management of the First World War, the public policy functions of central banks expanded relative to their banking functions. While several central banks also established statistical and economic sections between the wars, it was not until much later that their full impact was felt. The public service era of central banking was at its height between the 1940s and 1970s. Most central banks cooperated closely with their respective treasuries or ministries of finance. Monetary policy was regarded as an integral part of the government's macroeconomic policy and not a separate area of endeavour. This period also saw the growing infiltration of economists into the central banking world. Central banks recruited more graduates, including economics graduates, and devoted more resources to research. As early as 1961, half of the presidents of the Federal Reserve banks were professional economists (Whittlesey 1963: 38). In the 1960s, some central banks became involved in econometric modelling, an enterprise then in its infancy. Sherman Maisel, who served on the Federal Reserve Board between 1965 and 1972, felt that the views of professional economists on the staff were beginning to carry as much – and sometimes more – weight that those of Board members or even of the chairman (Nelson, R. H. 1987: 82), but this is debatable.

By the end of the twentieth century, the ties between central banks and governments had loosened somewhat. Economists were reaching the top much more frequently than before. The quantity of economic research conducted within central banks continued to expand (St-Amant et al. 2005). Between 1990 and 2005 the number of G10 central bank governors with backgrounds largely in the private sector dwindled; the number with strong public service backgrounds rose somewhat; but there was a big surge in former academics. 'In 1990, only one in ten governors had spent much (post-PhD) time in the academy. Among the current G10 governors [in 2005], six were once academics (to some degree)' (Simmons 2008: 183). During the twentieth century, central banking became a much more balanced profession in terms of the relative influence of its three constituent cultures. By the early twenty-first century, it began to look as though economics might become dominant.

As one Federal Reserve official explained in an interview with Donald Kettl (1986: 6), central bankers saw themselves as 'part of a special priesthood'. This was an apt description for a society of men. Only nine of the world's 173 central bank governors in 2001 were women. Victoria

Asfura (Honduras) noted that the world of finance, like the military and the church, was a male profession. Her counterpart in Bermuda, Cheryl-Ann Lister, explained that most of the politicians who appointed central bank governors were themselves male (Anon. 2001).

Helleiner (1994: 19, 198–201) argues that central bankers display some of the characteristics of a 'transnational epistemic community'. This term originates in political science (Haas 1992), and refers to an influential group of experts with a common scientific understanding of the world, a shared set of values and policy objectives, and a willingness to cooperate with each other. The notion that central bankers are an epistemic community has been employed most forcefully in discussions of European monetary integration in the late twentieth century (Verdun 1999). Whether or not this category is applicable to earlier generations is unclear (Kapstein 1992). While Eichengreen and Temin (2000) contend that central bankers in the early twentieth century had much in common, they add that many of their most cherished beliefs were misguided. Indeed they argue that central bankers in the 1920s and early 1930s displayed an incorrigible gold standard *mentalité*. This deep-rooted commitment to gold, which was shared by many economists and politicians, contained both intellectual and moral elements. After 1918 central bankers were eager to cooperate internationally in order to reconstruct and defend the gold standard (Clarke 1967), but this enterprise ended in disaster and recrimination in the early 1930s. Eichengreen and Temin conclude that the gold standard *mentalité* was at best pseudo-scientific. Even if we reject the idea that early twentieth century central bankers formed an epistemic community, there is merit in treating them as members of a professional community whose interests and loyalties sometimes transcended national self-interest.

Do personalities matter?

Some readers might think that individual central bankers cannot have much effect on policy decisions and outcomes, these being determined by impersonal economic forces and relationships. One might also ask whether the skills or force of personality of a general (such as Napoleon) can affect the outcome of a military campaign. The thrust of most econometric studies is to minimise the contribution of individuals to the functioning of the macroeconomy, and to stress impersonal relationships between variables such as the interest rate or the money supply, borrowing, spending, and inflation. However, it is not entirely clear that personalities are considered irrelevant even in mainstream economics: indeed the 2006 American Economic Association conference included a session entitled 'Alan Greenspan's legacy: an early look'. In this session, Calomiris (2006: 170) stated that 'Alan Greenspan played an important role in shaping major changes in the structure of financial regulation'. Benjamin Friedman (2006: 176) concluded by saying that 'The Greenspan era ... may stand as the modern-day pinnacle of "discretion", rather than "rules", in U.S. monetary policymaking.' Without a doubt it was Greenspan's discretion that counted, and the results, in Benjamin Friedman's (2006: 177) now unfashionable view were not only 'to be admired' but could become the 'envy' of future policy makers.

Siklos (2002: 81–127) argues that personalities are more likely to have an impact, whether for good or ill, on the conduct of monetary policy during times of crisis, such as the 1930s, than in periods of relative tranquillity, such as the 1990s, when it is possible to rely on routine procedures. The Taylor rule, for example, offers a routine that relates the policy interest rate to deviations from the desired level of inflation and changes in the output gap. Siklos's approach is persuasive, and individuals are likely to matter most during upheavals, but any implication that the age of crises is in the past would be wide of the mark.

Milton Friedman (1962) believed that individual central bankers could have a major impact on policy, and that this impact was nearly always deleterious, which is why he favoured the imposition on central banks of a strict monetary rule. In their monetary history of the USA, Friedman and Schwartz (1963) examined in detail the consequences of the change in – or disappearance of – leadership within the Federal Reserve System in the late 1920s, concluding that the effects were disastrous for the US economy. Meltzer (2003) endorsed this interpretation. Romer and Romer (2004), whose work extends into the Greenspan era, suggest that variations in the economic philosophies of Fed chairmen have influenced the success or failure of monetary management.

Of course, it is difficult to establish beyond reasonable doubt why a particular policy decision is made, let alone whose voice is the decisive one. Abrams (2006) has written an article based on conversations about monetary policy on the Nixon tapes. If individuals did not matter, there would be no reason to ponder the implications of every word uttered by Arthur Burns, chairman of the Federal Reserve Board, President Richard Nixon, and his budget director, George Schultz, and this type of article could not have been published in an economics journal. But whose words carried the most weight? The Fed was supposed to be autonomous from the executive, and monetary policy was supposed to be determined by the Federal Open Market Committee (FOMC) and not by the chairman alone. Yet Nixon evidently believed that the FOMC would follow Burns's direction: 'You can lead 'em[, Arthur]. You can lead 'em ... Just kick 'em in the rump a little' (Abrams 2006: 181). Ultimately, though, the tapes are inconclusive. Why was monetary policy loosened prior to the 1971–2 elections? Did Burns and the FOMC bow to pressure from the executive to stimulate demand for electoral reasons, or were they responding in good faith to changing perceptions of economic conditions? Since we cannot see into the minds of the key individuals, we cannot be sure of their motives. A comparable situation arose in New Zealand in the early 1990s. Under new legislation in 1989, the RBNZ was granted operational independence. During a recession in 1991, however, the government rebuked Don Brash, the governor, for running an excessively tight monetary policy. Brash, who had sole responsibility for monetary policy under the 1989 act, eased the central bank's policy settings later in the year. Brash justified this decision in terms of the changed outlook for inflation, and strenuously denied having been 'nobbled' by ministers (Singleton et al. 2006: 180–3). But there is no way of knowing whether Brash was influenced, either consciously or unconsciously, by external pressure.

Individuals do have the potential to influence the behaviour of central banks, and some of them are external to these organisations. Woolley (1984) suggests that politicians, Treasury officials, academic economists, bankers, and even journalists may all have some degree of influence. A recent book by Shih (2008) contends that swings in monetary policy and inflation in post-reform China have been driven by shifts in the relative power of factions within the communist leadership. The boundaries of central banks are no less permeable than are those of other institutions. The more numerous the players, the harder it is for economists to model the monetary policy game, and the greater is the scope for other disciplines, including economic history and political science, to make a contribution to understanding central banking.

Not so boring guys

In the 1970s and early 1980s, the average central banker was commonly depicted as a pushover for spendthrift politicians. It was against this background that Rogoff (1985) contended that society would gain from delegating responsibility for monetary policy to a 'conservative' central banker. Writing much later, Blinder (1998) questioned whether central bankers had ever been less than conservative. If at times they had accommodated the inflationary tendencies of governments, then for the most part it had been under duress. The notion that central bankers can be divided into hawks or 'inflation nutters' (Mervyn King 1997: 89) and ineffectual doves is simplistic. The remainder of this chapter is devoted to illustrating the variety of talents, philosophies, strengths, and weaknesses displayed by a range of central bankers over the past century. They are not chosen at random. All could have made much higher salaries in the private sector than they made from central banking.

The man of mystery: Montagu Norman

Few central bankers have aroused as much interest or controversy as Montagu Norman, the governor of the Bank of England between 1920 and 1944 (Sayers 1976; Boyle 1967; Clay 1957). There can be no doubt that Norman was inclined to monetary conservatism. He was an unflinching supporter of sound money and the gold standard, who continued to see merit in this system after it had begun to unravel in the early 1930s. Yet he acknowledged that governments could demand the final word on policy matters. Norman's career illustrates the role of external observers, including the media and scholars, in the construction of a central banking personality.

Norman was a merchant banker by trade, a partner in the respected firm of Brown Shipley. Personally, he was extremely shy, rather inarticulate, and somewhat mischievous. He struggled, as did Alan Greenspan, to give a lucid account of economic processes. Unlike Greenspan, however, Norman was not much of an economist; indeed he distrusted theoreticians, and his approach to central banking was largely intuitive. When Norman did make statements on the record, he could sound rather callous about problems such as unemployment.

The chapter headings of Andrew Boyle's (1967) biography are instructive: Norman was in turn the novice, the escapist, the possessed, the onlooker, the insider, the alchemist, the illusionist, the defendant, and the scapegoat. Norman appeared to cultivate his reputation for mystery, sometimes travelling incognito as 'Professor Skinner'. According to Einzig (1932: 101), Norman was no less a 'mystery man' in the public imagination than was Sir Basil Zaharoff, the famous arms trader or 'merchant of death'. That Norman was a transatlantic globetrotter who hobnobbed with other central bankers, especially Ben Strong of the FRBNY and Hjalmar Schacht of the Reichsbank, only fuelled public interest, not to say suspicion. Americans were alarmed by Norman's hold over Strong, and feared his influence on US monetary policy.

Norman was disinclined to explain his actions to outsiders. But the gold standard, the mechanism of which he was so enamoured, offered a high degree of transparency with respect to the aims and effectiveness of policy. Either the pound was convertible into gold or it was not, and in the latter case the monetary authorities must have failed. Norman was ill during much of the crisis in 1931 when sterling was forced off gold.

The maestro: Alan Greenspan

The public's fascination with monetary wizardry continued into the Greenspan era (1987–2006) at the Federal Reserve. As the end of Alan Greenspan's term in office approached, professional and academic praise was lavished on his management of US monetary policy (Kahn 2005). Relatively low inflation and unprecedented prosperity were the hallmarks of the Greenspan era. Financial crises were either sidestepped or, like the dotcom crash, contained. Greenspan had been the first US policy maker to recognise that productivity growth had accelerated in the 1990s. In this benign environment, he contrived to maintain price stability without resorting to stringent monetary policy. The sentiments expressed at the time of Greenspan's retirement appear effusive in retrospect, and it is worth pointing out that there were some sceptics even before 2007–9. Hartcher (2006) described Greenspan as the 'bubble man', and Batra (2005) condemned his policies as a gigantic 'fraud' that would ruin the world economy.

Maestro, the title of Bob Woodward's account of Greenspan's career (Woodward 2000), evokes images of wizardry. Under Greenspan, the Fed emitted a continuous stream of information, while central bank officials debated the outlook for the economy with market participants, the media, Congress, and academics. Greenspan was a familiar face on television, coming across as avuncular to some, lugubrious to others. Many observers were puzzled, though, that while Greenspan could achieve satisfactory policy outcomes, he was unable to communicate a straightforward message. Perhaps the source of Greenspan's reputation for wizardry lies in this contrast.

With many years of experience in the private sector as an economic consultant and forecaster, not to mention a Ph.D. in economics, Greenspan ought to have been able to express himself lucidly. Yet he seemed to revel in what he himself called 'constructive ambiguity'. Woodward (2000: 180–1) tells the story of Greenspan's attempts to propose to his girlfriend. She could not understand what he was trying to say, and he had to repeat his proposal twice. The climate of ambiguity at the Federal Reserve was exacerbated by the absence of a clear policy target, such as Brash's inflation target in New Zealand, or Norman's peg to gold between 1925 and 1931.

In retirement, Greenspan (2008) published a collection of memoirs and reflections on the future of the US economy and economic policy. The possibility that good luck (Mankiw 2006: 182) rather than great skill (Nelson 2007b: 168–71) accounts for the policy successes achieved under Greenspan cannot be ruled out, and in fairness it is far too early to form a definitive judgement. But Greenspan was very lucky to retire when he did.

The opportunist: Hjalmar Schacht

Schacht's career as a central banker began in glory and ended in controversy if not infamy (Weitz 1997; James 1999b). As president of the Reichsbank from November 1923 until 1930, Schacht was credited with restoring a measure of financial stability to Germany after the disastrous period of hyper-inflation. Schacht enjoyed close relations with Norman, and was viewed as one of the most brilliant central bankers of the 1920s.

In the early 1930s, however, Schacht came under a very different influence. He threw in his lot with Hitler, whom he affected to see as the economic saviour of Germany. As Hitler's Reichsbank president (1933–9) and minister of economic affairs (1934–7), Schacht played a leading role in designing and implementing the expansionary policies that assisted Germany to recover from the depression and rearm. Schacht's reputation as a financial wizard was enhanced by these developments. But he squabbled with the Nazis, and indulged in public criticism of their collectivist and inflationary economic policies. Furthermore, he disapproved of some of their social policies. Schacht was removed as Reichsbank president in 1939, but continued to be involved with the German government during the Second World War. Implicated in plots against Hitler, he was sent to a concentration camp in 1943. At the Nuremburg trials of Nazi leaders after the war, Schacht was acquitted of any direct responsibility for war crimes. He later published a self-exonerating autobiography (Schacht 1955). Robert Jackson, the chief US prosecutor at Nuremberg, summed up as follows: 'Schacht represents the most dangerous and reprehensible type of opportunism of the man of influential position who is ready to join a movement that he knows to be wrong because he thinks it is winning' (Jackson 1946). This assessment would be hard to better. Schacht had been arrogant enough to believe that he could tame the Nazis and bend them to his own purposes.

The prince: Yasushi Mieno

Yasushi Mieno was appointed governor of the Bank of Japan in December 1989. Against the advice of the Ministry of Finance, he ordered a sharp increase in interest rates in order to defuse rising inflationary pressure. Tighter monetary policy pricked the asset bubble that had emerged in the late 1980s, but propelled the Japanese economy into an era of stagnation. Mieno was lauded as 'central banker of the year' by *Euromoney* in 1991 (von Furstenberg and Ulan 1998: 203), yet his legacy is extremely controversial.

Mieno was one of the 'Princes of the Yen'. This central banking dynasty was started by Hisato Ichimada, who became governor of the Bank of Japan in 1946. An admirer of Schacht – he had spent three years in Germany in the 1920s – Ichimada wielded immense power during the reconstruction of the Japanese economy under US occupation. Given the severe shortage of credit in post-war Japan, Ichimada was in a position to approve or reject the investment plans of major firms. As a result of his seemingly limitless power, Ichimada was dubbed 'the Pope'. Like the Roman pope, he was also said to be infallible.

In 1954 Ichimada became minister of finance, a post from which he continued to support the Bank of Japan. Though the Bank of Japan appeared to be cowed by the government, Werner (2003) contends that its weakness was largely illusory. Ichimada established the tradition of alternating the governorship between senior officials of the central bank and the Ministry of Finance. Whenever the governor was a ministry man, the deputy governor was an internal appointee, who expected to succeed at the next changeover, and vice versa. Governors from the ministry tended to be marginalised by their deputies and by other senior central bank insiders.

According to one observer, 'Just as an heir to the shogunate would be chosen, the BOJ [Bank of Japan] governorship was always predetermined. When the time came, the BOJ princes would receive the "scroll" from the elder princes ... the handing over of the scroll is in effect like saying, "You will be king." And ... this initiation process starts early' (quoted in Werner 2002: 41–2).

Ichimada anointed Tadashi Sasaki as the Bank of Japan's first prince. Sasaki became deputy governor in 1962 and governor in 1969. He was followed by Haruo Mayekawa and then by Mieno. (Governors drawn from the Ministry of Finance were not regarded as princes.) Mieno was a devoted central banker, serving as deputy governor under Satoshi Sumita, whose lax policies fuelled the stock market and property boom of the late 1980s. By tightening so dramatically after taking over, Mieno demonstrated that he would not be bullied by the government (von Furstenberg and Ulan 1998: 174–206).

The conservative central banker: Don Brash

New Zealand provided a benchmark for central banking in the 1990s. The 1989 Reserve Bank Act enshrined price stability as the sole monetary policy objective of the RBNZ. It also created a novel form of central bank autonomy based on a contract between the governor and the minister of finance, who then negotiated a Policy Targets Agreement (PTA). In practice the crux of the PTA was an inflation target. Other than in exceptional circumstances, the government could not intervene once a PTA was in force; however, the governor could be reprimanded or dismissed for any breach of the target. Walsh (1995b) described these arrangements as a good approximation to an optimal central bank contract.

Brash, a prominent businessman and banker, was appointed as governor in 1988, and remained in office until 2002, when he resigned in order to stand for and enter Parliament. When Brash became governor, inflation had already been falling for several years, and the main features of the 1989 Act were already settled. While Brash was therefore not the architect of the New Zealand model, he was its enthusiastic champion. For example, he made several gruelling tours of the country to speak to small business owners about the central bank and the economy. On one visit, as he addressed farmers in a region affected by drought, heavy rain started to fall on the roof of the building. In a BBC radio interview in 1993, he stated unequivocally that he expected to be sacked if annual inflation rose above 2 per cent, the maximum permissible rate under the PTA (RBNZ 1993a: 286). This was the authentic voice of the conservative central banker … and a testable hypothesis. When inflation did exceed the upper bound of the target range for several quarters in the mid 1990s, Brash kept his job. As inflation was still much lower than it had been in the 1970s and 1980s, it would have seemed harsh to dismiss him. Brash was equally zealous in other areas. The RBNZ's approach to banking supervision was remodelled along lines approved by free market critics of bureaucratic intervention. Administrative costs were slashed, and the RBNZ became a leader in the drive for greater efficiency in central banking (Singleton *et al.* 2006).

The radical: Marriner Eccles

Marriner Eccles was an obscure Utah banker at the start of 1933. Within little more than a year, he would be the chairman of the Board of Governors of the Federal Reserve Board. Eccles had been talent spotted by the Roosevelt administration, which was eager to recruit people with new ideas and enthusiasm after the policy disasters of the previous few years. Nevertheless, he was an unusual central banker: 'Eccles held a Keynesian view long before that view became dominant among academics and central bankers. Mixed with that view were vestiges of older ideas about underconsumption, overinvestment, borrowing, speculation, and income distribution. Eccles repeated many times ... that the depression was due in part to inequality in income distribution' (Meltzer 2003: 477).

Furthermore, Eccles agreed with Congressman Goldsborough that, in the context of the depression, monetary policy was as ineffective as 'pushing on a string'. Eccles believed that the answer to depression and the accompanying high level of unemployment was a combination of increased government spending, financed by borrowing, together with the redistribution of income. These ideas were radical indeed for a central banker. On fiscal policy, Eccles was much more innovative than the Roosevelt administration, which continued to believe in balanced budgets. Milton Friedman later argued that Eccles 'played a far greater role in the development of what came later to be called Keynesian policies than did Keynes himself' (quoted in Israelsen 1985: 362).

At the personal level, relations between Eccles and the secretary of the Treasury, Henry Morgenthau, were difficult. But Eccles's critics maintained that he was too ready to concede the initiative in policy making to the Treasury. After the Second World War, however, when the risk of inflation started to outweigh the risk of deflation, Eccles called for the restoration of the Federal Reserve's freedom to control monetary policy. This irritated President Harry Truman, who decided not to reappoint him as chairman in 1948. Yet Eccles continued to sit on the Federal Reserve Board and his campaign for greater autonomy bore fruit in the Treasury–Federal Reserve Accord of 1951.

The compliant central banker: Nugget Coombs

H. C. (Nugget) Coombs, a professional economist and public servant, was thought to be a radical when he took over as governor of the Commonwealth Bank of Australia in 1949. But the radicalism of the 1930s would become the orthodoxy of the 1950s and 1960s. The task of the central bank in Australia in the Keynesian era was in essence to implement the monetary policy decisions of the government. Under the management of Sir Roland Wilson, the Australian Treasury was inclined to treat the central bank as a subordinate agency. Coombs, himself a firm Keynesian, appears to have taken these arrangements for granted (Coombs, H. C. 1981). When he did venture to criticise government policy it was always behind closed doors.

Coombs made few public appearances, and the publications of the Commonwealth Bank and the Reserve Bank of Australia (RBA) were singularly uninformative. (Until 1960 the Commonwealth Bank was

both a commercial bank and a central bank. The central banking arm
was then spun off in the form of the RBA.) As Coombs explained in a
newspaper article in 1968, the year of his retirement: 'I don't think it
makes good sense for a Central Bank to want to have both the role of
a private confidential adviser to government and an outspoken public
critic at the same time. These roles are incompatible' (quoted in Rowse
2002: 289).

Wilson, the domineering secretary of the Treasury, sat on the board
of the central bank, handing down policy and words of admonishment.
'Wilson rarely missed an opportunity to bring the Bank to heel. Although
Coombs was a brilliant and determined advocate, he resiled from the
use of aggression' (Schedvin 1992: 154), not least because he remembered the events of 1931, when relations between the Commonwealth
Bank and the government had broken down, prolonging the depression
in the opinion of some. Wilson restricted Coombs's access to ministers,
and demanded that the central bank report to him. Though aspects
of Coombs's relationship with Wilson were uncomfortable, not to say
humiliating, there was no fundamental clash over policy. Coombs
attached somewhat more emphasis to short-term stabilisation and fine
tuning, while Wilson stressed long-term growth and development, but
these were matters of detail. They sometimes disagreed over the timing
of changes in macroeconomic policy, but Coombs showed no reluctance to comply with the wishes of government. From the perspective
of ministers and Treasury officials, he was a model central banker.

The rebel: James E. Coyne

The Coyne affair 'came close to devastating the Bank of Canada'
(Muirhead 1999: 167). James Coyne was appointed governor of the
Bank of Canada in 1955. He was an insider, having been senior deputy
governor. As the Bank of Canada Act was somewhat vague concerning
the relationship between the government and the central bank, Coyne
had more room for manoeuvre than did Coombs in Australia. Indeed
there was little formal contact between the central bank and the government in Ottawa. The Bank of Canada ran a tight monetary policy by the
standards of the late 1950s. This approach alienated Donald Fleming,
the minister of finance, as well as many professional economists. But
the most unusual feature of Coyne's governorship was his outspoken
and very public censure of government policy. (This would have been
unthinkable in Australia.) The Bank of Canada's 1959 annual report
singled out loose fiscal policy as the most potent threat to economic
stability. Coyne returned to the attack in 1961, releasing a detailed and

wide-ranging critique of government policy, accompanied by recommendations for reform.

Ministers were incensed by Coyne's intervention in policy issues that in their opinion did not concern him, and even more by his readiness to air his dissent in public. Muirhead (1999: 168) describes Coyne as 'arrogant beyond measure'. The government counterattacked by expressing disapproval of the decision of the central bank's directors to double Coyne's pension. In addition, the government introduced a bill in June 1961, which if enacted would have declared vacant the office of governor. This measure was passed by the House of Commons. Coyne then made an emotional speech to the Senate's Banking and Commerce Committee. It became clear that the Senate would not support the government's bill to remove him. Nevertheless, Coyne realised that his position had become untenable and resigned (Howitt 1993: 466–9). Coyne regarded John Diefenbaker, the prime minister, as the 'evil genius' who had orchestrated his downfall (Macfarlane, D. 2008: 136). Having refused to play the compliance game, Coyne paid with his job.

The statesman: Manmohan Singh

It is not unknown for politicians to become central bankers or for central bank governors to advance to senior political positions. This traffic represents another side of the permeability of the central banking world. For example, Jelle Zijlstra served for many years as a government minister in the Netherlands, and then briefly as prime minister from October 1966 to March 1967, before becoming president of de Nederlandsche Bank in May 1967. An economics professor by background, Zijlstra combined his presidency of the Dutch central bank with the presidency of the BIS. He relinquished both posts in 1981 (Zijlstra 1985).

Manmohan Singh has achieved greater heights. After a successful career as an economist in academia and in public service, including a period as a director of the Reserve Bank of India in the late 1970s, Singh became governor of the RBI in 1982, a post that he held for three years. India was still a highly regulated economy – the 'licence raj' – and Singh had to work within an uncongenial policy framework (Jadhav 2003). Singh left the RBI in 1985 to become deputy chairman of the Planning Commission. As finance minister, between 1991 and 1996, he was the principal architect of the deregulation of the Indian economy, including the financial sector. Bhagwati (1993: 3–4) praised him for having, at long last, 'taken India on what Jawaharlal Nehru would have called her "tryst with destiny"'. After a stint as leader of the Opposition between 1998 and 2004, he became prime minister in 2004. While in opposition, Singh gave an interview to V. N. Balasubramanyam, in which he described the autonomy of the central bank as 'a state of mind. It depends very much on the vision, knowledge and experience of the Governor of the Bank. If the advice is of a high quality, it cannot be ignored by any Government' (quoted in Balasubramanyam 2001: 94).

Singh's case raises the question of how long one must work at a central bank in order to qualify as a central banker. Is three years enough? Singh's relative transience is illustrative of a wider trend away from lifetime employment in central banking. By the late twentieth century, recruitment and retention policies were becoming more flexible, and there were more points of entry and exit. Personnel now joined to do a specific job or improve their experience, and moved on after a few years. 'Career central bankers' were not extinct, but they were increasingly rare (Hickey and Mortlock 2002).

The professor: Ben Bernanke

We have already been introduced to three professorial central bankers: Arthur Burns, Jelle Zijlstra, and Manmohan Singh. Since the Second World War, it has become increasingly common for central bank governors to be drawn from the universities. The early twenty-first century has seen the continuation of this practice. For example, Mervyn King, a former economics professor at the London School of Economics, was appointed governor of the Bank of England in 2003.

Professor Ben Bernanke (formerly of Princeton University) succeeded Alan Greenspan as chairman of the Federal Reserve Board in 2006. As an academic, Bernanke was well known for his research on the macroeconomic history of the 1930s. 'To understand the great depression', Bernanke (1995: 1) contended, 'is the Holy Grail of macroeconomics.' While a student, he had been inspired by Friedman and Schwartz's *A Monetary History of the United States*. Bernanke's (2000) own book on the depression stressed the role of the credit crunch, which reflected weaknesses in the banking system and the declining creditworthiness of borrowers. Interviewed by Brian Snowdon (2002: 213), Bernanke said that monetary policy in the USA had become 'too personalised' in the Greenspan era, and suggested that thought should be given to the establishment of a more coherent framework for decision making, such as inflation targeting. By contrast, Greenspan was a sceptic of inflation targeting.

Bernanke was appointed to the Board of Governors of the Federal Reserve System in 2002. After two years in this role, Bernanke (2005: 1) expressed satisfaction 'that the intellectual challenges of my new job have been as rewarding as those I encountered as an academic.' Between June 2005 and January 2006 he served as chairman of the president's Council of Economic Advisers. He took over from Greenspan in 2006, but did not introduce inflation targeting. Another prominent economist, Gregory Mankiw (2006: 184) advised Bernanke to be 'as boring a public figure as possible' and decline the mantle of 'inscrutable wizard'. Mankiw hoped that the personality of the chairman would no longer distract attention from the role of the Fed as institution or the process of formulating and implementing monetary policy. Within a short space of time, however, Fed watchers had more serious concerns, as the USA and the rest of the world plunged into the worst financial turmoil since the depression. No one was better qualified than Bernanke to be at the helm in this situation.

Conclusion

Whereas in 1900 the central banker was a highly specialised type of banker, by 1950 he – as yet there was no she – needed to operate both as a banker and as a civil servant, and by 2000 he, or very occasionally she, was required to be proficient in three areas: banking, economics, and public service. Central banking was becoming a complex, hybrid occupation. In a loose sense, the main events in the evolution of the profession coincided with the first and second revolutions in central banking. Public service notions came to the fore during the revolution of the 1930s and 1940s, while economic skills became more important during the revolution of the late twentieth century.

As central banks came to play a more visible – if not always well understood or transparent – role in public policy, central bankers themselves were increasingly thrust into the news. Montagu Norman was the first star on the central banking stage in the 1920s. He was strongly supported by Hjalmar Schacht, who later turned out to be a villain, and by Benjamin Strong. The star system weakened in the middle decades of the twentieth century, when central bankers were expected to be dutiful public servants. But not all central bankers were content to be 'boring guys' and in the early 1960s James Coyne took on the Canadian government in a public slanging match. The star system returned with a vengeance in the late twentieth century. Central banks were now in the vanguard of the struggle against inflation, and central bankers were never far from the public eye. Alan Greenspan was the epitome of the central banking star or wizard in the 1990s.

Textbooks of monetary economics are loath to discuss the contribution of individual decision makers to the formulation and implementation of monetary policy. Decisions are assumed to be made by an impersonal entity, the central bank, which reacts in a mechanistic way to the flow of economic and monetary data and projections. Yet a case can still be made to the effect that individual policy makers have an impact, whether for good or ill, particularly in times of crisis. Moreover, in so far as the boundaries of central banks are permeable, these institutions could be seen as part of a wider network of policy-making relationships.

3 Wind in the willows: the small world of central banking *c.* 1900

> At the end of the nineteenth century ... 'central bank' meant scarcely more than a single bank distinguished from others by unique public responsibilities eclipsing its commercial interests.
>
> R. S. Sayers (1976, vol. I: 1)

> To mark the 100th anniversary of the publication of 'The Wind in the Willows' on 8 October 1908, the Bank [of England]'s Museum has opened a new, permanent display celebrating the career of its author, Kenneth Grahame, who worked at the Bank for thirty years ... John Keyworth, Curator of the Museum, said 'Grahame's Bank career is little-known, but it is very likely that his thirty-year career had some influence on his writing; either the direct influence of colleagues on the famous characters he created or the atmosphere of life at the grand old institution imbuing his work.'
>
> Bank of England (2008)

The central banking world was small and rather stuffy at the start of the twentieth century. But there were interludes of excitement. *The Times* of 25 November 1903 reported a 'Shooting Outrage at the Bank of England'. A visitor asked for the previous governor, and was taken to see the Bank's secretary, none other than Kenneth Grahame. He subsequently pulled out a gun and fired several times at Grahame. The shots missed, and the plucky central banker overpowered his assailant and locked him in a waiting room. According to *The Times* the gunman expressed 'Socialistic views' when interviewed by police, and was charged with 'Wandering, deemed to be a lunatic'.

Central banking was still an overwhelmingly European phenomenon in 1900, with a single offshoot in Japan (see Table 1). The USA did not have a central bank until 1914. This chapter describes the origins, ownership, governance, and management of selected central banks, and discusses their main functions and policy tools. Rather than attempting an exhaustive coverage, four case studies are presented, dealing with the Bank of England, the Banque de France, the German Reichsbank, and the Bank of Japan. This is not to deny the excellent work that has been done on central banks in other countries including Belgium, Portugal,

Table 1 *Founding dates of banks of*
issue and central banks

Sveriges Riksbank	1688
Bank of England	1694
Banque de France	1800
Bank of Finland	1811
Nederlandsche Bank	1814
Austrian National Bank	1816
Norges Bank	1816
Danmarks Nationalbank	1818
Banco de Portugal	1846
Banque Nationale de Belgique	1850
Banco de España	1874
German Reichsbank	1876
Bank of Japan	1882
Banca d'Italia	1893
Swiss National Bank	1905
Commonwealth Bank of Australia	1911
Federal Reserve System	1913

Source: Broz (1998: 237).

and Sweden (Buyst and Maes 2008a; Reis 2007; Wetterberg 2009). Excellent brief descriptions of the origins and histories of a wider range of European and other central banks can be found in Goodhart, Capie, and Schnadt (1994: 123–231).

It is traditional to begin the analysis of the period between 1870 and 1914 with a discussion of the gold standard, the dominant international monetary regime in 1900 (Bordo and Schwartz 1984). As Gallarotti (1995) explains, however, the international aspects of the gold standard were derived from the prior commitment of governments and banks of issue to monetary stability, which they held to require the convertibility of domestic currency into a fixed weight of precious metal. Given that the leading commercial and financial power, the UK, was already on gold, and that gold was widely perceived to be more stable in value than silver (not to mention paper), other countries had an incentive to adopt a gold standard.

By 1900 the debate over whether the objective of a bank of issue – a term still widely used (Conant 1896) – should be to generate profits for its shareholders or to serve the national interest had been settled in favour of the latter. What would the modern central banker find most jarring if transported back in time to 1900? The overriding commitment to gold convertibility rather than to domestic price stability would seem odd. Not until the First World War and its aftermath would policy makers begin to give much thought to other goals. The absence of explicit economic models and the paucity of economic and monetary data would also shock the modern central banker, since they are taken for granted today. Without such resources central banking was an art and not a science.

From pet banks to central banks

The nineteenth century was the first era of globalisation (O'Rourke and Williamson 1999). To a lesser degree it was also the first era of independent central banks, a term that sounds very modern but which was around in the 1920s (Kisch and Elkin 1932: 17). Central banks were more autonomous in 1900 than they would be in 1950. The main European central banks had considerable *operational* autonomy; sometimes this autonomy was de jure and sometimes it was de facto (Flandreau *et al.* 1998: 133–5, 138–9). Governments rarely told their central banks when to raise or lower the rediscount rate, then the principal lever of policy. Given the requirement that central banks must maintain gold convertibility, they did not have *goal* independence. But this really did not matter in an era when central banks believed in gold at least as strongly as did governments (Eichengreen and Temin 2000). Many of today's independent central banks also have operational but not goal autonomy.

The founders of the first banks of issue had no conception of central banking, let alone of central bank independence. Discussing the origins of the Bank of England, Lawrence White (1991: 39) stressed the government's wish 'to have a pet bank from which to borrow', especially during wartime. Quite a few European governments would establish special banks to assist them with financial problems, often of a war-related nature, and these institutions evolved into banks of issue (Broz 1998: 240–1). Many early banks of issue were owned either wholly or predominantly by private shareholders, but this was not always the case and, for example, the Royal Bank of Prussia, established in 1765, was state owned.

As a *quid pro quo* for supplying the state with loans and other services, these banks and their owners were awarded certain privileges, including the right – but not necessarily the exclusive right – to issue banknotes and earn seigniorage. They were also protected to varying degrees from competition by the imposition of restrictions on the entry and activities of other banks (Grossman 2001). Their charters were renegotiated from time to time in the light of changing circumstances. Governments were tempted to offer new privileges in return for additional loans, or alternatively to threaten their withdrawal unless such loans were forth-coming (Broz and Grossman 2004).

Relations between banks of issue (or proto-central banks) and gov-ernments were complex, anticipating many of the problems experienced in later periods. On the one hand, some autonomy from government was essential in order to reassure shareholders and depositors that they would not be cheated. On the other hand, governments feared that banks of issue would overexpand the issue of notes so as to boost seigniorage, in the process causing inflation and financial instability. (The temptation to overexpand the note issue should not be exagger-ated. Inflation would erode the real value of bank assets and undermine the confidence of depositors, and could also jeopardise renewal of the bank's charter.) A common solution to the threat of overissue was to compel banks of issue to back their notes with reserves of silver and/or gold, or in other words adopt a silver, gold, or bimetallic – silver plus gold – standard. Rules were also devised for sharing seigniorage and other profits between the shareholders and the government. The desire to curb profit seeking and protect the national interest (how-ever defined) was a major consideration in the design of banks of issue. Convertibility was at least in part a tool to constrain the behaviour of banks of issue (Flandreau 2007). The details of how much precious metal was required by law to back the note issue varied from country to country.

By the second half of the nineteenth century, the older banks of issue had consolidated their positions. They were the principal, if not always the exclusive, issuers of banknotes in their jurisdictions. Furthermore, they were major though not always dominant players in the financial markets, with private sector clients as well as their core government banking business. Other banks found it useful to make deposits at the bank of issue, which was typically regarded as a safe haven because of its government sponsorship. Deposits at the 'central bank' could be held as reserves and/or used for interbank settlement. Central banks offered rediscount and loan facilities to banks and certain other institu-tions. Lending and rediscounting were profitable lines of business for central banks.

In a banking crisis the clamour for rediscounts became shrill, pre-senting central bankers with a dilemma. Should they extend emer-gency assistance to other banks, or cling to their reserves and let the other banks collapse? Either response could be profitable for the cen-tral bank. A bank of issue that accepted the role of lender of last resort would expand its portfolio of securities and earn more income from interest payments. A bank of issue that let other banks fail could take over some of their customers. That it might be the duty of the bank of issue to act as lender of last resort had been discussed since the 1790s. In practice, however, this responsibility was accepted only with the greatest reluctance. Not until the first decade of the twentieth century was it widely acknowledged in the central banking world (Wood, G. E. 2000). Whether the central bank should assist individual banks, or focus on providing emergency liquidity to the banking system as a whole, remained a moot point. According to Goodhart (1988), central banks were in a unique position to judge when there was a genuine case for lender of last resort intervention. Routine contact with other banks enabled banks of issue to monitor their management, the quality of their assets, and their liquidity. Even so, there was no explicit prudential supervision by central banks before the twentieth century (Grossman 2006).

By the late nineteenth century, the transformation of banks of issue into central banks was well underway. Central banks were bankers' banks as well as bankers to governments. Most were committed to maintaining the convertibility of the national currency into precious metals. Though their relationship to the state was close, they enjoyed considerable autonomy. So long as convertibility was sacrosanct, the capacity of governments to manipulate central banks and monetary conditions was limited. There was an equally nuanced relationship between central banks and the rest of the banking sector. Drawing many of their senior personnel and shareholders from the world of high finance, central banks might be tempted to think that what was good for this community was good for everyone. On the other hand, many bankers continued to regard central banks as dangerous competitors even when such competition was largely in the past.

Who had the most influence over early central banks? Commenting on nineteenth-century France, Bonin (1992: 223) finds it 'difficult to assess the balance of power between the wishes of the state or the [central bank] Governor it appointed and the wishes of the directors, more or less representative of the world of business and finance'. Where convertibility prevailed, however, neither group could have a free hand.

Bank of England

The Bank of England was the first bank of issue to become a genuine central bank. Its headquarters on Threadneedle Street were at the heart of the world's most complex financial market place (Clapham 1944, vol. I: ch. 7; Sayers 1976, vol. I: chs. 1–4).

Ownership of the Bank of England was vested entirely in private hands until nationalisation in 1946. The governor, deputy governor, and directors were elected by the shareholders. The government limited the Bank's capacity to retain profits and pay dividends, but was otherwise loath to interfere, though it did have the right to demand loans under some circumstances. As a result of these ownership and governance arrangements, the Bank enjoyed substantial operational independence. The working relationship between the Bank and the government was fairly harmonious. Both shared a strong commitment to gold convertibility and fiscal conservatism. The Bank had no need to trumpet its independence, and the government had no reason to undermine it.

Culturally, the Bank of England was one of the pillars of gentlemanly capitalism (Cain and Hopkins 1993a, 1993b). This regime was an alliance, cemented by intermarriage, between the landed and the monied classes of south-east England. The Bank of England was an elite institution, and most of its governors and directors were recruited from the City of London. Some directors were also Members of Parliament. But it does not follow that relations between the Bank of England and other parts of the City were invariably cosy. The big commercial (or 'clearing') banks resented the Bank of England's influence over liquidity, even though they found it useful to have access to central banking facilities. Their resentment owed something to the fact that the Bank of England had until recently been a competitor. Despite having some branches in the provinces, the focus of the central bank was metropolitan and international. The Bank's cultural distance from the ultimate sources of national prosperity in provincial and Scottish manufacturing would attract much criticism in the twentieth century, but was not noticed before 1914 (Daunton 1992; Green 1992; Howe 1994).

Policy was made by the Bank's Treasury Committee (which was nothing to do with Her Majesty's or H. M. Treasury), which included the governor and deputy governor and other senior figures. The Bank was intensely hierarchical and paternalistic (de Fraine 1960), but the pace of work was not taxing. From a public choice perspective, the Bank might be described as a bureaucracy with a soft budget constraint.

The UK had been on the gold standard longer than any other country, convertibility having been restored in 1821 after an interlude during the Napoleonic Wars. The Bank of England operated under the Bank Act of 1844. Organisationally, it was divided into a note issue department and a banking department. The Bank was obliged to hold enough gold to redeem all of its notes on issue, excepting a small fiduciary issue of £14 million, at the rate of one ounce of gold to £3 17s. 9d. This rule was stricter than those in many other countries where it was common for the required gold backing to be well under 100 per cent. Certain other UK banks, especially in Scotland, retained limited rights to issue banknotes.

In practice, the Bank of England held more gold than the required minimum, so as to provide a buffer, albeit partial, against internal and external drains. Of course, the note issue was only a fraction of total deposits of the banking system. All bank deposits were in theory convertible into gold, though the reserves would soon have run out if this had been tested. During an internal financial panic, of which there were several in the nineteenth century, the Bank feared being drained of gold. Furthermore, any overall deficit on the balance of payments might if all else failed have to be met by gold shipments. Thus the gold reserves of the Bank of England were expected to meet internal and external drains.

The Bank of England provided deposit and settlement services to banks in the UK. It also rediscounted eligible securities and advanced funds to certain financial institutions. The discount houses, including Gilletts, acted as a buffer between the Bank of England and the clearing banks. Whenever there was a shortage of liquidity, the discount houses could borrow from the central bank. Gilletts did so roughly once a month, generally seeking an advance, but occasionally offering securities for rediscounting (Sayers 1968: 54–60). The interest rate charged by the Bank at the discount window was the 'Bank Rate'. This was set at a 'penal' level above the market rate for funds.

The objective of the Bank was to maintain convertibility by conserving its gold reserves. Typically, it adjusted the Bank Rate in order to manage the level of gold reserves and the ratio of reserves to liabilities, or liquidity (Giovannini 1986). When the Bank felt that the gold reserves and/or liquidity were too low – either because of developments at home or overseas – it was inclined to raise the Bank Rate. A high Bank Rate pulled funds into the UK from abroad, improving the balance of payments and attracting gold, which ended up at the Bank of England. Moreover, a high Bank Rate depressed domestic borrowing and activity, curbing the demand for banknotes, and enabling the Bank to manage with less gold. By contrast, when the gold reserves were deemed plentiful, the Bank might cut interest rates, though in this situation the incentive to act was weaker. How systematically the Bank reacted to changes in reserves and liquidity – how closely it played by the unwritten rules of the gold standard game – is a matter for debate. As the credibility of the UK's commitment to gold was rarely questioned before 1914 there was considerable scope for discretion.

Discount rate policy is more effective when the central bank can control market liquidity and force the private sector to visit the discount window. During the late nineteenth century this was often a problem. By 1900, however, the Bank had developed techniques for extracting liquidity by borrowing from the market on the security of government paper, or by selling securities (OMOs) for repurchase later (Bindseil 2004: 108–17, 145–6). Additional tools were available. Changes could be made to the eligibility of securities for rediscounting. The Bank also manipulated the gold devices: inducements were offered to importers of gold, while administrative costs and delays were imposed on exporters of gold. The reserves could also be replenished by purchasing or borrowing gold from abroad.

Walter Bagehot (1873), the author of *Lombard Street*, the most famous book on central banking, chided the Bank of England for shirking its duty as a crisis manager and lender of last resort. He argued that the Bank had on several occasions failed to act as a responsible central bank. During the crises of 1890 and 1906–7, however, the Bank acted more decisively than previously to avert panic. The Bank responded to the failure of Barings in 1890 by organising a consortium of City firms to guarantee the liabilities of this merchant bank, and even made a contribution of £1 million from its own funds. In addition, the gold reserves were boosted by borrowing and purchasing bullion. These measures proved effective. During the crisis of 1906–7 the Bank obtained further loans of gold from abroad. It continued to provide rediscounting services to the market during these episodes instead of withdrawing into a defensive shell (Kindleberger 1996: 147–40, 169–70; Clapham 1944, vol. II: 326–39).

The Bank of England was by far the most sophisticated and experienced central bank in 1900. Privately owned, with governors and directors appointed by the shareholders, the Bank enjoyed considerable operational autonomy within the overall constraints of the gold standard and the 1844 act. By 1900 the Bank saw itself as a public agency and not as a commercial operation, and was committed to upholding the stability of the banking system. In other words it had made the transition from bank of issue to central bank.

Banque de France

The Banque de France was set up in 1800, and was initially the pet bank of Napoleon Bonaparte. Over the nineteenth century, the Banque evolved into an accomplished central bank. But it was in some respects very different from the Bank of England. In particular, the fact that France lagged behind the UK in financial development had implications for the behaviour of the French central bank.

Though the Banque was in private ownership in 1900, it was by no means a profit-maximising organisation, and dividends were capped. Managerial control was exercised by three state appointees, namely the governor and two deputy governors, and fifteen directors elected by shareholders. The Banque possessed considerable de facto autonomy. It was not obliged to offer short term credit to the state, but it did have to invest half of any surplus in French government securities. Left-wing critics alleged that the Banque was dominated by shareholders and directors from the 'deux cent familles', or the financial elite. But this was an exaggerated claim, and in fact the Bank's shareholders and directors were drawn from a much wider social sphere (Plessis 1992: 147–50).

Certain limits were imposed on the Banque's issue of banknotes. But there was no rule specifying the amount of gold or silver required as backing for the note issue. France was legally on a bimetallic standard, and the Banque had the right to redeem its notes in silver or gold (Gallarotti 2005: 630). However, France had been a de facto member of the gold standard since 1878, and the Banque normally paid out gold.

One of the legacies of the Napoleonic era was the belief that it was the duty of the Banque de France to facilitate the provision of affordable credit to the French economy. To this end, the Banque focused on maintaining a low and very stable rediscount rate (the rate was usually between 3 per cent and 4 per cent). Contemporaries often remarked on the stability of the French rediscount rate, not least in comparison with the UK bank rate. In France the discount window was open to numerous industrial firms as well as to banks. Moreover, advances were made to many of these clients. The Banque was handicapped in the conduct of policy by the prohibition of OMOs. Its capacity to influence monetary conditions was also limited by the high liquidity levels of the Paris banks, which rarely needed to approach the discount window. Indeed the big Paris banks were loath to place deposits at the Banque (Bopp 1952; Bonin 2000). Interest rate stability was facilitated and underpinned by the Banque's high gold reserves, a luxury that its British counterpart did not enjoy. The Banque could afford to permit substantial changes in the level of reserves before adjusting the rediscount rate. When the Banque wished to strengthen the reserves, it often preferred to use the gold devices rather than change the rediscount rate.

The French provincial economy was hampered by a relatively primitive banking sector. With some reluctance, the Banque de France was persuaded to offer improved banking and transfer services in regional centres, though it did not welcome retail customers. In 1902, the Banque had 126 branches and 50 auxiliary offices, and connections in a further 234 towns, as well as a head office in Paris (Palgrave 1903: 143; Plessis

2007). Curiously, the Banque was more of a central bank to provincial France than it was to Paris where, as noted above, there was less need of its services.

The mantle of lender of last resort was accepted in the 1880s. The Banque made advances to the Paris and Lyons stock exchanges in 1882, with a view to preventing a crisis spilling over into the banking system. Advances were also made to several banks in 1882 after the collapse of the Union Generale. In 1889 and 1891 the Banque stepped in again to support and restructure ailing banks (Goodhart 1988: 121).

The Banque de France had much more of a developmental role than did the Bank of England, though this function was not embraced with any enthusiasm. Low and stable discount rates were a boon to the French economy. The Banque operated in a different environment to that which prevailed in the UK, but it was no less capable or successful than the Bank of England.

The Reichsbank

The Reichsbank was created in 1876, in the aftermath of the Franco-Prussian War, German unification, and Germany's adoption of the gold standard in 1871, helped by a substantial war indemnity from France. Conant (1896: 197) described the Reichsbank, which inherited many of the functions of the Royal Bank of Prussia, as 'entirely a private institution as to ownership, but essentially a public one in its management'. It was evident from the outset that the Reichsbank would be guided by the public or imperial interest and would not attempt to maximise returns to shareholders.

One of the Reichsbank's first tasks was to unify the currency. A second goal was to circulate the new banknotes, and a third was to facilitate inter-regional payments, to which end branches were opened across Germany and a clearing house was set up in Berlin. The central bank was also expected to provide rediscount accommodation at a modest rate to German business and the banks. By offering these services the Reichsbank contributed to the financial integration of Germany, and thus helped to foster the emergence of a new economic superpower (Goodhart 1988: 105–11).

On the face of it, the Reichsbank was not very independent. The Reich chancellor chaired the supervisory Curatorium of the Reichsbank. The Bank was actually managed by a Directorate, nominated by the Bundesrat and appointed for life by the Kaiser, and the chief executive was known as the president rather than the governor. On occasion the Directorate was given politically motivated commands. A famous incident occurred in 1887 when at the insistence of the government, and for reasons of foreign policy, 'the Reichsbank forbade the *Lombardierung* (use as a security deposit against loans) of Russian bonds' (James 1999b: 9). Moreover, the Reichsbank could be required to extend short-term credit to the government. Mostly, however, the government permitted the Directorate to run the central bank without interference. Even shareholders had some countervailing power: they had the right to be consulted over the direction of the Reichsbank, and could veto preferential transactions with the Reich or state governments. Holtfrerich (1988: 111) concludes that despite 'the legal subordination of the Reichsbank to the Reich ... the Reichsbank Directorate in fact enjoyed a considerable degree of autonomy', at least within the constraints imposed by the gold standard.

The Reichsbank was required to back its note issue up to a fixed limited with reserves of one-third in gold (or silver) and two-thirds in first-class bills. Additional notes required 100 per cent cash backing (Flandreau *et al.* 1998: 133). Reichsbank policy was to rediscount 'real bills', or bills arising from 'genuine' commercial transactions and not speculative activities. In 1900, about 63,000 firms or persons had either direct or indirect access to the discount window, and each had a separate credit line. As well as offering a rediscount facility, the central bank offered advances or 'Lombard' loans at a higher interest rate on the collateral of various private and public sector securities. The rediscount rate, which was closely shadowed by market rates, was the main tool of monetary policy. OMOs were conducted four times before 1914 (Giovannini 1986: 474).

Econometric evidence suggests that the Reichsbank adjusted the rediscount rate in response to changes in the ratio of its gold reserves to liabilities. When the Reichsbank's liquidity declined, it came under pressure to increase the rediscount rate. Between 1876 and 1913, however, the rediscount rate kept within the range of 3 per cent to 6 per cent, rising above 6 per cent only in the crisis of 1907 (Bindseil 2004: 129–35, 139; Sommariva and Tullio 1987: 101–18).

By the start of the twentieth century, the Reichsbank was beginning to act as a lender of last resort. When the Leipziger Bank and Dresdner Kreditanstalt collapsed in 1901, the Reichsbank intervened to avert contagion, though its liberality during this episode could have been a source of moral hazard (James 1999b: 13). Building on a long tradition of state banking, the Reichsbank evolved into a genuine central bank, offering a wide range of services to government and the private sector (Lexis 1910). It played a crucial role in binding the German economy together after the formation of the empire. Though the Reichsbank enjoyed less formal autonomy than did the Bank of England, its expertise was respected by the German government, and for the most part it was allowed to get on with the job.

Bank of Japan

Established in 1882, the Bank of Japan was the first central bank outside Europe. After the Japanese economy was opened to western influence in the mid-nineteenth century, there was a period of financial experimentation and instability. The creation of a European style central bank, ostensibly modelled on the Banque Nationale de Belgique (BNB), which in the opinion of the Japanese authorities was the state of the art, was an important event in the process of financial stabilisation and modernisation. Aspiring to become a modern state, Japan was determined to copy the best European institutions (Schiltz 2006). Banknote issue was consolidated in the hands of the new central bank, which began to offer a range of financial services to the government, as well as to the banking industry.

The similarities between the early Bank of Japan and the BNB and its western European peers should not be exaggerated. Whereas the BNB was privately owned and relatively autonomous, the Bank of Japan was to a large extent under the government's thumb. The state was a major shareholder. Private citizens needed to have permission from the minister of finance before they could acquire shares in the central bank. The policy of the Bank was dictated by the Japanese Treasury. Consequently, the Bank was not in a position to deny short term loans to the government. A second point of difference between the European and Japanese approaches flowed from the curious role of the Yokohama Specie Bank (YSB). The YSB, which was also a government controlled institution, handled the financing of overseas trade, the raising of official loans overseas, and the accumulation of precious metals. Special rediscounting facilities were offered by the Bank of Japan to the YSB. Thus there were two important banking institutions with a public policy role in Japan, and both were subordinate to the Treasury.

A third significant difference between the Belgian and Japanese experiences concerns relations between the central bank and the commercial banks. The BNB was willing to rediscount good quality commercial securities, at the market rate or above, when approached by anyone in the market. By contrast, the Bank of Japan interacted with a relatively small number of large banks – about 40 out of 2,000 or so banks in 1900. Though the Bank of Japan provided a rediscounting facility, it often made direct advances to clients, frequently accepting relatively illiquid securities as collateral. Until around 1903, the Bank of Japan furnished advances at interest rates below market.

The Bank of Japan became the lender of last resort during the crisis of 1890. The Bank made an important contribution to the development of the Japanese banking system. As in Germany, the central bank was involved in the development of the payments and inter-regional transfer systems, and branches were opened in a number of cities. But market interest rates remained high by western European standards, and to some extent regional variations in rates persisted, indicating that financial markets were less sophisticated than in Europe (Tamaki 1995: 57–73, 90–7; Ohnuki 2007; Goodhart 1988: 150–60; Patrick 1965).

After the successful war against China in 1894–5, Japan obtained a large indemnity in gold from the Chinese government. This indemnity was used as the basis for Japan's switch from the silver standard to the gold standard in 1897. Japan had been considering a move to gold ever since India made the transition in 1893. Advocates of the gold standard argued that sticking with silver, which was depreciating in value relative to gold, would be inflationary, but the surge in world gold supplies in the late 1890s meant that at the start of the twentieth century it was actually more inflationary to be on gold. The management of Japan's participation in the gold standard required close cooperation between the Bank of Japan and the YSB, dubbed the Siamese twins. There were high-level exchanges of staff between these institutions, though some jealousy was inevitable. Indeed, it was the YSB that opened an account at the Bank of England in order to facilitate official international transfers (Tamaki 1995: 82–5; Mitchener, Shizume, and Weidenmier 2009).

Though Japan was at an earlier stage of financial and economic development than the UK, France, or Germany, it was eager to adopt the form and, to a lesser extent, the substance of European central banking. In this respect it was in advance of the USA, which continued to debate the pros and cons of a central bank until the eve of the First World War.

International gold standard

This is not the place for a detailed account of the history and working of the gold standard. Readers are referred to the standard accounts (Bordo and Schwartz 1984; Eichengreen 1985, 1996: ch. 2; Officer 2001; Bayoumi, Eichengreen, and Taylor 1996), and only selected aspects are considered here. During the nineteenth century a number of countries followed the UK's example and made their currencies convertible into gold. This network evolved into the international gold standard in the final three decades of the century (Gallarotti 1995). China, Spain, and Brazil were the only large economies without gold convertibility in 1900. As the US case shows, however, it was possible to have gold convertibility without a central bank.

By the late 1890s, gold production was rising strongly because of discoveries in South Africa and Australia. As gold grew more plentiful it became easier for countries and their central banks to accumulate gold reserves and stay on the gold standard, though this did not stop peripheral members from falling off gold from time to time. The increase in gold supplies also led to rising price levels around the world. But gold was not the only form in which reserves could be held. Many central banks, including the Reichsbank, held some reserves in the core international currencies, especially sterling. As the UK's commitment to gold was believed to be unshakeable, sterling balances in London bank accounts were as good as gold, at least in the opinion of many central banks and other financial market participants. Their faith in the British would prove sadly misplaced after the First World War.

Many people – including some who should have known better – believed that the operation of the international gold standard involved large transfers of gold, ultimately between central banks, in response to imbalances in international payments. In reality, however, the flow of gold in settlement of deficits was quite small. Central banks could often avoid external drains by raising interest rates to attract inflows of short-term capital, or by tweaking the gold devices. Speculation tended to be stabilising because the commitment of the core central banks to the gold standard was credible. Instead of rushing to withdraw funds from a country with an external deficit, speculators increased their deposits in anticipation of higher interest rates. Marginal changes in interest rates were sufficient to reverse international imbalances. But this only worked for core countries whose commitment to gold was believed.

Since central banks were interested in domestic financial conditions, including the potential for banking instability, as well as in the external situation, and could count on stabilising speculation, they did not always raise interest rates in response to an external deficit. Similarly, inflows of gold could be sterilised in order to defuse inflationary pressure. In other words central banks did not always follow the 'rules of the game' – the somewhat misleading term often used to describe central bank behaviour under the gold standard. There was no formal gold standard 'regime' in 1900, only a loose network of countries and central banks with similar objectives and convictions.

The classic era of the gold standard was by no means devoid of currency, banking, or twin crises (Bordo 2007). Peripheral countries and the USA were more vulnerable than the advanced European nations, but no country was immune. For example, a financial crisis originating in the USA in 1907 led to a serious drain of gold from the Bank of England. Lifting the rediscount rate was not enough to halt this drain, and the Bank of England supplemented its reserves by borrowing foreign gold (Flandreau 1997). There was always a risk of conflict between the central bank's commitment to gold and its function as the domestic lender of last resort. When a central bank pumped liquidity into individual banks and/or the banking system, there was an increased risk of inflation and gold losses. Fortunately, major difficulties of this nature were avoided before 1914. A final threat arose from the rapid growth of foreign currency reserves. What if central banks with holdings of sterling decided that they wanted gold instead? The UK was in an increasingly vulnerable position, yet little thought was given to this problem.

The gold standard worked smoothly in the core countries before 1914 because shocks were modest, relative price levels did not diverge strongly, and policy objectives did not change. Only small adjustments to interest rates were necessary to make the system work with minimal adverse impact on the banking system and the real economy. During and after the First World War these benign conditions would no longer pertain.

Conclusion

Central banks were accountable to both governments and shareholders in 1900, but not in any standardised way. Central bank autonomy varied from country to country. A loose correlation between financial development and central bank independence may be observed in the cases described above. Perhaps the oddest feature of the central banking world in 1900 was the non-participation of the USA, though the USA was on the gold standard.

The interest rate on rediscounts (and advances) was the main policy tool of central banks. The gold devices also proved useful, but open market operations were relatively infrequent. The key policy objective was to maintain the convertibility of the currency into gold; indeed this goal was mandated by legislation. Central banks also played a role in the payment and settlement system. They received deposits from other banks, though the amounts involved might be quite small, and they facilitated inter-regional payments. Furthermore, central banks monitored the overall health of the financial system and from time to time acted as emergency lenders of last resort.

The international gold standard was successful because it evolved out of national monetary arrangements and was not a mechanism imposed from outside. Under pre-war conditions, the commitment to gold at existing exchange rates did not create undue stress on the real economy. Central banks were not given the task of smoothing domestic economic fluctuations or of eliminating employment. In any case, no central bank possessed the intellectual capital, and few had the institutional framework, required for the sort of economic management that would be popular in the mid twentieth century. After 1914 the world changed dramatically, and central banks faced new challenges. How they responded to these challenges is dealt with in later chapters.

4   Something for everyone: new central banks, 1900–1939

> It has generally been agreed ... that when the direction of public finance is in the hands of a ministry responsible to a popularly elected Legislature, a ministry which would for that reason be liable to frequent change with the changing political situation, it is desirable that the control of currency and credit in the country should be in the hands of an independent authority which can act with continuity ... indeed the only practical device for securing this independence and continuity is to set up a Central Bank, independent of political influence.
>
> Sir George Schuster, Finance Member of the
> Viceroy's Council, 1933
> (Simha 1970: 38–9)

The central banking gospel was spread far and wide between 1900 and 1939. The Federal Reserve System, which came into operation in 1914, has pride of place in this chapter. However, in the 1920s and 1930s central banks were established in a range of countries in central and eastern Europe, the British empire, and Latin America. The motives of those who set them up were many and various, and indeed they often disagreed over the nature of the benefits that they would confer. Questions of institutional design, governance, and goals proved equally controversial.

After 1918, central banking proliferated in the context of global political and economic turmoil. Post-war instability and reconstruction lasted until the mid 1920s. Following a brief respite, the world economy plunged into depression in the early 1930s, and had barely recovered by the outbreak of the Second World War in 1939. The next two chapters concern the activities of central banks between the wars.

Origins of the Federal Reserve System

Nineteen thirteen was a decisive year in the history of central banking, the Federal Reserve bill being passed in December. The Federal Reserve System (the Fed), which consisted of twelve regional Reserve

Banks in cities from Boston to San Francisco, and a Federal Reserve Board in Washington, commenced operations in 1914. War was declared in Europe in August, and the Reserve Banks opened in November (Meltzer 2003: 74). Created in response to concerns about the stability of the *domestic* banking system, the Fed was confronted by a major *international* disruption before it was on its feet.

Central banking was a controversial topic in the USA. The First and Second Banks of the USA (1791–1811 and 1816–36) fulfilled some rudimentary central banking functions until they fell foul of their critics. Opposition to centralised economic institutions was a persistent feature of American life. Politicians, farmers, and business leaders in the hinterland hated the 'money power', or the north-eastern financial establishment, and feared that any central bank would come under its sway. The US banking system developed in a haphazard manner, with a mixture of state-registered and nationally registered banks, and tight restrictions on branch banking. Under the national banking system a complex chain of relationships emerged between banks in different centres. Country banks had accounts at banks in reserve cities, while reserve city banks had accounts at banks in central reserve cities, the most important of which was New York. Interbank payments were cleared – calculated and approved – through private clearing houses, and settled by transfers between accounts at banks in reserve or central reserve cities. Holdings of gold were spread widely, but the main concentrations were in the hands of the US Treasury and certain New York banks.

National banks issued banknotes, the quantity allowed depending on their capital and the amount of US Treasury securities that they deposited with the comptroller of the currency. These banks faced strict reserve requirements in relation to deposits. Reserves could include banks' own balances at reserve city or central reserve city banks up to certain limits, as well as gold and silver, gold and silver certificates, and US government greenbacks (Champ 2007). Holders of banknotes and deposits could demand gold, compelling local banks to withdraw gold from banks in the reserve cities, and ultimately the central reserve cities. Central reserve city banks might be able to obtain gold from the US Treasury or from abroad, but their position could soon become delicate.

The New York banks had the capacity, at least up to a point, to act as lenders of last resort to the rest. Although they did provide emergency liquidity from time to time, they could not be relied upon consistently to do so. During the crisis of 1893 they left many regional banks in the lurch because they feared losing too much gold. Unlike the Bank of England or the Banque de France, the New York banks were not backed by central government, and did not have a public policy role. The US Treasury did inject liquidity at moments of crisis, but this was not its primary function. Clearing houses also helped by allowing special certificates to be used in the clearing and settlement process, and from time to time the New York banks staunched an outflow of gold to the public by enforcing the temporary suspension of convertibility. The propensity of the US banking system to descend into chaos was not its only problem. The inelasticity of the currency, which arose from the fixed link between the volume of national banknotes in circulation and the quantity of government debt, was highly inconvenient. At harvest time, the level of agricultural transactions rose and extra currency was needed. Since more currency was not forthcoming, interest rates soared and banks struggled to cope with withdrawals. The inelasticity of the currency rendered banks vulnerable to a run. In the eyes of many Americans at the start of the twentieth century, the lack of a central bank with the capacity to rediscount securities, respond to seasonal changes in demand for currency, and act as the lender of last resort was the Achilles heel of the US economy. But others were not convinced, holding that more limited reforms would suffice to increase the elasticity of the currency and reduce the incidence of crises (Wood, J. H. 2005: ch. 6).

The central banking debate gained impetus from the financial crisis of 1907. Panic spread in the wake of a run on the Knickerbocker Trust Company, a specialist New York bank that had been speculating in copper. As the crisis developed, many banks suspended payments to depositors (Friedman and Schwartz 1963: 156–68). The US Treasury and a group of bankers led by J. P. Morgan eventually rode to the rescue, supplying emergency liquidity to the banking system and the New York stock exchange, possibly averting a systemic meltdown. Even so, there ensued a recession with repercussions in Europe, as American investors and financial institutions sought to repatriate funds, leading to withdrawals of gold from the Bank of England and other central banks.

Perhaps a central bank would have responded to the Knickerbocker crash more effectively, smoothing its impact on the banking system and economic activity. At any rate, this was a plausible argument after 1907. The Aldrich Vreeland Act 1908 made provision for the creation of emergency liquidity. A National Monetary Commission (NMC) was also set up in 1908 to discuss the problems of the US monetary system. The NMC, chaired by Nelson Aldrich, a Republican senator was extremely thorough. The commissioners took classes on money and banking from a distinguished economist, A. Piatt Andrew (Caporale 2003: 319), and sailed to Europe to inspect some real central banks. Though sceptical at first, Aldrich grew convinced that America needed a central bank. But this was still a divisive topic among economists, politicians, and the public. Later generations are indebted to the NMC for commissioning some detailed studies of foreign monetary and banking systems that together provide the most comprehensive account of central banking in Europe before the First World War (Mitchell 1911).

After protracted deliberations, Senator Aldrich, Professor Andrew, and a group of leading New York bankers met on Jekyll Island, Georgia in November 1910 to draft legislation for a National Reserve Association (NRA). In an effort to defuse criticism, they proposed a scheme for a cooperative union of banks rather than a central bank. The NRA would have performed central banking functions, including the rediscounting of commercial bills. Banks that joined the NRA would have held most of their reserves as deposits with the association. Subscribing banks would in fact have owned the NRA. Fifteen branches were envisaged, with control vested in a central board. Members of the central board would have been elected by the branches, while the chairman and chief executive, or governor, would have been appointed by the president of the USA (Wicker 2005).

Aldrich wanted to strengthen the banking system, and enable New York to compete more successfully with London as a financial centre. These aims were shared by many north-eastern bankers. Lacking adequate facilities for rediscounting, the market for commercial paper in New York was primitive by the standards of London or Paris, and in consequence it was failing to attract international financial business (Broz 1999).

When the Democrats swept all before them in congressional and presidential elections in 1910–12, they depicted the Aldrich bill as a ploy to entrench the 'money power'. Given the proposal's origins on Jekyll Island, this was a plausible interpretation. Wall Street bankers were the bogeymen of the day, and the machinations of the 'money trust' were about to be investigated by the Pujo Commission. The Aldrich bill was thwarted. However, the Democrats indicated that they were open to proposals for a central bank that incorporated safeguards against undue centralisation and manipulation by the money power. President Woodrow Wilson, elected in 1912, and Secretary of State William Jennings Bryan agreed that a central bank could be useful, if run in the national interest (as they saw it) and not in that of the eastern financial establishment. Wilson, a high-minded lawyer and academic, was anxious to break up excessive concentrations of economic power.

Bryan had run for the presidency in 1896 as a friend of the farmers and a bitter opponent of the gold standard (Forder 2003). They were interested in a central bank that would supply liquidity to the regions, particularly in times of distress.

In 1912 Representative Carter Glass (Democrat), a former newspaperman, became chairman of a subcommittee of the House Banking and Currency Committee tasked with examining reform proposals. Committee members relied heavily on the advice of another economist, Henry Parker Willis, who helped them to formulate a new central banking proposal, involving a system of independent regional reserve banks with minimal coordination. Curiously, Wilson considered the Glass scheme to involve too much decentralisation, and insisted on greater coordination by a central board of government nominees. Wilson's modifications became the basis for the Glass Owen bill and the Federal Reserve Act 1913. Forder (2003) notes the differences between Wilson's understanding of central bank independence and that of economists and central bankers today. Wilson emphasised that the central bank should be *independent of the New York banking establishment*, and regarded the government's involvement as a guarantee of autonomy. By contrast, the Aldrich plan had envisaged a system run by bankers. The conventional view today is that a central bank should be autonomous from both politicians and bankers.

The goals of the 1913 Act were 'to provide for the establishment of Federal Reserve Banks, to furnish an elastic currency, to afford means of rediscounting commercial paper, to establish a more effective supervision of banking in the USA, and for other purposes' (Board of Governors of the Federal Reserve System 1994: 2). No provision was made for lending to the government – a key function of early banks of issue in Europe – and there was no mention of macroeconomic goals such as price stability.

The Federal Reserve System comprised twelve Reserve Banks, their locations selected after much wrangling, and a Federal Reserve Board in Washington (Sprague 1914). Each Reserve Bank was owned by 'member' banks in its region, membership comprising all national banks plus qualified (and interested) state registered banks. National banks could opt out by becoming state banks (Wood, J. H. 2005: 165). Initial subscriptions to capital were paid in gold or gold certificates. Member banks elected two-thirds of the directors of the Reserve Banks, the remainder being chosen by the Federal Reserve Board. Only half of the elected directors could be bankers. The governors or chief executives of the Reserve Banks varied in influence, the most important being the governor of the FRBNY.

The Federal Reserve Board was empowered to issue banknotes through the medium of the Reserve Banks, which had to maintain a gold cover against such notes of at least 40 per cent. Federal Reserve notes started to replace national banknotes during the First World War. Reserve Banks also had to maintain a minimum reserve ratio of 35 per cent in gold and other lawful money against member bank deposits (Hawtrey 1922a: 228). The government transferred much of its banking business to the Reserve Banks. Member banks were required to hold fixed proportions of total deposits as reserves at the nearest Reserve Bank, but reserve requirements were not as stringent as under the national banking system. There was a gradual transfer of bank reserves from existing reserve agents to the Reserve Banks. Only those reserves held at a Reserve Bank counted from 1917 (Scott 1914; Friedman and Schwartz 1963: 194). Reserve Banks were empowered to rediscount eligible securities and engage in OMOs (Small and Clouse 2004). These powers could be used to adjust monetary conditions so as to meet seasonal requirements, as well as to facilitate intervention by Reserve Banks as emergency lenders of last resort. Only 'real' bills, or bills representing genuine – agricultural, industrial, and commercial – as opposed to financial transactions, were eligible for rediscounting. The logic underlying this distinction was contentious.

There was little in the 1913 Act concerning the role of the Federal Reserve System in the payment system. Nevertheless, the Fed soon became active in this area, especially through the introduction of an improved cheque collection service, and the provision of facilities to expedite inter-regional transfers. Costly and slow procedures for collecting, processing, and clearing cheques had been a drawback of the national banking system. Member banks were able to settle interbank obligations through the Fed from 1918 onwards. By 1920, the Fed had branches in twenty-two cities, and was the only nationwide banking group (Gilbert 2000). The 1913 act also touched upon prudential supervision. It authorised the comptroller of the currency to examine each member bank twice a year, and the Fed to examine them at its discretion. Overlapping responsibilities would lead to persistent friction between the Fed and the comptroller (Robertson 1968: 105–12).

The Federal Reserve Board in Washington had seven members: the secretary of the Treasury, the comptroller of the currency, and five members appointed for ten-year terms by the president of the USA with the advice and consent of the Senate. The president chose the governor and vice-governor from amongst the Board members. At first the Board was supported by a small staff of forty-five. Willis was the first secretary to the Board (Dykes 1989).

The Federal Reserve System 'had something for everyone', according to J. H. Wood (2005: 165). In other words, it was a compromise between centralisation and decentralisation, between bankers and government. A messy arrangement was inevitable given political realities in the USA. As well as having a dearth of personnel and directors with practical experience of central banking, the Fed was hampered by the unclear division of authority between the Board and the Reserve Banks. Reserve Banks saw themselves as independent agents, while the Board was tempted to manage as well as coordinate them. Meltzer (2003: 75) observes that 'Tension between the Board and the reserve banks began before the System opened for business.' Because of the strategic position of the FRBNY, and the superior ability of its governor, Ben Strong (Chandler, L. V. 1958: 41), New York was inclined to dominate (Friedman and Schwartz 1963: 190) the system in the early years. At the prompting of Strong, who mistrusted the political appointees on the Board, the Reserve Banks established a Conference of Governors, later known as the Presidents' Conference.

Relations between the Fed, the US Treasury, and the government were far from easy. The powers of the Treasury and the Fed overlapped in some areas, and the Treasury was represented on the Federal Reserve Board by the secretary of the Treasury and the comptroller of the currency. Charles Hamlin, the first governor (chairman) of the Board, was a former assistant secretary of the Treasury. At Treasury insistence, the Board was at first based in the Treasury building in Washington, an arrangement that Willis described as a 'fundamental error in the process of organization', since it implied that the Board was a branch of Treasury (Clifford 1965: 79). There was conflict between Treasury and non-Treasury factions on the Board. While the Fed would soon assert a separate identity, it could not resist all government influence, especially during wartime.

In 1913 the US Congress had created one of the most powerful economic agencies in the world. The Fed would have to learn its business by trial and error, during the most turbulent period in monetary history, while struggling with a difficult organisational problem. Indeed the Fed resembled one of those poorly coordinated holding companies that were set up in the USA and the UK between the late 1890s and the First World War (Chandler, A. D. 1990: 75–8). As a result of the First World War and its aftermath, the Fed was soon drawn in activities not contemplated by the founders. Envisaged as a largely 'passive system' (Meltzer 2003: 73) responding to the fluctuating needs of business, the Fed was compelled to become more active.

Europe and Latin America

The Fed was not the only new central bank in the early twentieth century. Switzerland set up a central bank in 1905, while under the Commonwealth Bank Act 1911 Australia acquired a state-owned trading (commercial) bank that would gradually evolve into a central bank. After the First World War, which left a legacy of political and economic instability (Singleton 2007; Eichengreen 1992a, 1996: 45–92), there was a renewed drive to establish central banks, partly in order to restore a semblance of monetary order. The disintegration of the Austro-Hungarian, Russian, and German empires created opportunities to spread the central banking gospel. Plenty of encouragement and advice was offered by the Bank of England, the FRBNY, the Banque de France, and the League of Nations to nations that were contemplating opening a central bank. However, no single factor accounts for the rapid diffusion of central banking in the inter-war period (Helleiner 2003a: 140–62).

During the First World War the operation of the gold standard was suspended, as European governments attempted to stem outflows of gold. Nearly all currencies, except the US dollar, were floating by 1919. This situation alarmed most economists and policy makers in western Europe and north America, believing as they did that the gold standard had been vital for prosperity before 1914. They hoped that central banks would lock new and peripheral countries into a reconstructed gold standard in the 1920s. If new central banks could be insulated from domestic political manipulation, they would play a key role in overcoming high (or hyper-) inflation, which was the precondition for currency stabilisation and the introduction of some form of convertibility. If international investors could be assured by an autonomous central bank that irresponsible government policies would be thwarted, then loans for reconstruction and development would be forthcoming (Bordo, Edelstein, and Rockoff 1999).

Within the countries debating the formation of a central bank, there were many who shared the perspective of the international elite, but also many others with different motives for promoting central banking. At the most basic level, writes one historian of central banking in the former Austro-Hungarian empire, 'National monies required national central banks' (Schubert 1999: 222). A central bank might be desired as a symbol of national identity and modernisation. Furthermore, instead of constraining domestic politicians, a central bank might be used by them to stimulate economic activity and development, in defiance of advice from the Bank of England or other international authorities. Even in the core countries, doubts were emerging over the appropriateness of the traditional emphasis on central banks as guardians of the gold standard. A few economists, including Irving Fisher in the USA, and Ralph Hawtrey and John Maynard Keynes in the UK, argued that *domestic* price stability should have priority (Mehrling 2002). In short, the advocates of central banking called upon a variety of economic reasoning.

The central banking cause was boosted by the recommendations of the International Financial Conference at Brussels in 1920. Called by the League of Nations, this conference discussed solutions to the postwar financial crisis (omitting the question of German reparations). All countries were urged to balance their budgets, combat inflation, and work towards restoration of the gold standard. Having ruled out the introduction of an international currency, the delegates concluded that independent banks of issue (central banks) should be established in all countries (Davis 1920; League of Nations 1945: 12, 20). During the 1920s the League of Nations Financial Committee, which enjoyed close links with the Bank of England (Clavin 2003: 223), advanced a number of stabilisation and reconstruction schemes for central and eastern Europe. An autonomous central bank was a standard component of such schemes. Once the budget had been balanced, inflation overcome, and the (new) currency stabilised and linked to gold, the central bank would ensure the smooth running of the regime and defend convertibility. Montagu Norman and other central bankers provided the League and its clients with advice, personnel, short-term credit (on occasion), and help with the marketing of reconstruction loans. Inevitably there was some jockeying for position between the European central bankers, especially the British and the French.

For Norman and his peers, the extension of central banking into new lands was anything but a purely technical matter. Independent central banks would link the countries of eastern and central Europe more firmly into the liberal capitalist international economy. By promoting financial stability and facilitating rising prosperity, they would inoculate the successor states of the continental empires against communism and militarism, and thus underpin European peace and economic progress. If the new central banks could also be induced to follow British (or French) advice on the management of the international monetary system, then the national interests of the UK (or France) would also be served. In 1923, Norman looked forward to an 'ultimate solution for Eastern Europe', based on a liberal capitalist 'Economic Federation to include half a dozen countries on or near the Danube free of customs barriers' (quoted in Péteri 1992: 251).

The first League of Nations reconstruction scheme – for Austria – was to a large extent subcontracted to the Bank of England. Austria was cut down to size after 1918. The new Austrian republic was dogged by hyper-inflation and political instability, and increasingly cut off by tariffs from former markets in central Europe. The defunct Austro-Hungarian central bank was liquidated in 1919, leaving Austria, Hungary, and Czechoslovakia without central banks (Schubert 1999). The Austrian reconstruction plan, which formed the basis for the subsequent Hungarian plan, involved a loan guaranteed by European governments, and measures to balance the budget and achieve currency stability. A central bank, named the Austrian National Bank, was established in 1923. According to Sayers (1976, vol. I: 168), with respect to 'the constitution of the new National Bank the Austrians ... accepted the British view in its entirety: no government officials, directors elected by shareholders, no lending to governmental bodies, and a note issue with partial gold cover'. A precedent was created when the League of Nations insisted that the new central bank should have foreign advisers (Santaella 1993), the first of whom was Swiss. Such advisers kept in close touch with international organisations and central banks, especially the Bank of England. The Hungarian central bank, established in 1924, was modelled on its Austrian counterpart (Péteri 1992). Central banks were also set up in Czechoslovakia, Poland, Yugoslavia, the Baltic States, and even Danzig, though the extent to which the League and other outsiders were involved varied.

Stabilisation did not involve the adoption of the gold standard proper. The trend in the 1920s was towards the gold exchange standard, involving the convertibility of national currencies into reserve currencies, such as the US dollar and sterling, which were in turn convertible into gold, in the case of sterling between 1925 and 1931. National reserves were held increasingly in the reserve currencies. But even the gold exchange standard was short lived. The new central banks of Europe were no more able to cope with the shocks of the 1930s than were the Bank of England or the Fed.

But Europe was not the only receptive ground for the central banking creed. The term 'money doctor' refers to an expert, usually from the UK, the USA, or France, who diagnosed financial and monetary ailments in other parts of the world, and prescribed certain remedies, often including fiscal rectitude and the creation of an independent central bank (Flandreau 2003). In Latin America, experts from the USA predominated, the most famous being Professor Edwin Kemmerer of Princeton University (Drake, P. W. 1989). Though Kemmerer was not a representative of either the US government or the Fed, his work to bring financial reform and stability to Latin America was welcomed by the US authorities (Seidel 1972). Kemmerer was a one-man alternative to the League of Nations Financial Committee. An intrepid traveller, he sometimes encountered personal danger. For example, Kemmerer and his family had a narrow escape in 1922, when their steamer blew up on the Parana River between Paraguay and Argentina. Between 80 and 100 passengers and crew drowned or were burned to death. Kemmerer saved his wife by getting her to cling to a floating beer case (*New York Times* 1922).

Between 1917 and 1931, Kemmerer served as a financial adviser to the governments of Mexico and Guatemala, and personally led financial missions to Colombia, Chile, Poland, Ecuador, Bolivia, China, and Peru. In addition, he provided advice on central banking to South Africa, and worked with the Dawes Committee on German reparations and financial problems in 1924. Before the First World War he had been involved with the National Monetary Commission, and in 1918 he published *The ABC of the Federal Reserve System* (Kemmerer 1918). One of Kemmerer's most dramatic missions was to Colombia in 1923, where he was involved in setting up a central bank, the Banco de la República, in the midst of a financial crisis. Legislation foreshadowing a central bank in Colombia had already been passed in 1922 (Goodhart *et al.* 1994: 182–6); even so Kemmerer worked closely on the design and promotion of the Banco de la República. The Poles turned to Kemmerer and other American advisers when planning their own central bank, believing them to be more disinterested than European experts. Central banks were either established, or given greater autonomy, in most of the countries advised by Kemmerer. But these institutions were ill-prepared to hold back the onslaught of depression in the early 1930s. And sometimes there could be a long delay before Kemmerer's advice bore fruit. In China, for example, the Kemmerer mission recommended the formation of a central bank in 1929, but no action was taken until 1935. China was still without a proper central bank at the outbreak of war with Japan in 1937 (Trescott 1995).

Assessing the motives and legacy of Kemmerer and other interwar money doctors is a task fraught with ambiguity. Kemmerer saw himself as a disinterested advocate of sound money, good governance, democracy, and economic progress. In his presidential address to the American Economic Association in 1926 (Kemmerer 1927), he asserted that the USA was known to be a more objective source of advice on monetary issues than were the core European countries. In his view, the creation of better institutions, including central banks, would help governments in Latin America and other developing regions to achieve stability and attract US capital. For critics, however, central banks were part of a web that tied Latin American economies into an exploitative relationship with the USA, based ultimately on gold. One diplomatic historian goes so far as to portray Kemmerer as a representative of white American 'manliness' with a mission to supervise 'disorderly' and feminine countries:

The need to perform according to gendered codes – to devise systems that instilled duty, regularity, and responsibility – helped shape not only a powerful set of discourses about the superiority of (white) manhood and its natural destiny to supervise lesser beings. It also helped shape the emerging institutions of the global financial order: gold-exchange standard currencies, central banks, [and] scientific tariffs regularized accounting procedures brought by manly men. (Rosenberg 1998: 173–4)

But the emerging institutions of the global financial order in central and eastern Europe and Latin America were not exactly good advertisements for the superiority of liberal capitalism. The gold exchange standard was a burden during the depression, while central bankers in peripheral Europe and Latin America were totally out of their depth, as also were the 'manly men' in more prestigious institutions. Yet, with the assistance of radical surgery, most new central banks survived the debacle of the early 1930s, though several of those in Europe would disappear as a result of the Second World War and Soviet expansionism.

The British dominions

In *Central Banking in the British Dominions* (1940), A. F. W. Plumptre discussed the origins of central banking in Australia, South Africa, New Zealand, and Canada. He concluded that central banks had been set up for a mixture of reasons. Domestic policy makers aspired to financial and economic stability and wished to assert increased national autonomy. Meanwhile the Bank of England promoted central banking in the dominions because it wanted to underpin international monetary stability and cooperation, and to erect institutional bulwarks against monetary unorthodoxy (Plumptre 1940: 422–3; Sayers 1976, vol. I: 200–10, 1976, vol. II: 512–19; Cain and Hopkins 1993b: 90–2, 109–45). There was a blend of nationalism and imperialism in the motives of central banking advocates.

The arguments for and against central banking were complex, and the debate was often poorly articulated. Plumptre (1940: 201) felt that 'neither nationalism nor imperialism spoke with the still small voice of logic. Instead they spoke with many tongues, often babbling and contradictory'. The potential for muddle was compounded by the lack of a coherent theory of central banking, and by manifest policy failures in the USA, the UK, and continental Europe.

Each dominion central bank issued banknotes, offered settlement and rediscounting facilities to commercial banks, and provided banking services to the government, but in some other respects they were distinctive. Plumptre devoted a chapter to 'English' influence, but the importance of this factor is debatable. Dominion governments did not appreciate meddling by Norman and his associates. Finally, Plumptre (1940: 201) anticipated that the Bank of England's authority would wane: 'nationalism has time on its side; its influence is in the ascendant in the Dominions'.

The Commonwealth Bank of Australia (CBA) began life as a state bank rather than a central bank. It was set up by a Labor ministry to provide banking services to the Commonwealth (or Federal) government, and offer the public an alternative to the widely mistrusted trading banks. The government appointed a governor to manage the Bank and allowed him considerable autonomy. After the First World War, the CBA started to evolve into a central bank. From 1924, trading banks were required to maintain settlement accounts at the CBA. A board of directors was created to determine policy. Although directors were appointed by the government, they were not required to follow government direction. Advice was taken from the Bank of England on the correct operation of a central bank. During the slump, the CBA acquired gold from the trading banks, and started to control the exchange rate, which was fixed to sterling rather than gold. Australia was on a sterling exchange standard, but was linked indirectly to the gold standard when the UK was on gold. The CBA dramatically asserted its independence from the Australian Labor government in 1931, declining to accommodate a reflationary fiscal programme on the grounds that the purchase of more Treasury bills would be inflationary. For better or worse, the bank 'refused to cash any more government cheques' (quoted in Cornish 1993: 442). The CBA served as a bulwark against left-wing policies until the Second World War. But in any case its capacity to influence monetary conditions was limited by the lack of an active secondary market for commercial bills, Treasury bills, or other government securities (Giblin 1951; Gollan 1968; Schedvin 1992: 23–61).

The South African Reserve Bank (SARB) was established in 1921. Vague plans for a South African central bank had been discussed on the eve of the First World War. At the end of the war, the government began to consider the future of financial and exchange rate policy. Henry Strakosch, a leading figure in the Anglo-South African mining and financial nexus, was approached for advice, and he suggested the creation of a central bank. Despite some internal opposition, not least from the commercial banks, the SARB proposal was implemented. The SARB has always been privately owned. In the interwar period, shareholders elected a majority of directors, while a minority were appointed by the government. Commercial banks were required to keep a fixed proportion of their liabilities on deposit at the SARB. Most government banking business was transferred to the central bank. By agreement with the mining companies, the SARB became the monopoly purchaser of the dominion's gold production, facilitating control over the exchange rate. Efforts to develop a commercial bill market and a secondary market in government paper were largely unsuccessful. As in Australia, the overdraft system met the financial requirements of most businesses, and few commercial bills were issued (De Kock, G. 1954; Strakosch 1921). Sayers hints that Strakosch exerted considerable influence over Norman. The success of the SARB initiative may have persuaded Norman that it would be worthwhile encouraging central banking elsewhere in the empire. Both Strakosch and Norman sought to make the SARB as similar to the Bank of England as possible (Sayers 1976, vol. I: 203). W. H. Clegg, the first governor of the SARB, had been chief accountant of the Bank of England. Even so, the South Africans also looked to the Netherlands and the USA, including Professor Kemmerer, for guidance, and were not completely beholden to the British (Plumptre 1940: 58–63).

The situation in New Zealand was different again. Though the Reserve Bank of New Zealand (RBNZ) was established in 1934, towards the end of the depression, any suggestion that its purpose was to promote recovery would be misleading. The government's aim was the less ambitious one of separating the New Zealand and Australian banking and monetary systems. A number of trading banks had operations in both countries. They kept sterling reserves on deposit in London, and issued banknotes denominated in pounds in Australia and New Zealand. When London reserves accumulated, the banks increased their lending in New Zealand and Australia. When London reserves fell, they cut lending in both countries. During the slump, Australia's balance of payments weakened more sharply than New Zealand's, and Australia came to be regarded as financially unstable. The City of London made the false assumption that New Zealand was afflicted by the same weaknesses. Moreover, when the banks' London reserves were depleted because of the situation in Australia, they also cut lending in New Zealand. The New Zealanders believed that they were being punished for Australia's shortcomings.

A prominent Bank of England official, Sir Otto Niemeyer, was invited by the New Zealand government to advise them on exchange rate policy. He reported in February 1931, recommending the formation of a central bank (Niemeyer 1931). This report was welcomed by the government. Not only would a central bank be able to manage the exchange rate, but it could also achieve monetary separation from Australia. Furthermore, it could take over the task of issuing currency, and become a depository for bank reserves. The lending behaviour of the banks would then depend on monetary and economic conditions in New Zealand, and less on events in Australia or perceptions in the UK. However, the government regarded central banking as a technical matter and not a priority in the midst of the depression. Most trading banks opposed the establishment of a central bank, while the opposition Labour Party feared that it would be controlled by overseas financial interests. It was not until 1934, when recovery was underway, that the RBNZ commenced operations.

Two-thirds of the RBNZ's share capital was subscribed by the crown and one-third by private shareholders. The governor and deputy governor were appointed by the crown, as were the first seven directors. The scope for resisting government pressure was likely to be limited. In 1936 the new Labour government nationalised the RBNZ, and set out the state's powers over the bank more forcefully. Though fiscally conservative in general, Labour was more expansion minded than the previous administration. While the government did not attempt to exert day-to-day control over operations, it did compel the Bank to extend credit to the public sector, especially in support of the state housing programme and the dairy industry. Leslie Lefeaux, the first governor of the RBNZ, and a former deputy chief cashier of the Bank of England, was appointed on the recommendation of Norman. He deplored government policy but exercised little influence over unorthodox ministers. The RBNZ was the least independent of the dominion central banks in 1939 (Singleton et al. 2006: ch. 1; Hawke 1973: 12–81; Wright 2006).

The Bank of Canada owed its formation in 1935 to the widespread perception that the Canadian monetary system had been mismanaged during the depression, combined with a rather vague belief that a central bank would have done better. Whether or not a central bank would have helped Canada during the depression is debatable considering the poor performance of central banks in the USA and other countries. Even without a central bank, Canada avoided the banking collapses that plagued the USA. Attempts by the British to influence the design and management of the Bank of Canada were brushed off. Canada was more developed financially and more self-confident than the other dominions. Under the Bank of Canada Act, the chartered banks were compelled to hold minimum deposits at the central bank. As the capital market was relatively sophisticated in Canada, there was somewhat more scope for conducting monetary policy through the market than was the case in the other dominions. No attempt was made to fix the exchange rate, which had been floating since 1929. Established as a private corporation, the Bank of Canada passed into full state ownership in 1938, but actual political interference remained minimal (Bordo and Redish 1987; Cain 1996; Watts 1993: 1–41).

Plumptre felt that in some respects the formation of central banks in the dominions was premature, not least because of the underdevelopment of the capital markets, and the consequent lack of scope for OMOs such as those commonly used by the Bank of England. These are issues for developing countries today (IMF 2004: 11). Plumptre was hopeful that the new central banks would encourage the development of financial markets, but saw a potential obstacle in the behaviour of governments: 'Whether or not central banking [in the dominions] will … extend along more or less accepted lines or whether it will extend into increasingly direct forms of intervention in financial affairs, will depend upon the course of political developments in the various countries' (Plumptre 1940: 426). The dominion central banks, though supported, and often provided with key staff, by the Bank of England, did not become tools of the British monetary authorities. Niemeyer dismissed leaders in the dominions as 'colonial savages', and believed that they required control from London (Cain 1996: 342), yet these savages resisted such manipulation. By 1940, it was clear that they would become even less amenable to British influence in the future.

The Reserve Bank of India

Finally, we come to India, the jewel in the British empire. The British economist, John Maynard Keynes, floated a plan for a sort of central bank for India in 1913 (Simha 1970: 21–3), but there would be two decades of wrangling between the imperial authorities in London (including the Bank of England), the British-controlled government of India, and the Indians themselves before the Reserve Bank of India (RBI) became a reality in 1935.

The British had a strong interest in the financial stability of India. A sound banking system would encourage trade and enable the smooth transfer of payments between the two countries. These payments included substantial 'home charges' from India to the UK each year, covering debt service and administrative costs, including the pensions of retired colonial officials. The British desired a stable exchange rate between the rupee and sterling, one set at a level that would both facilitate the payment of home charges and encourage exports from the UK to India. They also wished to avoid a situation in which India was allowed to drain the British and world gold reserves – successful Indian families had (and still have) a large appetite for gold. The UK also had to bear in mind the recommendation of the Brussels conference to the effect that central banks should be established throughout the world. Although it could be argued that this recommendation was not meant for minor colonies in Africa or the Caribbean, there could be no doubt that India was an important component of the international economy. Indian politicians and business leaders saw advantages in the creation of a central bank, provided that it was under local rather than imperial control. As for the British, they spoke with many tongues, the authorities in Delhi often taking a more pro-Indian stance than those in London (Balachandran 1994).

During the 1920s central banking functions in India were divided between the government and the Imperial Bank of India (IBI), a very large bank created by the amalgamation of three regional banks in 1919. Although the IBI had private shareholders (both Indian and British), the majority of its directors were government appointees. The IBI was granted a monopoly over government banking business, including the management of the public debt. In addition, it held cash balances for other banks, and provided clearing house, remittance, and rediscounting facilities. In the 1920s the IBI was no less of a central bank than was the CBA. However, control over the note issue and the exchange rate rested with the Indian government. Many observers were troubled by these divided responsibilities. Montagu Norman worked very closely with the IBI, which he saw as an embryonic central bank. From Norman's rather odd perspective, the Bank of England and the Imperial Bank ought to 'marry' each other (Balachandran 1994: 629).

In 1926 the Hilton Young Commission on Indian finance and currency recommended the establishment of a fully fledged Reserve Bank of India to take over the central banking functions of the IBI and the government. The Commission recommended that the RBI should be privately owned with a majority of directors chosen by shareholders and a minority by the governor-general (Simha 1970: 26–8). The wrangling now began in earnest. Basically, the British wanted a privately owned central bank under their control, whereas Indian political and business leaders insisted on substantial Indian involvement in the direction of the bank, and the election of some directors by the national and regional legislatures. Political involvement (or rather the political involvement of Indians) in the governance of the central bank was anathema to the British. There was deadlock for several years, but a compromise, which seemed to favour the British, was cobbled together in 1933 (Simha 1970: 28–39).

At the time of its formation in 1935, the RBI was a privately owned central bank with shareholders dispersed all over India. There was a central board of direction of sixteen: seven directors, including the governor and deputy governors were appointed by the governor-general, and eight by the shareholders (and none by the legislatures). The sixteenth director was a non-voting government official. This gave the British an institution that was insulated from nationalist control, and the Indians an opportunity to buy shares, and sit on the board as representatives of the shareholders or the government (Simha 1970: 87–112). One British Treasury official hoped that the board would be 'white and sensible and not black and political' – curiously, though, he said nothing about the need for 'manliness' (Balachandran 1994: 638). In the event the first board included twelve Indians, including one of the deputy governors, and four Britons including an Australian; the Indians were presumably sensible ones from the British point of view. Norman still hoped for a 'hindoo marriage' with the RBI, but it was all rather messy. The British could not even agree amongst themselves; when the first governor, Sir Osborne Arkell Smith, an Australian, fell out with the government over the issue of exchange rate policy, a tap was placed on his phone. The correspondence of Arkell Smith as well as his alleged mistress was also read by the secret police (Balachandran 1994: 643).

Indians nevertheless achieved some prominent managerial positions, and in 1943, four years before independence, Chintaman Deshmukh became governor. The British had at least succeeded in creating a central bank in one of the world's largest developing countries, and within less than a decade had agreed to the appointment of an Indian to the helm. Despite the element of farce in Anglo-Indian relations, the creation of the RBI was an important event in central banking history.

Conclusion

Central banks were regarded as part of the solution to various problems in the early twentieth century: an inelastic currency and financial instability in the USA, hyper-inflation and political extremism in central and eastern Europe, the complexities of Anglo-Indian finance, and the entanglement of the Australian and New Zealand banking systems, to name but a few. From the perspective of Montagu Norman's office at Threadneedle Street, or of Ben Strong's at the FRBNY, the ultimate goal was to bind more countries into the liberal capitalist system based on fixed exchange rates, gold, sterling, and the US dollar. From the periphery, however, central banks were frequently viewed as symbols of national development and autonomy. Though the efforts of Norman and his supporters to rebuild the pre-1914 world were shattered in the early 1930s, a strong element of institutional continuity was preserved. The new central banks survived their battering, and in the 1930s and 1940s adopted more nationalist stances.

5 A series of disasters: central banking, 1914–1939

> Men are far readier to plead – to themselves as to others – lack of power than lack of judgment as an explanation for failure.
>
> Milton Friedman and Anna J. Schwartz (1963: 418)

> [I]t is a special characteristic of the art of central banking that it deals specifically with the task of an authority entrusted with the promotion of economic welfare.
>
> Ralph Hawtrey (1932: vi)

Central bankers failed abjectly to promote the public welfare at key moments in the interwar decades, especially during the depression of the early 1930s. They were made to pay for their shortcomings when the central banking world was thrust into its first age of revolution as one country after another rejected gold.

Maddison (1995: 65) portrays the entire period from 1913 to 1950 as 'a bleak age, whose potential for accelerated growth was frustrated by a series of disasters', including two world wars and the worst depression in history. This chapter focuses on the activities of central banks in a troubled world. How was central banking affected by war and depression? Were central banks equipped to cope with the unexpected? To what extent were they to blame for the depression of the early 1930s? How much of their autonomy could they preserve after the depression? Generally speaking, the First World War and the interwar decades were disastrous for central banks. War brought inflation, the suspension of the gold standard, and the subjugation of central bankers to governments. The early 1920s saw hyperinflation in some countries, most famously in Germany, and deflationary policies in others. Central bankers struggled to reconstruct the gold standard and reassert their autonomy. They were successful only temporarily, for the early 1930s saw renewed turmoil: output and prices fell dramatically throughout the industrialised world, unemployment rocketed, thousands of banks collapsed, and many countries were thrown off the gold standard. The inability of central banks to prevent or at least contain the slump was

69

embarrassing. Not surprisingly, there followed a widespread loss of confidence in central banks, and they came increasingly under government supervision.

The First World War

To most economists, the First World War (1914–18) was inherently senseless (Pigou 1921). It destroyed millions of lives and led to a drastic fall in economic activity in most European countries (Broadberry and Harrison 2005; Singleton 2007). Central banks played an important part in managing the war economy. As lenders of last resort, they provided liquidity to financial markets during the initial panic in 1914. As guardians of the gold reserves and government bankers they were vital to the war effort. Central bankers were called upon to advise governments on economic policy, to sell war loans, and to represent their nations in international financial negotiations. More controversially, they were required to purchase increasing amounts of short- and long-term government securities, a practice that boosted the money supply and resulted in inflation. As Montagu Norman (1932: v) put it: 'With the outbreak of war in 1914 the traditional practices of Central Banks were gradually abandoned under the pressure of political expediency.' Ferguson (2001: 156) adds that 'the war took central bank-state relations back to the eighteenth century'.

Government spending grew rapidly. Financing this expenditure was a problem in all belligerent countries. Taxes were put up, but the increase in revenue lagged behind the increase in government war expenditure. More government bonds were sold to investors at home and abroad, but the appetite for such issues was limited. The task of selling government debt was complicated by the reluctance of governments to borrow at interest rates commensurate with risk. Given that tax revenues and the proceeds of borrowing from the private sector and foreigners were inadequate to cover the rise in spending, governments were compelled to resort to the printing press. In brief, central banks were instructed to purchase Treasury bills (floating debt), thereby boosting the money supply and inflation. The 'inflation tax' ate into incomes and savings as effectively as did other taxes.

The Bank of England worked more closely with HM Treasury in wartime, and deferred to the government on many matters. When war broke out in August 1914, the Bank and the government agreed that the semblance of the gold standard should be retained in order to shore up confidence, but severe restrictions were imposed on gold exports. The Bank underwrote government loan issues, and was drawn into financing the war effort directly through the purchase of Treasury bills. In 1916, the Bank reminded the Treasury that such borrowing made it harder to contain inflation and manage the exchange rate (Sayers 1976, vol. I: 95–6). Lord Cunliffe, the governor, assisted the government's efforts to raise loans overseas. He visited Washington in April 1917 as part of a British economic mission to negotiate an intergovernmental loan (Sayers 1976, vol. II: 93–4). Cunliffe was a merchant banker by profession. He sported a walrus moustache, was not very bright, and had the reputation of an arrogant bully (Burk 2004). Moreover, he possessed a rebellious streak. While in the USA, he concluded that certain Treasury officials, including Keynes, were undermining his authority at home, and demanded their dismissal, but the government declined to act. Cunliffe then became involved in a dispute with the Treasury over the control of gold held by Canada on behalf of the UK. Chancellor of the Exchequer Andrew Bonar Law and Prime Minister David Lloyd George were incensed when Cunliffe sent directions to Ottawa about the use of this gold. According to Cunliffe, Lloyd George threatened to 'take over' the Bank. Cunliffe was forced to send a grovelling apology to Bonar Law, in which he acknowledged that the central bank must follow government orders for the duration. Sayers (1976, vol. I: 109) described this affair 'as the worst blot ever known on the relations between Governors and Chancellors'.

The Reichsbank supported the German war machine. Rudolf von Havenstein, the president of the Reichsbank between 1907 and 1923, was known as 'Generalgeldmarschall' (Feldman 1997: 32). He was more compliant than Cunliffe. The Reichsbank established a propaganda and marketing organisation to sell government securities to the public. Reichsbank policy was to disguise the fact that it was supplying the government with a huge amount of short-run accommodation. Germany was forced to abandon gold convertibility, but kept up the pretence of defending the value of the currency. Even sales of long-term government debt to the public were monetised because they were eligible as collateral for loans from 'loan bureaus' controlled by the Reichsbank. Banknotes issued by the loan bureaus counted as specie and could be used as backing for further currency issues. Germany struggled to borrow abroad, and at home faced the same resistance as its enemies did to higher taxation (Balderston 1989). Censorship was deployed to suppress criticism of the Reichsbank, and the term 'inflation' was banned. The Reichsbank said that prices were rising because of hoarding, which was nonsense. In reality the 'government and Reichsbank were paying for the war by printing more and more money' (Feldman 1997: 49). They had to print money even faster when the domestic appetite for war loans began to wane. By the final stages of the war, German investors had little hope of ever being repaid. The involvement of the Banque de France in war financing was rather more transparent, but only somewhat less inflationary. The legal limit on central bank advances to the state was raised by stages from 200 million francs in December 1913 to 24,000 million francs in February 1919. The Bank discounted Treasury bills and marketed large quantities of defence bonds (Mouré 2002: 32, 38).

War proved challenging for the Fed, even though the USA was neutral until April 1917. After an initial gold outflow, the US economy started to attract vast amounts of gold, as European demand for American primary products and munitions rose, and investors sought a safe haven for their capital. Between 1914 and 1918 the stock of monetary gold in the USA increased by 88 per cent (Meltzer 2003: 83). After the American entry into the conflict, the Fed played a key role in the drive to market government bonds (or Liberty Loans). The Fed extended credit at interest rates below market levels in order to enable member banks and their clients to purchase more Liberty Loans. Meltzer (2003: 88) explains that 'the reserve banks were the source of the [government] financing no more and no less than if they undertook the same volume of purchases directly'. The Fed also rediscounted Treasury certificates at a preferential rate. Objections by the Federal Reserve Board to the government's policy of borrowing at low interest rates were swept aside. At one point, the secretary of the Treasury, William McAdoo, threatened to take over the functions of the Reserve Banks if the Board became troublesome (Meltzer 2003: 86). Unfortunately the Fed was an 'engine of inflation' during the latter stages of the war and the immediate aftermath.

Working conditions in central banks deteriorated. Employees were not immune to the climate of revolt that swept the world after 1917. On 1 January 1919, staff at the Bank of England presented their grievances to management. They pointed out that after a long war there was 'bound to be a reaction accompanied by unrest, dissatisfaction, and yearning for better conditions of hours and pay', and requested the formation of a staff–management committee to look into these matters. Staff emphasised, however, that they were not motivated by 'any spirit of disloyalty or captious criticism', and hoped that, after settlement of their grievances, 'a feeling of harmony and goodwill may be restored' (Sayers 1976, vol. III: 51, 54). A mechanism for staff representation was duly set up at the Bank.

Large increases in the money supply had predictable consequences. Between 1914 and 1918, consumer prices rose by 69 per cent in the

USA, 100 per cent in the UK, 113 per cent in France, 204 per cent in Germany, 1,063 per cent in Austria-Hungary, and 1,334 per cent in Belgium (Maddison 1991: 300, 302). Inflation continued to gather pace in some countries in 1919–20, posing a big challenge for central banks and governments.

Inflation, deflation, and restoration of the gold standard

The world after November 1918 was very different from the world before August 1914. Central bankers were not the only ones who struggled to make sense of this world of sticky wages and prices and floating exchange rates. As children of the Victorian age, Norman and his peers were 'ill-prepared for confronting [the] new monetary situation' (Cassis 2006: 165). Most policy makers were convinced of the need to revive the gold standard at the earliest opportunity (Eichengreen and Temin 2000), but this goal would prove hard to attain. Even sterling came off gold and floated in 1919; the US dollar was then the only major currency still pegged to gold (Eichengreen 1992a: 100–24).

Controlling, if not reversing, inflation was a precondition for the stabilisation of exchange rates. Inflation threatened the stability of the banking and financial system. According to Keynes, inflation posed a serious threat to social cohesion and the survival of capitalism, because it discouraged saving and fostered resentment of entrepreneurs, who came to be seen as profiteers (Moggridge 1992: 333). Dealing with inflation proved a costly process. Central bankers believed that the restoration of their own independence would increase the credibility of anti-inflationary measures. There was a swing back to central bank autonomy in Europe and the USA in the 1920s (Kisch and Elkin 1932: 16–41).

Conventional wisdom insisted that returning to gold would improve business confidence and financial stability. A committee chaired by Lord Cunliffe put the argument for the gold standard in uncompromising terms (reprinted in Eichengreen 1985: 169–83). Insofar as the gold standard *mentalité* was ingrained in the minds of ministers and Treasury officials, it served as a prop for central bank independence. Attempts by the state to manipulate the central bank could be resisted on the grounds that they might hinder the resumption of convertibility. After the restoration of the gold standard, or rather the advent of the gold exchange standard – involving the indirect pegging of minor currencies to gold via the US dollar or sterling – central banks continued to warn against political interference. With a fixed exchange rate and open capital markets, a policy of monetary stimulation could lead only to an external crisis (Obstfeld, Shambaugh, and Taylor 2004).

Central bankers were suspicious of politicians, regarding them as incompetent, mendacious, and opportunistic, or prone to time-inconsistent behaviour. Pierre Quesnay, an adviser to Émile Moreau, the governor of the Banque de France, wrote the following summary of Montagu's Norman's philosophy in 1926:

The economic and financial organization of the world appears to the Governor of the Bank of England to be the major task of the twentieth century. In his view politicians and political institutions are in no fit state to direct with the necessary competence and continuity this task of organization which he would like to see undertaken by central banks, independent at once of government and of private finance ... [Central banks] would succeed in taking out of the political realm those problems which are essential for the development and prosperity of the nations: financial security, distribution of credit, movement of prices. (Quoted in Boyle 1967: 205)

Proponents of the gold standard argued that a brief, albeit sharp, interlude of deflation would suffice to restore the pre-war price level, and reverse the large shifts in relative income and wealth that had occurred since 1914. But this remedy did not work because of social and political changes. Labour shortages during the war had increased the strength and militancy of trade unions. Further cartelisation had occurred in some industries. Wages and prices were no longer as flexible as they had been before 1914. The war also brought about an extension of the franchise in many European countries. As poorer people gained the vote, support waned for zealous anti-inflationary policies involving large cuts in government spending, especially on benefits and food subsidies (Eichengreen 1992a; Eichengreen and Simmons 1995; Maier 1975). Central bankers were committed to reasserting their autonomy, deflating prices, and returning to gold. Politicians wished to restore the gold standard, but had to be sensitive to pressure from the working classes. There was political disunity, confusion, and resentment in Germany and central Europe. What a recipe for trouble!

In the USA, however, disinflation was accomplished relatively smoothly, perhaps because the rise of labour was less pronounced than in Europe. The Fed distanced itself from the government after the war. Monetary policy and fiscal policy were tightened in a concerted effort to defeat inflation. A sharp recession in 1920–1 was followed by the rapid recovery of employment and output. The price level fell, though not to pre-war levels. Perhaps the events of 1920–1 gave the Fed an exaggerated sense of its ability to read the economy and achieve benign outcomes (Parker 2002: 3–4). During the 1920s the American economy enjoyed rapid growth and low inflation. Given the weakness of many European economies and currencies, the USA accumulated gold. Instead of permitting the inflow of gold to be monetised, however, the Fed pursued a policy of sterilisation because it was anxious to prevent the re-emergence of inflation (Meltzer 2003: 139). This approach was inconsistent with the rules of the game, but countries accumulating gold had more leeway to pursue domestic goals than did those losing gold.

Conflict between the Federal Reserve Board and the Reserve Banks continued into the 1920s. Had it not been for the authority of Ben Strong at the FRBNY, the Board might have consolidated its control sooner. Strong was the dominant figure in the Fed until his premature death in 1928. A forceful personality, he had come to the FRBNY from Bankers Trust, one of the most dynamic corporations in the financial sector. His biographer records that after his divorce in 1920, 'Strong was not to have a normal family life. His devotion was to be centered on the Federal Reserve' (Chandler, L. V. 1958: 30). Strong's main rival was Adolph Miller, an academic economist by profession, who sat on the Board in Washington. Miller was an indecisive policy maker, and he had a different philosophy to that of Strong. Miller believed in the real bills doctrine, whereas Strong was a sceptic. Miller emphasised rediscount rate policy, but Strong was an advocate of OMOs. Though Strong favoured cooperation with foreign central banks, Miller was more insular and considered that Strong was too close to the British (Meltzer 2003: 245). Whether the apparent success of US monetary policy in the early and mid 1920s reflected Strong's influence and skill, benign circumstances, or good luck, is debatable.

The British managed to struggle back to gold at the pre-war parity, equivalent to $4.86, by 1925, at the cost of a protracted bout of deflation. Norman, who succeeded Cunliffe as governor, had insisted that there was no alternative. Winston Churchill, the chancellor in 1925, and no expert on financial matters, was uneasy about the course of action recommended by the central bank and the Treasury. Ultimately, however, Churchill swallowed his misgivings and deferred to his advisers, much to Keynes's disgust (Skidelsky 1994: 197–200). The effort to keep sterling on gold between 1925 and 1931 involved persistently tight monetary policy, which served to entrench unemployment (Moggridge 1969; Sayers 1976, vol. I: chs. 6, 7, 9). Churchill bitterly regretted the return to gold, and was loath to forgive Norman. 'I have gone the whole hog against gold. To hell with it!', he thundered in 1932, 'It has been used as a vile trap to destroy us' (quoted in Wood, J. H. 2005: 293). In retrospect, Norman accepted that $4.86 had been an overvalued rate (Collins and Baker 1999: 29).

Less well known than the 'Norman Conquest' of 1925 is the Bank of England's growing involvement in industrial matters during the 1920s, a field of action not normally associated with an independent central bank. At Norman's prompting, the Bank encouraged and underwrote reconstruction plans for some firms and industries. It did so partly to help clients, such as the arms manufacturers Armstrong Whitworth, and partly to avert bankruptcies that could have left the banking system in a precarious position (Sayers 1976, vol. I: ch. 14; Garside and Greaves 1996).

Several countries in central and eastern Europe, including Germany, Poland, Austria, and Hungary, experienced hyperinflation in the early 1920s. In 1922 clerks in Austria used banknotes as scribbling paper because they were effectively worthless (Pauly 1997: 53). Germany's hyperinflation has attracted considerable attention (Balderston 2002). Contemporaries often attributed this phenomenon to exchange rate depreciation and the German government's runaway budget deficit. Both reflected loss of control by the monetary authorities. The depreciating exchange rate raised import prices, and put the government under pressure to increase transfer payments and subsidies to compensate adversely affected groups. The rising budget deficit boosted demand for imports and shattered confidence in the paper mark on world markets (Eichengreen 1992a: 125–45). In order to make reparation payments, the authorities also had to convert paper marks into hard currency, intensifying the spiral of depreciation. Though a burden, reparations accounted for just one third of the increase in government spending as a share of net national product between the pre-war period and the early 1920s. The principal causes of the budget deficit were welfare spending (unemployment benefits, war pensions, and food subsidies), and the losses of the rail and postal systems (Ferguson 1996). Stalemate between left-wing parties, which would not accept cuts in spending, and right-wing parties, which would not tolerate large tax increases, was the root cause of the crisis. At the peak of hyperinflation, 133 firms were printing banknotes (Dornbusch 1987: 346–7). Savings were wiped out, contributing to the alienation that would be exploited by the Nazis.

The Reichsbank offered little resistance to inflation, notwithstanding the apparent strengthening of its independence under the Autonomy Law 1922 (Holtfrerich and Iwami 1999: 70–1). Max Warburg, a prominent Hamburg banker, placed some of the blame on Havenstein:

He was an extraordinarily sympathetic personality with an unbending sense of duty and honorable character, but not up to the present situation. Since the beginning of the war, obedience and subordination to the presumed superior authority, be it the General Staff, be it the Reich Finance Ministry, be it the Reich Economics Ministry, had become so much a part of his flesh and blood that, even where it would have been possible, he did not know how to maintain the independence of the Reichsbank. (Quoted in Feldman 1997: 795)

German politicians and central bankers were equally scared of taking action to control the deficit and halt the printing of money. Havenstein saw it as his duty to supply the credit demanded by German business and the government, even though this involved stoking inflation (James 1999b: 21). Not until 1923, when the currency was practically worthless, did the government pluck up the courage to embark upon drastic measures. With Havenstein refusing to step down, the government decided to bypass the central bank, and appointed Hjalmar Schacht as 'currency commissar'. When a heart attack at last removed Havenstein from the stage, Schacht was installed as Reichsbank president, despite the opposition of the central bank Directorate. On 15 November 1923, the Reichsbank ceased to rediscount Treasury bills, and the printing presses were turned off.

Feldman (1997: 796) notes that the Reichsbank changed course under 'the crack of Schacht's whip'. Various expedients were tried, James (1999b: 23) recording that in 1924 there were 'three parallel German central banks', the Reichsbank, the Rentenbank, and the Golddiskontbank. However, stability was restored to the currency, and the government reined in the budget deficit. A Banking Act was passed in August 1924, reorganising the Reichsbank and reasserting its independence, and introducing a new gold-backed currency, the Reichsmark. A fourteen-person central bank General Council (seven Germans and seven foreigners), was created as a bulwark against domestic political interference. One foreign member of the General Council was empowered to veto further note issues if he considered gold convertibility to be endangered (James 1999b: 24–5). As would often be the case – for example, in New Zealand in the 1980s – legislation to enshrine central bank autonomy and monetary stability followed rather than preceded the introduction of anti-inflationary policies.

France had some of the same budgetary and political problems as Germany, but the French contrived to avoid hyper-inflation, achieved stabilisation in 1926, and returned formally to gold in 1928, albeit at a much depreciated exchange rate. The Banque de France fought a lengthy battle to free itself from government manipulation in the 1920s, the balance of advantage swaying from side to side (Bouvier 1988: 81–6). One of the most blatant instances of state interference was the *faux bilans* case, which came to light in 1925 (Mouré 2002: 77–86). In the words of Kisch and Elkin (1930: 22): 'Acting under Government compulsion, the

Bank [of France] eventually exceeded the legal limit for advances to the Treasury and published balance sheets to hide the fact.' Significantly, they added that: 'Such extreme abuses of Government power are, of course, only possible when a country has ceased to be on a gold basis.'

Several central banks acquired new functions during the 1920s. Formal responsibility for the prudential supervision of banks was allocated to the Bank of Spain (1921), the Bank of Portugal (1925), and the Bank of Italy (1926). The Federal Reserve System continued to possess limited supervisory and monitoring powers, while other important central banks, including the Bank of England and the Reichsbank, lacked any formal supervisory authority (Grossman 2006).

The decade of the 1920s was turbulent for central banks. With immense effort, the façade of the gold standard, in the form of the gold exchange standard, was reconstructed (Eichengreen 1992a: 153–221). Some of the autonomy that had been lost between 1914 and 1918 was restored to central banks. Nevertheless, the recovery of the international economy was incomplete, and central banks were woefully unprepared to deal with further turbulence.

New thinking on central bank objectives

The 1920s saw the first stirrings of statistical and economic research within central banks. The Fed was a pioneer in this field (Yohe 1990). By the 1930s some smaller institutions, including the CBA, were opening their own tiny economics departments (Cornish 1993). Central bank statisticians and economists spent most of their time in the collection, processing, and presentation of financial and economic information. It was hoped that such information would enable policy makers to reach better informed decisions. There is little evidence to suggest that these hopes were realised. The thrust of internal research was to map and explain the nuts and bolts of the monetary system, but not to challenge the foundations of established thinking. For more radical thinking it was necessary to read or consult outsiders.

Developments in economic theory were pointing towards a reconsideration of the objectives of monetary policy. Before the First World War, the Chicago economist, Irving Fisher, and his counterpart in Stockholm, Knut Wicksell, had examined the merits of a policy based on the stabilisation of the domestic price level (Skidelsky 1994: 168–70). These ideas were taken up in the early 1920s by Ralph Hawtrey, a British Treasury official and economist, and Keynes, who had acquired some of the characteristics of a media don after his resignation from the Treasury over the conduct of the Versailles peace conference.

Countries on the gold standard were expected to live with temporary fluctuations in inflation, output, and employment, since it was through changes in prices and wages that adjustments to serious balance of payments disequilibria were made. But sticky wages and prices were throwing more of the burden on the real economy. In other words there was potential for conflict between external and internal stability. Seeking a compromise, Hawtrey (1932: 116–302) argued that the gold standard should be managed so as to avoid sharp fluctuations in the price level and in business activity. Hawtrey assumed a much more active role for central banks than did the dogmatists responsible for the Cunliffe Report. The debate over rules versus discretion in monetary policy was already underway. Hawtrey's approach was in some respects followed by the Fed in the 1920s. The US dollar was on gold, and the US balance of payments was in surplus, but the Fed was reluctant to allow the rapid monetary expansion that would normally follow in this situation, being concerned to restrain inflation and smooth domestic economic conditions. The only central bank to target price stability explicitly during the interwar period was the Riksbank, following Sweden's forced withdrawal from the gold standard in 1931 (Berg and Jonung 1999).

In *A Tract on Monetary Reform*, Keynes adopted a far more radical position. Why should jobs be sacrificed and firms bankrupted merely for the sake of convertibility? He concluded that when 'stability of the internal price level and stability of the external exchanges are incompatible, the former is generally preferable'. The gold standard was a 'barbarous relic' and an 'outworn dogma' (Keynes 1923: 163–4, 172, 173). After failing to convince Churchill to reject Norman's advice in 1925, Keynes launched a scathing attack on British policy in a pamphlet entitled *The Economic Consequences of Mr. Churchill* (Skidelsky 1994: 200–7). Keynes's thinking continued to evolve (Moggridge and Howson 1974; Bibow 2002). He began to doubt that stabilising the price level would suffice to smooth the business cycle or achieve full employment after a major shock. In some circumstances, monetary policy could become impotent. If nominal interest rates were already close to zero, but the price level was falling, so that real interest rates were rising, the traditional tools of the central banker would lose their power to counteract deflation. This was the famous liquidity trap. During the 1930s, Keynes gave pride of place to the role of fiscal policy in economic management. Central banks had been dethroned in many countries before the publication of the *General Theory* (Keynes 1936), not because of the triumph of Keynesian thinking, which remained controversial, but because of their disastrous performance in the depression.

Ben Strong had many long discussions with the Fed's economists, including Walter Stewart and Carl Snyder, as well as with leading academics, including Edwin Kemmerer (Chandler, L. V. 1958: 50–1). Stewart moved to the Bank of England as Norman's adviser in 1928. In the main, though, Norman and his officials were resistant to new ideas. When the Bank of England considered hiring an economist to work in its 'economic section' in 1925, the appointment of a sympathiser of Keynes was ruled out on the grounds that such a person 'would be worse than useless' (Hennessy 1992: 314).

With the onset of crisis in the early 1930s, the advice tendered by economists became increasingly divergent, giving central bankers some excuse for indecision. In a review of five books, each by a prominent economist, Winfield Riefler (1936: 707), himself a former Fed economist, concluded that the 'lack of agreement among experts on the subject of central banking has gone far beyond the bounds of desirable and stimulating intellectual controversy. It approaches an intellectual scandal, with shocking effects of the gravest import upon the formulation of public policies.' How could central bankers be expected to choose between the various nostrums on offer?

The depression

An economic downturn in Europe and the USA in the late 1920s turned into the deepest slump in history in the early 1930s. Millions of workers lost their jobs, thousands of banks closed their doors, prices plummeted, and trade collapsed. Germany and the USA bore the brunt of the depression, but every capitalist nation from New Zealand to Norway was affected. In 1931 the gold exchange standard began to disintegrate. No consensus emerged as to what had gone wrong. The extent to which central bankers were to blame for the slump was a moot point (and remains so), but they had indubitably failed to discover a solution (Parker 2002; Eichengreen 1992a: 222–86; Temin 1989; James 2001).

Whether the initial recession began in Europe or in North America, and whether the causes were monetary or non-monetary, are questions that continue to be debated. What matters most, though, is to explain how a normal recession became a catastrophe. Most accounts start with the USA. The Fed tightened monetary policy in 1928 in order to combat speculative exuberance, an action that is often portrayed as the opening scene in the drama. In the years that followed, the behaviour of the Fed was often incoherent. Persistent squabbling between the Reserve Banks (especially the FRBNY) and the Board, as well as amongst the members of the Board, did not help. Some leading figures at the Fed and in government welcomed the pricking of an apparent bubble; others favoured the aggressive injection of liquidity to promote recovery; others dithered. The Federal Reserve System (or parts thereof) engaged in monetary stimulation, using OMOs and cuts in the rediscount rate, on various occasions between 1929 and 1933, but these efforts were marred by irresolution and frequent backtracking. The extent to which the Fed was constrained by fears about the gold parity is also open to interpretation, though the USA was more secure in this respect than any other country except France (Hsieh and Romer 2006).

Various reasons have been offered for the US central bank's inability to avert disaster (Meltzer 2003: 271–413; Wood, J. H. 2005: 194–211). In retrospect, the Fed should not have relied on the level of member bank borrowing from Reserve Banks (the Riefler Burgess doctrine) as an indicator of when to change the stance of monetary policy. It was commonly believed that member banks were reluctant to borrow from the Reserve Banks, and would only come to the discount window when the economy was weak, which was the signal to relax monetary policy. Low member bank borrowing was taken to mean that conditions were fine and no change in policy was required. Unhappily the Fed's interpretation of member bank borrowing was back to front. In reality fewer real bills went into circulation and fewer were presented for rediscounting when business was depressed. The Fed's reliance on a poor indicator of business conditions hindered it from appreciating that the economy was deteriorating rapidly. In addition, the central bank failed to distinguish between nominal and real interest rates. Although the Fed cut the rediscount rate, real interest rates rose strongly in the early 1930s because of the falling price level. If the Fed had paid attention to the real interest rate, it would have seen that monetary conditions were very tight, and could have conducted further OMOs. In short, the Fed did not loosen policy aggressively enough.

A further grievous error was the Fed's neglect of its responsibilities as the emergency lender of last resort. According to Friedman and Schwartz (1963: 342–59), the top brass at the Fed attributed bank failures to bad management, and not to the downward spiral in the economy, even though lower level 'technical' officials, especially at the FRBNY, grasped the true situation. One-third of American banks failed in a series of crises between December 1930 and February 1933. Though the panics were regional rather than national affairs, their impact was substantial. The destruction of millions of deposits, and the public's growing preference for currency over deposits, contributed to the fall in the US money supply, and brought about a massive credit crunch.

Even sound businesses found it hard to borrow in the 1930s, as surviv-
ing banks became extremely risk averse, treating loan applicants with
greater suspicion, and preferring to stock up on government securities
rather than extend credit to the private sector (Bernanke 1983, 2000).
It was not so much a matter of rescuing one or two big banks, as might
have been the case in a country with a less atomistic banking industry.
Thousands of small and medium-sized banks were in trouble. Many
were insolvent as well as illiquid; though in the heat of battle it was hard
to be sure about the solvency of an individual bank. The proper role of
the lender of last resort in this situation was to make enough liquidity
available at the systemic level, but the Fed did not do so. From the monetarist perspective the best safeguard against depression would have
been to maintain a constant rate of growth of the money supply come
what may.

Friedman and Schwartz (1963: 412–13) concluded that better leadership could have made all the difference:

> If Strong had still been alive and head of the New York Bank in the fall of 1930,
> he would very likely have recognized the oncoming liquidity crisis for what it
> was, would have been prepared by experience and conviction to take strenu-
> ous and appropriate measures to head it off, and would have had the standing
> to carry the System with him. Strong, knowing that monetary measures could
> not be expected to produce immediate effects, would not have been put off
> the expansionary course by a temporary persistence of the decline in business
> activity.

This bold assessment is not shared by all. Wicker (1966) contended that
Strong was far from outstanding in his grasp of central banking principles, and argued that his handling of monetary policy in the 1920s does
not inspire confidence that he would have been any more capable in a
crisis than the rest of the lacklustre team at the Fed. Meltzer (2003: 281)
is measured in his assessment of Strong and his colleagues: while many
of the actions of the Fed's leaders appear 'ludicrous' in retrospect, they
were constrained by the intellectual orthodoxy of the times, handicapped by internal conflicts, and forced to reach decisions on the basis
of inadequate and outdated information. He doubts whether a fit and
healthy Strong would have made a decisive difference to the management of the US economy in the early 1930s (Meltzer 2003: 408–9).
Remarkably, though, the Fed believed that it had acted appropriately, and continued to assert 'its lack of responsibility for the collapse'
(Meltzer 2003: 413).

The depression was more than just an American phenomenon.
Eichengreen (1992a, 1992b) investigates the chain reaction around the
world. The transmission mechanism was the gold standard. When the

Fed tightened monetary policy in 1928, capital flowed from Europe to the USA. As the American economy slowed, demand for European (and world) exports declined, and US citizens and companies continued to run down their foreign assets. Pressure was put on the external balances of many countries and on the gold and foreign exchange reserves of central banks. Having fought so long and hard to rebuild the international monetary system, the Europeans were determined to defend their gold parties to the last. 'Central banks losing reserves, though they could delay the day of reckoning, were soon forced to defend gold convertibility. Adherence to the gold standard required that reserve losses be allowed to reduce domestic money, credit, prices, and, ultimately, economic activity' (Eichengreen 1992a: 247).

Governments tightened their belts. Bankruptcies and unemployment rose dramatically throughout Europe and further afield. It was not simply pride that caused the Europeans to behave in this manner: they believed that the maintenance of convertibility would bring more benefits in the long run than would depreciation. After the experience of the 1920s, currency depreciation was associated with high inflation. Perhaps this was not sound economic reasoning at a time of falling prices, but the desire of policy makers to take no chances with unorthodox policies is understandable.

Between August 1929 and September 1934 there were banking crises in Argentina, Austria, Belgium, Czechoslovakia, Egypt, Estonia, France, Germany, Hungary, Italy, Latvia, Mexico, Poland, Romania, Sweden, Switzerland, Turkey, and the UK, as well as the USA, according to one definition of this phenomenon (Oliver 2007: 196–8). The ability of the central bank in a country on a fixed exchange rate to act as an emergency lender of last resort is limited unless external reserves are truly massive. They face a dilemma: should they inject liquidity in order to save the banking system, or withdraw liquidity in order to protect the exchange rate?

The year 1931 witnessed a major banking crisis in Europe, which precipitated the UK's departure from gold. The crisis started with the collapse of a major bank, the Credit Anstalt, in Austria in May. Foreigners sought to withdraw their funds from Austria, and to protect themselves the Austrians froze access to some of these funds, including deposits by the British (Bordo and Schwartz 1996: 449). The Austrian National Bank and the government stepped in at great expense to save the Credit Anstalt, which though insolvent as well as illiquid was considered too big to fail (Schubert 1992). Events in Austria reduced confidence in the German banks, which had not fully recovered from the effects of hyperinflation. Facing the classic dilemma, with both convertibility and the banking system under threat, the Reichsbank chose initially to focus on the external situation, tightening monetary policy by imposing stricter restrictions on access to the discount window. In July, however, the Danat Bank collapsed, and the Dresdner Bank indicated that it was on the brink. The government ordered a lengthy bank holiday, and during this interlude the authorities introduced exchange controls. Henceforth, the 'convertibility' of the Reichsmark was maintained by administrative controls over access to gold and foreign currency. As far as the rules of the game were concerned this was blatant cheating. Following the bank holiday, the Reichsbank applied a less stringent discount policy. Bank mergers were arranged, while the state and the Golddiskontbank, a Reichsbank subsidiary, purchased major stakes in several large banks (James 1986: 288–323; Schnabel 2004; Balderston 1991).

British banks had made significant deposits in Germany, which they could no longer easily withdraw. Contagion threatened to envelop the UK banking industry and end sterling's participation in the gold standard. Membership of the gold standard had crippled British industry since 1925. Responding to an accelerated drain of gold during the summer of 1931, the Bank of England urged ministers to introduce further measures of retrenchment, and suggested that the government seek overseas loans (Kunz 1987; Sayers 1976, vol. II: 387–415). Ever since the First World War exchange rate policy had been a matter for discussion between the government and the Bank of England. Before 1914 the central bank had been left alone to manage the UK's membership of the gold standard. By the 1920s, however, there *were* alternatives to the gold standard, even if some of them were unpalatable. Sayers (1976 vol. II: 387) noted that in 1931 the key policy decisions were taken by ministers and not central bankers. Norman's views carried weight, but even he understood that the government would have the last word on matters of national interest. At a meeting with the new chancellor, Philip Snowden, in 1929, Norman had acknowledged that the governor's 'was the technical and financial side – [while] the Chancellor's was the political and fiscal side' (Kynaston 1995: 28).

The position in the summer of 1931 was unprecedented. George Harrison of the FRBNY advised that a sharp increase in Bank Rate could have the 'perverse' effect of reducing confidence in sterling, if interpreted as a sign of panic (Sayers 1976, vol. II: 405). Bank Rate was not raised above 4.5 per cent during the crisis. Despite political turmoil, the government imposed fiscal cuts, and borrowed overseas from central banks and a consortium led by Morgans, but these measures were ineffective. A 'mutiny' (actually a protest) in the navy over wage cuts was taken as another sign of British disarray. A small group of Treasury and Bank of England officials concluded that the cost of further resistance would be prohibitive. (Norman was indisposed during the worst of the crisis.) Prime Minister Ramsay MacDonald made the decision to 'suspend' the gold standard in September. His action was designed in part to safeguard the remaining gold reserves, and there was hope, especially at the Bank of England, of an eventual return to gold. The banking sector survived largely unscathed. Grossman (1994) concludes that leaving gold was the most effective way of averting a banking crisis; it also helped to have a robust banking structure and a responsible lender of last resort.

After the British abandonment of gold, there was a slow drift towards floating around the world, as other countries realised that staying on the gold standard was making their plight more difficult. Central banks no longer inspired much awe after 1931. They floundered during the depression, unsure what to do for the best, clinging to the old recipe of the gold standard, retrenchment, and, in the USA, the real bills doctrine. When unemployment rocketed, and the prices collapsed, this recipe lost credibility, and so did its supporters.

Recovery and loss of independence

The countries that left the gold standard early, including the UK, Sweden, and Japan started to recover soonest, while those that held on to gold for grim death, including France, remained depressed for much longer. The USA occupied an intermediate position, floating in 1933, and then returning to gold at a depreciated exchange rate in 1934. Depreciation gave a kick start to recovery. Of at least equal importance was the loosening of monetary policy once policy makers realised that high interest rates were no longer needed to protect the balance of payments. Germany chose a different path, maintaining its gold parity, and reflating behind a barrier of exchange controls (Eichengreen 1992a: 287–399).

The recovery cannot be described in detail here; our purpose is rather to discuss how central banks fared in the post-gold standard world. Governments were tempted to take a closer interest in the monetary policy arena. Politicians who rejected the gold standard *mentalité*, and showed little interest in central bank independence, came to power in several core countries, including the USA (Franklin Roosevelt), Germany (Adolf Hitler), and France (Leon Blum). The role, influence, and governance of central banks were all brought into question. For example, legislation in 1936 tightened the government's grip over the Banque de France (Mouré 2002: 222–6).

Even in the UK, where political developments were less dramatic, economic policy makers adopted new priorities. According to Montagu Norman: 'When the Gold Standard was abandoned, there took place an immediate redistribution of authority and responsibility' between the Bank of England and the Treasury (Kynaston 1995: 28–9). In 1932, the government, acting on Treasury advice, introduced a cheap money policy, insisting that Bank Rate be capped at 2 per cent, where it remained until the outbreak of war in 1939. With the formation of the Exchange Equalization Account (EEA) in 1932, the government assumed tighter control over exchange rate policy. The EEA's function was to intervene in the foreign exchange market in order to avoid undue fluctuations in the exchange rate, and ensure that sterling's trajectory was consistent with government policy – thus the British float was 'dirty'. The Bank of England and the Treasury collaborated in the management of the EEA, and the Bank conducted all transactions on its behalf, but the ultimate say on sterling policy now rested with the government (Eichengreen 1992a: 304). The government's strategy was to facilitate economic recovery by running an accommodating monetary policy. The central bank's cooperation was requested rather than demanded, and no change was deemed necessary in central banking legislation. Norman and the Bank of England accepted the new environment. They had no choice.

In the USA, the revolution in the central banking framework was more tangible. The first Glass Steagall Act 1932 widened the range of paper eligible for rediscounting by the Fed, and permitted government securities, temporarily at first, to be used as backing for the note issue, though at first limited use was made of these powers. The advent of the Roosevelt administration in 1933 was followed by a more fundamental change in strategy and personnel. Roosevelt became president in the middle of a banking crisis, caused in part by perceptions that he would devalue the dollar. Roosevelt's monetary philosophy was not as radical as that of some of his supporters. Even so, he presided over important changes that undermined the Fed's independence. Under the Thomas Amendment 1933, the president was granted powers to change the gold value of the dollar, and to instruct the Fed to conduct OMOs including in government paper. The Federal Reserve Board was also empowered to adjust reserve requirements, which had been fixed under the 1913 act, subject to presidential agreement. In April 1933, an embargo was placed on gold exports, effectively floating the dollar. This decision provoked the outrage of the entire Federal Reserve Board, but procured a rapid and timely depreciation. In January 1934, Roosevelt reattached the dollar to gold at a rate of $35 per ounce compared with the pre-1933 rate of \$20.67 per ounce (Wood, J. H. 2005: 213–14; Eichengreen 1992a: 331–2, 336). Also in January 1934, the government nationalised the gold reserves of the Fed, and created an Exchange Stabilization Fund (ESF), along similar lines to the British EEA. The US Treasury now controlled intervention in the foreign exchange market, using the FRBNY as its fiscal agent (Bordo, Humpage, and Schwartz 2007).

In November 1934, the Roosevelt administration appointed an economic radical, Marriner Eccles, as governor of the Federal Reserve Board (or 'chairman of the Board of Governors' in the parlance of the 1935 Banking Act). Eccles believed that reflationary fiscal policy was the key to recovery. Doubting the ability of monetary policy to achieve recovery, he did *not* blame his predecessors' passivity for causing the slump (Meltzer 2003: 465). He was also of the view that the central bank should act in support of the general economic strategy of the government. In practice this meant keeping interest rates moderately low. Before accepting appointment, Eccles extracted a commitment from Roosevelt to implement sweeping reforms in the Federal Reserve System. Eccles's agenda involved the centralisation of power in the hands of the Board. Steps had already been taken in 1933 to restrict the ability of Reserve Banks to influence open market policy. Eccles demanded further curbs on Reserve Bank autonomy, alleging that these institutions represented private banking interests. In short, he wanted to convert the Fed into a real central bank, controlled by the Board in Washington. George Harrison was treated to a lecture when he came to congratulate Eccles on his appointment. Eccles told Harrison that had taken the job 'for the purpose of carrying out an important legislative program, which you in all probability are going to oppose' (quoted in Meltzer 2003: 470).

The Banking Act 1935 was a triumph for Eccles. The Board's control over the key Federal Open Market Committee (FOMC) was confirmed, while the right of individual Reserve Banks not to participate in OMOs authorised by the FOMC was rescinded. Instead of consisting of the twelve Reserve Bank governors, the FOMC now comprised seven members of the Board and five Reserve Bank presidents. (Reserve Bank governors became presidents; the Federal Reserve Board became the Board of Governors and its members became governors; the governor of the Board became the chairman.) The Board was also given authority to vary the required reserve ratio of member banks without the prior agreement of the president of the USA. Furthermore, the Board received the power of veto over the appointment of Reserve Bank presidents. Although the secretary of the Treasury and the comptroller of the currency were removed from the Board, in reality the Fed was developing a closer relationship with the government. Not all of

Eccles's objectives were met, however, and his request for control over all bank examinations was rejected. The prudential function continued to be shared with other agencies (Clifford 1965: 125–62; Meltzer 2003: 463–90). The 1935 Act did not redefine the objectives of the Fed. Eccles had wanted a mandate to stabilise 'production, trade, prices, and employment', but there was too much disagreement on this issue, and the Fed's original objectives were left unchanged (Wood, J. H. 2005: 220–2).

Other reforms in the mid 1930s included the separation of commercial from investment banking under the second Glass Steagall Act, the creation of the Reconstruction Finance Corporation (RFC) to help rebuild the banking industry, and the establishment of the Federal Deposit Insurance Corporation. The RFC was in effect the brainchild of Eugene Meyer of the Federal Reserve Board, and he became the first head of this institution (Nash 1959). Regarding the introduction of Federal deposit insurance, however, the Federal Reserve System made no comment (Meltzer 2003: 433).

Monetary policy was mostly accommodating after 1934. The Fed cooperated with, and indeed deferred to, the Treasury in most cases. Unsterilised inflows of gold through the ESF helped to underpin monetary expansion in the mid 1930s (Romer 1992: 774), giving the Treasury a direct role in monetary policy. A major policy error occurred in 1936–7, when the Fed, alarmed by the growth in 'free reserves' – banking reserves in excess of minimum requirements – doubled the required reserve ratios. Unfortunately, the level of free reserves proved to be no less fallible than the quantity of rediscounts as an indicator of monetary conditions. The 1936–7 tightening contributed significantly to the recession of 1937–8 (Meltzer 2003: 490–534).

Under the Nazis, the Reichsbank played a prominent role in the German economic recovery and rearmament programme. Hitler brought Schacht back as Reichsbank president in 1933 and made him minister of economics in 1934. While there was no formal change in the status of the Reichsbank until 1939, legal niceties counted for little under the Nazis and the central bank came under increasing pressure to conform to government policy. Hitler encouraged his barons, including Schacht, to fight among themselves for power and influence. Schacht was at first an enthusiastic supporter of the Nazi economic programme, with its emphasis on public works, rearmament, and the control of external transactions. Credit was manufactured in various ways by the Reichsbank, some of them heavily disguised in order to distract attention from their potentially inflationary consequences. For instance, the Metal Research Company (Mefo) was set up by four large armaments firms with a view to financing rearmament. Mefo issued bills in payment for work done by arms firms and subcontractors. Mefo bills were the equivalent of cash because they were eligible for rediscount at the Reichsbank. In addition, the Reichsbank assumed control of all debt and interest payments from German residents and firms to foreigners. Foreign creditors were paid only to the extent that it suited Schacht, and often had to accept payment in inconvertible currency. These policies did produce an economic recovery, albeit of an unbalanced kind (James 1986: 343–419; Weitz 1997: 145–261).

Reichsbank staff, and other Germans, held a range of opinions about the Nazis. In his memoirs, Schacht (1955: 391) claimed to have discouraged Nazi attitudes and behaviour within the central bank. By 1936–7, he was convinced that rearmament had gone beyond what was needed to restore Germany's great power status. Moreover, he disliked the Nazis' autarchic aspirations, and was worried about rising prices. In an apparently stormy meeting with the Führer in 1937, Schacht refused to supply further credit in aid of rearmament (Weitz 1997: 315). Friction with the Nazis led to Schacht's dismissal from the positions of minister of economics in 1937 and Reichsbank president in 1939. The Reichsbank Act 1939 finally eliminated the fiction of central bank autonomy in Nazi Germany.

Gauging the extent of a central bank's independence is an art rather than a science, as mid-twentieth-century scholars recognised (Kriz 1948). Clearly, though, the trend in the 1930s was towards greater government involvement. Not surprisingly, this went furthest in totalitarian states, though Schacht was by no means as compliant as Hitler would have liked. In democracies such as the USA and France, changes in legislation and personnel foreshadowed closer cooperation between governments and central banks. For the most part these changes occurred by consensus in the UK. The new framework was most visible in the area of exchange rate policy where in the UK and USA the central bank was compelled to share control with the government in the form of the EEA and ESF respectively.

Conclusion

Central banking was one of many industries to experience dramatic and unsettling changes in fortune between 1914 and 1939. The public policy role of central banks became more pronounced in this period, initially because of wartime needs, and later because of the emerging, though less than coherent, doctrine that national economies should in some sense be managed. The older gold standard *mentalité*, to which nearly all central bankers subscribed, persisted into the 1930s, even though it took no account of the changes in the behaviour of key groups such as trade unionists, business leaders, voters, and politicians. Central bank independence was much more contingent in the 1920s than it had been before 1914, and ebbed away after the disasters of the early 1930s. Whether central bankers believed that they knew what they were doing between 1929 and 1933 is an interesting question, however their actions were often inconsistent and misdirected. They did nothing to alleviate the economic crisis; indeed their policies made it worse. As a result they lost face, and it is not surprising that governments began to insist on greater involvement in the formulation of monetary and exchange rate policy. Of course, with some people it took a long time for the penny to drop. When the UK left gold in 1931, Chancellor Snowden is reported to have said in astonishment: 'nobody even told us we could do that' (quoted in Williamson 2004: 23). Central bankers such as Norman, Strong, Eccles, and Schacht needed to be much more politically attuned than their predecessors had been before 1914. Some policy decisions now required agreement between central bankers and political leaders, unpalatable as this might have been to governors of the stamp of Norman. Central bankers were not yet civil servants, but in order to survive they had to adapt and take the wishes of governments into account.

We might conclude by returning to Hawtrey and Friedman and Schwartz. That central banking was an endeavour with implications for general economic welfare, rather than a technical function, became increasingly apparent between 1914 and 1939. But this did not make it any easier for central bankers (or their ultimate political masters) to identify the policies that would best serve the public interest. Whether the failure of central banks was due primarily to incompetence, as Friedman and Schwartz suggest, or to a combination of difficult circumstances and the constraints imposed by a particular intellectual milieu, remains an open question, but not a unique one. Military historians continue to debate the same issues in relation to the conduct of the First World War.

6 The mysteries of central bank cooperation

> Events so moved as to bring ... central bankers together, sometimes face to face, more often in correspondence by letter and cable or on the telephone, in repeated attempts to resolve international monetary problems.
>
> S. V. O. Clarke (1967: 17)

> Between all 4 [of us] much talk and increased personal understanding & friendliness. But, sooner or later fundamental differences of position ... CBk cooperation melancholic[,] rather a pretence! than deep reality.
>
> Montagu Norman, 1927 (Sayers 1976, vol. III: 98–9, 100)

Montagu Norman, the leading proponent of cooperation amongst central bankers in the 1920s, judged the response of some of his peers to be rather lukewarm and superficial. Nowadays central bank cooperation is taken for granted. Central banks exchange information, opinion, advice, and personnel. They provide each other with banking facilities. They may even coordinate their policies, for example in the spheres of prudential supervision and exchange rate management. Central bankers meet regularly at international conferences, and are served by their own trade journals, including *Central Banking*, as well as by specialist academic publications such as the *International Journal of Central Banking*. One hundred years ago, however, there was very little interaction between central banks. This chapter examines the history of central bank cooperation up to 1939, discusses the motives for cooperation (and non-cooperation), and assesses the record of achievement and failure. As space is not available for a comprehensive narrative of events, readers in search of this level of detail are referred to Sayers (1976), Eichengreen (1992a), Clarke (1967), Meyer (1970), and Toniolo (2005).

H. A. Siepmann, a Bank of England official, wrote in 1943 that central bank cooperation was a 'gospel' with its own 'apostles' (quoted in Mouré 2002: 150). Paul Einzig (1931) was far more cynical, portraying leading European central bankers as members of their country's financial general staff, engaged in a struggle for mastery in Europe. In truth, whether they were apostles of cooperation or financial warriors depended on the circumstances. As in private business relationships, moreover, the distinction between cooperation and collusion, or indeed manipulation, was in the eye of the beholder. Isolationist Americans were suspicious whenever representatives of the Fed, and in particular Ben Strong, were on friendly terms European central bankers. The behaviour of some western European central bankers during the Czech gold crisis in 1939 left many observers with the impression that they were colluding with Nazi Germany.

As the cost of communications fell and the speed of travel rose, the frequency of interaction between central bankers increased. The financial turmoil of the interwar decades provided an incentive for central bankers to meet and talk to one another more often. On the other hand, the problems – both economic and political – confronting them were so severe that the chances of reaching a common position, let alone of achieving tolerable results, were greatly reduced. The interwar period did see the establishment of a loose framework for cooperation, not least in the form of the Bank for International Settlements (BIS), which became a sort of club for central bankers, though not necessarily a very comfortable one in a period when Europe was divided between weak democracies and aggressive totalitarian states. Perhaps of equal, if not greater, importance than attempts at multilateral cooperation was the forging of bilateral relationships between central banks, including between the Bank of England and elements of the Federal Reserve System.

Why cooperate?

According to the theory of the price specie flow mechanism – the traditional theory of monetary adjustment under the gold standard – there was no need for cooperation between banks of issue or central banks. Gold flowed into (or out of) the country when there was a balance of payments surplus (deficit), causing inflation (deflation), a loss (increase) in competitiveness, and the correction of the initial disequilibrium. In practice, however, central banks used the rediscount rate and other techniques to correct balance of payments disequilibria, and, especially after 1918, to manage the aspects of the domestic economy. Moreover, they also intervened from time to time as lenders of last resort. Given that central banks made policy choices and were not entirely passive, there was at least the potential for them to coordinate such choices. Even when central banks played by the rules of the game, increasing the rediscount rate in reaction to an external deficit and cutting the discount rate in reaction to a surplus, they were engaged in an implicit form of cooperation.

In the event of a large outflow of capital, the gold and foreign exchange reserves could run down rapidly, necessitating drastic deflationary measures, and perhaps even threatening the maintenance of convertibility. A period away from the gold standard would not be the end of the world, but it would be seen as a national disgrace, and the central bank would do everything in its power to avoid this outcome. The central bank could borrow or buy gold or foreign exchange from other central banks or the market. In so far as other central banks provided assistance on commercial terms, the degree of cooperation involved was limited. As well as seeking profit, however, the lender might have in mind the strengthening of the gold standard as a regime. Central banks sometimes faced a sort of prisoner's dilemma. If several central banks were worried about losing gold, they might be tempted to engage in a bidding war for funds, pushing up interest rates and depressing economic activity. This is what happened in the early stages of the depression. Cooperation, whether formal or tacit, offered a way out of this impasse, but cooperation was not always forthcoming. Central banks took part in other games too. In 1921, for example, the Bank of England and the Banque de France played each other at football (Cottrell 1997: 67).

Between 1914 and 1939 the problems of the international monetary system grew in severity. How was this system to be returned to a sound basis after the First World War? How were currencies to be stabilised at realistic levels? How were threats to the stability of the reconstructed system to be overcome? It was widely believed that an increase in central bank cooperation was required to answer these questions. But what form was such cooperation to take, and what were the chances of it succeeding?

The cooperative framework

The notion that central banks should cooperate systematically rather than on an ad hoc basis emerged during the 1920s. The Bank of England was the principal advocate of cooperation. Unfortunately, Norman's enthusiasm for cooperation often aroused the suspicion of some other central banks and governments, and in particular of the French. This section outlines several of the proposals for cooperation that were floated, but not necessarily implemented, in the inter-war era, and discusses some of the practical aspects of cooperation.

In preparation for the Genoa Conference in 1922, the Bank of England drew up a set of guidelines for the development of closer relations between central banks. First, central banks should consult one another and avoid actions that might inconvenience one another. Secondly, they should open accounts only at other central banks, partly so that all transactions were visible to the host central bank. Thirdly, the Bank of England offered to hold sterling balances for other central banks, an arrangement designed to facilitate the smooth operation of the gold exchange standard. Fourthly, central banks should be as independent as possible from their governments (Sayers 1976, vol. I: 157–9). Siepmann argued that independence was conducive to cooperation because it highlighted the difference between central bankers and government officials. Central bankers were a 'caste apart' with 'a professional and corporate responsibility, and … interests which transcended those of national particularities' (quoted in Mouré 2002: 151). Siepmann appears to have envisaged a kind of epistemic community, but this was not fully realised in the 1920s and 1930s.

Hardly any central bankers attended the Genoa Conference, which was an intergovernmental affair. Nevertheless, the gold exchange standard and the principle of central bank independence were endorsed. A resolution was also passed to the effect that there should be 'continuous co-operation among central banks of issue'. Delegates recommended that the Bank of England should convene an international conference of central bankers to discuss the framework for such cooperation (Hawtrey 1922b: 290). The Bank of England then drew up another set of guidelines for consideration at the proposed meeting. Though cooperation should be continuous, it should not be allowed to restrict the autonomy of participants. Cooperation should involve the exchange of confidential information relating to matters such as rediscount rates, the stability of the exchanges, and gold movements. Central banks should conduct their foreign banking operations through other central banks and should not seek to profit from the provision of banking services to their peers. The right of a central bank to make withdrawals from an account at another central bank should not be restricted. Each central bank should attempt to ensure that there was a free market in forward exchange in its jurisdiction (Péteri 1992: 240; Sayers 1976, vol. III: 75). In the event, the conference was postponed indefinitely, not least because of the reluctance of other central banks to accept British leadership or enter into any new commitments.

After the collapse of the first attempt to establish a multilateral cooperative framework, there was a retreat to ad hocery, an approach that did have some merits. Both Strong and Norman realised how difficult it would have been to reach a consensus at a conference attended by numerous delegations. They were inclined to prefer a less formal type of cooperation based on agreement among the major central banks: the FRBNY (as proxy for the Fed), the Bank of England, the Banque de France, and, perhaps, the Reichsbank (Chandler, L. V. 1958: 40–1). And for a few years this is more or less what they got.

Not until 1930 did the multilateral approach gain renewed traction, in the form of the BIS. According to the statutes of the BIS, its primary function was to promote central bank cooperation. (The origins and initial traumas of the BIS are discussed below.) In its *Fifth Annual Report*, the BIS set out its vision for cooperation amongst central banks. Cooperation was in the best *long- term* interests of all parties, and should be continuous rather than intermittent. Central banks should try to develop agreed monetary doctrines and return to a universally accepted international standard (ideally the gold standard); they should endeavour to understand each other's problems; they should avoid harming one another; they should establish reciprocal banking relations, collect and exchange data, cooperate on technical matters, and help small countries to set up central banks and encourage them to pursue sound policies. Finally, central banks should work together to improve the international monetary system (Toniolo 2005: 1–3). These principles went somewhat further than those envisaged by Norman in the early 1920s, and were not fully realised until much later. But they are still relevant today (Cooper 2008: 78–80).

The *Fifth Annual Report* of the BIS also noted that successful cooperation depended on regular contact and exchange of information. BIS meetings, which were held ten times a year in Basel, were attended by central bankers from across Europe (Toniolo 2005: 3–4). Though not a member of the BIS, the Federal Reserve System was represented indirectly at meetings. Central bankers also met in other forums. A central bank conference at Paris in 1928 was devoted to economic and monetary statistics and information (Mouré 2002: 172). Central bankers participated in major international conferences, including the World Economic Conference 1933, alongside politicians and government officials (Clavin 1992). But they were not the leading lights at world gatherings. The standard account of the Genoa Conference (Fink 1984: 232–42) shows that political and security issues occupied the minds of the political leaders, while monetary questions were consigned to 'expert' committees including Treasury officials, bankers, and central bankers. The Bank of England was represented at Genoa by Sir Charles Addis, a director (Sayers 1976, vol. I: 157), but he was outranked by Sir Robert Horne, the chancellor.

Central bankers also visited each other, and corresponded 'by letter and cable or on the telephone' (Clarke 1967: 17). One of Schacht's early acts as president of the Reichsbank was to visit London to seek Norman's support. Norman went to the trouble of greeting Schacht personally at Liverpool Street station. They got on well, and Norman became godfather to one Schacht's grandchildren (Schacht 1955: 194, 203). In 1927, Norman, Schacht, and Charles Rist of the Banque de France crossed the Atlantic by liner for a summit with Strong on Long Island. Norman and Schacht sailed together on the *Mauretania* (Sayers 1976, vol. 1: 337), and believed they were travelling 'incognito'. The *New York Times*, however, crowed that 'Their efforts to avoid attracting attention defeated their own purpose!' (Chandler, L. V. 1958: 375), and there was feverish press speculation about the talks. Strong made a number of visits to Europe during the 1920s. In between meetings, Norman and Strong maintained a regular correspondence, though this did not preclude disagreement when their perceived national interests diverged. Strong regarded Norman as 'a dear queer old duck', whatever that meant (quoted in James 2002: 205). Norman was assiduous at keeping in touch with (or badgering) other central bankers. He sent out regular 'Empire letters' to his counterparts in the central banks and quasi central banks of the British empire (Hennessy 1992: 296).

The age of transatlantic air travel was in the future. Yet, in July 1930, Hans Luther, the intrepid and by now desperate Reichsbank president, flew to London for discussions with Norman on Germany's financial plight (Toniolo 2005: 104). Face-to-face meetings were important for building trust and long-term relationships in international commerce (Miller 2003). We have no reason to believe that they were any less valuable in the central banking world. Strong wrote to Norman in 1921 that 'Our success in accomplishing anything depends so much upon … personal relations', and warned that if Norman were to retire it would be difficult to replicate those relations with his successor (quoted in Mouré 2002: 149). Norman proposed the formation of a central bankers' club in 1925, but no progress was forthcoming until the creation of the BIS in 1930 (Toniolo 2005: 30). The cooperative framework established between the wars was not particularly reliable, but it may have been the best that could be achieved at the time.

Obstacles to cooperation

The fifth report of the BIS was not entirely sanguine about the prospects for cooperation, and noted several obstacles. Central banks were secretive, proud, and often nationalistic. They also set great store by their 'independence' whether real or imaginary. Such traits were not conducive to a spirit of cooperation. Even if central bankers wished to work together, the BIS feared that they might be hampered by the hostile nature of international relations in the mid 1930s (Toniolo 2005: 4).

Economic theory suggests that while cooperation can generate net benefits in some circumstances, it may be difficult to initiate and sustain unless sanctions can be imposed on outsiders or turncoats. Cooperation may be beneficial when there are large externalities, or when a crisis requires decisive action (Toniolo 2005: 10–13). A smoothly functioning international monetary system is a public good (Kindleberger 1986), conferring large benefits that are non-rivalrous in consumption. Moreover, in the absence of a hegemonic power with the ability to enforce a sharing of costs, such benefits are non-excludable. An effective international monetary system contains risk and uncertainty, lowers transaction costs, smoothes the process of adjustment to imbalances, and provides some cushioning against shocks. Because a serviceable international monetary system (or standard) is a public good, each nation has an incentive to consume the benefits without contributing to the cost of maintenance. Such costs include any loss from foreign exchange intervention, and any loss of output arising from the tailoring of economic policies to the requirements of the international standard. The international monetary system will be neglected unless nations and their central banks undertake to share the costs and cooperate.

After 1945, there was an undisputed hegemon, the USA, and powerful international financial institutions, including the International Monetary Fund and the World Bank, over which the USA exerted considerable influence. In principle, the USA could reward cooperation by providing more official capital flows, and punish non-cooperation by discouraging such flows. The British had not consciously sought to exert hegemony before 1914, except over their empire. As explained in Chapter 3 above, the international gold standard before 1914 was the manifestation of the desire of the core countries for domestic monetary and financial stability. Between 1918 and 1939, there were far more financial crises than before 1914 or after 1945, but no hegemon or leader, despite the aspirations of Montagu Norman to this role. Modest international financial assistance was available to help countries to stabilise their currencies or defend their parities, but few sanctions were available to punish misbehaviour; indeed all major powers misbehaved by the standards of the day. The UK abandoned the gold standard in 1931; Germany imposed exchange controls; the USA suspended participation in the gold standard in 1933; France hoarded gold instead of letting it flow back into the system. Of course, they all believed that they had good reasons to pursue such policies. Essentially the costs of maintaining the gold-based international monetary system had become excessive. Whether or not the costs could have been reduced to an acceptable level by a more substantive programme of cooperation in order to limit the scramble for gold is debatable.

Though valuable, personal relationships were no substitute for agreement on policy, and such agreement was often lacking. Central bank cooperation after 1918 was hindered by rivalries over war debts, reparations, trade, prestige, and power. None of these rivalries was purely economic. Inter-war central bankers desired to cooperate, but only on their own terms. As Clarke (1967: 29) pointed out, all were 'first and foremost *national* central bankers'. At one level, interwar central bankers were slaves of the gold standard. At another level, however, they were quick to identify national interests – as interpreted by themselves and not by politicians – with the interests of the world. The result was a fragile sort of cooperation, marred by misunderstanding and quarrels (Clarke 1967: 32).

Few bonds were as close as those between Norman and Schacht or Norman and Strong, and even these relationships were contingent. Central bankers could be catty about one another. In his notes on the Long Island summit, Norman recorded that 'B[enjamin] S[trong] admires S[chacht] as a despot or tyrant: no personal sympathy: little personal understanding' (quoted in Sayers 1976, vol. III: 96). When Strong was succeeded at the FRBNY by George Harrison, relations with the Bank of England cooled, a factor that Eichengreen (1992a: 209, 220) regards as of some importance. Almost inevitably, the French and the British viewed one another with suspicion. Émile Moreau, the governor of the Banque de France between 1926 and 1930, described Norman as 'an imperialist seeking world domination for his country ... [by making] sterling the universal instrument of exchange' (quoted in Meyer 1970: 31). The French regarded Norman, who felt that Germany should be assisted to recover from the war and not be burdened with an excessive reparations bill, as dangerously pro-German (Sayers 1976, vol. I: 185–8). British perceptions of Moreau were equally jaundiced. Siepmann found him 'Devoid of imagination and generally of understanding; but a magnificent fighter, for narrow and greedy ends' (quoted in Mouré 2002: 156). The more atavistic aspects of international monetary relations were highlighted by Einzig (1931), who took great objection to the French policy of amassing large gold reserves, allegedly with a view to creating havoc in the rest of Europe.

In fact the motives of interwar central bankers were multifarious. They intended to rebuild the gold standard and restore stability at home and abroad; they wished to serve their nations, though not as the lackeys of politicians; and, last but not least, they desired to further their own careers and reputations. This made for a complex game.

Cooperation before 1920

The extent of central bank cooperation before 1914 has aroused some controversy. According to Eichengreen (1995: 104), 'Co-operation was episodic but occurred when the system's anchor currencies came under attack.' There was some informal coordination of rediscount rate changes, with other central banks following the lead of the Bank of England, the so-called conductor of the orchestra, though the degree of orchestration is open to question (Eichengreen 1996: 33). Central banks sometimes cooperated by rediscounting bills for one another and/or by lending each other gold. During the Baring crisis of 1890, the Bank of England obtained gold from the Banque de France and the Bank of Russia. When US participation in the gold standard was threatened in 1895, European central banks intervened to support the dollar. The Reichsbank and the German banking system obtained assistance from the Bank of England and the Banque de France in 1898. During 1906 and 1907 the Bank of England turned once more to the Banque de France for aid, and the Reichsbank received help from the Bank of Austria. The Banque de France gave further help to the Bank of England in 1909 and 1910. Eichengreen argues that central bank cooperation was grounded in a common determination to preserve the gold standard. Cooperation was increasing in intensity in the decade before the outbreak of war.

Flandreau (1997), however, contends that central bank cooperation before 1914 was a mirage: 'what has been interpreted as cooperation was the product of the selfish interest of central banks'. There was no international community of central bankers, and their attitude to one another 'oscillate[d] between hatred, neglect, and indifference' (Flandreau 1997: 737). The Banque de France profited from extending loans to the Bank of England and from the rediscounting of British securities (Mouré 2002: 147). The French also realised that by helping to avert a banking or exchange rate crisis in the UK, they were insuring the French banking system and gold reserves against contagion. Cooperation, in so far as it existed, was unilateral.

Priscilla Roberts (1998: 587) credits the First World War for the growth of 'trans-national links ... between the New York Federal Reserve Bank, the Bank of England, the Morgan firm [the US bankers to the French and British governments] and, to a lesser extent, the Banque de France'.

Ben Strong was an internationalist, unlike many of his colleagues at the Fed. He played an important role in the development of wartime cooperation; not only was he inclined to favour the Allies, but he also wished to attract business to New York. At Strong's instigation, the Fed loosened certain regulations in order to facilitate the access of Allied governments to the New York capital market, despite opposition from pro-German elements, including Paul Warburg. Within Europe, there was a growing, though still prickly, relationship between the Bank of England and the Banque de France. During the First World War it was the turn of the British to extend aid to the French. A telegraph line was installed between the offices of the governors of the Bank of England and the Banque de France in 1916, though Cunliffe characteristically had little time for the French (Mouré 1992: 262, 2002: 148). Gold was moved from the vaults of the French central bank to the Bank of England as guarantee for a British loan. Strong visited Europe during the war for discussions in London and Paris. As a result of these talks, a correspondent relationship was established between the FRBNY and the Bank of England (Chandler, L. V. 1958: 93–8). They opened reciprocal accounts, provided one another with banking services on favourable terms, and undertook to exchange information. In 1918 the FRBNY opened an account at the Banque de France, but this was the limit of their cooperation (Mouré 1992: 262). The FRBNY and the Bank of Italy also entered into an arrangement in 1917 (Toniolo 2005: 17). Strong's interest in collaborating with European central banks was strengthened by his wartime experience (Roberts, P. 2000: 68), but this does not mean that he neglected US interests.

The 1920s

Given the lack of consensus over the extent of central bank cooperation before 1914, it comes as no surprise to find more disagreement over whether cooperation increased or declined after 1918. Eichengreen (1992a) argues that there was a decisive fall in cooperation in the interwar period, which he believes had disastrous consequences for the world economy. Clarke (1967), however, contended that the mid 1920s saw a brief golden age of central bank cooperation. Borio and Toniolo (2008) suggest that central bank cooperation rose in the 1920s, but fell back in the 1930s. They identify three factors influencing the intensity of cooperation: the state of international relations in general; the prestige and independence of central banks – more prestige and more independence would give central banks greater freedom to cooperate; and the 'technicality' of the situation – as the problems facing central banks become more complex there would be a greater need for cooperation. In the 1920s international relations were less conducive to cooperation, but this consideration was outweighed by rising central bank independence and the growing technicality of the position. In the 1930s international relations were even worse and the prestige and independence of central banks were very much reduced. But it is not clear how the three factors introduced by Borio and Toniolo should be weighted. Alternatively it might be said that while a little cooperation was sufficient to maintain the international monetary system before 1914, after 1918 the problems facing the system were so serious that they could not be mastered despite an increase in cooperation.

Post-war international monetary problems were debated in a climate of extreme political tension (Singleton 2007). The Treaty of Versailles assigned responsibility for the war to Germany. The European Allies, led by France, were determined to extract maximum reparations in gold from Germany. At the same time the USA insisted on the repayment, though not in full, of wartime loans to Europe. The American government declined to join the League of Nations and appeared bent on washing its hands of Europe. Much of central and eastern Europe was in disarray after the collapse of the Austro-Hungarian and Russian empires. The place of the Soviet Union in the international system was yet to be determined. The UK and France vied for dominance of the European continent, and clashed over the future of Germany. French policy was to keep Germany as weak as possible. The British were more inclined to acknowledge the merits of a prosperous, democratic Germany.

Without Strong's leadership, the Fed might not have bothered to cooperate with European central banks. Strong, however, understood that the US economy was not self-contained, and would benefit from economic recovery in Europe (Chandler L. V. 1958). Like nearly all of his contemporaries, he believed that the restoration of gold convertibility was an integral part of the recovery process. He accepted the need for some redistribution of world gold reserves from the USA to Europe, though he was aware that the American public (and many of his colleagues in the Fed) would not countenance policies that sacrificed apparent US national interests – including low inflation and the retention of high gold reserves – for the sake of foreigners. Strong was wary of being regarded as a soft touch for Norman and other Europeans. For example, after expressing support initially for Norman's proposed international conference of central bankers in 1922, he started to backtrack. Strong realised that the Fed would be outvoted by European central banks, and presented with embarrassing requests for assistance, at such a conference (Clarke 1967: 36–40).

As discussed in Chapter 4, major central banks, including the FRBNY, promoted stabilisation programmes for some of the smaller (and new) European countries, and helped them to set up central banks. Even a modest credit or loan from central banks was interpreted by financial markets as a signal of confidence in the beneficiary. Even so, there was competition, especially between the British and the French, over the direction of such initiatives, not least in the case of Romania (Meyer 1970). Kindleberger (1987: 301) was scathing in his assessment of Anglo-French relations: 'The rivalry between the Bank of France and the Bank of England over which should take the leadership in restoring independence to central banks and stabilization of currencies in Eastern Europe would be pathetic, had it not run risks of instability for the system as a whole when the French threatened to withdraw balances from London.'

The German stabilisation of 1924 was equally controversial. Norman, who had made several small loans to the Reichsbank in the early 1920s, was determined to play a key role in any operation to stabilise the mark. He hoped to fix the mark to sterling (which was still floating), but the Dawes Committee, the international body set up to consider German reparations and finances, decided that it should be fixed to gold. A Bank of England director, Sir Robert Kindersley, sat on the Dawes Committee, but Norman's views did not prevail. Though disappointed, Norman welcomed the Dawes Plan as a whole, including the proposal to safeguard the Reichsbank's autonomy. Norman agreed to underwrite and market the London portion of the Dawes Loan, through which capital was raised for Germany. The Bank of England's involvement in the Dawes Loan, in a merchant banking capacity, helped ensure its success (Clarke 1967: 45–70; Sayers 1976, vol. I: 175–83). Norman's interest in German stabilisation has been described as 'an important example of the unreality of any rigid line between central banking and international politics' (Sayers 1976, vol. I: 182).

In order to assist the UK's return to gold in the mid 1920s, the Fed loosened monetary policy, offered a $200 million stand-by loan to the Bank of England, and used its influence to arrange an intergovernmental loan to the UK (Eichengreen 1992a: 190–2; Meltzer 2005: 171). Perhaps the most 'celebrated/notorious' (Cooper 2008: 77–8) instance of cooperation among core central banks in the 1920s was the Long Island summit of 1927. Despite internal opposition, especially from the Federal Reserve Bank of Chicago, the Americans agreed to cut the rediscount rate so as to relieve pressure on the British balance of payments, and reduce the need for further tightening in the UK. The French and German central banks also undertook to avoid actions that would weaken sterling for the time being (Meltzer 2003: 175–8, 220–4). Prior to this summit the British had believed that the Banque de France was systematically and capriciously forcing them to disgorge gold (Eichengreen 1992a: 210–12). There can be no doubt that there was intense rivalry between the British and the French. Eichengreen (1984) contends that at times, instead of cooperating, they competed to attract gold by pushing up interest rates. While helpful to the British in the short run, the Long Island measures did not correct the fundamental misalignment of exchange rates, reflecting in part an overvalued pound and an undervalued franc.

Clarke (1967: 41–2) noted that whereas the Fed was prepared to help the Bank of England in 1927 when the US economy was weak and a lower rediscount rate could be justified on domestic grounds, it was not willing to help the British when the US economy was in the throes of a speculative bubble in 1928–9. In other words, central banks were happy to cooperate when it suited them, but not when the price was high. He concluded that central bank cooperation was a qualified success until the middle of 1928. Thereafter the record was largely one of failure, as the international central banking community was progressively overwhelmed by the magnitude of the problems confronting them, starting with the downturns in the US and German economies (Clarke 1967: 220).

Establishing the BIS

The BIS was a by-product of wrangling over German reparations. Another international committee, chaired by Owen Young, a US banker, started looking into the reparations question in February 1929 (Kindleberger 1987: 65–8). Young's proposals included the raising of a commercial loan for Germany on international markets, a cut in annual reparations payments, and the establishment of an international bank to collect them and pay Germany's creditors (Simmons 1993).

Hjalmar Schacht of the Reichsbank and Émile Francqui, a Belgian banker, drafted plans for the international bank. The blueprint for the BIS was a compromise between the competing schemes. The BIS would be owned by central banks, and they would open accounts at it. As well as managing the reparations process, the BIS would promote cooperation and facilitate transactions between central banks. The details of these additional functions – which were destined to become core activities – were left vague, and would be worked out in practice. Schacht envisaged an embryonic World Bank, making development loans to underdeveloped countries, but this idea was rejected as too ambitious by most central bankers (Toniolo 2005: 24–60).

Norman was delighted with the BIS scheme, which promised to realise his ambitions for a central bankers' club. Moreau also endorsed the BIS proposal, with the proviso that it must not be permitted to compromise the freedom of action of central banks (Toniolo 2005: 38). Basel in Switzerland was chosen as a safe, neutral location for the headquarters. The BIS secretariat was international, with some officials seconded from central banks, but many junior positions occupied by Swiss. The British provided the largest foreign contingent, followed by the French. Staff members were expected to set aside national loyalties, and did so some of the time, but rivalry between the European contingents was hard to contain. At the outset there was wrangling over senior management positions. Pierre Quesnay, the former head of economic research at the Banque de France, took the post of general manager. A small economic research department was established under Per Jacobsson, a Swede. Senior central bankers, including Norman and Moreau, were appointed to the board of directors (Toniolo 2005: 61–6).

All but two of the twenty–two founding members of the BIS were European central banks. The exceptions are interesting: the Bank of Japan was represented by a consortium of Japanese commercial banks, and the FRBNY was represented by a consortium of US banks. The US government, true to its isolationist principles, insisted that the USA had no direct interest in German reparations, and refused to be drawn into the tortuous world of intra-European finance. To the chagrin of the FRBNY, it forbade any direct Fed involvement in the BIS. However, the BIS persuaded J. P. Morgan & Co, the First National Bank of New York, and the First National Bank of Chicago to subscribe to the capital of the BIS. Gates W. McGarrah resigned as chairman of the FRBNY to become the inaugural president and chairman of the BIS (Toniolo 2005: 44–8). Thus FRBNY participation was in essence through proxies. Japanese law prevented the Bank of Japan from holding BIS shares directly, and it asked a group of fourteen Japanese banks to purchase them on its behalf (Toniolo 2005: 68).

With the cessation of reparations payments in June 1931, the BIS lost the function that had brought about its birth. In order to survive, it had to focus on other, less well defined, albeit important, functions.

The 1930s

The underlying desire to cooperate did not desert central banks in the 1930s. Relationships that had developed over the previous two decades were not abandoned. Similarly, old rivalries, for example between the Bank of England and the Banque de France, continued. Eichengreen

(1992a: 10–11, 393) argues that only a massive increase in the level of central bank (and intergovernmental) cooperation could have saved the gold standard in the early 1930s. As unemployment soared and prices and output dropped, the monetary authorities' commitment to defending the gold standard lost credibility. Concerted international action was required in this situation. Central banks and governments should have agreed on an international package to loosen monetary policy. Instead of scrambling for gold, they should have collaborated to reduce interest rates and increase the money supply. That they failed to do so reflected a lack of agreement on the causes of the crisis. In the UK the depression was treated as an unfortunate external shock; in France it was attributed to lax monetary policy in the UK and the USA in the 1920s; in America there was no consensus view. Without a common interpretation of events it was difficult to imagine a collaborative solution (Eichengreen 1995). But cooperation along the lines advocated by Eichengreen would not necessarily have averted the intensification of the depression. Cooperating in order to save the gold standard was pointless if the regime was fatally flawed (Temin 1989).

During the global financial crisis of 1931 neither the BIS nor individual central banks were inactive. Credits were channelled through the BIS to the Austrian National Bank (100 million schillings), the National Bank of Hungary (three separate credits totalling $26 million), the Reichsbank ($100 million), the Bank of Danzig (£150,000) and the National Bank of Yugoslavia ($3 million). The BIS made a financial contribution to each of these credits alongside one or more central banks (Toniolo 2005: 108–9).

But the assistance provided was meagre. The German credit, announced on 26 June 1931, was exhausted by 5 July, and repayment was due on 16 July. In the event, there were nine renewals, each of three months' duration, though the Reichsbank could not take these renewals for granted. Creditors were anxious to limit their commitments, while those seeking assistance were inclined to underestimate their requirements. The Reichsbank president, Luther, had originally contacted Norman on 22 June with a view to borrowing $100 million for three weeks. Norman insisted that the FRBNY be brought in, and they in turn insisted on the involvement of the Banque de France. It was George Harrison of the FRBNY who, in conjunction with McGarrah, decided that the German credit should be offered under the auspices of the BIS. Another reason for the inadequacy of crisis assistance was the political situation. Luther visited London and Paris on 9 July and 10 July respectively for urgent talks, as the repayment date for the BIS credit was fast approaching. Luther now wanted up to $1 billion.

Norman said that the position was so serious that only intergovernmental action could save the day. In Paris, Luther met P. E. Flandin, the minister of finance, and Clément Moret, the central bank governor. The French said they were prepared to renew the existing credit, but would oppose additional borrowing unless Germany ceased to pursue a customs union with Austria, abandoned plans to build a new battleship, renounced territorial claims in Poland, and stopped pressing for more concessions on reparations. For their part, the Americans demanded the further tightening of monetary policy in Germany. The result was a deadlock that could not be broken by further discussions (Toniolo 2005: 101–6; Eichengreen 1992a: 275–8). On 13 July the German banking crisis began to unfold. Blocked in all other directions, the Germans imposed restrictions on international transactions. This was the first major crack in the reconstructed gold standard. Arguably the BIS did all that it could have done in the circumstances. It was reliant on the goodwill of the major powers, and lacked either the authority or the resources to chart an independent course.

The Banque de France was more supportive of the Bank of England than it was of the Reichsbank during the 1931 crisis. Moret assured the Bank of England on 25 July that the British would be given all the help that they required, provided the Americans made a similar offer. The Banque de France and the FRBNY each agreed to provide a credit worth £25 million. The British awarded Moret a knighthood for his part in the unsuccessful defence of sterling's parity. Having been assured that their sterling balances were safe, the Banque de France and other central banks were outraged when sterling left gold and depreciated in September 1931. The gold value of sterling balances was slashed. The Bank of England declined to pay compensation to any sterling balance holder except the BIS. (The Banque de France eventually secured compensation from the French government.) Losses on sterling balances in September 1931 caused the resignation of the governor of the Dutch central bank. British actions were resented, and long standing misgivings about the gold exchange concept were borne out, however the cause of central bank cooperation was not set back permanently (Mouré 1992: 274–6; Eichengreen 1992a: 280–5; Sayers 1976, vol. II: 414–15; vol. III: 258–61).

In June 1933 the last great set piece of interwar economic diplomacy, the World Economic Conference, was held in London (Eichengreen 1992a: 317–37). Though primarily an intergovernmental affair, there was extensive central bank and BIS involvement in conference preparations. Many central bankers attended as members of their national delegations. They were 'required more for their technical skills than for their expertise in formulating effective monetary policy' (Clavin 1992: 309), and had few new ideas to offer. Most were still mesmerised by gold and longed for the stabilisation of exchange rates in relation to gold, which was hardly to their credit. The conference itself was an utter fiasco. Roosevelt's decoupling of the dollar from gold in April 1933 suggested that he did not attach a high priority either to the impending gathering or to the search for a collaborative solution to the international crisis. The US president sent a dismissive message to the conference in which he attacked 'the old fetishes of so-called international bankers' and indicated that nations should sort out their domestic economies before trying to reconstruct the international monetary system (Meltzer 2003: 443–50). Delegates were appalled both by the American float and by Roosevelt's apparent contempt for their efforts. However, Roosevelt's analysis was in essence correct, and there are no grounds for believing that the conference would have come up with a workable plan in the absence of his intervention.

After 1933 central banks continued to cooperate on a bilateral basis and to a limited extent through the BIS. The stock of central banks had fallen dramatically. Politicians did not care what their central bankers talked about when they visited Basel. The BIS remained stubbornly, if not pigheadedly committed to the resurrection of the gold standard (Toniolo 2005: 136). Though the BIS did exhibit some of the features of a club in the 1930s, it could not insulate itself from the national and ideological rivalries that would see its members taking different sides in the Second World War. That BIS members on both sides of the ideological divide – democratic and totalitarian – found it worthwhile to keep in touch is as good an indication as any that a central banking community, albeit a far from satisfactory one, was in the process of being established (Toniolo 2005: 159–200).

When limited agreement was reached on action to counteract short-run fluctuations in the value of the dollar, the pound, and the franc in 1936, the parties concerned were the US, British, and French governments, and not the FRBNY, the Bank of England, and the Banque de France (Mouré 2002: 242–3). The so-called Tripartite Agreement confirmed the loss of status of central banks in an area of policy of long-standing importance to them. Intergovernmental cooperation was starting to overshadow central bank cooperation.

Toniolo, the historian of the BIS, is open about the organisation's shortcomings. A low point was reached in March 1939, when the BIS consented to transfer the ownership of part of the Czech gold reserves, which were on deposit with the BIS but held at the Bank of England, to the Reichsbank, following the German invasion of Czechoslovakia.

Directors of the Czech National Bank were seized and threatened by the invaders, who were accompanied by a Reichsbank 'commissioner', and ordered to send a message instructing the BIS to pay the gold into the Reichsbank's account. The Czech central bank directors were able to make it known that they were acting under duress. BIS management dithered over the instruction and consulted the British and French central banks. The Bank of England and the Banque de France could in all probability have vetoed the transfer but they chose to do nothing. Ownership of the Czech gold was allowed to pass to the Reichsbank, which sold some of it to the Bank of England but swapped most of it for gold held at the Dutch and Belgian central banks. The gold was then transported from Belgium and Holland to Germany. When news of these events reached the press there was uproar (Toniolo 2005: 204–14). Central banks and the BIS were made to appear craven or sinister by this affair. Blaazer (2005) places much of the blame on Norman, who was determined to maintain good relations with Germany. From Norman's perspective, it was more important to cooperate with (or appease) the Reichsbank than to prevent the theft of gold from the central bank of a country under German occupation.

Conclusion

Central banks had more reason to cooperate after 1918 than they had done before 1914. The international monetary system was in disarray and required more attention and maintenance than ever before. Central bankers were the obvious people to sort out, or at least attempt to sort out, a difficult situation. The main advocates of central bank cooperation were Norman and Strong. Norman's commitment to cooperation was the firmest, but without the support of Strong the Americans might have shown no interest in working alongside the Europeans. Cooperation did have some successes, especially in the form of the currency stabilisations of the 1920s and the establishment of new central banks. But cooperation was always contingent on its not interfering unduly with the pursuit of other objectives. And it was weakened by suspicion and rivalry, especially between the British and the French.

During the early 1930s central bankers continue to cooperate, not least through the medium of the BIS, but their efforts were feeble, given the magnitude of the problems confronting the international monetary system. In any case it is by no means clear that the attempts made to patch up the gold standard were worth the effort. Perhaps what the world economy needed was greater flexibility in exchange rates and monetary policy, not to say a coordinated programme of reflation. But these were not realistic options for a central banking community that was still wedded to the gold standard *mentalité*. The BIS, which was the only institutional manifestation of central bank cooperation, became a talking shop for central bankers who were nostalgic about the gold standard. This was not much of an achievement. Central bankers – except, perhaps, Marriner Eccles – simply did not have the answers, and by the mid 1930s they were bypassed by the real policy makers in government. The 1930s was a bleak decade for central bankers. They were the apostles of a discredited religion. They still had work to do as the intermediaries between governments and banks, but they no longer dictated economic strategy and no longer shaped the international monetary system.

7   The first central banking revolution

> [T]he Federal Reserve system is so unimportant, nobody believes anything that Marriner Eccles says or pays any attention to him.
>
> President Franklin D. Roosevelt, December 1940
> (quoted in Meltzer 2003: 556, n. 286)

> After all, it is not the theoretical constitution of the Institution that matters, but the spirit in which the partnership between the Ministry of Finance and the [Reserve] Bank is worked. The success of the partnership will, in the ultimate analysis, depend on the manner in which Government desires to be served and provides opportunities accordingly.
>
> Chintaman Deshmukh, Governor of the Reserve Bank of India,
> 1948 (quoted in Jadhav 2003: 18)

The world of central banking was transformed by a spate of nationalisations beginning in 1936, and by the assertion of more governmental influence over monetary and banking policy during and after the Second World War. Central banks became less autonomous in the middle of the twentieth century. The period from the mid 1930s to the late 1940s may be termed the first revolution in central banking, and its beginnings were discussed in the previous chapter. New institutional arrangements were imposed after the depression, and in some cases new leaders – most notably Eccles himself – were appointed. Though it might be tempting to see the 1930s and 1940s as an era in which central banks were conquered and occupied by governments, the new ethos was in fact one of partnership. Central banks were not supine, and in 1951 the US Fed reasserted some of the powers that it had given up in the 1940s. In West Germany the lack of consensus over central banking amongst the political elite in the 1950s enabled the Bank deutscher Länder (BdL) and the Bundesbank to pursue a distinctively independent course. For the most part, central bankers accepted that they were now the partners, often the junior partners, of government with respect to the formulation of macroeconomic policy. In other words they adjusted to the new environment. The stalwarts of the gold standard era retired, and were succeeded by a new generation of central bankers with more tolerance for modern concepts of economic management, and more inclination to work with governments.

Whether the new regime was genuinely Keynesian is fortunately not the issue here (Congdon 2007), though it is a convenient label. Postwar central bankers did not regard themselves as government stooges, and it would be unfair to portray them in such terms. Until the late 1960s, moreover, policy outcomes were benign. The first central banking revolution did not lead to rampant inflation in the 1950s and early 1960s. Both inflation and unemployment were low, and there were hardly any banking crises (Goodhart, Hofmann, and Segoviano 2004: 593).

This chapter focuses on the changing relationship between central banks and governments in the mid twentieth century; the following chapter considers their evolving functions, techniques, and internal organisation. We begin, however, with a discussion of central banking in the Second World War.

The Second World War

The role of central banks between 1939 and 1945 was to assist governments with the war effort, not least through the marketing (and purchase) of government securities and the management of the exchange rate. Marriner Eccles remarked that in wartime the 'Federal Reserve merely executed Treasury decisions' (quoted in Meltzer 2003: 382). Central banks acquired large portfolios of government paper through a combination of rediscounting and direct purchases, and as a result were compelled to turn on the printing presses. Despite tax increases, price controls, and credit rationing, inflation was experienced in all belligerent countries. Capie (2007: 166–8) notes that the worst cases of inflation during the Second World War and its aftermath occurred in Greece, Hungary, and China. In Greece, the German invaders demanded large payments from the government, which were met by increasing the money supply. In Hungary, the price level rose by 3^{1025} between July 1945 and August 1946, apparently because the Soviet occupiers, who were eager to ruin the middle classes, turned a deaf ear to central bank requests for remedial action. The Chinese situation was complicated because the war with Japan overlapped with the civil war and revolution. Inflation continued to surge after 1945. 'As one association of [Chinese] university professors observed [in 1948], they were now being paid less than coolies or the men who shovelled manure in the countryside' (Spence 1981: 315).

The wartime activities of the Reichsbank (renamed the Deutsche Reichsbank in 1939) have aroused widespread interest and condemnation (Marsh 1993: 122–41; James 1999b: 41–9). Walther Funk, the Nazi economics minister, replaced Schacht as Reichsbank president in 1939. Other Nazis were promoted or appointed to senior positions. One of these gangsters, Rudolf Brinkmann, kept a loaded revolver on his desk. Funk was too busy to devote much time to running the central bank, and this task was assigned to Emil Puhl. Entering the central bank as a clerk in 1913, Puhl had worked his way up through the ranks. He had also become a Nazi. While the extent of Puhl's ideological commitment to the Nazis is unclear, he was an accomplice in some of their crimes. Reichsbank officials were involved in the monetary management of occupied territories such as Poland. The Reichsbank became a receiver of stolen goods. When the Nazis seized the gold reserves of occupied countries they deposited them at the Reichsbank. Between August 1942 and January 1945, the Reichsbank received seventy-six deliveries of property, including jewellery, foreign exchange, financial securities, and gold tooth fillings, confiscated by the Nazi SS from concentration camp inmates. Some of this property was resold through the Berlin Municipal Pawn Shop and the proceeds credited to the account of an SS officer. But part of this swag was purchased from the SS by the Reichsbank. When Germany needed to make payments to allies such as Romania or neutrals such as Spain and Portugal, gold was transferred from the Reichsbank to the Swiss National Bank. The Germans and the Swiss pretended that these transactions involved only gold that had been acquired legitimately. In the final stages of the war, gold was withdrawn from the Reichsbank and hidden along with other loot. Some went to a salt mine at Merkers where it was discovered by the Americans (Bradsher 1999). But the whereabouts of part of the Nazi treasure remains an intriguing mystery. Funk and Puhl served time in prison after 1945. But many German bankers, including prominent Reichsbank officials, were rehabilitated. A blind eye was turned to their activities between 1933 and 1945, apparently because their skills were needed to rebuild the economy and they were deemed not to have been enthusiastic Nazis (Marsh 1993).

War brought government and central bank officials into closer contact than ever before, as they worked together on problems of economic and monetary management. In Australia, for example, Nugget Coombs, who was at that time a Commonwealth Bank economist, was seconded to the Treasury. Leslie Melville, the chief economist of the CBA, also took several important advisory posts, and led the Australian delegation to the Bretton Woods monetary conference in 1944 (Schedvin 1992: 105). Giblin (1951: 261–3) remarked that it was easier for economists in the central bank and the government service to cooperate than it was for officials trained in other disciplines – economists spoke the same language.

Central banks: slaves or partners?

There were relatively few state-owned central banks before 1936, the main exceptions being Sweden, Finland, the USSR, Bulgaria, Uruguay, Iceland, Australia, China, and Iran. Between 1936 and 1945, however, the central banks of Denmark, Canada, New Zealand, Bolivia, and Guatemala were nationalised, and new state-owned central banks were set up in Ireland, Poland, Thailand, Ethiopia, Costa Rica, Paraguay, Nicaragua, and Afghanistan. After the Second World War, a further round of nationalisations extinguished the private shareholdings in the central banks of the UK, France, East and West Germany, the Netherlands, Norway, Czechoslovakia, Yugoslavia, Hungary, Romania, Argentina, India, Indonesia, Egypt, Spain, El Salvador, and Peru (De Kock, M. H. 1974: 304–5).

Whether or not a central bank is in state ownership is not necessarily a reliable indicator of the extent to which it is controlled by the government, yet a clutch of nationalisations in a short period of time is indicative of a shift in government–central bank relations. Even when there was no transfer of ownership, new legislation in many instances redefined or clarified the relationship between the central bank and the government. Previous legislation, especially in the case of older central banks, tended to be vague in this area (Kriz 1948: 565–6).

Leslie Lefeaux, governor of the RBNZ, panicked in 1936 when the Labour government revealed plans to nationalise the central bank. However, Montagu Norman, Lefeaux's former boss at the Bank of England, sought to reassure him:

You know that I share your view that anything that tends to reduce the true independence of a Central Bank is unwelcome. But let me repeat my conviction, which I am sure is yours also, that fears aroused by apparently sweeping legislative changes may be proved groundless by the willing collaboration and prudent administration of the people concerned with putting them into effect. (Quoted in Singleton 2009: 9)

Norman realised that the nature of the game was changing and that resistance would be futile. Central banks could still hope to guide policy if they were prepared to enter into a partnership with governments. Norman's colleague, Sir Ernest Harvey, added:

I need not remind you that ultimate authority regarding credit and currency must rest with Governments ... But when this is appreciated both by the Central Bank and by the Treasury the Central Bank has unrivalled opportunities for pressing its views on the Treasury thus gradually provoking recognition of them. Even if state-owned the Bank does not necessarily lose its power of independent initiative. (Quoted in Singleton 2009: 8)

Lefeaux was too hidebound to be convinced, but he was succeeded in the 1940s and 1950s by governors who accepted the need for cooperation with the government.

Schedvin (1992: 63–4) depicts the Commonwealth Bank Act 1945 as a landmark in the history of central banking. While this may be an exaggeration, the Australian legislation of 1945 helped to set the tone for post-war central banking, just as the Reserve Bank of New Zealand Act 1989 set the tone for the 1990s. The Commonwealth Bank Act outlined ambitious, quasi-Keynesian goals. As well as ensuring the stability of the currency, the central bank was required to promote the full employment, prosperity, and welfare of Australians. The governor was expected to work closely with the secretary to the Treasury, with the government having the last word. Comparable legislation elsewhere stressed the right of the government to determine the broad direction of central bank policy. But this power was tempered by injunctions to seek consensus and, in some cases, including those of Australia and the Netherlands, by an appeals mechanism, through which the central bank could protest against government instructions. The Australian disputes mechanism, introduced in 1951, enabled the central bank governor to appeal to the Executive Council (Schedvin 1992: 149–55), which had to explain its decision to Parliament. Though this procedure was not used, it had the potential to embarrass any Australian government inclined to push the central bank too far.

To some extent, nationalisation and legislative reform set the seal on the new relationship between governments and central banks that emerged after the collapse of the gold standard. According to Miroslav Kriz, himself a FRBNY staff member, these changes did not necessarily involve the subjugation of central banks. The quality of the relationship with government was crucial. Kriz emphasised 'partnership'. 'Independence' was an unrealistic aspiration, while 'subordination' was a feature of totalitarian societies. He concluded that the relationship between central banks and governments was 'subtle', reflecting the 'conditions obtaining in particular countries' (Kriz 1948: 580).

Why were so many governments anxious to assert ownership, in the broadest sense, over their central banks in the mid twentieth century? After the depression there was a turn to the left in most democracies, which persisted into the 1940s and was reinforced by the success of wartime economic planning. Central banks were symbols of a discredited and anachronistic policy regime based on the obsession with gold. They were no longer trusted to serve the public interest without supervision. Many economists and politicians feared that the global economy would slip back into depression after the war. They regarded it as essential, therefore, that all aspects of economic policy should be coordinated and directed towards averting this outcome. Central banks could not be allowed to thwart government policy. That there would be no serious downturn after 1945 could not have been known in advance.

Fiscal policy was considered to be the strongest leg of macroeconomic policy in the 1940s and 1950s. The followers and interpreters of Keynes believed that monetary policy was a comparatively weak tool, and doubted whether macroeconomic stability could be procured by adjusting interest rates. Central banks were offered a supporting role in economic policy, and no longer occupied centre-stage. Governments desired low and stable interest rates in order to reduce the burden of servicing a bloated public debt, stimulate the job market, encourage reconstruction and development, and help powerful interest groups including exporters, farmers, and home purchasers. Interest rates were kept low by direct regulation and by accommodating monetary policy. Since low interest rates were likely to encourage spending, fuel inflationary pressure, and weaken the balance of payments, most governments imposed administrative controls on bank lending and access to foreign exchange. By the 1950s, macroeconomic policy makers, including central bankers, were aiming for the multiple objectives of full employment, low inflation, a stable balance of payments, and high economic growth.

The Radcliffe Report on the British monetary system in 1960 provided the most exhaustive statement of the argument that monetary policy was a sideshow (Capie in press: ch. 3). In adopting this position the members of the Committee went far beyond Keynes, who had argued that monetary policy was effective in most but not all circumstances. The Radcliffe Committee downplayed the influence of the stock of money on the economy, and emphasised the even more slippery concept of liquidity (Kaldor 1960). The Committee advocated closer cooperation between the Bank of England and the Treasury. The type of partnership envisaged was towards the subservient end of the spectrum: the policies of the central bank 'must be from first to last in conformity with those avowed and defended by Ministers of the Crown' (Committee on the Working of the Monetary System 1959: para. 768). The Committee's assumptions and conclusions were rejected by many overseas critics, especially by Americans (Sayers 1961; Gurley 1960). Though much of the Radcliffe Report seems impenetrable to a modern reader, it is none the less indicative of an influential strand of thinking in the 1950s and 1960s.

Amongst mainstream (Keynesian) economists and politicians there was a growing sense of confidence in the late 1950s and early 1960s that the macroeconomic problem was being mastered. Compared with the 1930s, this was a period of stunning economic success. Arguably, the climate of optimism reached its apogee during the Kennedy era in the USA. The work of Bill Phillips, a New Zealand economist, was interpreted as evidence of a manageable trade-off between inflation and unemployment. The 'Phillips curve' appeared to simplify the lives of macroeconomic policy makers, though Phillips himself did not intend that his findings should be used as a guide to policy (Leeson 2000). Post-war Keynesian orthodoxy did not convince everyone. One of the lesser known sceptics at the time was the young Paul Volcker, who was in the early stages of a career that would take him to the chairmanship of the Federal Reserve Board in 1979 (Volcker 2000). As the 1960s wore on, and macroeconomic instability grew, the volume of dissent increased.

Post-war central bankers accepted that macroeconomic policy should be coordinated, and in the main acknowledged the right of ministers to determine the overall thrust of policy. Karl Bopp, who was on the staff at the Federal Reserve Bank of Philadelphia, conceded that governments were sometimes right and central bankers wrong on policy (Bopp 1944: 263–4). Bopp was comfortable with the notion of multiple objectives for a central bank: 'As I mulled over alternative objectives, I found myself coming out with a combination of the price level and employment' (Bopp 1954: 17). Central bankers, he pointed out, could not ignore the intellectual and political environment. 'It should not be surprising that central banks have seldom pursued policies too far out of line with what the public has really expected of them. Fundamental habits of thought usually change slowly and central bankers are influenced by the same forces that affect the population of which they are a part' (Bopp 1954: 12). Central banks should be neither independent from nor subservient to governments. 'I believe that a shift in emphasis from insistence upon rights, sovereignty, and independence to comprehension of duties and responsibilities for social welfare would aid in establishing relationships between the two institutions appropriate to existing conditions' (Bopp 1944: 277). In the mid twentieth century it was possible to argue that policy-making institutions could together work for the public good without courting ridicule. Nugget Coombs was even more enthusiastic about the post-war consensus. After his appointment as head of the CBA in 1949, Coombs worked to 'establish the "Keynesian" conceptual framework as the language of communication between myself and my colleagues, between the Bank and the Government/Treasury complex, and between the Bank and its commercial bank clients' (Coombs, H. C. 1981: 147–8). Despite the Keynesian leanings of some central bankers, they did not go as far as some economists, politicians, Treasury officials, and members of the Radcliffe Committee did in regarding monetary policy as toothless. Central bankers lobbied for moderation in the use of direct controls and for greater flexibility in interest rate policy.

While Keynes is remembered primarily for his contributions to theory and public debate, he also held firm views on the design of central banks and on the relationship between central banks and governments. He had begun to address these topics before the First World War in proposals for Indian monetary reform. In the 1930s Keynes broadly endorsed the British Labour Party's policy of nationalising the Bank of England. He believed that after nationalisation the Bank of England should have equal status with the Treasury. Furthermore, he felt that the central bank should be run by 'experts' and not by ministers or Treasury officials. While the goals of monetary policy should be set by the state, the central bank should have considerable autonomy in the implementation of policy. Thus Keynes anticipated the distinction between goal and operational independence. He differed from some later thinkers, however, in maintaining that the relationship between the central bank and the government should always be cooperative (Bibow 2002).

The nature of the partnership between government and central bank evolved in different ways in different countries. It was more equal in some countries than in others; sometimes it was close, sometimes distant; and there were squabbles, some of them quite bitter. Ultimately, though, government–central bank relationships *were* based on cooperation in the mid twentieth century.

Bank of England

It is far from clear that nationalisation in 1946 made much difference to the role of the Bank of England in policy making (Collins and Baker 1999: 17–19). Montagu Norman, who retired in 1944, had accepted that the government should have the final say on important matters of monetary and exchange rate policy. The Bank of England did not resist socialisation in 1946; indeed it cooperated with the government in drafting the necessary legislation (Fforde 1992: 4–30). If the central bank had stayed in (nominal) private ownership it might not have pursued a radically different policy after 1945.

Norman's response to nationalisation was typically enigmatic. After visiting the Bank of England in 1946, he remarked that his old colleagues tried to 'pretend it is the same place' (quoted in Kynaston 1995: 30), but he evidently had some doubts. If nothing else, the Bank had lost a certain amount of status. Nationalisation had symbolic importance for the Labour Party, not least because the 'Old Lady of Threadneedle Street' was held partially responsible for the interwar depression. Taking over the Bank of England was also the first step in a wider programme of nationalisation, extending to the 'commanding heights' of the economy including transport, mining, and utilities (Singleton 1995). Only mild opposition was offered by the Conservative Party.

Richard Sayers (1958: 69), the historian of the interwar Bank of England and a key figure on the Radcliffe Committee, felt that nationalisation encouraged the 'professionalization' of the Bank of England. Managerial control now rested with 'the Governor and a small group of professional central bankers', comprising a deputy governor and four executive directors, and there was less scope than previously for part-time directors to interfere. A more recent historian of the Bank, however, concludes that it was on the whole still run by crusty old buffers (Capie in press).

The Bank of England Act 1946 was vague concerning details of the relationship between the central bank and the Treasury (Cairncross 1988: 50). It is difficult to be sure how monetary policy was formulated in the UK. While the Treasury was given reserve powers to direct the governor, in practice these were not used. Policy was discussed at meetings between the governor and the chancellor and Treasury officials. They did not always arrive at a consensus. In the late 1940s, for example, the Bank was critical of the Labour government's policy of 'cheap money' or low interest rates (Howson 1993), but this policy was not abandoned. With the advent of a Conservative government in 1951, some flexibility was restored to interest rate policy. Whatever its point of view, however, the Bank never questioned that interest rate policy was ultimately a matter for the government (Fforde 1992: 398–409). Capie (in press) argues that interest rate decisions were taken by the Bank and not by the chancellor until the mid 1960s, and that the Bank retained considerable autonomy. But the Bank could not have followed a strategy that was seriously at odds with that of the government. Much depended on the character and persuasive powers of the governor. The Bank knew more or less how far it could go, while the government was inclined to defer to the Bank's superior knowledge of financial markets. The Bank of England continued to reign over the banking system. According to the Treasury's legal advice, the 1946 Act did not empower the government to issue directives to the banking industry, and instead it had to approach the banks through the medium of the Bank of England. As post-war monetary policy relied on moral suasion, or cajoling the banks to adjust the quantity and direction of lending, the Bank of England occupied a strategically important position.

Relations between the central bank and the Treasury were mixed. There was more cooperation over balance of payments policy than over domestic economic policy. Bitter squabbles between the government's 'West End' (Treasury) and 'East End' (central bank) advisors erupted from time to time. On becoming chancellor in 1955, Harold Macmillan expressed surprise at the infrequency of contact between Treasury and central bank officials, and began regular meetings with staff from both institutions (Peden 2000: 440), but tensions remained.

Governmental dissatisfaction with the Bank's implementation of monetary policy in 1955 – a squeeze on credit had failed, necessitating the reversal of pre-election tax cuts – was an important factor in the decision to commission the Radcliffe Report. Either the Bank had misunderstood the government's intentions in 1955, or else, as critics maintained, it had deliberately backpedalled. Allegations (later judged false) that two part-time Bank of England directors with posts in the City had used inside information to profit from impending changes in interest rates added to the pressure for a full-scale enquiry into the activities of the central bank (Cairncross 1988: 55–7; Fforde 1992: 700–3). Alec Cairncross (1998: 203), who sat on the Radcliffe Committee, concluded that this investigation was a 'watershed' in relations between the Bank of England and the government, quashing any lingering doubts that the chancellor was in charge. Capie (in press) is more cautious, arguing that there was little overt change in the relationship as a result of the Radcliffe Report.

Lord Cromer, the governor in the mid 1960s, almost provoked a crisis when he attempted to insist on an increase in interest rates, despite the opposition of the Labour government. Cromer threatened to appeal to the public if denied. Prime Minister Harold Wilson made it clear that if Cromer did speak out in public, it would mean the end of the Bank of England. Cromer backed down. He was not reappointed for a second term, and returned to the family merchant bank, Barings (Orbell 2004).

His successor, Leslie O'Brien, publicly criticised the government's economic policy in 1968, and suggested that it had lost the confidence of
the City. This outburst led to another furore, though O'Brien kept his
job (Schenk 2004: 336–7).

The central bank continued to promote the development of the
City of London as an international financial centre, and to press,
often in opposition to the Treasury, for the loosening of controls on
capital account transactions. Cromer had particularly close relations
with the City because of his merchant banking connections. The
Bank of England facilitated and encouraged the development of the
Euromarkets, through which the dollar and other offshore currencies
were borrowed and lent, and resisted pressure to regulate participants.
Consequently, the Bank contributed to the reinvigoration of the City of
London in the 1960s and thereafter (Burn 1999; Schenk 2004; Cassis
2006).

Given the British predilection for allowing institutional relationships
to evolve irrespective of formal arrangements, it is difficult to assess the
degree to which the Bank of England's autonomy was constrained by
nationalisation. There was a partnership, though not always a harmonious one, between the central bank and the government in the post-
war decades, just as there had been in the interwar period. It was up
to the Bank to show initiative and assert a measure of autonomy when
it could, and it did so most effectively in its relations with the City of
London.

The Fed

The seminal event in the history of the Fed in the post-war era was the
1951 Accord with the US Treasury. Mayer (2001: 83) regards the signing of the Accord as the most important event in the history of central
banking. Whether or not such hyperbole is justified, the Accord was
clearly 'a major achievement' (Meltzer 2003: 712).

In 1942 the Fed had undertaken to maintain an interest rate of no
more than 0.375 per cent on Treasury bills, and no more than 2½ per
cent on government bonds. When these upper limits were threatened,
the Federal Reserve System stepped up open market purchases. After
the war these maxima persisted. Not only did low interest rates ease
the cost of government borrowing, but they also protected the holders of war bonds from capital losses, and, it was believed, insured the
country against a renewed slump. Another measure at this time was
the Employment Act 1946, which gave the government and the Fed a
mandate, albeit an imprecise one, for minimising unemployment. In

the later 1940s, central bankers, led by Allan Sproul at the FRBNY, became worried about the inflationary potential of permanently low interest rates. Although in 1947 the Treasury had accepted the need for some flexibility in short-term rates, it vigorously opposed any action that might undermine the 2½ per cent cap on long-term rates. Matters came to a head when China entered the Korean War in late 1950, sweeping aside US forces and raising the spectre of another world war. The Fed anticipated that these events would require yet more government borrowing, which, under current policies, would sooner or later be monetised. It stepped up calls for the interest rate ceiling to be lifted and for rates to be allowed to find their own level.

Relations between the Fed and the government deteriorated in 1951 following two acts of duplicity by the executive. On 18 January, the secretary of the Treasury, John Snyder, announced that the chairman of the Board of Governors, Thomas McCabe, had recommitted the central bank to the 2½ per cent ceiling. McCabe had made no such commitment. On 31 January the FOMC met with President Harry Truman. After this meeting the government announced, incorrectly, that the FOMC had agreed to comply with government policy on interest rates. Eccles, who remained on the Board of Governors after ceasing to be chairman in 1948, was incensed by this misrepresentation. He released the FOMC's account of the 31 January meeting, flatly contradicting the administration's version of events. On 19 February the Fed informed the Treasury that without a new policy agreement, the FOMC would act on its own initiative, meaning that it might let interest rates rise. The government relented. It was anxious to avert a major internal rift in wartime, and estimated that it lacked the congressional and public support that would be required to confront the Fed. In short, a compromise was reached that enabled the Fed to regain control over interest rate policy (Hetzel and Leach 2001a; Meltzer 2003: 699–712; Sproul 1980: 49–88).

The wording of the public statement accompanying the Accord, in March 1951, was rather anodyne: 'The Treasury and the Federal Reserve System have reached full accord with respect to debt-management and monetary policies to be pursued in furthering their common purpose to assure the successful financing of the government's requirements and, at the same time, to minimize monetization of the public debt' (quoted in Meltzer 2003: 711). How far the Fed would be prepared to go in asserting its newfound autonomy remained to be seen. It was never envisaged that the Fed would set itself up in direct opposition to the government. Sproul's (1980: 73) position was essentially that the Fed and the Treasury were 'co-equals in the area of their overlapping responsibilities'. Indeed, he regarded it as the duty of 'informed and responsible men' in these agencies to communicate and find common ground.

Interest rates did not need to rise strongly in the immediate wake of the Accord, as inflation soon receded. For most of the 1950s and early 1960s the economic environment was relatively benign, and there were few occasions for serious disagreement between government and central bank. By the mid 1960s, however, the potential for conflict was increasing, in view of the inflationary pressure associated with government spending on the 'Great Society' and the Vietnam War. William McChesney Martin Jr., who had helped to negotiate the Accord in the capacity of assistant secretary of the Treasury, succeeded McCabe as chairman of the Board of Governors in April 1951 (Bremner 2004). Critics expected Martin to be a government stooge, but he became a strong defender of central bank autonomy; indeed in one early encounter Truman accused him of being a 'traitor' to the administration (Bremner 2004: 91). Martin stayed in office until 1970, and is often remembered for his wisecrack that the job of the central banker is to take away the punch bowl just as the party is warming up. He brought the FRBNY to heel, while raising the profile of the other Reserve Banks, and followed a monetary policy characterised as 'leaning against the wind', which involved 'moving short-term interest rates in a way intended to mitigate cyclical fluctuations and maintain price stability' (Hetzel and Leach 2001b: 58).

Martin spectacularly defied President Lyndon Johnson in 1965, raising the rediscount rate in a belated response to signs of growing inflationary pressure, an action that provoked an angry outburst from the administration. Martin did not back down, despite a session in the 'wood shed' with the president. Sylla (1988: 33), however, suggests that the Federal Reserve may have taken fright after this incident, becoming reluctant to challenge the government again. On the whole Martin was more accommodating in the 1960s than in the 1950s, often deferring to advocates of expansionary policy in the Kennedy and Johnson administrations as well as in the FOMC itself. Martin believed in seeking consensus (Romer and Romer 2004: 137–8) and in cooperating with the government. As government priorities changed, this approach became harder to reconcile with the search for price stability. Martin was dismayed by the rise in inflation during his final years in office.

The Bundesbank

Widely considered to be the independent central bank par excellence, the Bundesbank, established in 1957, had tortuous origins. Indeed it was by no means certain in the early post-war years what sort of central banking arrangements would be deemed appropriate for West Germany, the state created from the UK, US, and French zones of occupation.

At the end of the war, the Americans were keen to suppress the Reichsbank. Landeszentralbanken (LZBs) were set up in each of the West German *Länder* or regions in 1947–8. The Americans envisaged the creation of a loose coordinating board at the peak of this network in a manner reminiscent of the early Federal Reserve System. The British, however, favoured a more centralised structure, and the outcome was a compromise. The year 1948 saw the formation of the Bank deutscher Länder (BdL). Though the LZBs were strongly represented in the BdL, there were substantial concessions to the British viewpoint (Holtfrerich and Iwami 1999: 91–3). A new currency, the Deutsche Mark (DM), was introduced in 1948, and later came to symbolise West German prosperity.

The Allies insisted on the BdL's freedom from German political control, largely because they wished it to be overseen by the Allied Bank Commission, and not out of any interest in central bank independence. As the Allies' desire to control the BdL receded, this embryonic central bank gained in de facto autonomy. The BdL was meant to be a stopgap until the new West German government could design a permanent central banking structure, but the Germans appeared to be in no hurry to reach a conclusion. The Allies relinquished their powers over the BdL in 1951, begging the question of the BdL's relationship to the West German government. Within the West German government and parliament various opinions were expressed on the central banking question. Some politicians favoured an independent central bank, while others sought a more compliant institution. As there was no consensus, the BdL was permitted to retain considerable autonomy, with the vague proviso that it should take government policy into account. Though this arrangement was not intended to pre-empt a final settlement, the BdL was able to consolidate its position as an aspiring independent central bank (Bibow 2009; Berger 1997).

One controversial feature of the BdL, and also of the Bundesbank in its early years, was the continuity of staff from the old Reichsbank. Marsh (1993: 159) comments that, until 1969, at least half of the directorate of the West German central bank comprised former Reichsbank officials. Such persons were of course implicated to a greater or lesser extent in the activities of the Third Reich. For example, Karl Blessing, the Bundesbank president between 1958 and 1969, and one of the world's most respected central bankers, had orchestrated the Reichsbank's takeover of the Austrian National Bank in 1938. He joined the Nazi Party in

1937, justifying this action on the grounds that moderates were needed in the party as counterweights to the extremists (Marsh 1993: 52–4). But this sounds suspiciously like another case of opportunism. That there was no complete break with the past is not surprising, given West Germany's need for experienced central bankers, and it was no different in other spheres of post-war German life.

Konrad Adenaeur, the West German chancellor, was the most powerful advocate of a compliant central bank. Ludwig Erhard, the economics minister, disagreed with Adenauer, up to a point. In Erhard's opinion, the government should not have the authority to issue directions to the central bank. However, he envisaged that the central bank would wish to cooperate closely with the government. Erhard's vision was similar to that of Sproul, who trusted in the capacity of 'informed and responsible men' to reach good conclusions. Curiously, it was not only Erhard and other right-wing 'ordoliberals' who upheld the principle of central bank independence in the 1950s. Provoked by Adenauer's attacks on the BdL, left-wing parliamentarians also sought to insulate the central bank from government manipulation (Bibow 2009).

The 1957 Bundesbank Act transformed the BdL, from 1958, into the Deutsche Bundesbank, a public sector central bank. Under the 1957 legislation, 'the *main duties* of the Bundesbank [were] those of regulating the amount of money in circulation and of credit supplied to the economy with the aim of safeguarding the currency, as well as arranging for the execution of domestic and international payments' (Stern 1999: 126). The central bank was to support government economic policy in so far as this did not undermine the performance of its main duties. The Stability and Growth Act 1967 outlined a clutch of macroeconomic objectives for the West German state, including price stability, high employment, external equilibrium, and economic growth. Though the Bundesbank was exhorted to take these objectives into account, the Stability and Growth Act did not override the Bundesbank Act (Stern 1999: 128).

It would be inaccurate to suggest that the Bundesbank enjoyed unfettered independence. The federal government retained the power to defer decisions of the Bundesbank council for up to two weeks. More importantly, exchange rate policy was determined by the government. Nevertheless, the Bundesbank was more autonomous than most central banks, and this owed something to the fact that the majority of Bundesbank council members were in effect selected by regional governments (Lohmann 1998). So far as domestic monetary policy went, the Bundesbank possessed a high level of autonomy in the context of its primary mission to safeguard the value of the currency. On the other hand, domestic monetary policy and exchange rate policy were interdependent. Government decisions (or indecision) on the exchange rate had implications for domestic monetary conditions under an adjustable peg system such as Bretton Woods. Stern (1999: 154) writes of a 'subtle and balanced regulation of the relationship between the Federal Government and the Bundesbank' and attempts 'to unite independence and cooperation'.

The rather vague accountability of the Bundesbank to the executive and parliament sits uncomfortably with late twentieth-century approaches to central bank independence, such as the Reserve Bank of New Zealand Act 1989. Having said that, the Bundesbank achieved its main goals, and succeeded in building up a strong base of public support, or 'stability culture'. While the Bundesbank was not immune to political intrigue, it resisted most attempts by central government to influence policy decisions (Neumann 1999).

Bank of Japan

Until 1998 the Japanese central bank operated under a legal framework established during the Second World War, and modelled on the Reichsbank Act 1939. Article 1 of the Bank of Japan Law 1942 stated that 'the purpose of the Bank of Japan shall be to adjust currency, to regulate financing and to develop the credit system in conformity with policies of the state so as to ensure appropriate application of the state's total economic power'. Article 2 reiterated that 'the Bank of Japan shall be operated exclusively with a view to accomplishing the purposes of the state' (quoted in Werner 2003: 54).

The longevity of the 1942 law owed more to the absence of consensus over a replacement than it did to its merits. Relations between the Bank of Japan and the Japanese government were much closer, though not necessarily any easier, than the equivalent relationships in the USA and West Germany. The fact that the post-war Bank of Japan continued to operate under legislation designed to meet the requirements of financing a world war contributed to the perception that the Bank of Japan was one of the least autonomous central banks in the developed world. Before 1998 Japan showed up very poorly in measures of legal central bank independence (Dwyer 2004: 249). However, the formal legal position is only one aspect of the multifaceted question of central bank autonomy. Government–central bank relationships are rarely mechanistic. The Bank of Japan, like the Bank of England, could usually make its weight felt within the policy-making community.

Unlike in Germany, the institutions of state did not disappear in Japan in 1945. The US occupation authorities ruled Japan through existing organs, including the Bank of Japan. (However, the Yokohama Specie Bank was closed and converted into a private sector institution, the Bank of Tokyo.) Complex discussions took place between the Americans, the Japanese government, and the Bank of Japan over the shape of post-war banking and monetary policy structures. The Americans and the Japanese central bankers agreed that the government's absolute power over the Bank of Japan should be curbed. The Finance Law 1947 placed limits on the central bank's obligation to provide accommodation to the government. Proposals for a separate monetary policy board with powers over the central bank were discussed but thwarted. Instead a policy board was created within the Bank of Japan in 1949 (Holtfrerich and Iwami 1999: 86–91, 97–100). The Bank of Japan and the Ministry of Finance were rivals as well as partners and they often seemed to be locked together like sumo wrestlers while they vied for control over monetary policy.

Lack of transparency has always been one of the distinguishing marks of Japanese monetary policy. Werner (2003: 2) argues that the Bank of Japan pretended to be under the thumb of government in order to disguise the fact that the central bank played the crucial role in the formulation of monetary and credit policy through 'window guidance', a mechanism over which the Ministry of Finance could exert no influence. After 'Pope' Ichimada left the Bank of Japan to become minister of finance in 1954, he lobbied for the reform of the central bank law with a view to enhancing formal central bank autonomy. Support was garnered from industrial and banking groups and parliamentarians, and a government committee recommended that price stability be proclaimed as an objective of the central bank. After Ichimada lost power in 1958 the supporters of the status quo rallied, and the proposed legislation was dropped in 1960 (Werner 2003: 65–8). But this did not represent a decisive defeat for the Bank of Japan, which continued to assert control over the quantity and allocation of credit, while hiding behind its legal subordination.

The rather murky and ambiguous relationship between the Bank of Japan and the government functioned adequately over a period of decades. Japan's economic performance between the 1950s and the late 1980s was extremely impressive, and the Bank of Japan won respect for its contribution to this record (Cargill, Hutchison, and Ito 1997). Despite the eventual souring of the Japanese miracle around 1990, central bank reform was not seriously considered again until 1995 (Dwyer 2004: 249).

Conclusion

The 1930s and 1940s witnessed an upheaval in the central banking world that amounted to a revolution. Some central banks were nationalised. New legislation was imposed on many central banks that were already in state-ownership. The terms of the government–central bank relationship were set out in greater precision than ever before. Moreover, governments sought greater influence over central banks with a view to achieving improvements in economic management. Given the disasters of the interwar period, this was a reasonable reform programme.

It would be unfair, however, to conclude that the typical central bank became a mere adjunct of the government machine. One or two particularly self-effacing governors, such as Nugget Coombs in Australia, came close to subservience at times, but many other governors and central banks managed to preserve a considerable degree of autonomy. The Federal Reserve System successfully reasserted its independence from the US Treasury in the early 1950s. The Bundesbank was from the outset a strongly independent central bank. Even the Bank of England and the Bank of Japan found ways of influencing policy. In Canada (see Chapter 2 above), Governor James Coyne was extremely outspoken in his criticism of government policy in the early 1960s, in the process becoming one of the most notorious figures in central banking history. Coyne was not alone. Even Leslie O'Brien at the Bank of England publicly chided the British Labour government over its policies in 1968.

Cooperation rather than subservience or independence was the dominant theme in government–central bank relations between the Second World War and the 1960s, at least in the developed world. Politicians such as Ludwig Erhard and central bankers such as Allan Sproul saw cooperation or partnership as the ideal. So long the positions of governments and central banks on the policy issues of the day were relatively close, cooperation was feasible most (though not all) of the time. Central bankers accepted the need for economic management and the coordination of monetary and fiscal policy. They may not have liked the tendency for many academic economists and politicians to deride monetary policy, but cooperation was a sustainable strategy, especially in an era of low inflation and generally tranquil economic conditions. It was not until much later that serious problems emerged.

8   No time for cosmic thinkers: central banking in the 'Keynesian' era

[T]he central banker today is a public servant as well as a banker. His role is to operate one of the instruments of public policy for the attainment of the economic objectives of the community.
Louis Rasminsky, Governor of the Bank of Canada, 9 November 1966
(Rasminsky 1987: 75–6)

[I]t is clear from the evidence that the Treasury do not *know* whether or not the Bank [of England] in the conduct of its own affairs, is efficient … and they do not know what return it gets on its money.
British Parliamentary Select Committee on the Nationalised Industries,
1969–70 (quoted in Hennessy 1995: 209)

By the 1950s the main central banks were large organisations with thousands of employees, working predominantly in routine tasks such as currency processing and distribution. The 1940s had seen rapid internal expansion in response to the increased burden of regulating the financial system. For example, employment at the Bank of England doubled from 4,120 in 1939 (Hennessy 1995: 205) to 8,250 in 1950 (Vaubel 1997: 204). Many central banks acquired substantive new functions, including the administration of exchange controls, and in some cases new or increased responsibility for banking supervision. Though there was some levelling off and contraction in central bank employment in the 1950s, when the most draconian wartime and early post-war regulations were relaxed, the upward trend resumed in the 1960s. Recruitment of professional staff was stepped up as central banks extended their statistical and economic research functions and began to develop forecasting sections. Yet the bulk of central bank workers continued to be in the less specialised operational areas.

This chapter focuses on the activities of central banks in the industrialised world in the mid twentieth century. How did they implement monetary and exchange rate policy? How did they interact with the rest of the banking sector? What was their role in encouraging the development of financial markets? How (and for whose benefit) were they managed? How did they develop their research capabilities? Siklos

(2002: 12–14) describes the half-century after 1945 as a time of 'experimentation' in central banking. The policy and regulatory frameworks established in the 1940s appear ad hoc from a twenty-first century perspective, but they proved reasonably effective until the mid 1960s.

Monetary policy implementation

At the beginning of the twentieth century, the rediscount rate had pride of place in the armoury of central banks. Nowadays monetary policy revolves around the manipulation of a short-term interest rate, which is either fixed or targeted by the central bank (Borio 1997: 13–14). But in the mid twentieth century the monetary authorities placed much less reliance on the adjustment of an interest rate to attain their objectives (Bindseil 2004: 203). This reflected doubts – which were stronger in some countries – about the effectiveness of interest rates as a tool of economic management, combined with the belief that interest rates should be kept low and stable to encourage investment and economic growth.

M. H. De Kock (1974) devoted five chapters of his classic work on central banking to instruments used in the 'control of credit' or monetary policy. These chapters dealt with discount rate policy, open market operations, variable reserve requirements, 'other methods' including selective and quantitative controls on lending and 'moral suasion', and exchange controls. In 1963 the BIS published a survey of eight European central banks, listing and describing their instruments for the implementation of monetary policy. The Banque Nationale de Belgique (BNB), for example, had 'at its disposal' the discount rate, money market intervention, the reserve ratio, foreign exchange operations, quantitative and qualitative controls, and 'its position as adviser to the government and the banks' (BIS 1963: 38). Unfortunately, the purpose of certain regulations was rather hazy. Goodhart (2004: 342) notes that in the UK: 'Cash and liquidity required ratios were maintained, though whether their function was related to monetary policy or to financial stability was never very clear; nor was their efficacy, in either disguise.'

The international dimension of monetary policy was a major complication. This was true whether the balance of payments was chronically weak, as in the UK, or persistently strong, as in West Germany. The ability of the British monetary authorities to focus on domestic objectives was restricted in the 1950s and 1960s by the need to defend an overvalued exchange rate (Ross 2004). West German monetary policy makers faced an almost equally intractable problem. The DM was undervalued, creating large external surpluses that threatened price stability. Otmar Emminger of the Bundesbank described the balance of payments as an *Ersatz-Notenbank* or 'substitute central bank', which pumped money into the economy. When the Bundesbank tightened monetary policy in order to counter inflationary pressure, market interest rates rose, and even more capital flowed into West Germany (Franke 1999: 391).

Given the potential for conflict between domestic and external priorities, it was important to make the most appropriate assignment of policy tools. Some theoretical guidance was provided by Mundell and Fleming in the early 1960s. In an economy with a pegged exchange rate and capital mobility, the task of achieving domestic balance is best left to fiscal policy, while monetary policy should be assigned to the maintenance of external balance (Thirlwall 1980: 124–9; Mundell 2000: 333; Boughton 2003). In practice, however, capital account restrictions were widespread, and there was no clear cut assignment of tools to objectives. Monetary policy was expected to contribute to domestic as well as to external economic management (Thirlwall 1980: 132–3).

Interest rate policy was perceived to be somewhat more effective in containing inflation than in stimulating a faltering economy. But even in the area of inflation control, there were fears that monetary restraint would prove either inadequate to the task, or too costly in terms of lost output and jobs. Statutory or voluntary prices and incomes policies were advanced as a supposedly painless and more effective remedy. In fact they were neither. Opposing contemporary assessments of incomes policies are found in Rockwood (1969) and Brittan and Lilley (1977).

Nevertheless the rediscount rate was an important signal of the monetary authorities' intentions. Greater flexibility crept into interest rate policy in the late 1940s and early 1950s. The authorities were inclined to 'lean into the wind', raising interest rates when aggregate demand was considered excessive, and reducing them when unemployment increased. Market interest rates were also influenced by OMOs, changes in reserve requirements, moral suasion, and, last but not least, market conditions. Central banks usually attached more significance to interest rate policy than did their Treasury counterparts. For example, the Australian central bank repeatedly urged the government to make more use of interest rate variations (Schedvin 1992: 308–14), but the Treasury demurred, leading one observer to describe interest rate policy as the 'blind spot' of the Australian monetary authorities (Holder 1965: 95).

An important feature of the post-war decades was the emphasis on implementing monetary policy through the manipulation of quantities (including bank reserves, liquidity, and bank lending, but not the money supply) rather than by variations in interest rates. Bindseil (2004: 242) regards this approach as part of a longer 'quantitative detour' in monetary policy implementation, lasting from the 1920s into the monetarist era of the 1970s and early 1980s.

But there were occasions when interest rates did occupy centre-stage. In the early 1960s the Kennedy administration was intent on reducing net capital outflows and on stimulating domestic investment and growth. Under 'Operation Twist' the Fed was induced to conduct OMOs in order to tweak the yield curve or the relationship between market interest rates on securities of different duration. The Fed sold short-term securities with the intention of raising short-term interest rates and bolstering the international position of the US dollar, and bought longer-term securities so as to dampen long-term interest rates and encourage growth. This strategy, which met with mixed success, was dismissed by critics as a gimmick, and viewed with scepticism within the Fed (Bremner 2004: 162, 180–1; Beckhart 1972: 384–6).

Reserve requirements were prominent in most countries. Though originally introduced for prudential reasons, they started to evolve into monetary policy tools in the 1930s. The USA in 1933 was the first country to give the monetary authorities the power to vary reserve requirements. New Zealand was not far behind in 1936 (Goodfriend and Hargreaves 1983; Feinman 1993; Sayers 1957: 85–91). By varying the reserve requirement, the central bank could reduce or increase the amount of 'free' reserves available to commercial banks for credit creation. (Free reserves could also be affected by other measures such as OMOs.) Manipulating the level of free reserves was central to the thinking of the Federal Reserve System in the post-war decades. A variant of this approach – the targeting of free liquid reserves – was employed by the Bundesbank between 1958 and the early 1970s (Holtfrerich 1999: 320–1). In Italy, the compulsory reserves regime, introduced in 1947, 'expressly sought to create a system to be used for monetary control, even though it was based on powers attributed to the monetary authorities for banking supervision purposes' (Gelsomino 1999: 175). Commercial banks could also be required to hold variable minimum ratios of liquid assets (such as government bills and securities) to deposits. In some countries, including Australia and the UK, commercial banks were asked to make non-interest-bearing 'special deposits' at the central bank when additional monetary stringency was required (Ross 2004: 305–6).

The impact of controls over bank reserves and liquidity was weakened by banks' access to the discount window when reserves were running low, and by the fact that they were highly liquid after the Second World War, having stocked up on government bills and war loans. In countries with persistent external surpluses, such as West Germany, attempts to exert monetary control through variations in minimum reserve requirements were nullified by the growth in bank reserves arising from capital inflows. The Bundesbank responded by engaging in swaps, removing DMs temporarily from commercial bank balance sheets and replacing them with equivalent amounts of foreign exchange. But according to Holtfrerich (1999: 322, 391) this policy was not pursued with sufficient vigour.

Other controls were even more direct. Monetary authorities commonly issued guidelines or instructions concerning the permissible quantity and direction of bank lending (Dow 1970: 235–42). Such guidelines had two purposes. First, they were used to restrain aggregate spending at a time of low real interest rates. Secondly, they were supposed to encourage meritorious or politically desirable spending, such as capital formation in export industries and the housing sector, whilst limiting spending on luxuries such as holidays and consumer goods. One economist feared the emergence of a frivolous 'milk bar' economy in Australia in the absence of measures to channel resources into productive activities (Copland 1949). The old idea that certain economic activities were unproductive was alive and kicking.

Many controls originated during the Second World War:

By spring 1942, the list [of items covered by Regulation W, requiring down payments and limiting the length of consumer loans] included new and used goods, shoes, hats, and haberdashery. Monthly charge accounts were covered also. The regulations became so detailed that the [Federal Reserve] Board agreed to exempt the Boy Scouts and railroad employees required to use a precision watch. (Meltzer 2003: 602, n. 34)

Some controls were retained in peacetime, resulting in considerable inconvenience for consumers, businesses, and banks (Merrett 1998: 137–9). Given the fungibility of money, the ingenious could evade the spirit of the controls while following the letter. Borrowing for the purchase of 'essential' new machinery might free up retained profits to pay for the construction of an 'inessential' corporate headquarters or a chain of milk bars.

Window guidance, or the imposition of limits on lending by *individual* banks, was one of the 'primary instruments of monetary policy as practiced by the Bank of Japan' (Cargill, Hutchison, and Ito 1997: 30). Introduced in 1954, window guidance applied principally but not solely to city banks, or large commercial banks in major centres. The guidance was adjusted monthly or quarterly according to the central bank's assessment of the need for expansion or constraint. There is some debate over the extent to which the Bank of Japan used this mechanism to influence the distribution of lending between sectors and firms (Vittas and Wang 1991: 8). The Ministry of Finance used its own powers to influence the direction of lending (Okazaki 1995). Though window guidance was in a sense only advice, banks could not afford to flout the wishes of the Bank of Japan, which controlled access to the discount window and decided whether banks could open new branches (Rhodes and Yoshino 1999).

Moral suasion, the western equivalent of administrative guidance, was part of every central banker's toolbox, especially in states with highly concentrated banking sectors. The more concentrated the banking industry, the fewer the banks that needed swaying. Central banks sought to influence the lending of banks by lecturing them in public and chatting to them in private. In the UK the entire system of controls over reserves, liquidity, and lending was based on moral suasion. The Bank of England preferred to regulate by consent. Harold Macmillan, while chancellor, described this as the 'British way of running the banking system' (quoted in Fforde 1992: 660). As in Japan, however, British banks understood that outright refusal to cooperate would be punished (Capie 1990: 133). Ultimately, the central bank or the government could enforce compliance. Nugget Coombs had a similar philosophy to that of the Bank of England, regarding the Australian trading banks as a family with the Commonwealth Bank as its head. Coombs moved towards a policy of regulating by consensus rather than by formal rules in the mid 1950s, obtaining the consent of the banks to a gentleman's agreement on liquid government security ratios (Rowse 2002: 223; Schedvin 1992: 196–7; 212–20). Less reliance was placed on moral suasion in countries such as the USA where the banking system was fragmented (Adams 1957: 133).

Breton and Wintrobe (1978) argued that commercial banks had an additional reason for responding positively to moral suasion. By cooperating with the central bank, they could acquire valuable information about the condition of the monetary system and the thinking of the monetary authorities. The task of managing a banking cartel was simplified by acceptance of central bank leadership in relation to interest rates and the volume of lending. The post-war era was marked by strong elements of collusion in the banking industry, especially in economies dominated by a handful of commercial banks.

Exchange control, or the rationing of foreign currency, was the final policy tool. During the Second World War most governments introduced exchange controls in order to conserve scarce currencies such as the US dollar. Requests for foreign currency were processed by the commercial banks, often under the supervision of the central bank. For nations with chronic balance of payments difficulties, the effective management of the foreign reserves was critical. Though the regulation of capital flows was condoned by the International Monetary Fund (IMF), member countries were obliged to restore current account convertibility as soon as possible after the war. In the event, however, many retained current account restrictions until well into the 1950s, citing the 'dollar gap' in justification (Mikesell 1954; MacDougall 1957; Eichengreen 1993). Central bankers were ambivalent towards exchange controls, acknowledging their value in the defence of the external reserves and the exchange rate, but looking forward to a time when they were no longer necessary. Critics argued that exchange controls were used to protect inefficient industries. Current account convertibility was reintroduced by the major European countries in December 1958, by which time the dollar gap had closed. In addition, West Germany took some steps to liberalise capital account transactions. Japan introduced qualified current account convertibility in 1964 (Helleiner 1994: 51–77; Schenk 1994; Kaplan and Schleiminger 1989). Australia followed the Europeans in adopting current account convertibility, but New Zealand continued to restrict such transactions in order to insulate the economy from external shocks, an approach that became increasingly anomalous in the 1960s and 1970s.

Different rules and practices applied in each country with respect to the provision of financial accommodation to the government by the central bank. Accommodation could be supplied either directly or indirectly through the purchase of government paper on the secondary markets where they existed (Leone 1991). There were strict controls on central bank lending to governments in some jurisdictions, including West Germany, but lax controls in others, including France until 1959. M. H. De Kock (1974: 34–56) drew attention to the large increase in central bank lending to governments between 1945 and 1970. Such lending contributed to inflationary pressure in the 1960s.

Reliance on administrative controls instead of market-based techniques to implement monetary policy was not a matter of choice in some countries. Where secondary markets for commercial and government paper were underdeveloped, the scope for influencing interest rates through OMOs was limited. Even in some relatively sophisticated economies, including Canada, Italy, Japan, and Australia, there were serious gaps in financial markets in the early 1950s. Central banks endeavoured to overcome these deficiencies. The Bank of Canada promoted the emergence of a broader short-term money market in 1953–4, partly with a view to facilitating greater reliance on OMOs in Treasury bills, though older methods of monetary control continued to have priority in Canada, especially the movement of government funds between the central bank and commercial banks (Watts 1972, 1993: 94–8). The aspirations of central banks were not always appreciated by governments. The Bank of Japan was interested in fostering a Treasury bill market, but the Ministry of Finance would not entertain the idea, preferring to borrow on terms that were easier to control through the government bond syndicate. In order for a short-term market to have operated effectively, moreover, there would have had to be some flexibility in interest rates, probably leading to a rise in the cost of borrowing, but this was unacceptable to the Ministry of Finance (Rosenbluth 1989: 51–2, 63–4, 79, 98–9). Inspired in part by the Canadian example, the Australian central bank promoted the development of a short-term money market in the 1950s. Overcoming Treasury scepticism, an official short-term market was opened in 1959, but it remained underutilised for another decade because of continued restrictions (Schedvin 1992: 248–70).

How effective was monetary policy between the end of the Second World War and the late 1960s? Outcomes were satisfactory, despite the vast discrepancy between the objectives and techniques of policy then and best practice today. The 1950s and 1960s constituted a golden age for the world economy. Growth was strong throughout the developed world, especially in Japan and the countries that in 1958 formed the European Economic Community (EEC). Inflation rates were moderate notwithstanding rapid economic growth, though they began to creep up in the late 1950s – from 1957 according to one article (Fischer et al. 2002: 876). Furthermore, there were no serious banking crises. Nothing could have been more unlike the inter-war period.

Reliance on direct controls in monetary policy implementation did have significant drawbacks. Banks were constrained in their lending decisions and forced to hold more liquid assets, including government securities, than they wished to hold. Restrictions on the banking sector encouraged disintermediation, or the growth of non-bank financial institutions which were potentially more unstable. At the same time, regulation produced an environment in which banking cartels flourished and banks made satisfactory profits without increasing their efficiency (Ross 2004). Compliance costs rose. In April 1971, the governor of the RBNZ summed up the situation: 'the system is becoming more and more complicated and the arbitrariness of it is becoming more obvious' (quoted in Singleton et al. 2006: 27).

But nothing should be allowed to detract from the fact that post-war monetary policy was hugely more successful than monetary policy in the

1920s and 1930s, and that inflation was not a critical international concern until the late 1960s. In praising US monetary policy in the 1950s, Romer and Romer (2002b: 121) conclude that the Fed was successful in containing prices and 'actually quite sophisticated' in its thinking. They find that the aims of the Fed in the 1950s, and the 'understanding' of policy makers, were 'remarkably similar' to those of the Fed in the 1990s. Restoring current account convertibility was a significant achievement for monetary policy makers outside North America, and would not have been possible if inflation had been out of control. Not until the second half of the 1960s did this benign environment start to disintegrate.

Relations with banks

The new stress on administrative controls and moral suasion altered the relationship between central banks and the banking industry, and provoked some resentment amongst commercial bankers. The postwar years also saw the growing involvement of some central banks in prudential supervision. It is difficult to encapsulate the relationship between central banks and commercial banks, which was marked by elements of collusion and coercion as well as of cooperation.

Governments and legislatures asserted a greater interest than before in moulding the structure of the financial system. Their motives ranged from the prudential to the populist. The administration of structural controls was often delegated to central banks, implicating them in the consequences. In the USA, for example, new regulations in the 1930s had a major impact on the structure of the banking industry. The separation of commercial from investment banking was achieved in the second Glass Steagall Act (officially the Banking Act 1933). The 1933 and 1935 Banking Acts empowered the Fed to place ceilings on the interest paid on time and savings deposits (Regulation Q). No interest was permitted on demand deposits. One of the aims of Congress, in establishing Regulation Q, was to encourage country banks to focus on lending to local communities by making it unprofitable for them to hold large balances at banks in financial centres. By restraining price competition for deposits, Congress also hoped to reduce the temptation to engage in risky lending. Regulation Q was extended to thrift institutions in 1966, and at the same time the interest rate ceilings were allowed to bite in order to ease the burden on certain classes of borrower. Thrifts were permitted to offer slightly higher interest rates than commercial banks, so as to encourage the reallocation of deposits and an increase in mortgage lending (Gilbert 1986). Regulations took on a life of their own, becoming increasingly baroque as they were modified to address new situations. The distortions caused by Regulation Q troubled some observers in the 1950s and 1960s, but this measure remained in force until 1986. Addressing the American Finance Association and the American Economic Association in December 1966, Allan Sproul (1967: 144) lamented the way in which Regulation Q had been 'stretched to serve as a handmaiden to general monetary policy ... and as a yo-yo device to switch funds' between different types of financial institution.

Some central bankers shared the concern of governments about structural issues. In the early 1960s, Guido Carli, the governor of the Bank of Italy, accepted that competition between banks should be restricted. He was particularly anxious to protect small and medium-sized regional banks from competition offered by large nationwide banks (Alhadeff 1968: 39). Between 1918 and 1967 the Bank of England and the British Treasury made it known that they would oppose any mergers between the 'Big Five' UK clearing banks (Cottrell 2003: 45, 54–5).

Whatever the rationale for controls, a cooperative attitude on the part of commercial banks was required for their smooth implementation. Karl Klasen (1957: 25) of Deutsche Bank, the largest West German bank, felt that the central bank was 'always dependent on the cooperation of the commercial banks'. This made it all the more important for the central bank to possess moral authority. As a precondition for 'moral suasion or [the] exertion of psychological influence', added Klasen (1957: 41), 'close contact must exist between the central bank and the commercial banks'. Though 'tensions' with the commercial banks could arise when 'excessive demands' were placed on the central bank by the government, cooperation was the norm in West Germany (Klasen 1957: 42). The same principles applied in the UK, perhaps even more so because of the voluntary nature of British regulation. Regular consultation and frequent lunches helped to maintain a degree of consensus. This was just as well, for according to Fforde (1992: 696) the 'rather ramshackle monarchy over which [the Bank of England] presided could not accommodate much discontent without courting disobedience to the monarch and a damaging decline in the standing of the central institution'. In 1957 Cameron Cobbold, the governor of the Bank of England, claimed that he could convene a meeting with senior representatives of the banking industry within 'about half an hour' (Roberts, R. 1995: 180). The chairman of the Committee of London Clearing Bankers (CLCB) was 'consulted by the Governor of the Bank of England continuously', the CLCB held its meetings at the central bank every quarter, and there were frequent lower level contacts (Ellerton 1957: 117).

In New Zealand, regulation of the banking industry reached an unusual intensity for a developed capitalist country. Controls were employed for monetary policy reasons as well as to create protected markets for different classes of institution. Trading banks were hindered from competing directly with community-owned trustee savings banks and the Post Office Savings Bank. Consequently, the market share of the trading banks declined. The regime became increasingly elaborate as old loopholes were closed and new ones were found. Though the trading banks resented tight controls, they maintained cordial relations with the central bank (Holmes 1999: 36–45). The RBNZ was still 'the best friend they had within the official policy making system' (Holmes 1999: 37), but this was not saying much. As well as being tasked with the implementation of monetary policy, central banks sometimes acted as representatives of the banking industry in government circles. Such relationships were multifaceted.

Largely because of regulations on interstate and branch banking, the US banking industry did not display the oligopolistic tendencies that were evident elsewhere. At the district level, there was close contact between the Federal Reserve Banks and commercial banks. Indeed commercial banks with membership of the Federal Reserve System had a say in the governance of the Reserve Banks. At the national level there was consultation between the Federal Reserve Board and banking industry associations, but the relationship was not as close as it was in some countries.

Woolley (1984: 69–87) saw little evidence to suggest that the Fed was captured by the banking industry. The Fed had to be sensitive to a number of constituencies, including Congress and the president, as well as the Treasury and other business groups, such as farmers and manufacturers, each with their own policy preferences (Kettl 1986). As a result it was insulated from control by any one constituency, including the bankers. Moreover, capturing the Fed would not have been enough, since there were several regulatory and supervisory agencies. In some other countries there was more scope for collusion between central banks and banking industries in the 1950s and 1960s. Though regulation held back the most innovative banks, it helped the banking system as a whole to achieve healthy profits at little or no risk. Low interest rates brought excess demand for credit, enabling banks to select only the best applicants for loans. Goodhart (2004: 342) contends that because of regulation 'banking was an extremely safe, and boring, occupation between 1945 and 1973'. Banking cartels even proved useful to the authorities. Carli, for example, found it convenient to leave the control of deposit and lending rates to the Italian banking cartel (Alhadeff 1968: 349). No urgency was attached by the authorities to achieving improvements in bank efficiency. A risk-averse approach was understandable following the interwar debacle, which was never far from the thoughts of the first post-war generation of top bankers, central bankers and politicians: 'oligopolistic conditions ... seemed a fair price to pay for soundness and stability in the banking system' (Onado 2003: 170).

The Japanese practice of *amakaduri* (or the descent from heaven), whereby retired Ministry of Finance and central bank officials were appointed to senior positions at major banks and other enterprises created opportunities for collusion with their former colleagues, for example in the setting of lending targets under window guidance (Horiuchi and Shimizu 2001). On the other hand, relationships that might seem collusive to some may be oppressive to others. Reflecting on Swedish experience in the 1960s, Olsson and Jörnmark (2007: 206–7) conclude that the 'banks became something like circumscribed subjects to the Governor of the Central Bank'. The head of the Riksbank 'was forced to develop very special and close relationships with the private bank managers, whom he regularly met to either persuade or threaten'.

The efforts of the CBA to improve relations with the Australian banks were undermined for some years because the CBA was itself a major trading bank. Other trading banks resented the fact that the CBA was both regulator and competitor – umpire and player in cricketing terminology (Rowse 2002: 215) – though in practice the commercial and central banking divisions were run separately. Governor Coombs favoured the retention of the dual function, partly on the grounds that it would be handy in the event of another depression. But political pressure from the trading banks ensured that the CBA was split in 1960, the central banking functions being allocated to the new RBA. This separation defused tension between the central bank and the trading banks (Schedvin 1992: 271–94).

Central banks and other financial institutions sometimes cooperated over the provision of industrial finance. At the end of the Second World War the Bank of England and City institutions set up two companies, the Finance Corporation for Industry and the Industrial and Commercial Finance Corporation, to overcome perceived bottlenecks in industrial finance. While these bodies assisted companies in a number of industries, they were particularly interested in promoting small businesses and new industries. They had a sort of development banking (Fforde 1992: 704–27) or venture capitalist (Roberts, R. 1995: 175) role. In New Zealand, the RBNZ subscribed 30 per cent of the capital of the Development Finance Corporation (DFC) in 1964. The DFC was designed to 'provide finance and advisory services for new and expanding industries' that could not obtain funding on reasonable terms elsewhere (Morrell 1979: 113). Whether the DFC was really necessary, or merely a political stunt, is open to debate (Hawke 1985: 271). Since the bulk of the DFC's capital was subscribed by trading banks and insurance companies, it involved some cooperation, albeit of a hesitant nature, between the central bank and the private sector. The RBNZ's involvement with the DFC was short lived with the corporation entering government ownership in 1973. The CBA also asserted a developmental role, setting up an Industrial Finance Department in 1945, to make advances to small businesses. In addition the CBA provided credit to the financially troubled State Electricity Commission of Victoria and other public sector entities in the early 1950s (Schedvin 1992: 5, 67, 199–200). In other words the Australian central bank became the lender of last resort to an electricity board. If this seems odd from today's perspective, it was consistent with the philosophy that a central bank was a flexible tool of state policy.

Prudential supervision was not an unduly pressing concern in the post-war decades. Given that banks were tightly regulated and cartelisation was rife, depositors faced little risk. Until the mid 1970s the Bank of England had only one senior official involved in what might be termed prudential supervision, and no clear mandate (Goodhart, Capie, and Schnadt 1994: 26; Fforde 1992: 749–79). In some countries, including Belgium (Buyst and Maes 2008b), France, and Switzerland, the central bank was not entrusted with prudential supervision. In the USA, bank supervision continued to be shared by the Fed and government agencies. Responsibility was also shared in West Germany, where the Federal Banking Supervisory Office delegated the day-to-day task of supervision to the central bank (Franke 1999: 253–61). The Ministry of Finance supervised Japanese banks, but the Bank of Japan also conducted onsite inspections of those banks to which it offered current accounts (Japanese Bankers Association 2001: 46).

Some central banks did become more active in the prudential sphere. The Bank of Italy's responsibility for prudential supervision was confirmed in 1947, when it fully reabsorbed the duties that had been given to the Credit Inspectorate in 1936 (Gelsomino 1999: 175). Though the Dutch central bank had long possessed an informal supervisory function, it received legislative backing for this role in 1948 and 1952. The 1952 Act for the Supervision of the Credit System distinguished between the Dutch central bank's mandates to engage in monetary supervision or monetary policy, business supervision for the safeguarding of bank creditors, and structural supervision for the improvement of systemic efficiency and stability (Prast 2003: 168–90; BIS 1963: 249–52).

Table 2 *Central bank personnel, 1950–90*

	UK	France	Italy	Switzerland	West Germany Total	Direktorium	USA FR System	FR Board
1950	8,250	12,185	8,421	415	9,570	1,778	18,571	563
1955	7,450	11,429	7,370	397	11,110	2,153	19,693	576
1960	7,110	11,406	7,233	393	10,647	1,967	20,527	598
1965	7,350	12,496	7,336	414	11,450	1,960	19,335	667
1970	7,700	14,850	7,549	432	12,734	2,113	23,126	1,016
1975	7,900	14,935	8,073	462	13,545	2,463	27,960	1,460
1980	7,000	16,065	8,645	516	14,825	2,705	25,733	1,498
1985	5,470	17,349	9,261	583	15,077	2,762	24,929	1,520
1990	5,140	17,176	9,229	547	(17,519)	(2,939)		

Source: Vaubel (1997: 204).

Nowadays it is universally accepted that central banks should promote a stable *and* efficient banking sector. In the final quarter of the twentieth century the stress was on efficiency, but in the third quarter the key objective was stability, and this was often achieved through regulation and moral suasion instead of through prudential supervision. The overwhelming weight given to stability was not indicative of immaturity, but rather it was an expression of the public's aversion to uncertainty and its fear of banking collapses after the events of the 1930s. As a by-product of the distinctive post-war approaches to monetary and banking policy, central banks and commercial banks were brought into closer touch than ever before. Relations with the commercial banks were multifaceted, encompassing elements of cooperation, collusion, and coercion.

The central bank as an institution

The argument that central bankers are self-serving empire builders (Toma and Toma 1986) receives only partial support from the employment figures shown in Table 2. Staffing at each of the British, French, Italian, and Swiss central banks actually declined during the 1950s, though it picked up again in the 1960s. Only the Federal Reserve System showed an inexorable rise during the 1950s and 1960s. One interpretation of these figures might be that the Fed was in a better position than some European central banks to assert its autonomy.

Vaubel (1997) contends that in the second half of the twentieth century there was a positive relationship between central bank independence (as measured by the institution's power to set the salaries of senior officials and to spend 'profits') and central bank employment. Milton Friedman (1986: 27) once lamented that the 'Fed is not subject to an effective budget constraint. It prints its own money to pay its expenses.' After 1947 the Fed was under no legal obligation to transfer surplus revenue to the Treasury, but did make significant payments voluntarily. Shughart and Tollison (1986) contended that the Fed attempted to maximise its own rewards, as proxied by employment within the System. Monetary policy was compromised, they claimed, because the Fed profited from (inflationary) open market purchases of interest bearing securities. Taking a different line of attack, Acheson and Chant argued that in the 1950s and 1960s the Bank of Canada implemented monetary policy in a deliberately complex and opaque manner in order to avoid being held accountable for its mistakes as well as for its spending (Chant and Acheson 1986; Acheson and Chant 1986).

What are we to make of such criticisms? Central bankers did become more like civil servants in the mid twentieth century, and cannot have been immune to the usual bureaucratic incentives. Yet it is difficult to believe that Bill Martin or Lord Cromer was motivated by the desire to maximise central bank profits or to raise armies of clerks and typists. Each could have multiplied his salary by moving into the private sector. Top central bankers were at least as interested in achieving policy successes as they were in covering up errors and scrambling to survive. Influence, reputation, and a place in history were what mattered to them. Their reputations depended on achieving policy successes, or at least on fighting for what they perceived to be virtuous policies. At the same time, they had little incentive to worry about internal costs in an environment of lax budget constraints (Willett 1990). Central bankers lower down the hierarchy are the ones most likely to have behaved like petty bureaucrats. As late as 1982, an assistant governor described the RBNZ as a 'comfortable old slipper' with working conditions and scones that were the 'envy of visiting Treasury officers' (quoted in Singleton et al. 2006: 237). In any case, the position might not have been much better in the cartelised banking industry in the 1950s and 1960s.

Most central banks continued to be opaque rather than transparent. As well as being self-serving, central bank secrecy suited the executive, which was anxious to demonstrate unanimity within the policy-making community. Sir Roland Wilson of the Australian Treasury 'set limits to what Governor Coombs could say about economic policy' in public (Rowse 2002: 211). An Australian journalist remarked in 1967 that the RBA's annual report was so terse and cryptic that it was as hard to understand as the Book of Revelation (Schedvin 1992: 342). Of course, there were outbursts of dissent, for example by Governor Coyne in Canada, but they were infrequent. By the rather low standards of the day, the Fed was actually one of the most transparent central banks (Bindseil 2004: 2). The Banking Act 1935 compelled the Federal Reserve Board and the FOMC to include in the Board's annual report 'a complete record of all action taken, the reasons for the action, and the votes'. (Meltzer 2003: 486). Fed leaders during the 1960s were under constant pressure from some Congressmen, especially Representative Wright Patman and Senator William Proxmire, to defend their policy decisions and alleged waste of resources. Evidently, 'A hearing before either of these gentlemen was something of an ordeal. Word of a new invitation to testify before either one was typically greeted around the Board with the institutional equivalent of a sigh' (Stockwell, E. 1989: 26). Greater transparency was accompanied by greater vulnerability to criticism. However, the continued growth in staff numbers indicates that the Fed's critics were ineffective.

Rising staff complements were at least in part the result of external forces, especially in the 1940s. Growing state intervention in the financial system created more work for bureaucrats. Some new administrative functions, including the management of exchange controls, were delegated to central banks. The acquisition of new labour intensive duties did not always please central bankers. For example, the Bank of England initially regarded its role in the administration of exchange control as an 'unwelcome' burden or nuisance (Hennessy 1995: 205), though it acknowledged that controls were necessary during the war and post-war dollar shortage. Falling central bank employment in several countries in the 1950s reflected the gradual relaxation of some wartime controls. The rise in employment in the 1960s and 1970s is much easier to explain in terms of the tendency of bureaucracies to reproduce, as individual departments clamoured for more resources in the context of loose budget constraints. Even so, some central banks accepted the need for limited internal reform. The Federal Reserve Board established an Office of the Controller in 1953 in order to improve internal auditing and budgeting, and then appointed external auditors. These initiatives were designed to head off Congressional scrutiny (Stockwell, E. 1989: 16–17). In 1968, the Bank of England appointed McKinsey & Company, a management consultancy, to report on organisational matters. As a result of the McKinsey report the Bank introduced a new Manpower Services (including computing) Department and an improved system of budgetary control (McKenna 2006: 182–5: Hennessy 1995: 207–9).

Mystery and privilege may well have attached to the lives of senior central bankers, but many of the operational functions of central banks were extremely tedious. One of the functions assigned by the New Zealand government to the RBNZ was the management of the registry for government stock. As one worker in this department recalled, there were long periods of idleness. 'Five of us used to sit there in Registry, poised for files to arrive so that we would have something to do. The boredom at times was incredible' (RBNZ 1994). Central banks were formal, rather stuffy institutions, though rather less so in Australia and New Zealand. Women still faced discrimination and could not expect to achieve high position. In New Zealand, they were ejected from the reserve bank's pension scheme as soon as they married.

Rise of the economists

Central banks expanded their research activities at an accelerating pace in response to the demand for accurate and timely financial statistics, the growing (though not unchallenged) prestige of economics, the increased availability of trained economists and econometricians, and the advent of computer modelling. Governments too were employing more economists, a trend that started in the Second World War. Economics was becoming a profession (Coats, A. W. 1981).

The Fed was in the vanguard. Sproul built up the research department at the FRBNY, hiring the best economics graduates from leading universities (Ritter 1980: 9–10). The Kennedy and Johnson administrations were inclined to appoint Keynesian-leaning economists to the Federal Reserve Board. With the appointment of Sherman Maisel in 1965 economists achieved a majority on the Board. Inevitably, this trend provoked some resentment among non-economists who felt that their own contribution was not valued as highly as before (Stockwell, E. 1989: 21). The 1960s also saw the emergence of econometric modelling at the Fed. However, modelling and forecasting were still considered rather outré activities (Mayer, T. 1999: 18), and it was not until the 1970s that they were fully accepted. Bill Martin, whose own Ph.D. was in finance, appointed economists to vacant presidencies of the Reserve Banks, but remained ambivalent about econometric modelling. At Maisel's suggestion, Martin agreed in 1966 to allow econometric forecasts – one for the macroeconomy and one for money and credit – to be introduced into FOMC discussions. Perhaps justifiably, Martin had little confidence in early econometric forecasts, which were often seriously flawed. Martin also deprecated 'statisticalitis', and the division of the Board between those who spoke economics and those who spoke English (Bremner 2004: 192, 253, 269, 271).

Research at the Bank of Canada also took a more quantitative turn in 1966 with the development of an econometric model of the Canadian economy. This was initially known as HOSS after the four main contributors, Helliwell, Officer, Shapiro, and Stewart. Helliwell (2005–6: 35) remembers that 'boxes of computer cards were sent off every night by bus to the Université de Montréal computer centre, to be returned the following morning'. Later on, data was sent at night via modem to a computer at Salt Lake City. As there were frequent glitches, researchers had to stay at the Bank until late into the night 'fuelled by large tins of cookies'. Econometric research at the Bank of Canada and other central banks involved extensive collaboration between in-house researchers and academics. By the first half of the 1970s, econometric modelling was in full swing in the central banking world (Masera, Fazio, and Padoa-Schioppa 1975). Central bank econometric models were not intended solely for forecasting, and often proved more useful when used to simulate the effects of alternative policies (Singleton et al. 2006: 74–5).

Economists were few in number and relatively low in status at the Bank of England in the 1940s and 1950s. The situation began to change after publication of the Radcliffe Report, which was critical of the Bank's deficiencies in statistics, economic research, and publications. Despite resistance from conservatives within the Bank to the term 'research', which sounded too 'American' and academic, there was considerable expansion after 1959, and a new Economic Intelligence Department was established in 1964 (Hennessy 1992: 316–23). The appointment of Charles Goodhart as economic advisor in 1968 strengthened the Bank's economic and econometric capabilities (Goodhart 1984: 1–19). Early Bank of England forecasts were made with a model 'developed first by the London Business School' (Bank of England 1976: 444), another instance of collaboration with academics.

At the Bank of Japan, graduates received in-house training in economics irrespective of whether their degrees were in economics or other disciplines. The most promising recruits were then sent overseas for postgraduate study in economics (Komiya and Yamamoto 1981: 271–2). Economists brought new insights and a different type of logic to the work of central banks. Graduate recruits with an economics degree were not employed exclusively in central bank research departments, but this was where many of them found a niche.

Central bank economists were expected to do practical research. Sproul had no time for economists who liked 'cosmic thinking and metaphysical roundabouts' (Ritter 1980: 10). Central banks tended to hire economists of moderate views rather than the ideologically driven. Embarrassing the governor or the government would not have been a good career strategy for a central bank economist. Compliance was especially prized at the Bank of Japan. According to one insider, the Bank of Japan Research Department in the 1960s was stacked with 'yes men' and run on semi-military lines (Werner 2002: 47–9). At the same time, central banks with credible in-house economic expertise, such as the Bank of Norway, were in a stronger position to argue against unpalatable government policies (Bergh 1981: 166).

Conclusion

Between the Second World War and the mid 1960s, central banks in developed western economies achieved impressive results in comparison with the preceding and following periods. Inflation was contained and there were no banking crises to threaten financial stability. These outcomes were obtained using ad hoc methods including extensive direct controls. For the most part, central banks worked in close concert with governments. By the late 1960s the cosy world that had been constructed in the 1940s was beginning to disintegrate, but this does not detract from the successes of the previous twenty years. Efficiency in financial markets was sacrificed for greater security after 1945. Even so, financial markets continued to develop, often with the encouragement of central banks. Central banks themselves experienced growth during the 1940s and 1960s (and in some cases the 1950s as well). Top central bankers were more interested in posterity than in empire building, but they had no incentive to rein in costs when faced by lax budget constraints. By the 1940s central bankers had become public servants as well as bankers. The economists were on the march by the 1960s, and central banks were in the process of being transformed into the multidisciplinary organisations with which we are familiar today.

9   Rekindling central bank cooperation in the Bretton Woods era

> The United Nations Monetary and Financial Conference recommends the liquidation of the Bank for International Settlements at the earliest possible moment.
> Resolution V of the Final Act of the Bretton Woods Conference, 1944
> (quoted in Baer 1999: 361)

> The September 1960 annual meeting of the IMF registered concern about the dollar's exchange rate. Kennedy's election, two months later, did little to reassure markets. It is in this context that the United States 're-discovered' the BIS.
> Claudio Borio and Gianni Toniolo (2008: 45)

The international connections and activities of central banks aroused considerable suspicion during the 1940s, not least amongst some of the framers of the Bretton Woods settlement. Special hostility was reserved for the Bank for International Settlements, which had been tainted by its pre-war enthusiasm for the gold standard, and by the perception that it was a collaborator of the Axis powers. The Bretton Woods agreements were intergovernmental, and central banks were assigned a largely subordinate, technical role in their functioning. Between 1945 and the end of the Bretton Woods exchange rate system in the early 1970s, however, central banks and the BIS fought to rebuild their influence in the international arena. Their success, though not immediate, owed much to the shortcomings of Bretton Woods and its principal agent, the International Monetary Fund (IMF). By the 1970s, central banks were well on their way to regaining the status that they had lost in the 1930s and 1940s.

The BIS at war

When war broke out in September 1939, central bankers on both sides, as well as in neutral countries, were keen for the BIS to remain in business. Nobody could predict how long hostilities might last, and it was hoped that the BIS would be involved in financial reconstruction.

Central banks instructed their nationals on the BIS staff to work harmoniously with colleagues from enemy countries (Jacobsson 1979: 141). After the German invasion of western Europe in 1940, however, it was harder to keep up appearances. Thomas McKittrick, the president of the BIS, admitted that some staff and their families 'were coming to hate each other' (quoted in Toniolo 2005: 222).

With fewer transactions involving central banks, staffing levels were cut and the BIS became even more of a talking shop cum research institute. Toniolo (2005: 229–30) suggests that BIS membership gave a fig leaf of respectability to career central bankers from the Axis nations. Italian central bankers supported the BIS as a counterpart to German financial power. Governments on both sides were more wary, fearing that the BIS would be manipulated by their enemies.

The BIS tried to remain neutral, devising elaborate protocols to avoid transactions that could be construed as aiding the war effort of either side (Toniolo 2005: 215–17). That these protocols did not always succeed is acknowledged in the official history of the BIS (Toniolo 2005: 257–9). McKittrick, an American banker, was elected president of the BIS on the eve of war, and stayed at his post until 1946. McKittrick was reappointed in 1943, though he was no longer a neutral citizen, because his presence was tolerable to both the Allies and the Germans (Toniolo 2005: 224–6). The wartime BIS was a 'magnet for information' (Jacobsson 1979: 151). In the course of their duties, BIS officials visited Berlin, London, Washington, and other capitals, thereby gaining a unique insight into the thinking of the warring nations. Per Jacobsson, the economic advisor to the BIS, who was a Swede, went to Berlin in 1943 to discuss the British and American proposals for post-war monetary reconstruction with the German authorities (Toniolo 2005: 231). On such occasions BIS personnel could not avoid telling their hosts something new about the other side, even if it was only gossip. Jacobsson's own sympathies were with the Allies. After returning from a trip to the USA in 1942, he was visited by Emil Puhl of the Reichsbank, who asked what the Americans were saying about Germany. Jacobsson then reported on this meeting to his friend, Allen Dulles, the European head of the Office of Strategic Services, the forerunner of the Central Intelligence Agency (Jacobsson 1979: 152–4). In response to approaches from Japanese board and staff members, Jacobsson tried unsuccessfully to mediate between Tokyo and Washington in 1945 (Jacobsson 1979: 169–77).

The BIS continued to execute a limited number of transactions for central banks. For example, it arranged for the transfer of some western European gold reserves to the USA prior to the German takeover. But it was also involved in some rather dodgier transactions. In 1941, the

BIS facilitated the transfer of gold from the Banque de France, which was under German influence if not control, to the Bank of Portugal in exchange for Portuguese currency, which might have been used to assist the Axis. Questionable payments were also made on behalf of the Reichsbank to Hungary and Yugoslavia, and on behalf of the central banks of Romania and Bulgaria, both Axis supporters (Toniolo 2005: 238–45).

Under pressure from powerful belligerent nations, the BIS had to compromise in order to survive. The same was true of neutral states such as Switzerland, Sweden, Portugal, and Spain. With the contraction of routine banking business, the BIS became heavily dependent on income from its pre-war investments in Germany. These investments were a legacy of the Bank's involvement in the Young Plan. The BIS ignored warnings that gold looted from the Banque Nationale de Belgique was being used by the Germans to pay interest. It later transpired that gold stolen from the Dutch, as well as a small amount from holocaust victims, was also transferred to the BIS in payment of interest (Toniolo 2005: 247–52; 257–8). According to Schloss (1958: 117), however, the BIS would have been no less vulnerable to criticism if it had refused German gold: the management 'would have been subject to the charge of aiding Germany by permitting her to retain gold ... and of disregarding the interests of the Bank's creditors'. In other words, the BIS could not avoid obloquy of one sort or another. In 1948 the BIS agreed to return 3,740 kg of looted gold to the original owners. After this concession, the US assets of the BIS, which had been frozen during the war, were unblocked (Toniolo 2005: 278).

Rightly or wrongly, the BIS came to be seen as a rather shady and undesirable organisation, not only in the USA but also in some European nations. Within the Federal Reserve System, only the FRBNY showed any sympathy for it (Toniolo 2005: 267). The unwillingness of the BIS to condemn the Axis was interpreted, perhaps conveniently, as a form of treachery. Paul Einzig (1960: 240), one of the noisiest critics of the BIS, subsequently recanted and admitted that it had been 'scrupulously neutral'. The BIS would have been in a far stronger position to influence post-war developments if it had relocated to the UK in 1939 or 1940 and sided wholeheartedly with the Allies, but there is no indication that these options were considered.

Bretton Woods

The Bretton Woods conference, held at the Mount Washington Hotel in New Hampshire in July 1944, represented a low point in the status and influence of central bankers. The purpose of this conference, attended by delegations from over forty Allied and neutral nations, was to design an international monetary regime that would save the post-war world from repeating the errors of the 1920s and 1930s. In a cynical moment, J. M. Keynes, the leader of the British delegation, described Bretton Woods as a 'vast monkey-house' staged by President Roosevelt (Cesarano 2006: 167). Much of the thinking behind the settlement was rooted in Keynes's analysis of interwar economic problems and their remedies (Cesarano 2006: 206). Bretton Woods was based on the principle that the international monetary system needed managing in such a way as to preclude the extreme gyrations capital flows, exchange rates, and output that had blighted the 1920s and 1930s.

Conference delegates were presented with two alternative plans, one attributed to Keynes, and one to Harry White, an American academic and Treasury representative. Both envisaged a regime of fixed or 'pegged' exchange rates, supported by an international scheme to provide credits to nations with temporary balance of payments deficits. Such credits would enable the deficit countries to retain their pegs without the need for drastic deflation, though some internal adjustment might still be necessary. Keynes and White differed over the design of the international scheme. Keynes proposed a Clearing Union, or a sort of international central bank, with the power to issue its own currency and extend generous amounts of credit to deficit countries. He foresaw a major role for national central banks in the management of this system. White's proposal was less ambitious, and involved a fund that could lend a limited amount of member countries' currencies to debtors. Under the White Plan, which was less generous than the Keynes Plan, deficit countries would have to start deflating sooner and more vigorously. The White Plan was more explicitly intergovernmental in scope, and assumed a smaller role for central banks. Supporters of White rejected Keynes's scheme as inflationary, while supporters of Keynes condemned White's scheme as penny pinching and potentially deflationary.

The final settlement was closer to the White Plan than to the Keynes Plan. The US dollar was fixed to gold at the rate of US$35 per ounce. Other countries fixed their exchange rates to the US dollar either directly or indirectly through pegs to the British pound or the French franc. The USA held its external reserves in gold, whereas other member countries could hold gold, US dollars, sterling, or French francs. Exchange rates could be altered only in cases of 'fundamental disequilibrium' (which was not clearly defined). IMF consent was required for devaluations or revaluations of more than 10 per cent. Signatories to Bretton Woods were required to deposit a combination of gold and their own currency into the IMF. Deficit countries could borrow from the IMF, but only up to certain limits. Members of the Bretton Woods system were permitted to restrict capital account transactions – fear of the destabilising effects of hot money flows was universal. But they were expected to restore current account convertibility shortly after the end of the war. Being the largest contributor, the US government dominated the IMF, particularly in the early years. In addition to the IMF, an International Bank for Reconstruction and Development (the World Bank) was established to help rebuild war damaged economies. The principals of the IMF and the World Bank were governments and not central banks, though many central bankers were seconded to these bodies as representatives of their governments. In other words, central bankers were allowed in through the back door, but did not control the Bretton Woods institutions (Van Dormael 1978; Gardner 1980; Eckes 1975; Cesarano 2006; Bordo and Eichengreen 1993; Helleiner 1994: 25–50).

James (1999a: 323–4) explains that the 'IMF's origins lay in the perception of a failure of central banks in the inter-war period: in the memory of the imposition of intolerably harsh deflation as part of adjustment in a fixed [exchange] rate system'. Central bankers were not trusted to design an exchange rate regime for the post-war world. Yet it was still taken for granted that a system of (more or less) fixed exchange rates was desirable. The most influential contemporary study of exchange rate policy concluded that fluctuating exchange rates had exacerbated global instability in the interwar period (Nurkse 1944). In retrospect we might question whether this was the correct lesson to draw.

Aspects of the Bretton Woods settlement amounted to monetary heresy by the standards of the 1920s. Indeed Bretton Woods was a mixture of Keynes's economics and New Deal populism, the latter embracing suspicion of bankers (of all sorts) and faith in planning. Neither the Keynes Plan nor the White Plan was satisfactory from the more conservative viewpoint of the BIS. Jacobsson believed that inflation and not deflation would be the main macroeconomic threat after the war. In this context, the weakness of the Keynes Plan was that it could be highly inflationary. On the other hand, the White Plan, though apparently less inflationary, excluded from influence the traditional guardians of monetary rectitude, namely central bankers (Jacobsson 1979: 178–85). But the opinions of the BIS hardly mattered by this stage.

Some central bank officials attended Bretton Woods. They did so as members of national delegations and not as independent representatives. Keynes himself was a director of the Bank of England. The Australian delegation was led by Leslie Melville, head of economics at the CBA, who was kept on a tight leash by the government (Cornish 1993). Marriner Eccles served as a member of the US delegation, and the Fed contributed personnel to the conference staff (Meltzer 2003: 617). The Fed did not exert much influence at Bretton Woods. The White Plan was floated by the US Treasury, which was profoundly suspicious of foreign (and perhaps domestic) central bankers. Rather lukewarm support was offered by the Fed. The majority view at the Fed was that it would be best to go along with the Treasury, either because international cooperation was a good idea in principle, or because it would be imprudent to defy Secretary Morgenthau and the government. But strong dissent was expressed by Sproul and his mentor John Williams of the FRBNY. Sproul and Williams regarded the White and Keynes plans as unworkable, since they overlooked the problems of transition from war to peace, and would not subject deficit countries to enough discipline once the transition was complete. Williams (1978), an academic economist as well as vice-president and director of research at the FRBNY, thought that the post-war settlement should be based on bilateral cooperation between the USA and the UK, the managers of the world's key currencies. The FRBNY's misgivings were shared by the New York banking community. Unwilling to be gagged, Williams declined to attend the Bretton Woods conference. Subsequently the FRBNY criticised the conference resolutions in public, arousing the ire of Eccles and the Treasury (Meltzer 2003: 612–27). In the end, the 'Federal Reserve never formally considered the Bretton Woods Agreement and was not asked to do so' (Meltzer 2003: 585). Louis Rasminsky of the Bank of Canada made the most constructive contribution of any central banker at Bretton Woods. Canadian policy was to avoid a breach between the British and the Americans, and Rasminsky assumed the mantle of go-between and mediator (Muirhead 1999: 98–112).

The Bank of England shared some of the FRBNY's doubts about the Bretton Woods proposals, especially the lack of adequate transitional arrangements. The British also deprecated the US Treasury's insistence on a rapid push to current account convertibility (Fforde 1992: 49–62). It would take the British export industries at least five years to recover from the war. Wartime sales of overseas assets had reduced inflows of interest and dividends. Moreover, several Commonwealth countries had built up large sterling credits (sterling balances) by supplying the UK with commodities and services during the war which they would attempt to spend, possibly in North America, afterwards. How could the UK restore current account convertibility in such circumstances? Furthermore, the Bank of England regarded Bretton Woods as an attempt to confirm the US dollar as the world's principal currency, and thus to downgrade sterling. Only one Bank of England official, George Bolton, was present at Bretton Woods. He watched proceedings and Keynes's theatrics with 'amused detachment' (Fforde 1992: 61). Though the British were at least as divided as the Americans over Bretton Woods, they and most other countries endorsed the resulting agreements. But it would take New Zealand, with its paranoia about international bankers, until 1961 to follow them down the Bretton Woods road (Singleton 1998). The Soviet Union also declined to ratify Bretton Woods.

Cheered on by Harry White and the US Treasury, the Norwegian delegation to Bretton Woods proposed that the BIS should be wound up prior to the establishment of a new international monetary regime. They demanded an investigation into the war record of the BIS. Ansel Luxford, the chief legal adviser to the US delegation, argued that IMF membership should be confined to those nations whose central banks denounced the BIS. Only the British and Dutch delegations expressed any sympathy for the BIS. Keynes, as was his wont, found the American position exasperating, and Luxford's intervention was branded as 'idiotic' by the leader of the Dutch delegation (Beyen 1949: 177). After considerable wrangling, both the Norwegians' proposed investigation into the BIS and Luxford's suggestion were dropped. A compromise resolution, calling for the BIS to be liquidated 'at the earliest possible moment', was endorsed. The widespread antipathy towards the BIS had several sources. Besides allegations of collaboration with the Germans, the BIS was dismissed as a relic of gold standard ideology, and feared as a potential rival to the IMF. White and the US Treasury detested the BIS because it appeared to be a European clique. The US government was keen to proceed to liquidation at the end of the war, but the Europeans began to drag their feet. Central banks had not been well represented at Bretton Woods. After the conference, the European central banks, including the Bank of England, began to rally round the BIS, and lobbied their governments on its behalf. Faced with European indecision, the Americans concluded that liquidation was not worth pursuing (Toniolo 2005: 267–82; Schloss 1958: 118–21; Kahler 2002).

From reconstruction to convertibility

President Roosevelt died in April 1945. His successor, Harry Truman, was more sympathetic to Williams's key currency framework, and more prepared to listen to the New York bankers. After the Bretton Woods exchange rate pegs were set in 1945–6, the focus of American policy shifted to achieving the convertibility of sterling as the first step towards multilateral current account convertibility. The US government extended a US$3.75 billion loan to the British, and stipulated that there must be an early date for the resumption of convertibility. July 1947 was selected as the deadline – far too soon in the opinion of Keynes, the Bank of England, and others in the UK. The sterling balances of India, Pakistan, and Egypt were partially blocked in order to reduce pressure on the UK's reserves. Current account convertibility was reintroduced on schedule in July 1947, but the gold and dollar reserves soon fell so low that convertibility was suspended in August 1947, this time until 1958 (Cairncross 1985: 121–64). Having observed the sterling fiasco, other countries decided to maintain extensive restrictions on current account transactions. A major devaluation of European currencies including sterling occurred in 1949. Progress towards the full implementation of the Bretton Woods system had stalled. Exchange rates had been pegged, and the IMF and World Bank had opened for business, but most countries except the USA continued to rely on exchange controls to defend their pegs.

Where did this leave central banks and the BIS? The false start of the Bretton Woods system did not restore central bankers to a dominant position in international financial diplomacy. Unlike in the 1920s (Ahamed 2009), the contours of international monetary policy continued to be shaped at the intergovernmental level. Central bankers were consulted on most issues, and asked to implement decisions made by governments and the IMF, but they did not take the lead. Nevertheless, central bankers continued to visit one another, and corresponded over the major problems of the day. BIS board meetings resumed in late 1946.

Central bankers also went on secondment to the IMF and the World Bank. Large countries could in effect appoint their own executive directors and alternates to the boards of the Bretton Woods institutions. Between 1948 and 1966, the positions of executive director and alternate for Australia at the IMF and World Bank were combined. Each position rotated between the Treasury and the central bank, with the central bank always supplying one of the two appointees (Schedvin 1992: 109). This sort of cooperative arrangement was common. Smaller countries were herded into groups, and invited to elect an executive director, often taking it in turns to fill this position.

Sterling area countries – consisting of the British Commonwealth and Empire minus Canada plus a few hangers on such as Iceland – pooled their gold and dollar reserves. Overseas sterling area countries were expected (and colonies were compelled) to exchange their dollar earnings for sterling at the Bank of England. Sterling thus acquired could be held on deposit at the Bank of England or in the form of Treasury bills or other marketable sterling securities (Reserve Bank of New Zealand 1963: 16). Sterling area countries could in principle draw upon the gold and dollar pool to make payments to the USA, Canada, or other 'hard currency' countries. In practice, however, the access of India, Pakistan, Burma, Ceylon, Iraq, Egypt, and the colonies to the pool was restricted. The only constraints on the white members of the sterling area were moral (Bell, P. W. 1956; Schenk 1992; Schenk 1994; Schenk 2010; Singleton and Robertson 2002). Regardless of the pros and cons of the sterling area, its functioning required close cooperation between central bankers, especially in their capacities as government advisors and overseers of exchange control regulations. The Bank of England, the custodian of the gold and dollar pool, sat like a spider at the centre of this web.

Once the threat of liquidation had receded, the BIS started to rebuild, and to seek new ways of serving its members and exerting influence. Working relationships were established between the BIS and the Bretton Woods institutions. When the World Bank opened a European mission in August 1947, it was housed in the BIS headquarters. In 1948 the BIS helped the World Bank to place a bond issue with Swiss banks and acquired some of these bonds for its own portfolio. BIS representatives started to attend the annual meetings of the IMF and the World Bank in 1948. Relations with the FRBNY remained cordial, and even those with the US Treasury began to thaw (Toniolo 2005: 300–1).

A month before the UK's experiment with convertibility in July 1947, the US Secretary of State, General George Marshall, announced a new aid package for Europe, later known as the Marshall Plan. The goal was to reinforce European recovery and create a stronger bulwark against communism. Aid payments would be conditional on agreement by the recipients to cooperate with their neighbours, and to commence the process of liberalising intra-European trade and payments. The convertibility crisis of July and August gave added impetus to Marshall's proposals. Indeed the UK would become the largest beneficiary of Marshall Aid. A Committee [later Organisation] for European Economic Co-operation (OEEC) was set up by the Europeans in response to the American offer. France, Italy, and the Benelux countries (Belgium, the Netherlands, and Luxembourg) began work on a scheme for the monthly bilateral settlement of trade surpluses and deficits. This smaller group, known as the Committee on Payments Agreements, sought technical assistance from BIS officials after an IMF representative failed to turn up for an important meeting. The BIS helped with the drafting of the Agreement on Multilateral Monetary Cooperation, which was signed in November 1947. Moreover, he BIS was selected as agent for payments under this and two subsequent schemes (Toniolo 2005: 301–8; Jacobsson 1979: 192). Central banks were keen for the BIS to take on this role, believing that it would be in a stronger position than any other agency to resist political interference (Helleiner 1994: 54; Fforde 1992: 177–8, 205–6).

Though limited in scope, the November 1947 arrangement was a step towards more intensive European monetary cooperation. It also provided the BIS with an opportunity to carve out a new niche. The Americans were anxious to intensify European monetary and trade cooperation because of the importance of a strong and united western Europe as a political, economic, and military partner, even if the result was further discrimination against the dollar and US exports (Hogan 1987; Milward 1984). A further round of negotiations between European governments and central banks, the US government, the Fed, the IMF, and the BIS was convened in order to design a less flimsy European payments agreement. By the late 1940s the Americans were more concerned about western European recovery than about the niceties of multilateralism. The IMF agreed to tolerate the proposed European Payments Union (EPU), even though as a regional arrangement it was at odds with the ethos of Bretton Woods. In principle the BIS also favoured a multilateral rather than a regional framework, but it could not afford to quibble when presented with an opportunity to work with the EPU (Toniolo 2005: 333).

When the EPU came into operation in 1950, it received a grant of US$350 million in Marshall Aid funds for use as intra-European credit (Eichengreen 1993: 26). In short, the EPU resembled a regional IMF, incorporating nearly all western European countries, including the UK, and, indirectly, the overseas sterling area and its French and Dutch counterparts. Members in temporary deficit with the rest of the EPU could obtain credit up to predetermined limits. Final settlement was made in dollars and gold. Exchange controls on current account transactions within the EPU were to be liberalised by stages as part of this scheme (Kaplan and Schleiminger 1989). In the event, the EPU proved remarkably successful.

The Belgians suggested that the EPU might be run by a committee of European central bankers, but this idea did not appeal to the central bankers themselves, for they had no desire to establish a rival to the BIS. Instead an intergovernmental EPU Management Board was formed, with the BIS acting as the fiscal agent, 'keeping the books and funds' (Schloss 1958: 124). When central bankers gathered in Basel for the monthly BIS meetings, those representing EPU member states were able to discuss the affairs of the union and seek advice from BIS staff. The actual contribution of the BIS to the EPU went somewhat beyond keeping the books. During the West German payments crisis of 1950–1, when there was a risk of the Germans exhausting their borrowing rights, the EPU Managing Board invited Per Jacobsson of the BIS and Alec Cairncross of the OEEC to visit Germany to report on the economic situation. Partly as a result of their policy recommendations, West Germany and the EPU surmounted their difficulties (Dickhaus 1998: 168).

Several BIS personnel were assigned to EPU duties. They received information from member central banks and, assisted by mechanical calculating machines (not computers), calculated the monthly net position of each central bank, 'the amounts of gold or dollars it would pay or receive, and the size of the automatic credit it would obtain or grant' (Kaplan and Schleiminger 1989: 339). When the EPU needed to make payments to central banks, the BIS withdrew funds from a US Treasury account. When central banks made payments to the EPU, the BIS either invested the funds received in US Treasury bills or bonds, or kept them in an account in Basel. Gold held in BIS accounts in several international centres was earmarked for the EPU. Central banks were offered gold accounts at the BIS to facilitate settlement. At this time, gold and US dollars were interchangeable.

The EPU was wound up in 1958, when European currencies finally attained current account convertibility with the US dollar. Several factors contributed to this achievement, including the improved performance of European vis-à-vis US industry, and the high levels of investment and aid flows from the USA to Europe and the rest of the world. While the contribution of the EPU should not be exaggerated, it certainly bolstered European unity and self-belief, and acted as a stage towards convertibility (Eichengreen 1993). Through its involvement with the EPU, the BIS demonstrated that it could make a valuable contribution to the management of the international monetary system, a point that was eventually conceded by its oldest critic, the US government. The US authorities also sought the cooperation of the BIS when making a loan to the European Coal and Steel Commission, the forerunner of the EEC, in 1954. An FRBNY observer attended BIS meetings when the agenda was of interest (Toniolo 2005: 318–20).

When Jacobsson was invited to move from the BIS to become managing director of the IMF, in December 1956, the atmosphere was very different from that in 1944 when the BIS had been an outcast. By the mid 1950s the major economic powers were collaborating in small groups, as predicted by John Williams, and using the services of both the IMF and the BIS to deal with international monetary problems. In some respects the BIS could provide a more convenient service, being less cumbersome and bureaucratic than the IMF (Helleiner 1994: 96). Central bankers were at last making a comeback. Jacobsson discussed the IMF offer with his colleagues at the BIS, and all but one advised him to decline. Sir Otto Niemeyer, who had been on the BIS board since 1932, warned him that the IMF had no future and that he would be wasting his time there (Jacobsson 1979: 283–4). Niemeyer's advice was not very good, and Jacobsson took the new job, but the fact that anyone could think that the BIS had better prospects than the IMF was indicative of how much the world had changed in a short time.

Bretton Woods in action

Current account convertibility proved not to be the 'promised land'. Old problems mutated in the 1960s, and new ones materialised. Central bankers, government officials, and politicians became embroiled in an ever more frantic attempt to save the Bretton Woods system. According to Cooper (2008: 88) the 1960s saw 'the real birth of multilateral central bank cooperation envisioned but stillborn in 1930'. But central bankers and governments failed again, and between December 1971 and mid 1973 the world drifted from pegged to floating exchange rates. Fortunately, the crises of the 1960s and 1970s were not as bad as the crises of the 1920s and 1930s, and the spirit of central bank cooperation did not depart. An engaging account of transatlantic financial diplomacy, which gives more credit to central bankers than to Treasury officials or politicians, is provided by Charlie Coombs (1976), senior vice-president of the FRBNY between 1961 and 1975. Robert Solomon (1982), also a Fed official, offers an alternative narrative of the fall of the Bretton Woods exchange rate regime. Space is not available below to give a detailed narrative of events.

As world economic activity expanded, the need for additional international reserves became obvious. At the same time, confidence was dwindling in the traditional reserve currencies of sterling and the US dollar. The volume of US dollar and sterling reserves was increasing relative to the ultimate reserve – the gold hoard of the US government. If the reserve ratio of any bank falls too far, deposit holders may panic. The same principle applies in international monetary affairs. US balance of payments deficits in the 1960s compelled the central banks of other members of the Bretton Woods system to accumulate US dollar reserves. Not only did governments and central banks grow uncomfortable with large US dollar holdings, but their acquisition involved pumping more money into their economies, thereby fuelling inflationary pressure. Action by central banks to sterilise monetary inflows by selling bonds pushed interest rates up further, drawing in yet more US dollars. The imposition of restrictions on capital outflows by the US government (which had previously avoided such controls) failed to stem the tide. Spending on the Vietnam War intensified the US balance of payments problem in the second half of the 1960s. Meanwhile, the US government found it difficult to acquire more gold reserves because the official price of US$35 per ounce was unattractive to suppliers. Increasing the gold price – in effect devaluing the dollar – would have been humiliating for the Americans and alarming for foreign dollar holders. Furthermore, a higher gold price would have given windfalls to politically unpopular gold producers including South Africa and the Soviet Union (Eichengreen 1996: 113–35; Aldcroft and Oliver 2001: 102–20; James 1996: 148–259; Gavin 2004).

From December 1960 onwards, Charlie Coombs of the FRBNY began to attend BIS Board meetings regularly, though the FRBNY still did not become a full member (Toniolo 2005: 364–5). The USA only took its seat at the BIS in 1994. Bank of Canada and Bank of Japan observers also went to Board meetings in the 1960s. The presence of a senior US central banker in Basel was a sign of the straits in which the Americans found themselves as the dollar weakened. As Gavin (2004: 88) points out, the 1960s was a decade of US financial vulnerability and not one of hegemony. European support was needed to save the dollar, and the best place to meet European central bankers was in Basel. The US Treasury began intervening in the foreign exchange markets in March 1961, for the first time since the Second World War. In February 1962, the Fed was authorised to engage in foreign exchange operations on its own account (Bordo, Humpage, and Schwartz 2007: 125). The cooperation of other central banks was welcomed and sought. In March 1961, for example, the FRBNY accepted an offer from Guido Carli of the Bank of Italy to sell it US$100 million worth of Italy's gold reserves (Toniolo 2005: 369). US acceptance of Italian help provided further evidence of how far the international economy had changed since the era of the Marshall Plan.

Various ruses were employed to defend sterling and the US dollar, but they could not remove the underlying imbalances. Central banks began to intervene in the gold market in November 1960 in order to prevent the market price from rising substantially above US$35 per ounce. Such intervention was deemed necessary to maintain confidence in the US dollar. The so-called 'gold pool', which comprised the

US, British, French, West German, Belgian, Italian, Dutch, and Swiss central banks, was formalised in 1961. It operated in the London gold market until 1968, losing gold in some phases and buying it back in others (James 1996: 159–60; Eichengreen 2007: 35–71).

Another method of protecting weak currencies was the system of central bank swaps, devised by an official of the Banque de France (Cooper 2008: 90–1). Swaps involved simultaneous spot and forward transactions. For example, the Fed would obtain the use of francs for three months, while the Banque de France obtained the use of an equivalent value of US dollars for the same period. Swaps were often renewed but most were repaid in less than a year. The swap network expanded rapidly. By the end of 1962, the Federal Reserve had a swap network totalling US$900 million with nine central banks and the BIS (Bordo, Humpage, and Schwartz 2007: 127). Charlie Coombs was in charge of swap operations at the FRBNY.

Central banks also provided each other with short-term loans and credits. For example, the Bank of England obtained 'Basel credits' worth US$910 million from a group of eight European central banks in 1961. Further central bank credits were required by the Bank of England between 1964 and 1968, but they could not prevent sterling from undergoing a 14.3 per cent devaluation against the US dollar in 1967. The French franc required similar support from other central banks and the BIS in 1968–9 (James 1996: 161–5, 183–97). As in previous periods, the intensity of cooperation and the level of goodwill between central banks fluctuated.

As part of their defensive operations, central banks and the BIS monitored and attempted to guide the development of the euromarkets, through which offshore currencies, especially the US dollar, were lent and borrowed. The growth of the euromarkets was symptomatic of the resurgence of international capital flows in the 1960s (Cassis 2006: 219–23; Battilossi 2000). Some central banks and the BIS were concerned about the macroeconomic effects of the euromarkets, their impact on the exchange rate system, and their implications for banking stability. The desire to control the euromarkets was tempered, however, by the determination of several central banks, including the Bank of England, to promote the development of financial centres in their countries. A number of central banks also placed their own funds in the euromarkets, a practice discouraged by the BIS in the early 1970s (Toniolo 2005: 452–71).

The governments of the main capitalist countries were reluctant to place too much reliance on the IMF, and often collaborated bilaterally or through relatively small groupings such as the BIS. Nevertheless, the

IMF contributed in several material ways to the campaign to uphold the Bretton Woods system. Under the General Agreement to Borrow (GAB) in 1961, the IMF supplemented its resources by borrowing from ten wealthy governments, known as the G-10. The G-10 became a third arena for cooperative endeavour alongside the IMF and the BIS. Central bank governors from the G-10 countries participated in G-10 meetings. After exhaustive negotiations about the reform of the international monetary system, a new type of international reserve asset, the Special Drawing Right (SDR), was created by the IMF, the first slice being disbursed in 1970 (Eichengreen 1996: 118–20; Solomon, R. 1982: 128–50).

G-10 central bank governors (or their representatives) and the members of the gold pool (essentially the same people) came together at the monthly BIS meetings (Baer 1999: 351). Though still in some respects rivals, the BIS and the IMF kept in close touch, and shared a common commitment to the fixed exchange rate system. As managing director of the IMF, Jacobsson visited Basel on a number of occasions (Jacobsson 1979: 293, 335, 338, 365, 390). BIS officials and prominent central bankers also made regular visits to the IMF in Washington. Indeed there was a central banking circuit with stops in Washington, New York, Basel, London, Paris, and Frankfurt, the home of the Bundesbank. IMF initiatives such as the SDR scheme were discussed at length by the BIS. The Bundesbank and the Bank of Japan became much more prominent in the central banking world in the 1960s. Not only did these central banks represent the two most dynamic large economies, but they were the ones most inconvenienced by major inflows of US dollars. Membership of the BIS was widened to include a few central banks from outside Europe, including the Bank of Canada, the Bank of Japan, and the RBA in 1970, and the SARB in 1971 (Toniolo 2005: 361). But there was no place for central banks from developing countries such as India. Basel was a rich man's club and a far more intimate one than the IMF (Toniolo 2005: 363–9; Simmons 2008: 175). The central banking world was becoming an epistemic community with a shared intellectual vision and values, as well as a common policy prescription involving the control of excess demand and the more effective management of budgets. Loyalty to this community could sometimes transcend national positions (Helleiner 1994).

All efforts to preserve the fixed exchange system came to nought in the early 1970s. As the Bank of Italy noted it in its annual report for 1968, the 'proper functioning of the international monetary system requires that the United States' and the United Kingdom's balances of payments be restored to equilibrium' (Carli 1993: 267). But stating the problem was not the same as finding a solution. US dollar weakness in the second half of the 1960s was exacerbated by the policies of General De Gaulle, the French president, who decided to cash in his dollars for gold, by the failure of desperate attempts to defend sterling's parity in 1967, and by the military adventure in Vietnam. The gold pool was terminated in 1968, when the US government decided that it would henceforth sell gold only to other central banks. Other countries became increasingly worried about the inflationary consequences of accumulating US dollars. Canada floated its currency again in 1970 (the Canadian dollar had also floated between 1950 and 1962). Against the advice of the Bundesbank, which would have preferred the restriction of inward capital flows, the West German government floated the DM in May 1971 (von Hagen 1999: 411–12). The Netherlands followed suit.

President Richard Nixon unilaterally 'suspended' the convertibility of US dollars held by foreign central banks in August 1971. Notwithstanding the efforts of some foreign central banks to support the US dollar, some countries had been drawing large amounts of gold from the USA, and Nixon was not prepared to allow this to continue. Arthur Burns, who had succeeded Bill Martin as Chairman of the Federal Reserve Board, warned that closure of the 'gold window' would put the survival of capitalism in the balance, but Nixon and John Connally, the secretary of the Treasury, laughed this off, and expressed indifference to the reaction of other countries. It was obvious that the system was now rudderless. Within two weeks the Bank of Japan had ceased to intervene to hold down the yen (James 1996: 216–21). Under the Smithsonian Agreement of December 1971 new parities were set for other currencies against a devalued and still inconvertible US dollar. As the Smithsonian Agreement began to disintegrate in March 1973, Otmar Emminger, the vice-president of the Bundesbank, claimed to hear 'the death knell for the Bretton Woods parity system' (quoted in James 1996: 242), though this was hardly as bad as the end of capitalism. A new era of fluctuating exchange rates was beginning.

By the end of the 1960s, central bankers had become very frustrated. Though most clung to the shibboleth of fixed exchange rates, they were increasingly prepared to consider modifications, including wider bands around the Bretton Woods parities, crawling pegs, involving regular small adjustments to parities, and temporary floats (Toniolo 2005: 430–3). More ambitiously, some of the Europeans, including Carli, imagined an EEC monetary area, with fixed exchange rates between member currencies, and a collective float against the US dollar (Carli 1993: 373). After retiring from the Fed in 1970, Bill Martin proposed the establishment of a world central bank, probably based on the IMF (Bremner 2004: 280–3, 290; Martin 1970). There was no easy answer to the strains that had built up in the international monetary system. Until governments, and in particular the US government, brought spending under control, it would be difficult to sustain any system of fixed exchange rates without recurring crises.

Many years earlier Milton Friedman (1953) had argued that it was futile to peg exchange rates. He believed that the price of a currency should be determined by supply and demand, in the same way as the prices of other assets. This thesis had no appeal to central bankers, and most ignored it. The commitment of central bankers to fixed exchange rates was a hangover from the gold standard, according to Friedman (Cesarano 2006: 185–6), and he feared that they were still fixated on gold. This was not solely the view of the monetarist right. In the Kennedy administration, Under-Secretary of State George Ball described the attitudes of the European central bankers as 'pre-Herbert Hoover' or stuck in the 1920s (quoted in Gavin 2004: 78).

Pegged exchange rates appealed to central bankers because they implied a constraint on domestic fiscal and monetary expansion. However, when other policy goals, including domestic economic objectives and war, were deemed more important, governments were prepared to take risks with the exchange rate. Elected representatives had the right to take such risks, and there were few advocates of a return to a world in which domestic economic policy was permanently subordinated to the exchange rate. Central bankers had no option but to accept this state of affairs, and to hope for a passable compromise. Once the fixed exchange rate system had been shattered in 1971–3, governments and central banks were compelled to wrestle with the new problem of containing inflation in the absence of an external 'nominal anchor'. Friedman believed that he had the solution to this problem as well, but most central bankers were less sure.

Conclusion

A key principle of the Bretton Woods conference in 1944 was that the design and oversight of the international monetary system was an intergovernmental affair. Central bankers were components of the national economic policy community, and they were expected to participate in the Bretton Woods institutions on that basis. The architects of Bretton Woods ruled out the recreation of an international cabal of central bankers, which they believed, not entirely fairly, had wreaked havoc in the 1920s. The BIS was attacked as a relic of the gold standard and as an Axis collaborator. After the war, the international monetary system failed to develop as the supporters of Bretton Woods had intended. Global financial recovery and stability could not be procured by the Bretton Woods institutions alone. The US began to support bilateral and regional recovery initiatives in Europe. In their desire to promote a strong western Europe as a counterweight to the Soviet bloc and market for US products, the American authorities condoned the lowering of tariffs and exchange controls on a regional basis. The BIS latched onto the resulting European Payments Union, forging a new role, and establishing political credit in Washington.

Despite the resumption of current account convertibility in 1958, the Bretton Woods system continued to misfire, primarily because of the progressive weakening of the US dollar in the 1960s, which in turn reflected the comparative decline of the US economy and heavy US external commitments. True US financial hegemony was a phenomenon of the 1940s and 1950s. In order to preserve fixed exchange rates after 1960, the US and other governments were prepared to use whatever tools came to hand. As well as replenishing the resources of the IMF through the General Agreement to Borrow, they turned to central bankers for help. An extensive network of central bank swaps and credits developed in the 1960s. The BIS participated in some of these operations. It also offered a meeting place in which the world's leading central bankers could discuss international monetary problems without politicians looking over their shoulders. Though it proved impossible to save the Bretton Woods exchange rate regime, central bankers and the BIS demonstrated that they had a special area of expertise, and could be useful to governments – much more useful than had been envisaged in 1944.

10 The goose that lays the golden egg: central banking in developing countries

The role of the central banker is necessarily greatly influenced by the system of government, by the stage of economic development, and by the organisation of financial markets.

Louis Rasminsky, Governor of the Bank of Canada, 1966
(Rasminsky 1987: 57)

The central banks of South and East Asia are ... an expression of monetary independence by new states anxious to solve the immense problem of poverty in these regions.

S. Gethyn Davies (1960: vii)

The Khmer Rouge celebrated the revolution in 1975 by blowing up the Cambodian central bank (Clark 2006: 15), but the Khmer Rouge were exceptional. A national airline, a steel industry, and a central bank – preferably state-owned – were regarded as strategic assets by most developing economies after 1945. Central banks had opened in a few developing countries, including India, Argentina, and Colombia, before 1939. The 1940s witnessed central banking reforms in several developing countries, including Paraguay, as well as the creation of some new institutions (De Kock, M. H. 1974: 10–12). The age of decolonisation, between 1945 and 1970, was also an era of central bank proliferation. Most were built from scratch, but in some cases, including Indonesia and Taiwan, they were adapted from existing institutions. As Richard Sayers (1957: 110) remarked, in a speech at the National Bank of Egypt in 1956, the Brussels Conference in 1920 had called for the establishment of central banks everywhere.

The central bank often dominates the financial system in low-income nations, commanding assets that may rival those of the entire commercial banking system. As the economy develops, however, the relative weight of the central bank usually falls (Levine 1997: 715–17). This chapter charts the spread of central banks in the developing world, discusses their status and objectives, and assesses their effectiveness. The primary focus is on the period up to the 1980s, leaving discussion of late twentieth-century developments, including aspects of financial liberalisation, rising central bank independence, and inflation targeting, until later chapters.

Louis Rasminsky, quoted above, perceived that central banks reflect the societies in which they operate. It would be unrealistic to expect a central bank in Africa or Latin America in the 1960s to have behaved like the Bundesbank. Nevertheless, central bankers in developing countries were not passive. They were better educated, as well as more 'conservative' in their economic thinking, than their political masters, and at least they tried to restrain the excesses of governments.

The glass was half full to some observers, half empty to others. Speaking at the tenth anniversary of the Bank of Jamaica in 1970, Andrew Brimmer (1971: 781), a member of the Board of Governors of the Fed, expressed satisfaction that, in addition to taking 'innovative steps … to help foster economic development', many new central banks had 'performed most of the traditional central banking functions [with respect to macroeconomic and financial stability] … with considerable skill'. Writing much later, however, Fry, Goodhart, and Almeida (1996: 112) lamented that in 1970, 'the central bank in a typical developing country was subservient to its government and used, in the main, to fill a large gap between government expenditure and conventional tax revenue'.

What central banks said they were doing and what they actually did were not necessarily the same. According to Rasminsky (1987: 57), central bankers in developing nations were responsible for 'improving the structure of financial institutions so that the maximum amount of domestic savings may be mobilised for economically constructive purposes and the pressures for inflationary financing of development thereby reduced'. Fry, Goodhart, and Almeida (1996: 112) concluded that in practice many central banks were agents of financial repression through which 'Governments pre-empted the supply of domestic saving by preserving a sheltered market for their own bills and bonds'.

The developing world was far from homogeneous: some governments were better than others, and some central banks were more successful than others. There was much more diversity in the third world – which embraced 'developmental states' such as South Korea and Taiwan, communist regimes such as the People's Republic of China, and incompetent dictatorships such as Indonesia in the first half of the 1960s – than there was in the first world.

American enthusiasm, British caution

The Americans and the British were frequently at odds over the spread of central banking through the developing world in the 1940s and 1950s

(Helleiner 2003b). The US authorities were optimistic about the future of emerging nations, and eager to support pro-capitalist nationalist movements, but their British counterparts still saw the developing world through imperial spectacles. Whereas the Americans were enthusiastic about new central banks, the British were sceptical, dragging their feet.

When asked to advise the Paraguayan government on monetary reform in 1941, a team of Fed officials, including Robert Triffin (who would later achieve eminence as an economist), concluded that the deflationary prescriptions of the interwar money doctors were no longer valid. They argued that the central bank should give priority to domestic economic stability and the promotion of economic development. In short, monetary policy should insulate economic activity from external shocks and not amplify those shocks. Triffin and his colleagues saw it as inevitable that central banks in developing nations would be asked to lend to their governments. Indeed they believed that central banks could make an important contribution by funding development programmes. Not only did such advice reflect the New Deal–Keynesian philosophy of the day, but it appealed strongly to existing and potential US clients. US influence on central bank design was particularly strong in Latin America and in parts of Asia, including the Philippines, and, to British chagrin, Ceylon (Helleiner 2003b).

The Central Bank of the Philippines was established in 1949 following a report by the Joint Philippine–American Finance Commission. It was given 'extensive powers to manage the currency and credit system and to promote the expansion of the national economy ... [and] empowered to grant extraordinary advances to the government ... to finance productive and income-producing projects' (Castillo 1948: 361). Central bank advocates, such as Andres Castillo, dismissed claims that the Philippines were not ready for a central bank and that competent staff were not available. Filipino central bankers might be inexperienced, but they could 'lean heavily on the experience of central banks elsewhere'. Moreover, the central bank charter spelled out essential procedures in 'great detail'. Running a central bank was evidently a matter of routine. 'Under normal conditions, even an inexperienced management, if it obeys the provisions of the law, will not be able to endanger the stability of the Bank' (Castillo 1948: 362). This was a truly remarkable and wholly unrealistic position.

From the perspective of the Bank of England and the British government, the prospect of central banks in states approaching independence was troubling. Was a central bank really necessary in the Gold Coast, Malaya, or Nigeria (Schenk 1997)? Colonial monetary arrangements were in the hands of currency boards, which ensured a one-to-one relationship between sterling reserves and internal currency creation (Schwartz 1993; Krozewski 2001). If currency boards were replaced by central banks under local control, the door would be open to inflation, balance of payments instability, and financial crisis, all of which would damage British business interests, and intensify demands on the sterling area's dollar pool. At first the British tried to stop the formation of central banks in colonies nearing independence. When this stance became untenable, they endeavoured to make sure that the central banks were modelled and staffed along conservative lines. J. B. Loynes, the Bank of England official who advised the Gold Coast on the development of banking institutions, acknowledged that 'my aim has been to give the people here something which looks fairly imposing but which, if applied, should not be too dangerous' (quoted in Stockwell, S. E. 1998: 110).

The UK could not thwart the central banking aspirations of Ceylon, which became independent in 1948 after 150 years of British control. The new government in Colombo did not trust the Bank of England to provide impartial counsel on the replacement of the currency board with a central bank. John Exter, a Federal Reserve economist, who had previously advised the Philippines on central banking, was invited to Ceylon for this purpose. Exter impressed his hosts so much that he was appointed the first governor of the Central Bank of Ceylon in 1950. The central bank was given extensive powers to manage monetary conditions with the purpose of stabilising the domestic economy. Ceylon's decision to seek US advice was a slap in the face for the British with their narrower conception of appropriate monetary arrangements (Karunatilake 1973; Gunasakera 1962: 259–90).

Matters were different in territories still under British control. The Bank of England was obstructive in Nigeria, dismissing proposals for a central bank in 1952. Finding an ally in the World Bank, however, the Nigerians continued to press their colonial masters. The UK gave way eventually, and the Central Bank of Nigeria was created in 1958, two years before independence. The Bank of England took a close interest in the design of this central bank. Statutory limits were imposed on money creation, though these were abolished in the 1960s (Uche 1997). It also took a favourable World Bank report on the prospects for a central bank to stir the British into action in Malaya. When sovereignty was transferred to the pro-business Malayan elite in 1957, work was already underway to draft a central bank constitution. In return for continued military support, the Malaysians undertook to remain in the sterling area and pursue conservative financial and monetary policies. The Bank Negara Malaysia opened for business in 1959, and for several years thereafter proved a cooperative partner of the Bank of England (Schenk 1993).

It would take too long to discuss the founding of every new central bank, but it is important to say something about China and Brazil, two of the largest developing countries. The Central Bank of China (CBC) had been powerless to avert hyperinflation during the revolutionary period. When the Communists achieved power in 1949, the CBC fled to Taiwan with Chiang Kai-Shek, remaining dormant until 1961. The Communists had set up a monobank, the People's Bank of China (PBC), on the mainland in 1948. All private sector banks were absorbed into the PBC after the revolution. The PBC was an arm of the communist state, and its primary duty was to fund government programmes under the system of five-year plans. During the two main periods of radicalisation – the Great Leap Forward (in fact a great leap backwards) of 1958–60, and the Cultural Revolution of 1966–76 – the PBC faced increased political interference at the national level, and lost control over personnel and credit decisions at the provincial level. Chinese economic policy, including anti-inflationary policy, descended into chaos during these episodes (Wei 1992: 41–50).

Brazil lacked a central bank until March 1965. The central banking question was almost as controversial in Brazil after 1945 as it had been in the USA before 1914. Plans for a Brazilian central bank had been mooted at the time of the First World War. Otto Niemeyer, the Bank of England's roving money doctor, proposed a central bank in 1931. A commercial bank, the Banco do Brasil, performed some of the functions of a development bank and central bank in the mid twentieth century, often in conjunction with government agencies, most notably the Superintendency of Money and Credit (SUMOC), formed in 1945. According to Marichal and Diaz Funtes (1999: 296–301), the Banco do Brasil pretended to implement policies handed down by SUMOC, whilst actually feathering its own nest. SUMOC was bullied by both the Banco do Brasil, with which it shared accommodation, and the Ministry of Finance. Monetary control was sacrificed in order to accommodate large budget deficits. Political divisions and the desire of the Banco do Brasil to retain pre-eminence set back the decision to create a central bank. SUMOC was at length split into the Central Bank of Brazil and the National Monetary Council in 1965. The purpose of the National Monetary Council was to absorb political pressure on monetary policy makers. It proved ineffective in this role, and Brazil continued to suffer chronic inflation (Maxfield 1997: 121–33; Goodhart, Capie, and Schnadt 1994: Appendix B, 226–9).

Several multinational central banks were set up amongst groups of very small and very poor nations. In 1962 certain former French colonies in Africa established monetary unions with the assistance of the French authorities. The West African Monetary Union (WAMU) was managed by the multinational Banque Centrale des États de l'Afrique de l'Ouest (BCEAO), and the Central African Monetary Area (CAMA) was managed by the multinational Banque des États de l'Afrique Centrale (BEAC). WAMU and CAMA used modified versions of the old colonial currency, the CFA franc (le franc des Colonies Françaises d'Afrique), which was pegged to the French franc. Together WAMU and CAMA constituted the CFA franc zone. The CFA franc zone central banks were based in Paris, along with their external reserves. In 1972–3, however, BCEAO moved to Dakar, and CEAC shifted to Yaoundé (Sacerdoti 1991; Fielding 2002). In the former British West Indies, the Eastern Caribbean Central Bank was established in 1983 by Antigua and Barbuda, Dominica, Grenada, Montserrat, St. Kitts and Nevis, St. Lucia and St. Vincent and the Grenadines. The larger former colonies in this region, including Jamaica and Trinidad, did not join this group and kept their own central banks (Nicholls 2001).

Delegates to the 1920 Brussels Conference would have welcomed the spread of central banking through large swathes of Africa, Asia, and Latin America. But they would have been aghast at the involvement of central banks in aspects of development planning and financing, and horrified at their subordination to unstable governments.

Relations with the state

A large colour photograph of President Ferdinand Marcos appears at the front of the volume commemorating the twenty-fifth anniversary of the Central Bank of the Philippines. The notoriously corrupt dictator resembles a jovial but aging Elvis Presley. In a congratulatory message, Marcos hopes that the anniversary volume will teach Filipinos about central banking, and 'inspire the Central Bank to scale greater heights of achievements worthy of its position, power and personality as the nation's premier financing [sic] institution' (quoted in Central Bank of the Philippines 1974). In practice, the central bank could do little to resist Marcos, whose policies stoked inflation. Though the central bank pledged unswerving loyalty to the dictator, the true feelings of senior staff may be discerned by reading between the lines of the main text: 'A review of the first quarter-century of the Central Bank's monetary policy indicates that, by and large, monetary policy was used as a foil to fiscal policy, and sometimes as a substitute for it. The growth of money supply was largely of internal origin' (Central Bank of the Philippines 1974: 44).

Central banks in third-world (and communist) countries were usually less independent – or less capable of resisting political pressure – than their counterparts in the developed world (Cukierman and Webb 1995). Anyone who imagined that central banks in post-colonial Africa could be independent was suffering from 'naivety' (Killick and Mwega 1993: 75). Short of revolution, political checks and balances barely existed in many developing countries. The niceties of central bank legislation and governance were overridden whenever ministers wished to confer favours on their banking cronies or needed monetary accommodation to meet the budget deficit. Central bankers were highly accountable – they risked dismissal (or worse) for failure to do the bidding of powerful politicians.

Formal indices of central bank independence (CBI) understate the degree of subordination of developing country central banks, not least because they attach too much weight to legislative window dressing. CBI indices can produce some odd rankings. According to one study, in the 1980s the central bank in Zaire (now the Democratic Republic of the Congo) was more independent than the central bank in Belgium (Cukierman 1992: 390). Moreover, some of the information embodied in CBI indexes is ambiguous. The average time spent in office of the governor is usually taken to be a good indicator of CBI, but longevity could reflect timidity and compliance in some instances (Maxfield 1994: 560).

According to Mas (1995), CBI is unlikely to emerge before the establishment of a sophisticated financial framework and modern political institutions. On the basis of Asian and Latin American experience, Maxfield (1997) concludes that governments stress CBI when they need to impress foreign lenders, but often revert to manipulation at other times. CBI might not be feasible in countries where it is difficult to raise revenue from direct taxes or to borrow from the public. Between 1979 and 1993, OECD governments borrowed 3 per cent of their net credit needs from their central banks, whereas governments in developing countries borrowed 45 per cent of their net credit needs from their central banks. The central bank is the goose that lays the golden egg for the government (Fry, Goodhart, and Almeida 1996: 28, 38). There are in fact several types of golden geese. The relatively autonomous free-range goose can bring in seigniorage revenue of up to 1 per cent of GDP. By imposing an inflation tax on citizens, the battery farm goose can generate seigniorage worth between 5 and 10 per cent of GDP for an extended period. Finally the force-fed goose can engineer an inflation tax that yields up to 25 per cent of GDP for the government until the inevitable collapse.

Bank Indonesia is one of many central banks that have at times been compelled to serve the interests of political cliques. The Java Bank, the bank of issue of the Netherlands East Indies, was nationalised in 1953, and renamed Bank Indonesia. Any continuity with Java Bank was transitory. Towards the end of the 1950s, Indonesia descended into economic chaos because of the policies of President Sukarno. There was a rapid changeover of personnel at the central bank, especially at senior levels, and a loss of competence. Senior appointments were made on the basis of patronage, and the real incomes of staff were allowed to decline. Hamilton-Hart (2002: 43) remarks that, 'Like other state organizations ... the central bank was eventually overwhelmed by the politics of the time ... How much the bank was functioning at all between 1960 and 1965 is doubtful'.

Following the downfall of Sukarno and the advent of Suharto's 'New Order' in 1966, Bank Indonesia was permitted to rebuild. The central bank became more technocratic and meritocractic than other Indonesian agencies. Economists trained overseas were recruited to the staff. Even so, Bank Indonesia was embroiled in the financial shenanigans of the Suharto regime, supplying funds to state banks responsible for lubricating government patronage and crony networks. Bank Indonesia did little to supervise such banks, and its officials were complicit in actions deemed corrupt elsewhere. Such behaviour was in part a consequence of the low salaries paid to central bankers compared with executives in the private sector. In short, Bank Indonesia 'combined a formal commitment to technocratic expertise with internal systems that were responsive to informal, sometimes even unspoken, patterns of influence' (Hamilton-Hart 2002: 65).

The boundaries between government, central bank, and other financial institutions were even more permeable than in developed nations. Government–central bank relations reflected a variety of idiosyncratic circumstances, as Zhang (2005) shows in a comparison between Thailand and Taiwan. Painful memories of hyperinflation enabled the CBC to assert some autonomy after its reformation in 1961. The autonomy of the Bank of Thailand was largely respected by authoritarian and technocratic governments between the 1950s and 1970s, but the shift towards populist democracy brought increased political interference in the 1980s. However, the Thai central bank was not spineless, and its leaders stood up to the government on some issues. In the mid 1980s the Bank of Thailand squabbled with the government over the budgetary implications of defence spending, the bail-out of financial institutions, and the conduct of banking supervision. This conflict led to the removal of Nukul Prachuabmoh from the governorship in 1984, and the appointment of Kamchorn Sathirakul, a close associate of the finance minister (Maxfield 1997: 84–5).

Sadly, the ultimate sanction for an errant central banker is death. After resigning as governor of the Bank of Uganda, Joseph Mubiru wrote a letter to the press that upset Idi Amin, the new president (and self-proclaimed king of Scotland), who threatened to have Mubiru tortured. The ex-Governor is thought to have been murdered at Makindye Police barracks in October 1972 (Glentworth and Hancock 1973: 251; Anon. 1975).

British opposition to the establishment of central banks in developing countries, though essentially self-serving, also appears to have been based on a realistic assessment of political conditions in parts of the developing world. Be that as it may, central banks became key sources of economic expertise in countries where such expertise was at a premium. Moreover, they did at least make an effort to foster economic development and restrain inflation.

Central banks and development

In an article published in 1957, Arthur Bloomfield of the FRBNY admitted that the most pressing economic challenge for governments in the developing world was the generation of economic growth rather than the achievement of price or exchange rate stability. Bloomfield (1957: 195) nevertheless went on to say that central banks could contribute most effectively to the development process by maintaining financial stability and control. Of course, he understood that this would not exhaust the ambitions of their political masters.

Independence leaders were very optimistic. As Kwame Nkrumah stated in 1949: 'If we get self-government we'll transform the Gold Coast into a paradise in ten years' (quoted in Aldcroft 2007: 312). Central banks tried to promote economic development in several ways. First, they encouraged the development of financial markets and institutions. Second, they sought to manage and channel financial flows and the balance of payments in accordance with the wider developmental goals of government.

Central bank involvement in the promotion of economic development was not a novelty after 1945. Several European central banks had operated extensive branch networks in the nineteenth century in an effort to stimulate financial development. They had also extended credit to industrial firms (Epstein 2005). As discussed above (Chapter 8), the central banks of some advanced countries, including the UK and Australia, were active, albeit to a limited extent, in a developmental role after the Second World War.

The cultivation of a modern banking and financial sector is a 'critical and inextricable part of the growth process' (Levine 1997: 689). Information and transaction costs will fall, savings and investment will rise, and innovation will flourish within a sophisticated financial system. Banking and other financial services are underprovided in developing countries because the risks of provision are perceived to be too high relative to the returns. Sayers (1957: 118) felt that central banks should promote the emergence of private financial institutions, and, if necessary, 'fill the gaps'. Bhatt (1974: 64), a World Bank economist, considered that the central bank 'should not be merely a lender of last resort: it has to be a lender of early resort' in order to facilitate the growth of the banking system.

Central bankers sometimes assumed a direct role in the establishment of new commercial banks and the nationalisation of existing ones. Following independence in 1947, the State Bank of Pakistan – the nascent central bank – convinced the government of the need for a large commercial bank that could perform the business functions formerly conducted by the Imperial Bank of India. The state-owned National Bank of Pakistan was founded for this purpose in 1949. Zaid Husain, the central bank governor, became president of the National Bank, cementing the close links between the two institutions (Husain 1992: 130–3). In 1955, the Indian part of the Imperial Bank was in essence nationalised as the State Bank of India. The RBI, which itself had been nationalised in 1949, became the dominant shareholder in the State Bank (Balachandran 1998: 318–54). State ownership of commercial banks was common in developing countries, as well as in more advanced economies (La Porta, Shleifer, and Lopez-de-Silanes 2002). Several – often many – of the domestic counterparties of new central banks were in the public sector.

Central banks also facilitated the emergence and expansion of commercial banks through the provision of payment and settlement services, including clearing house facilities. The central bank offered a safe depository for bank reserves as well as a source of routine and emergency liquidity. The Bank of Thailand, for example, advanced loans to commercial banks that could offer collateral in the form of government bonds, and rediscounted promissory notes relating to certain types of commercial transaction. Clearing, settlement, and funds transfer facilities were available at Bangkok and through the central bank's regional branches and provincial and district treasuries (Bank of Thailand

1992: 179–80). The Thai central bank endeavoured to 'stimulate private savings', not least by encouraging 'commercial bank branch opening in rural areas' (Bank of Thailand 1992: 164). These initiatives led to the growing involvement of central bankers in the monitoring and supervision of domestic counterparties. In some countries central banks also took the lead in promoting the modernisation of payment systems (Fry, Goodhart, and Almeida 1996: 56–60; Sanchez-Arroyo 1996).

Central banks and governments were keen to establish securities markets and stock exchanges. In most cases such markets were either negligible or non-existent in 1945. Potentially, they could offer the business sector and the state an alternative to bank (and central bank) borrowing. The use of OMOs as a monetary policy tool required the prior existence of securities markets (Drake, P. J. 1977). By the 1970s the Central Bank of the Philippines was making regular use of OMOs using its own certificates of indebtedness (Aghevli *et al.* 1979: 800, 806). But in many countries the efficient operation of securities markets was hampered by the desire of governments to retain control over interest rates. Governments wanted to be able to borrow cheaply, and some were reluctant to expose investors to the risk of the capital losses that accompany rising rates. It proved difficult to achieve an interest rate low enough to accommodate borrowers (especially the state) and high enough to encourage savers. The Taiwanese authorities sought to promote the wider holding and trading of government bonds in the 1960s, but their methods were self-defeating. Private investors were given the right to sell bonds to the central bank at par so as to insulate them from risk. Meanwhile, bonds held by the commercial banks were not traded because they were required to satisfy minimum securities ratios (Khatkhate 1977). The Nigerian central bank behaved in an equally contradictory fashion in the 1960s: in order to encourage investment in government securities pains were taken to ensure that their market price never fell below par. But investors doubted that this policy would last, and continued to shun the bonds (Brown 1966: 160–1). Markets for fixed interest securities developed slowly, especially in the least advanced countries, a problem that continued to exercise the IMF in the early twenty-first century (Laurens 2005). In the more highly developed Asian and Latin American countries, however, this obstacle had been overcome by the 1990s (Borio and McCauley 2002).

India's first five-year plan, in 1951, emphasised that in a 'planned economy', the central bank must extend its functions, taking on 'a direct and active role, firstly in creating or helping to create the machinery needed for financing development activities … and secondly, ensuring that the finances available flow in the directions intended' (quoted in

Jadhav 2003: 17). The central bank was clearly part of the governmental economic apparatus and not a free agent. A responsibility for agricultural finance, including the provision of seasonal credit and support for marketing, had been incorporated in the act creating the RBI in 1935. Financial underdevelopment had long been – and would continue to be – a constraint on the Indian economy and living standards. The RBI took its involvement in rural finance very seriously. In 1955 a third deputy governor was established with a mandate for overseeing rural credit programmes. Both short-term and long-term credit were made available by the RBI for rural projects and agencies, including cooperatives and rural land banks. These responsibilities became increasingly onerous and time consuming, and in 1982 most of them were spun off into a new agency, the National Bank for Agricultural and Rural Development, which was a joint venture between the RBI and the Indian government. Extensive support was also offered to industry through development institutions (Chakrabarty 2003; Balachandran 1998: 229–315, 513–89).

Some central banks subscribed capital to industrial and agricultural development banks. More commonly, central banks provided credit to such institutions, as well as to agricultural cooperatives, and helped to create markets for their securities. Extensive resort was had to direct controls over commercial bank lending in order to channel credit towards the development agencies. Where ceilings were imposed on bank lending, special allowance was made for 'priority' lending to meritorious sectors. Reserve requirements and required portfolio ratios were adjusted to reward financial institutions for helping to fund development projects. Central banks encouraged the purchase by the private sector of bonds issued by development institutions, offering to rediscount such paper at a favourable rate. Exchange controls and import deposit requirements were used to discriminate in favour of essential imports, whilst the exchange rate was often manipulated to boost short-term export returns. Brimmer (1971) offers a contemporary perspective on these activities.

South Korea was one of the world's most dynamic economies in the second half of the twentieth century (Amsden 1989). The central bank achieved a balance between the promotion of economic development and the procurement of macroeconomic stability. Founded in 1950, the Bank of Korea (which replaced the Bank of Chosun, a Japanese colonial institution) carried out a full range of central banking functions. Staff numbers rose from 1,122 in 1950 to 4,593 in 1982. The relationship between central bank and government was one of partnership. South Korea was an ambitious developmental state from the early

1960s, and the technical expertise of the central bank was valued. Bank of Korea staff drafted the first Five-Year Economic Development Plan of the military government in 1962, which identified priority sectors including agriculture, energy, cement, and steel. Advances were made by the Bank of Korea to development institutions including the Korean Development Bank. In the mid 1960s crucial decisions – typical of the Asian miracle economies – were taken to stimulate exports by making the exchange rate more competitive, and encourage savings by ensuring that real interest rates were positive. The central bank saw the maintenance of macroeconomic stability as vital to the creation of an economic climate conducive to high growth (Chung 2000).

While direct intervention by central banks in the development process *could* be effective, Brimmer (1971: 789) found that the overall record was 'rather mixed'. Later commentators were far more critical, their views reflecting the swing in the intellectual pendulum, starting in the 1970s, from development planning to liberalisation (Khatkhate 1991: 17). Was action to channel credit justified by market failure, or did it merely create new and equally troublesome distortions? Central banks risked capture by special interest groups: development and export finance provided by the Peruvian central bank in the 1950s and 1960s was slanted in favour of the powerful cotton growers, whereas producers of food crops were starved of credit (Frankman 1974). Since many of the techniques used to push credit into favoured sectors were also tools of monetary control, confusion was introduced into policy making (Aghevli et al. 1979). Quasi-fiscal lending added to inflationary pressure. One critic identified 'a clear conflict of interest between [a central bank's] primary monetary and prudential role and its secondary and acquired developmental role', and envisaged the partial divestiture of secondary functions either to the government or the private sector (Chandavarkar 1992: 138). The World Bank and the IMF were 'powerful purveyors of ideas' (Hodd 1987: 340) of the 'market friendly' variety to central banks in the developing world. The IMF also affected thinking in developing countries through its training programmes, and by its often controversial involvement in financial rescue and stabilisation programmes (Killick 1984), which included the setting of monetary targets (Aghevli et al. 1979: 812).

Outcomes varied dramatically. African economic performance was disastrous from 1970, but parts of Asia experienced an economic 'miracle' (World Bank 1993). Elsewhere, including Latin America and India, economic performance was in between these extremes. Until the financial crisis of 1997, the Asian miracle countries won praise for combining planning and state intervention with export-led growth and the maintenance of macroeconomic stability. India, by contrast, was a relatively closed economy until the 1990s. Space is not available here for an analysis of these contrasts in performance. Many processes and actors were involved. Central banks could and – where permitted – did make a positive contribution to policy formulation and implementation.

Central banks sat at the 'technocratic' end of the bureaucratic spectrum in the developing world (Chandavarkar 1992: 138). As early as the 1940s, the Central Bank of China had a substantial research department and a well-stocked library (Trescott 2007: 269). Central bankers were armed increasingly with western postgraduate degrees, and in a position to offer their governments reasoned economic advice, a commodity that was often very scarce. Foreign advisors, including IMF representatives, were liable to be treated with suspicion, but domestic central bankers could at least get a hearing (Hodd 1987: 341). Brimmer (1971: 789–90) identified the advisory role as a key function of central banks in the developing world. Central bankers were not to blame if governments with different priorities rejected their advice.

Central bankers have received less recognition than they deserve for the policy successes of some developing countries. The standard account of the South Korean economic miracle ignores the Bank of Korea, except as a valuable source of economic statistics (Amsden 1989). In a survey article on public policy and financial markets during the Asian miracle, Stiglitz and Uy (1996) heap praise on governments for achieving rapid financial development and relative macroeconomic stability, but barely mention the contribution of central banks. Hamilton-Hart (2002) goes some way towards redressing the balance in her comparative study of central banks in South-East Asia. Central banks were an integral component of the developmental apparatus. By promoting the growth of financial markets and institutions, they contributed to the development process. At the same time, however, attempts by governments and influential groups to use central banks for the promotion of sectional economic interests could hamper their work.

Inflation

Inflation was already acknowledged as a problem in developing economies in the 1950s. Not only were some central banks helpless in the face of government demands for monetary accommodation, but they were reluctant to deny credit to the private sector, fearing a political backlash against measures that might restrain (nominal) economic growth. Lacking 'tradition and prestige' new central banks were wary of anything that could 'jeopardize their limited status in the community' (Ahrensdorf 1959: 298).

Generally speaking, the primary cause of inflation in the developing world was the desire of governments for central bank credit – in short 'money supply soared' (Capie 2007: 176) in many countries. It was cheaper and more convenient for the state to borrow from the central bank than from other lenders. The central bank could also be tapped for quasi-fiscal advances. The fact that inflation diminished the real burden of accumulated domestic government debt was a big temptation for profligate rulers. Inflation weakened the balance of payments, however, and was liable to cause rapid currency depreciation, intensifying the burden of external debt.

The legal status of the central bank typically had less bearing on its capacity to curb inflation than did the quality of its informal relationship with political leaders and their attitude to inflation. Despite scoring poorly in terms of formal autonomy, the Bank of Thailand exerted considerable influence over policy, particularly before the 1980s, as a result of its involvement in the state budget planning processes. Thai governments had their hands in the till at the microeconomic level, but they were relatively tough on inflation (Maxfield 1994). Reporting on the East Asian economic miracle, the World Bank (1993: 348) concluded that macroeconomic 'stability and low inflation were necessary preconditions for rapid growth', and that 'the key element was the management of the fiscal deficit'. The aversion of most East Asian governments to inflation created an environment in which monetary policy could be effective. When central banks in East Asia did extend additional credit to their governments, they were inclined to reduce credit to the private sector by about two-thirds of this amount (Fry, Goodhart, and Almeida 1996: 41). The absence of sophisticated money markets meant that direct methods, such as variable reserve requirements and lending caps, were often employed to fight inflation (Dorrance 1965; Page, S. 1993), but for many years this was also the case in western economies.

When the price level rises more than 50 per cent per month for a considerable period of time there is said to be hyperinflation. Fischer, Sahay, and Végh (2002: 840) identify fifteen cases of hyperinflation between 1956 and 1996. The first outbreak was in Bolivia in 1984–5 (Sachs 1986). All but two cases (Ukraine and Serbia) were in developing countries. There was a strong association between war or civil unrest and hyperinflation. More common than hyperinflation was chronic inflation, involving persistently high inflation over many years, with inflation rates sometimes topping 100 per cent per annum without necessarily accelerating into hyperinflation. Chronic or persistent inflation was almost *de rigueur* in Latin America, and harder to end than hyperinflation (Pazos 1972; Végh 1992; Reinhart and Savastano 2003). Inflationary pressure exacerbated balance of payments difficulties and caused currency instability.

Indonesia in the 1960s provides a celebrated example both of the failure of monetary control in a developing country, and of the successful reimposition of such control after a change in regime. According to the Jakarta consumer price index annual inflation reached 1,500 per cent in the year to June 1966 (Tomasson 1970: 47). Whether the Indonesian inflation qualifies as hyperinflation is a moot point, but at the very least there was a period of extremely high inflation. After building up since 1957, inflationary pressure accelerated in the early 1960s. Indonesia faced internal revolts as well as military confrontation with the Malaysians, the British, and the Dutch. Nominal government spending, especially on the military, mushroomed, but tax and other revenue lagged. The government of President Sukarno, the army, and the communists were locked in a power struggle. By comparison, the central bank was a marginal player. The 1953 Bank Indonesia Act, which required the central bank to keep a 20 per cent ratio of gold and foreign exchange to advances, was relaxed in 1957. Bank Indonesia was compelled to finance the budget deficit in an inflationary manner. In 1961 Bank Indonesia was forbidden to publish regular weekly reports on the grounds that these would encourage speculators (Mackie 1967: 22, 33). There were similarities between Indonesia in the 1960s and Germany in the early 1920s, not least because there was no agreement at the highest political levels on how to bring the budget under control. Inflation was damaging but not disastrous for most Indonesians. Peasants were partially insulated by rising prices for their crops. Those suffering most were employees on fixed incomes. Government officials could survive only by taking bribes, moonlighting as chauffeurs or night watchmen, and sending their wives out to work (Mackie 1967: 83–5).

Inflation fell rapidly between 1966 and 1969, after a tumultuous change of regime in Jakarta. The new government, led by Suharto, sought aid and advice from the IMF and other agencies, and took control over the budget. Instead of focusing on meeting the government's residual financing needs, the central bank now concentrated on ensuring that there was sufficient credit to keep the business sector running. The Indonesian stabilisation was remarkably successful, and was achieved without a major recession (Tomasson 1970; Sutton 1984).

High inflation is ultimately a political problem, the Indonesian crisis of the mid 1960s being a case in point. When the budget deficit cannot be managed, governments turn to their central bankers for assistance, requiring them to switch on the printing presses, whatever the legal niceties and governance arrangements.

Central bank cooperation

Central banks in developing countries were active in international networks. First, some governments in the developing world were parties to monetary agreements and understandings with the former colonial powers. Second, new central banks sought technical advice and training from more experienced institutions. Third, they wished to present a common front, especially at the regional level.

By contrast to the close monetary and financial ties between France and its former African colonies, arrangements in the former British empire were somewhat looser. The management of the sterling area was the main objective of central bank and intergovernmental cooperation in the Commonwealth. Member states and their central banks were expected to collaborate to preserve the dollar pool and protect the external value of sterling. Communication between Commonwealth central banks was often conducted through the Bank of England. By the 1960s, however, interest in the sterling area relationship was waning. Tension was rising between the British and the remaining large holders of sterling, including Malaysia and Singapore, which were starting to switch into other reserve currencies including the US dollar. The sterling area ended in 1972, but the CFA franc zone marched on (Robertson and Singleton 2001: Schenk 2008). Even after 1972 the professional ties between the Bank of England and Commonwealth central banks persisted. In the 1990s the Bank of England continued to host meetings of former sterling-area central bank governors (George 1996: x).

Training facilities for central bankers from developing countries were provided by the major central banks. The Bank of England offered courses for Commonwealth central bankers (Hennessy 1992: 308–11). The CBA was instrumental in establishing the South East Asia New Zealand Australia (SEANZA) central banking group in 1957. SEANZA mounted regular training courses and convened meetings of central bank governors (Schedvin 1992: 210–11). Over the years SEANZA conferences and courses were held in a range of countries from Nepal to South Korea to New Zealand. They were important for building understanding amongst the disparate nations of the region. At the SEANZA course in Manila in 1970 there were speakers from Australia, New Zealand, the UK, the IMF, and the World Bank, as well as from developing countries including the Philippines, Pakistan, Malaysia, and Mexico. Topics discussed included development banking and rural banking in the Philippines, as well as basics such as national income accounting and the instruments of monetary policy. SEANZA encouraged the sharing of ideas and experience (Central Bank of the Philippines 1970). The IMF founded a Central Banking Service in 1963 to provide technical assistance to member countries, and in 1964 set up the IMF Institute to train economic officials, including central bankers, especially from developing countries (de Vries 1987: 102–5).

A Center for Latin American Monetary Studies (Centro de Estudios Monetarios Latinoamericanos or CEMLA) was founded in Mexico City in 1952 as a collaborative venture among Latin American (and later Caribbean) central banks. CEMLA was involved in training, research, and the dissemination of central banking ideas.[1] South East Asian central banks, including the Bank of Thailand and the Central Bank of the Philippines, began to call for greater regional cooperation in the early 1960s, not least with a view to lobbying more effectively and coordinating their voting in the IMF, the World Bank, and the nascent Asian Development Bank. For several years this initiative was hampered by military confrontation between Indonesia and Malaysia, but a South East Asian Central Bank group (SEACEN) was emerging by 1966–7. As well as promoting regional interests in the international agencies, SEACEN had a strong emphasis on central banking education. A SEACEN training centre was established in Kuala Lumpur in 1972, under the auspices the Bank Negara Malaysia. The SEACEN Centre was an Asian initiative, independent of western central banks.[2] The latter group had their own club, the BIS, from which developing country central banks were excluded.

Conclusion

By the 1960s the aspiration of the Brussels Conference of 1920 to see central banks established all over the globe had been realised. Yet central banks in the developing world were a very mixed bunch. The People's Bank of China, the Reserve Bank of India, and the Banque Centrale des États de l'Afrique de l'Ouest did not have a great deal in common. Central banks in the developing world faced immense challenges. On the one hand they were expected to promote the growth of stable, efficient, and modern financial institutions and systems, and to encourage broad-based economic development. On the other hand, they had to operate in highly personalised political environments, and were often

[1] www.cemla.org/about.htm (accessed 30 October 2008).
[2] www.seacen.org/about/history.aspx (accessed 30 October 2008).

under pressure to grant favours to government cronies and provide monetary accommodation to cover high budget deficits. The methods employed by central banks included a battery of direct controls, most of which would have been anathema to central bankers in the 1920s. Outcomes varied enormously. Some East Asian countries enjoyed spectacular success between the mid 1960s and mid 1990s, achieving rapid economic growth and macroeconomic stability. Elsewhere, particularly in Africa, there were equally spectacular failures. Some countries – Indonesia being a good example – experienced disaster and success at different times.

Professional central bankers were among the intellectual and bureaucratic elite in developing countries. They sought, often in vain, to restrain bad governments, and to cooperate with good governments. There was little scope for the exercise of central bank autonomy, but central banks in well-managed countries, including the developmental and quasi-developmental states of East Asia, proved capable of exerting a beneficial influence over the formulation of economic policy. Central banks did their best in trying circumstances, which is all that could be expected of them.

11   The horse of inflation

> The horse of inflation is out of the barn and already well down the
> road. We cannot return the horse to the barn ... but we can prevent it
> from trotting too fast.
>
> William Martin, Chairman of the Board of Governors of the Federal
> Reserve System, 1967 (quoted in Bremner 2004: 252)

> [I]nflation is a lot like alcoholism. When you drink, the good effects
> come first, and the hangover comes the next morning.
>
> Milton Friedman, 1977 (quoted in Nelson, E. 2007b: 161)

Inflation was one of the most serious economic challenges confronting
the developed world between the late 1960s and the 1980s. But it was
not the only problem. Exchange rates fluctuated unpredictably after the
collapse of Bretton Woods, whilst the banking crisis made a comeback.
Economic growth decelerated after the early 1970s, unemployment rose
to a post-war peak in the early 1980s, and two oil crises confused policy makers. Macroeconomic theory was in flux as Keynesians fought it
out with the monetarists. Each of these developments impinged upon
the political or intellectual milieu of central banking. In so far as inflation was a monetary phenomenon, central bankers had to take some of
the blame, though they could point out that responsibility for monetary policy was shared with government. In the long run, however, the
great inflation provided central banks with more opportunities than
threats. All else having failed, monetary policy was called upon to overcome inflation. Deane and Pringle (1994: 3, 4) explain that sometime
around 1980 'central banks started to come in from the cold'. Before
long 'monetary policy became virtually the only game in town'. The
power and prestige of central bankers rose to heights unknown since
the 1920s.

Inflation is more important than Vietnam

Inflationary pressure stirred in the late 1950s, strengthened markedly
in the second half of the 1960s, and exploded in the 1970s. According to

184

Meltzer (2005: 158), the turning point for the USA came in 1965, 'the last year of strong productivity growth and the first year of rising inflation'. Perhaps this was also a symbolic turning point for Keynesianism. On 31 December an image of Keynes appeared on the cover of *Time* magazine. He was the first dead person to achieve this accolade. Yet Keynesian doctrines, or the doctrines commonly attributed to Keynes, were already in question (Collins, R. M. 1996: 402).

The year 1968 was another troubling one for US policy makers (Collins, R. M. 1996). The economic situation was overshadowed by political events such as the Tet Offensive in Vietnam, student revolts, the Soviet invasion of Czechoslovakia, and the assassinations of Martin Luther King and Bobby Kennedy, but it was nonetheless disturbing. The Johnson administration had reduced taxes and boosted spending on Vietnam and the Great Society social programmes. Monetary policy was relatively accommodating, reflecting optimistic projections of economic growth. One of the most visible symptoms of economic malaise was the collapse of the gold pool – another expression of waning international confidence in the dollar. Policy makers feared rising economic instability. Speaking in Copenhagen in 1969, Chairman Martin stated that it was 'more important to settle the problem of inflation than to settle the war in Vietnam' (quoted in Bremner 2004: 272). Martin was well aware that these problems were connected. He had protested against the Johnson administration's attempts to conceal the cost of the war. In 1967 he had leaked projections of war costs to the press (Bremner 2004: 204–5, 224–5, 233).

Inflationary pressure was rising in many countries, partly for domestic reasons and partly as a result of monetary inflows from the USA. Speaking in 1970, the West German finance minister, Karl Schiller, said: 'Inflation is like a drug. For a short time it makes our society feel "high" … Then it becomes apparent that the 'trip' has not solved any problems, and even created new ones' (quoted in Nelson, E. 2007a: 46–7). Table 3 illustrates the rise and fall of inflation in some industrial countries. Inflation was universally higher in the 1970s than in the 1960s, but lower in the 1980s than in the 1970s. There were significant differences between countries. Switzerland and West Germany contained inflation more successfully than did Italy, the UK, Australia, and New Zealand. Countries with relatively high inflation also experienced greater inflation volatility. The costs of inflation are difficult to quantify (Fischer 1994: 270–7). High inflation is often but not always associated with poor economic growth; not always because Italy enjoyed one of Europe's strongest growth rates despite rampant inflation, whereas Switzerland faltered badly in the growth race despite

Table 3 *Average annual inflation in selected countries, 1960s to 1990s (%)*

	1960s	1970s	1980s	1990s
USA	2.8	7.9	4.7	2.8
Canada	2.7	8.1	6.0	2.0
Japan	5.8	9.1	2.1	0.8
France	4.1	9.7	6.4	1.7
Italy	2.9	14.1	9.9	3.8
Switzerland	3.3	5.0	3.4	2.0
UK	4.1	13.8	6.6	3.1
West Germany	2.6	5.1	2.6	2.4
Australia	2.5	10.5	8.1	2.2
New Zealand	3.8	12.5	10.8	1.8

Source: Borio and Filardo (2007: 43).

keeping inflation in check. Inflation also generates uncertainty, and causes large swings in relative income and wealth. The 1970s saw widespread industrial unrest as workers fought to gain compensation for past and anticipated inflation. Periods of high inflation (or rapid disinflation) are socially divisive.

Inflation and the economists

Central bankers could not count on economists for either a settled analysis of the causes of inflation or an agreed suite of policy recommendations. The period from the mid 1960s to the mid 1980s witnessed a bitter struggle between Keynesians and monetarists. The official history of the Bundesbank describes the principal German advocates of these competing schools as 'matadors' (Richter 1999: 545). With some exceptions, including the fervently monetarist Federal Reserve Bank of St Louis (Hafer and Wheelock 2001), central banks followed rather than led the debate. Keynesian ideas were resilient in central banking circles in the 1970s and early 1980s, not least in the Bank of England (Capie in press). Capie, Goodhart, and Schnadt (1994: 82) observe that central bankers were very human in their tendency 'to blame failures on factors beyond their own control'.

In the standard Keynesian paradigm of the 1950s and 1960s inflation was either 'demand pull' or 'cost push' in origin. Demand pull inflation occurred when aggregate demand pressed upon productive capacity, bidding up wages and prices. In modern parlance, the output gap was moving from negative to positive. Cost push inflation was attributed to the power of trade unions to raise wages, the ability of firms to increase the price of intermediate and final products, and the power of foreigners, including cartels such as the Organisation of Petroleum Exporting Countries (OPEC), to increase the cost of imports. Currency devaluation also raised import costs. Keynesians believed that policy makers could use the Phillips Curve as a basis for selecting a politically desirable combination of inflation and unemployment.

Monetarism put central bankers in the firing line in a way that Keynesianism did not. The term 'monetarism' was coined by Karl Brunner (Congdon 2007: 156), but it was disliked by the doyen of monetarists, Milton Friedman (1985). Monetarists held that inflation could not occur unless the money stock was permitted to increase faster than productive capacity. This conclusion followed from the quantity theory of money (Friedman, M. 1956). Its validity depended on the stability of the velocity of circulation or the demand for money (Laidler 1969). Monetarists rejected the Keynesian analysis of inflation. They denied that fiscal stimulus (one source of demand pull) could generate inflation, unless financed by central bank purchases of government debt, or the provision of additional money to enable commercial banks and their customers to purchase such securities. Trade unions and cartels could alter relative prices, but could not cause inflation without the assistance of the monetary authorities.

Monetarists regarded the oil crises of 1973–4 and 1979–80 (Beenstock 2007) as supply shocks that reduced potential output in net oil importing countries. Looser monetary policy in this situation would exacerbate inflation without restoring the previous level of output. By contrast, Keynesians were inclined to view the oil crises in terms of higher withdrawals from the circular flow of income, causing recessions, which could be overcome by reflation, provided that the accompanying increase in fuel costs was inhibited by prices and incomes policy from feeding through into general inflation.

Monetarists acknowledged that there could be a temporary trade-off between inflation and unemployment, but denied its persistence. They believed that there was a natural rate of unemployment, determined by microeconomic factors including benefit levels and other structural features. (The level of the natural rate was debated.) If the monetary authorities pushed unemployment below the natural rate, inflation would rise, diminishing real wages. After a short interval, money wages would be bid up, as workers demanded compensation. This would lead to declining profitability and more lay-offs. Unemployment would return to the natural rate, but – and this is the crucial point – inflation would be higher than before. If the authorities were determined to keep unemployment below the natural rate, they would have to live with accelerating inflation. The Phillips curve became steeper with the passage of time and was ultimately vertical. Inflationary expectations, formed on the basis of recent experience, also played an important role in monetarist analysis. As firms and workers grew to expect the continuation of inflation, they brought forward price increases and wage demands. The more explosive the trajectory of inflationary expectations, the faster any monetary stimulus would feed through into inflation (Phelps 1967; Friedman, M. 1968; Bordo and Schwartz 2006).

Monetarists tended to be critical of central banks: if inflation was rising then central banks must be doing something wrong. Friedman complained that monetary policy was erratic and short term in focus because central bankers endorsed and implemented the fine-tuning approach of governments. Policy actions were mistimed and falsely calibrated. He also felt that the Federal Reserve System was arrogant, ignoring or at least fobbing off criticism. In 1981 Friedman concluded: 'I have no doubt that the United States would be better off if the Federal Reserve had never been established' (*New York Daily News*, 22 May 1981, quoted in Nelson, E. 2007b: 161–2).

Rational expectations theorists offered a new perspective. Robert Lucas (1973) argued that economic actors used all information to hand and the best available economic reasoning to predict the effects of any policy change. Thus they would react immediately to the announcement of a monetary stimulus, bringing forward the impact on inflation and eliminating the temporary boost to output. Only a miscalculation by economic actors or a complete monetary surprise could affect output. Lucas (1976) also contended that rational expectations rendered useless the models commonly employed by central banks, which assumed adaptive expectations. The implications and validity of rational expectations were widely debated (Fischer 1980).

Another influential theoretical development of the 1970s was the concept of dynamic or time inconsistency, which stemmed from the work of Kydland and Prescott (1977). They explained that the monetary authorities had an incentive to behave opportunistically. If the public could be persuaded (or conned) that the authorities were hawkish on inflation, then inflationary expectations and wage and price demands would recede. Once workers and employers were locked into low wage settlements, the monetary authorities could set aside their commitment to price stability, and instead boost the money supply in order to achieve a temporary reduction in unemployment ... probably in the run up to an election. But any improvement would be short-lived and next time the authorities would not be trusted.

The international transmission mechanism for inflationary impulses was another major concern. Keynesians maintained that an increase in aggregate demand in a big country (or group of countries) could bid up world prices. Inflation could also be propagated by cost-push pressures: there was a boom in most commodity prices in the early 1970s followed by two oil price hikes. Monetarists focused on the role of fixed exchange rates in the transmission of inflation (Frenkel and Johnson 1976; Cross and Laidler 1976). When inflation rose in the USA, American goods and assets became less attractive vis-à-vis their (say) West German counterparts. West Germany would experience a balance of payments surplus. In order to prevent appreciation of the DM, the Bundesbank would have to purchase the excess supply of US dollars, increasing the West German money supply and causing inflation. If the Bundesbank were to sterilise the inflow by selling bonds, interest rates would rise, attracting even more US capital and bringing about a further increase in the money supply. With freely floating exchange rates, however, the domestic money supply would be completely insulated from external effects. But no country, except New Zealand after 1985, had a freely floating currency.

The solutions to inflation advocated by Keynesians and monetarists also differed. Keynesians supported the fine tuning of fiscal and monetary policy. When inflation picked up, governments should raise taxes and/or trim government spending, but when unemployment rose they should throw the policy levers into reverse. An obvious difficulty with this prescription was that in the 1970s inflation and unemployment often coincided. Stagflation – inflation combined with stagnation – was not envisaged in the Keynesian version of the Phillips curve. For Keynesians, cost push inflation should be fought with controls, either voluntary or statutory, over wages and prices.

Monetarists were adamant that the only answer to inflation was control of the money supply. Milton Friedman (1960) recommended a policy rule involving a fixed percentage annual growth of a selected monetary aggregate. There were several alternative monetary aggregates, though monetarists generally favoured the narrowest. Price stability could be achieved by setting the target monetary growth rate equal to the average rate of growth of real GDP. A monetary aggregate was an intermediate target, offering indirect control over spending and inflation. Monetarists were predisposed to support a floating exchange rate so as to insulate the money supply from international influences, thereby simplifying the task of the central bank. But floating without an alternative nominal anchor such as a monetary target was considered dangerous. The risk of triggering a currency crisis acted as a constraint on expansionary policies under a fixed exchange rate, but gradual depreciation under a floating rate did not attract as much attention.

Monetarists opposed the fine tuning of the monetary aggregates. Any sort of fine tuning was destabilising in their eyes because of lags and uncertainties in measurement, policy formulation, and implementation. It was far better to give the markets some certainty about monetary growth over the medium term. Monetary targeting as practised, however, involved considerable use of discretion. Targets were adjusted frequently, much to the disgust of the theorists. Milton Friedman (1985: 15) complained that the 'rhetoric of the monetary authorities has indeed been monetarist, but their policies have not been or, to be generous, have been only partially so'.

Keynesians argued that inflation should be reduced gradually in order to soften the transitional impact on jobs and output. But rational expectations theorists and some monetarists felt that the transitional costs of disinflation would be mild because price and wage setters would reduce their demands immediately upon the announcement of tighter monetary policy. But would such a policy announcement be believable (or credible) given the authorities' previous opportunism? This could be a problem. Without moderation in wage and price demands any reduction in money growth would bring about a surge in unemployment, as feared by the Keynesians.

Most central bankers strongly endorsed the view that money was important, after all money was their business. But they were reluctant to commit themselves to a rigid and exclusive theoretical perspective such as monetarism (Meek 1983). Gordon Richardson, the governor of the Bank of England, indicated, in a speech in 1976, that control of the money supply, while desirable, was only part of the story. 'I think it must be right to aim publicly for a growth in money supply which will accommodate a realistic rate of economic growth but not accommodate, more than in part, the rate of inflation. [But] Monetary and fiscal policy – and I would add incomes policy – each have their part to play and should form a coherent whole' (quoted in McClam 1978: 7).

Richardson was a 'practical monetarist', not a true 'believer'. Along with his peers in the central banking world, Richardson simply wanted governments to take inflation more seriously and cooperate with central banks to impose tighter monetary policy (Fay 1988: 73). Richardson would get more than he bargained for when a true believer, Margaret Thatcher, came to power spouting dogma in 1979. Monetarists found the eclecticism of central bankers infuriating; indeed this was in marked contrast to the narrowness of central bankers' vision in the age of the gold standard.

Explaining the great inflation

Just as much of the literature on the great depression focuses on the US experience, so do many studies of the great inflation. This is not to neglect the importance of the international dimension in either case: the gold standard was crucial in the propagation of the depression, while the Bretton Woods system was instrumental in the early stages of the great inflation.

The institutional framework and preferred monetary policy tools continued to differ from country to country (Holbik 1973; OECD 1974). However, these details mattered less than the way in which monetary policy was formulated, and the resolve with which it was implemented. Meltzer (2005) divides research into the causes of the great inflation into four categories, which attribute the blame to politics, theoretical errors, the use of incorrect data, and neglect of money growth, respectively. Meltzer's own account of the great inflation draws on each of these factors. In addition he criticises the decision-making procedures of the Fed, and the inadequacies of successive chairmen. Allowing inflation to persist for fifteen years was a more serious offence than letting it start. Weise (2008: 1–4) offers similar explanatory categories: political constraints; misperceptions due to mismeasurement of economic variables; and misperceptions due to theoretical confusion. Underlying both classifications is the assumption that inflation is ultimately a monetary phenomenon. Cost push may have played a supporting role by generating theoretical confusion as well as political pressure for an accommodating monetary policy, but it did not actually cause inflation.

Orphanides (2002; 2003; 2004) discusses the mismeasurement approach. Before the 1980s US policy makers were inclined to overestimate the degree of slack in the economy, and consequently failed to tighten monetary policy sufficiently. In effect, the Fed overlooked an upward shift in the natural rate of unemployment in the 1970s, and did not grasp that the deceleration in productivity growth in the late 1960s and early 1970s was a permanent phenomenon. The problem was not a shortage of analysts. In the early 1970s the Board of Governors had 'over 200 economists who directly or indirectly provide[d] policy-makers with information used in the formulation of monetary policy' (Lombra and Moran 1980: 11). Unfortunately, neither the accuracy of the statistical series that they constructed, nor the conclusions of their econometric exercises, could be relied upon. The Board had to draw upon experience, anecdotal evidence, and gut feeling, and often made the wrong decisions. Even in the 1990s and 2000, economic briefings and forecasts would take policy makers only so far, and they could not dispense with the exercise of judgment (Singleton *et al.* 2006: ch. 6). According to Meltzer (2005: 149), US monetary policy makers also misinterpreted the 1973–4 oil crisis, treating it as a deflationary shock that should be countered by a monetary stimulus, and not as a permanent transfer of income to OPEC, a mistake avoided by the monetary authorities in West Germany, Switzerland, and Japan.

Romer and Romer (2002a) and Nelson, E. (2005a) contend that conceptual misunderstandings led to the policy errors that exacerbated inflation. Nelson describes this as the monetary neglect hypothesis. Policy makers were confused by the variety of theories of inflation. Some still believed that the Phillips curve trade-off was operationally viable. Jacob Frenkel (1994: 327), governor of the Bank of Israel, later lamented that 'most politicians … especially Finance Ministers, were born with a Phillips curve in their head'. Those attracted to cost-push theory and incomes policy questioned whether monetary policy could control inflation. In essence, central bankers and other policy makers were too slow to recognise that inflation was first and foremost a monetary phenomenon. But this raises some troublesome questions. If policy makers were not using the best available theory, they cannot have had rational expectations, and thus were dumber than trade unions and households.

An internal report on 'Inflation in New Zealand', dated 1972, and attributed to the chief economist of the RBNZ, shows how difficult it was for some central bankers to settle on an explanation of this phenomenon. Inflation had been rising since 1967, and appeared to have multiple causes. Cuts in price subsidies, higher taxes, and increased charges for government services had raised the price level in 1967. Rising import costs and the increased receipts of commodity exporters after the November 1967 devaluation of the New Zealand dollar also helped to get inflation started. Growing consumer and business confidence and liquidity then caused an upsurge in expenditure. In 1968 labour shortages and the unravelling of New Zealand's unusual system of wage setting by Court of Arbitration resulted in strong upward pressure on wages. Firms passed higher wage costs on to consumers. A wage–price spiral was operating by the early 1970s. Without this spiral the level of aggregate demand would not have sufficed to sustain inflation. Government salaries were indexed to private sector salaries, intensifying wage-push pressure. Higher international liquidity associated with US balance of payments deficits also spilled over into New Zealand. The balance of payments was propelled further into surplus by a commodity price boom in the early 1970s. The RBNZ's econometric model assumed a close link between wage and price increases.

The chief economist attached considerable importance to institutional causes of inflation, including the end of harmony in wage setting, as well as the vulnerability of New Zealand to imported inflation. The fact that inflation was a global problem had encouraged complacency within government. It is interesting that the chief economist was concerned about liquidity – a term that harked back to the Radcliffe Committee – rather than monetary growth (RBNZ Archives 1972). Ed Nelson (2005b) provides additional commentary on monetary policy neglect in New Zealand.

Even the Bundesbank was receptive to cost-push notions in the early 1970s. In a speech in 1971, Karl Klasen, president of the Bundesbank, noted that wages were growing faster than could be explained by the strength of demand, which was actually softening. He welcomed plans for consultation between labour, capital, and the state over wages (Nelson, E. 2007a: 47). According to the Bundesbank's annual report of 1972: 'Monetary policy alone cannot avert the danger of inflationary expectations gaining strength' (quoted in Nelson, E. 2007a: 54).

Political explanations of the great inflation have always appealed. Governments were reluctant to tighten monetary policy, fearing job losses and electoral punishment. At certain junctures presidents Lyndon Johnson and Richard Nixon tried to bully the Federal Reserve System into following an accommodating policy. Perhaps the Fed was overly anxious to cooperate with the government, and unwarrantably slow to insist on its autonomy. On the other hand, there was no clear public mandate for tough anti-inflationary policies in the USA in the 1970s (DeLong 1997; Weise 2008). The public did not become seriously alarmed about inflation until 1980–1 according to Gallup poll evidence (Meltzer 2005: 147).

There is no reason to treat the explanations above as mutually exclusive. The situation was complex, and the main actors (as well as the minor ones) were liable to change their minds. In the early 1970s, for example, Arthur Burns, the chairman of the Fed, advocated an incomes policy. Romer and Romer (2004: 139–41) argue that Burns supported an incomes policy because he doubted the capacity of tight monetary policy to overcome wage-push inflation. Labour unions might not lower their wage demands in response to higher interest rates if they cared more about wages than jobs, or if they expected the authorities to backtrack on interest rates. An incomes policy, however, could reduce inflationary expectations and wage demands. A wage-and-price freeze was implemented in 1971, but it had no lasting effect on inflation. Weise (2008) refers to a lecture by Burns in 1979, after his retirement, that puts a different complexion on the matter.

[T]he Federal Reserve System had the power to abort the inflation at its incipient stage fifteen years ago or at any later point, and it has the power to end it today. At any time within that period, it could have restricted the money supply and created sufficient strains in financial and industrial markets to terminate inflation with little delay. It did not do so because the Federal Reserve was itself caught up in the philosophic and political currents that were transforming American life and culture. (Burns 1979: 156)

Either Burns had changed his mind and forgotten his views of 1971, or his original advocacy of incomes policy was insincere, or the Fed in 1971 was overcome by conceptual confusion and the fear of upsetting the government by insisting on tighter monetary policy. No doubt this does not exhaust the possibilities.

Nations in chronic balance of payments surplus, such as West Germany and Japan, shared some of the dilemmas of US policy makers. They also had to contend with the international dimension of inflation. In other words they were compelled to import inflation from the USA under the Bretton Woods system. Their reluctance to continue importing inflation was one reason why the fixed exchange rate regime was allowed to collapse (Bernanke et al. 1999: 43).

Fighting inflation was not as straightforward as the monetarists sometimes claimed it to be. Inflationary expectations could not be managed directly. In a tight labour market, trade unions could obtain large pay increases and firms could pass higher costs on to their customers. Accommodating the wage–price spiral was very tempting when the alternative might be a substantial rise in unemployment and deepening social divisions. Moderation by wage and price setters could alleviate the immediate impact on output and employment of tighter monetary policy. It is understandable that some central bankers advocated prices and incomes policy and fiscal restraint, even if the results were disappointing. Tackling inflation head on was a mission for the resolute.

Managing inflation

Some politicians and economists, and the occasional central banker, such as Ray White of the RBNZ (Singleton et al. 2006: 78), were resigned to permanent inflation by the mid 1970s. They drew up indexation schemes, the purpose of which was to dampen the inflation-induced redistribution of income and wealth (Fischer 1994: 277–8), but these ideas gained limited traction.

The macroeconomic policy cycle became more volatile in the 1970s. Governments and central banks would start to deal with one problem, say rising unemployment, but then have to divert their energies to cope with another problem, such as inflation or rapid currency depreciation. This was no longer fine tuning but crisis management. Unanticipated events, including the oil crises, threatened to overwhelm decision makers. The end of Bretton Woods did not usher in a world of freely floating exchange rates. Floating was dirty: central banks and governments still intervened in currency markets in order to push exchange rates in politically desired directions (Eichengreen 1996: 143). Moreover, efforts were made to fix intra-European exchange rates and adopt a common float against the rest of the world. Greater exchange rate flexibility helped to cushion weaker economies from external shocks, whilst insulating stronger economies somewhat from unwanted monetary inflows. But with the demise of fixed exchange rates the traditional nominal anchor for monetary policy was lost. What was there now to stop policy makers from creating ever more inflation?

In some major economies, including the UK and Italy, annual inflation surged above 20 per cent in the mid 1970s, and in some eyes appeared to be heading for Latin American levels. However, countervailing forces were gathering strength. The more visible and troublesome the problem of inflation, the greater was the incentive for governments and central banks to do something about it. In some cases they were sustained by external help, even if this was rarely appreciated by them at the time. When the UK was forced to borrow from the IMF in the midst of a currency crisis –the pound was sinking rather than floating – in 1976, the 'letter of intent' to the IMF from Chancellor Denis Healey set out targets for domestic credit expansion (DCE). Without such commitments the IMF might have walked away (Burk and Cairncross 1992: 107).

Central banks had begun, albeit slowly, to pay more attention to monetary and credit aggregates in the 1960s. After 1966 the Federal Reserve System took the course of the monetary aggregates into account when setting target ranges for short-term interest rates and net free bank reserves. Internal (unannounced) growth targets for the monetary aggregates were set from 1970, but remained contingent on money market conditions, and subject to frequent adjustment (OECD 1974: 47–9). The combination of monetary targets and incomes policy under Burns betrays the Fed's eclecticism rather than its monetarism. Indeed, when the wage–price freeze lowered inflationary expectations the monetary target was loosened (Lombra and Moran 1980: 22). Critically, the objectives of policy remained short term.

Monetary targets were announced publicly in a number of countries in the mid 1970s, including the USA, Canada, UK, Australia, Japan, and several continental European countries. West Germany and Switzerland led the way, proclaiming monetary targets in December

1974 (McClam 1978; Griffiths and Wood 1981; Fratianni and Salvatore 1993). By announcing a target the authorities hoped to show that they meant business, or establish credibility. If the authorities' commitment to the target was believed, inflationary expectations and exuberance in the labour and product markets would recede. Some central banks, including the Swiss National Bank (Rich 2003), adopted monetary targeting with enthusiasm, but several others did so reluctantly. The RBA bowed to pressure from the Australian government to introduce monetary 'projections' – a weak type of monetary targeting – in 1976, but saw little merit in this approach when the Australian dollar was still on a fixed exchange rate (Guttmann 2005: 70–98).

According to Friedman (1982: 102), Japan was the 'outstanding example' of a developed country following monetarist principles. (In the less developed world he praised Chile. West Germany also received some credit.) During the early 1970s the Bank of Japan started to use the M2 monetary aggregate as an indicator of demand pressure. Interest rates were raised in 1973, though not in time to prevent annual inflation rising above 20 per cent in 1974. By the end of 1975, however, annual inflation was back below 10 per cent. Unlike many other countries, Japan did not loosen monetary policy in response to the first oil crisis. Cost-push ideas were not allowed to divert policy makers from confronting inflation. The Bank of Japan started to announce 'forecasts' of M2 growth in late 1978. Governor Teiichiro Morinaga hinted that the central bank would respond to high money growth by increasing interest rates. Monetary policy was forward looking by the end of the 1970s, with the Bank of Japan tightening in anticipation of projected inflation (Nelson, E. 2007a; Hamada and Hayashi 1985). The adoption of a broadly monetarist framework did not require the abandonment of window guidance, though this approach was increasingly played down.

The precise target (e.g. central bank money, M1, M2, M3) varied from country to country. Some central banks opted for a stated percentage growth in the chosen aggregate, others for an acceptable range. Targets were not set in stone: indeed they were adjusted frequently, especially after they had been missed. Policy makers in most countries continued to shift their focus between unemployment, inflation, and the balance of payments instead of allocating a specific policy lever to each macroeconomic objective. Even the most determined exponents of monetary targeting were prepared to compromise when faced by large swings in other important variables such as the exchange rate. The Swiss National Bank temporarily abandoned the targeting of M1 growth in 1978, after an alarming appreciation in the Swiss franc, and substituted an exchange rate target. In 1979 the Swiss reverted to a monetary target. Announcement of the target was resumed in 1980 when a variant of the monetary base was adopted in place of M1 (Bernanke *et al.* 1999: 62).

Monetary targeting was implemented using the standard tools of monetary policy, ranging from the rediscount rate through OMOs to reserve requirements and administrative controls. However, there was a growing emphasis on OMOs. Two strategies presented themselves. Under the first, the central bank focused on maintaining the short-term interest rate that was compatible with the money supply target given the position of the demand for money function. Under the second, the central bank determined the money supply independently and let the interest rate find its own level. Monetarists preferred the second approach and were inclined to recommend control of the narrowest aggregate, the monetary base. By contrast, most central bankers preferred to smooth interest rates for the convenience of financial market participants, including governments, and found monetarist proposals disconcerting (Capie *et al.* 1994: 85). The upshot was often a fudge. But this was not the only complication. It was relatively easy to control a narrow monetary aggregate such as the monetary base, but the link from the monetary base to spending and inflation was tenuous. Controlling a broader aggregate such as M3 was very much harder, but arguably more relevant to the control of spending and inflation.

Monetary targeting gradually fell out of favour in the 1980s. Hitting the targets proved embarrassingly difficult. The velocity of circulation (or demand for money) became less predictable in the early 1980s (Capie, Goodhart, and Schnadt 1994: 31) because of the development of new financial products including interest bearing current accounts, the growing use and sophistication of computer and communications technology, and the drive towards financial deregulation. The early 1980s saw an international recession and mass unemployment. Tighter monetary policy quelled inflation, but at the cost of deepening this recession. The high transitional costs of disinflation stemmed from wage and price rigidities that were more persistent than some monetarists had anticipated. In other words the public doubted the resolve of monetary policy makers. Monetary targeting was in some respects a cover for an old-fashioned policy of deflation implemented by central bankers and a new wave of politicians who took the scourge of inflation more seriously than their predecessors. In the next sections we look in more detail at the control of inflation in West Germany, the UK, and the USA.

West Germany

Following the end of the Bretton Woods system the Bundesbank began to work towards a new strategy for maintaining the value of the DM. The exchange rate was not completely free because of Western Germany's participation in the 'snake', the forerunner of the European Monetary System (EMS). Domestically, the Bundesbank was under pressure to accommodate wage increases and higher oil prices. In 1973, however, the Bundesbank asserted that its main priority was fighting inflation (Issing 2005: 331). But how could low inflation be achieved in the environment of the mid 1970s? One option was to focus on control of the money stock, but it could not be taken for granted that this proposal would gain the upper hand at senior levels of the central bank. Von Hagen (1999: 425) argues that the decision to announce a monetary target was driven by tactical considerations. In 1974 support was growing within the Bundesbank for relaxing monetary policy in order to revive growth and employment. At the same time German central bankers were anxious not to give the public and wage negotiators the impression that they were going soft on inflation. In December 1974 the Bundesbank announced that it would aim for 8 per cent annual growth in central bank money (CBM), a broad monetary aggregate, in 1975. As CBM was rising at the rate of 6 per cent per annum during 1974, this represented a modest relaxation. Adoption of the targeting framework was meant to convey the Bundesbank's commitment to a more systematic approach to monetary control.

Monetary targeting explains only part of the Bundesbank's success in restraining inflation. The West Germans were comparatively inflation averse long before monetary targeting was introduced. Some monetary expansion occurred during the oil crisis, but not as much as elsewhere. The targeting strategy introduced in December 1974 was 'experimental' (Issing 2005: 330) for the first few years. The Bundesbank accepted that a small amount of inflation was unavoidable and built this into the targets. Deviations from target were justified from time to time on the grounds that low inflation was not the only concern of policy makers. This was the stance taken in 1977 when real growth was weak and the DM was appreciating.

The CBM target was overshot every year until 1979. Von Hagen (1999: 42–3) suggests that the Bundesbank might not have persevered with monetary targeting in the absence of a new development, namely the EMS. Established in 1978 with the endorsement of the French and West German governments, the EMS was a further attempt to peg exchange rates within Europe. If monetary targeting had been abandoned at this juncture, the public might have concluded that the Bundesbank viewed the EMS as an insuperable obstacle to the control of inflation. At the very least, the advent of the EMS strengthened the hands of the supporters of monetary targeting within the Bundesbank.

Between 1979 and 1981, the Bundesbank tightened the monetary targets in response to a new outbreak of inflationary pressure. This proved to be another decisive episode for the targeting regime. The Bundesbank was not deflected from tight money by the second oil shock, a stagnant economy, or rising unemployment. Only when inflation was receding in 1982 did the Bundesbank relent somewhat (Baltensperger 1999: 441–54). What mattered most in West Germany (and in other countries) was not the adoption of a monetary targeting framework, but rather the underlying resolve of the authorities to control inflation (Issing 1997). West Germany persisted with monetary targets until the late 1990s and the formation of the European Central Bank.

The United Kingdom

Though the 1974–9 British Labour government introduced monetary targets, it was not until the election of the Conservatives, led by Margaret Thatcher, in 1979 that fighting inflation became the top priority and monetary targeting took centre-stage (Britton 1994). Thatcher made no secret of the fact that she was attracted to monetarist doctrine. In her view the Bank of England was ideologically impure and lacking in backbone – 'wet' in the lingo of the 1980s. Thatcher preferred to take advice from leading monetarist academics, including Alan Walters (1986), as well as from the Treasury. The Bank of England and Gordon Richardson, who remained Governor until 1983, were marginalised in policy discussions; nevertheless the central bank was responsible for implementing the government's monetary policy (Kynaston 1995: 31–2).

Inflation was accelerating when the Conservatives came to power, peaking at 22 per cent per annum in May 1980. The new government announced a target of 7 to 11 per cent growth in sterling M3 (£M3) for the 1979–80 year. Interest rates were increased to levels deemed consistent with the achievement of this target. In 1980 the government published a Medium Term Financial Strategy, which included plans for increasingly stringent monetary targets as well as fiscal retrenchment. Elements of the government were eager to introduce monetary base control, but the Bank of England resisted this suggestion on the grounds that it would cause undue instability in interest rates. The Thatcher government accompanied monetary targeting with a programme of financial liberalisation. Many of the remaining direct controls over the banking sector – these had already been trimmed in the early 1970s – were abolished, as were exchange controls. Together with financial innovation, the trend towards financial deregulation and increased competition made it harder for the authorities to manage £M3, and the early targets were overshot. A debate ensued over whether £M3 was a good indicator of the tightness of monetary policy (Goodhart 2004: 354). Even so, inflation started to fall. Higher interest rates, combined with sterling's status as a petro-currency, brought about a rapid appreciation in the exchange rate, a serious recession, and the worst unemployment since the 1930s. In 1982 the government announced targets for M1 and private sector liquidity (PSL2) as well as £M3, encouraging cynics to suggest that this increased the chances of hitting at least one of them (Howson 1994: 251).

In the mid 1980s the Conservative government experimented briefly with monetary base control. But it proved difficult to make any sort of monetary target stick. The link between money growth and inflation in practice was very imprecise. The monetarist framework was wound down, and in 1987 the government ceased to announce monetary targets. Inflation had been slain (at least temporarily) by tight monetary policy and slackness in the real economy. Monetary targeting had in essence been a symbol of the government's determination to overcome inflation by any means. Believing that inflation had been quashed, the government loosened monetary policy in the second half of the 1980s, and gravitated towards a strategy of shadowing the DM – an informal exchange rate target.

The USA

The Volcker disinflation was equally dramatic. Paul Volcker was appointed as the chairman of the Fed's Board of Governors by President Jimmy Carter in August 1979. He succeeded William Miller, who is generally remembered as an ineffective and compromising chairman. Volcker, an inflation hawk, subscribed to a pessimistic view of the natural rate of unemployment. He was convinced, moreover, that inflation would respond eventually to the creation of slack in the economy.

Since 1975 Congress had required regular consultations with the Fed on its plans for the monetary and credit aggregates (Volcker 1978). Under the Full Employment and Balanced Growth (or Humphrey–Hawkins)

Act 1978 the FOMC had to set goals for the monetary and credit aggregates, and defend them before Congress. In practice, the Fed set targets
for both monetary growth and a short-term interest rate, the federal
funds rate. Whilst these targets were supposed to be compatible, it was
actually quite difficult to achieve them both at once, and when push
came to shove 'the trading desk was instructed to give precedence to
the federal funds rate target' (Mishkin 1995: 562). In October 1979,
Volcker introduced radical new operating procedures, based on controlling the path of non-borrowed bank reserves (Hetzel 2008: 151–71).
OMOs would be conducted so as to render the level of non-borrowed
reserves consistent with the announced targets for M1A, M1B, M2, M3
and commercial bank credit. The targets for non-borrowed reserves
were not revealed (Gilbert and Trebbing 1981). The federal funds rate
was allowed to fluctuate within wide bands. In essence, Volcker had
switched from an interest rate target to something approaching a monetary base target.

Volcker set out his philosophy in the March 1980 Federal Reserve
Bulletin:

In the past, at critical junctures for economic stabilization policy, we have usually been more preoccupied with the possibility of near-term weakness in economic activity or other objectives than with the implications of our actions
for future inflation ... The result has been our now chronic inflationary problem ... The broad objective of policy must be to break that ominous pattern ...
Success will require that policy be consistently and persistently oriented to that
end. Vacillation and procrastination, out of fears of recession or otherwise,
would run grave risks. (Quoted in Romer and Romer 2004: 145)

In reality Volcker's Fed was not always as single-minded as his mani-
festo promised. Interest rates rose sharply between August 1979 and
April 1980, but the Fed then hesitated in the light of a weakening real
economy and panic in the Carter administration. Not until the end of
1980, after the election of a more supportive president, Ronald Reagan,
did Volcker and the Fed return to the attack on inflation (Goodfriend
and King 2005). At the end of 1980 inflation was running at 12 per
cent per annum. The federal funds rate was permitted to rise by 600
basis points in November and December alone. Monetary stringency
was maintained during 1981, the Fed opting to sacrifice recovery
from the 1980 downturn in order to smash inflation. It is unlikely that
Martin or Burns, let alone Miller, would have acted with Volcker's
resolve.

Having witnessed a significant fall in inflationary pressure in
1982, the Fed reverted to 'business as usual' in October. Henceforth

monetary targets were given less prominence. Indeed the Fed covertly resumed the management of the federal funds rate. Volcker became more responsive to the level of slack in the economy. This was a slap in the face for monetarists, and a sign that the Federal Reserve, like many other central banks, was essentially pragmatic. Monetary targeting had been deployed for a purpose and then returned to its box. Friedman (Nelson, E. 2007b: 168) was singularly unimpressed, yet Volcker had achieved his primary objective.

Conclusion

The horse of inflation was allowed to bolt in the late 1960s and 1970s because of a combination of political constraints, theoretical turmoil, measurement problems, and monetary neglect. Until the collapse of the Bretton Woods regime, moreover, the US exported inflation to Europe, Japan, and other areas of the world. The solution to inflation would not be found until inflation was recognised as the critical macroeconomic problem, a more urgent one even than full employment or growth. West Germany, Switzerland, and Japan reached this point in the mid 1970s; the UK, the USA, and many other countries reached it a few years later. To some extent this shift in priorities reflected a changing of the guard, especially in the UK and the USA, with the advent of Thatcher and Volcker. It is not surprising that West Germany, with its distinctive monetary history, was in the forefront of the battle against inflation. A change in the intellectual climate brought renewed emphasis on inflation as a monetary problem, while a change in the political climate reflected greater aversion to inflation.

Monetary targeting provided the Bundesbank and its peers with a new anti-inflationary policy framework, but for most central bankers it remained a technique rather than an ideology. The monetarists found lukewarm and backsliding converts in the world of central banking. Reflecting on British and American experience with monetary targeting, Charles Goodhart (1989: 377) notes that whatever its theoretical and practical defects, this approach facilitated 'much tighter [monetary] policies, high interest rates (US) and a higher exchange rate (UK), than would have been adopted under more discretionary management. This did cause such severe deflation that inflation and inflationary expectations and psychology were tamed, if not broken.' The cost was much higher, especially in jobs, than had been anticipated. To use a phrase that gained currency in a different context in the 1990s, policy makers 'just did it' (McCallum 1995).

The great inflation and disinflation restored central banks to a vital place in the economic policy community. Almost everyone now accepted that monetary policy mattered, and that central banks were the professionals in this field. The status of central banks rose between the 1960s and 1980s, despite their reluctance to embrace hardline monetarism, and the embarrassment of missed monetary targets. Central banks had indeed come in from the cold.

12   The second central banking revolution: independence and accountability

> So complete is the consensus which now exists over the desirability of central bank independence that it is possible to forget how quickly it emerged.
>
> James Forder (2005: 843–4)

> In your deliberations on the future charter for central banking in Europe, I commend to you the example of New Zealand – though in so doing, I am conscious that my remarks may sound somewhat arrogant in view of the shortness of our history of central banking, and the recent nature of our adoption of the framework.
>
> Don Brash, Governor of the RBNZ, at Bank of England Tercentenary Symposium, 1993 (Brash 1994: 315)

The doctrine of central bank independence (CBI), as developed in the 1980s and 1990s, acquired an almost mystical status. The growing emphasis on CBI was one of the two principal characteristics of the second revolution in central banking, the other being inflation targeting. Central banks attained a higher level of prestige and influence in the 1990s than at any time since the 1920s. According to McNamara (2002), at least thirty-eight countries were granted 'legal' CBI between 1989 and 1999. Her list includes developed, developing, and transitional countries, but not those where CBI assumed a less formal character.

CBI is a difficult concept to define and measure; the associated concepts of accountability and transparency are no less slippery. Forder argues that 'those with the most to gain from central bank independence are central banks' (Forder 2002: 52). Yet the most ardent proponents of CBI were academic economists and politicians. Central bankers themselves could not afford to participate in what was after all a political debate on the nature of the relationship between the central bank and the state. The style of CBI varied considerably. Some countries enshrined CBI in new legislation, others reinterpreted existing legislation to permit greater autonomy; but for some CBI was little more than window dressing. Why did so many central banks achieve greater autonomy in the late twentieth century? What form did CBI take? And how were independent central banks held accountable? These are some of the questions examined below. Pride of place will go to the RBNZ, the pioneer of a new type of CBI.

The arguments

Central bank independence and accountability are not new ideas. Government–central bank relations were discussed in a sophisticated manner in the interwar period by Kisch and Elkin (1932) and Keynes (Bibow 2002). Nor is the debate over the autonomy and accountability of policy making institutions confined to central banking. Similar issues crop up in public sector auditing (Green and Singleton 2009) and military campaigns.

After 1945 most central banks were accountable to ministers, but not to society as a whole except in a sense during major probes such as the Radcliffe enquiry in the UK or the Porter Commission enquiry in Canada. National variations in central bank autonomy were significant but hard to pin down. The Bundesbank was highly independent and barely accountable to anyone. Though the Bank of England lacked formal independence, it retained considerable prestige and the capacity to influence events behind the scenes. The Federal Reserve System was ultimately accountable to Congress. Critics said that the Fed was in reality either a tool of politicians *or* an unaccountable bureaucratic empire.

According to Goodhart, Capie, and Schnadt (1994: 48–9), central banking history is marked by alternating periods of high and low independence. The pendulum swings in response to dissatisfaction with the status quo. The mid twentieth century saw the repudiation of the brand of CBI associated with the gold standard. In the late twentieth century, however, a new type of CBI was forged in reaction to many years of political interference and inflation. CBI today is rather different from CBI before 1914. In many (but not all) cases, the relationship between the central bank, the government, and society is now set out with greater precision. 'Instrument independence' or operational autonomy is distinguished from 'goal independence' or the capacity of the central bank to set its own objectives. It is now accepted that CBI should be combined with arrangements to ensure 'accountability', though there is no consensus as to the form of accountability. Transparency is often viewed as vital for accountability and for the smooth implementation of monetary policy (Siklos 2002). The contemporary focus on transparency is a genuine innovation (Geraats 2002).

Central bank reform coincided with a wider programme of public sector restructuring in the late twentieth century. Rejection of Beatrice

Webb's vision of public servants as a '"Jesuitical corps" of ascetic zealots' was central to the thinking of public sector reformers (Hood 1995: 94). Studies of the 'new public management' in the 1980s and 1990s discuss accountability and rules versus discretion in the context of the public sector as a whole (Hood 1995: 96). Advocates of public sector reform regarded civil servants and politicians as self-interested actors. Civil servants spent taxpayers' funds on their own empires, while politicians manipulated public sector agencies to buy votes. Under the principles of the new public management, public sector entities were (if not privatised) to be run in a businesslike manner. Managers were given clear objectives, and ministers were expected to refrain from interfering in operational matters. Public sector managers were held to account for their performance in relation to targets. The link between central banking and public sector reform was explicit in New Zealand (Singleton *et al.* 2006: ch. 5) but not well articulated elsewhere.

New public management and CBI are not identical. Most central banks, including those owned by the state, denied being members of the public sector proper. Central bankers were more successful than civil servants at parrying the charge that they were self-interested bureaucrats, perhaps because of their carefully cultivated mystique and prestige. The bureaucratic critique of central banks, which blossomed in the 1970s, was curiously peripheral to the CBI debate in the 1980s (Forder 2002: 52). Rogoff's (1985) proposal that monetary policy should be delegated to a 'conservative central banker' evokes an image of central bankers as selfless foes of inflation.

Economists and political economists explain the resurgence of CBI in different ways. Whereas economists emphasise public recognition of the economic benefits of CBI, political economists look for the political motives of those who redesigned central banks (King, Michael 2005: 95).

A string of almost canonical articles on CBI and accountability was published from the mid 1970s onwards. Kydland and Prescott (1977), followed by Calvo (1978), and Barro and Gordon (1983a), predicted that monetary policy would be implemented in a time inconsistent manner when central banks had discretion, especially when they were under the sway of governments. How could the authorities commit themselves to anti-inflationary policies, and establish credibility in the eyes of the public? Barro and Gordon (1983b) thought that a reputation for inflation aversion could be earned over time by resisting temptation. Arguably this was what the Bundesbank had done. Rogoff (1985) suggested delegating monetary policy to an independent central banker (or central bank) with preferences that are more inflation averse than those of society in general. Conservative central bankers would be in a better position to establish credibility, but how were they to be held accountable for results, and what would prevent the state from overriding their decisions? Persson and Tabellini (1993) favoured a contract between the central bank and the government that would rule out political interference. Walsh (1995b) argued that the contract should specify a precise objective, and that the governor should be punished, possibly by dismissal, if it was missed. Walsh addressed the question of accountability in an uncompromising way, and his solution was not meant to appeal to central bankers. Lohmann (1992) accepted that CBI must be contingent. Ministers should be able to override an independent central bank in special circumstances, but only if this was done with full public scrutiny. The distinction between goal and instrument independence was made by Debelle and Fischer (1994): the state should set the objective (or objectives) of monetary policy, while allowing the central bank freedom in operational matters. The benefits of CBI in terms of lowering inflation without causing serious damage to the real economy were demonstrated empirically, notably by Cukierman (1992: 347–455), though not to universal satisfaction.

During the 1990s the debate over CBI and accountability overlapped with that on inflation targeting (Blinder 1998). Both debates were informed increasingly by experience, not least by the dramatic reforms in New Zealand. Ultimately, however, there are no final answers to the questions posed by CBI and accountability, and this was recognised by some economists and practitioners, including Mervyn King (2004) who, as governor of the Bank of England and a former professor of economics at the London School of Economics, had a foot in both camps. Whatever the current benefits of delegating monetary policy to an independent central bank, the institutional framework cannot be set in stone. Not only is it impossible, said King, to tie the hands of later generations in the area of institutional design, but it is impossible to predict what arrangements and policies will be most effective and appropriate in the future.

There was an undercurrent of criticism, but it was relatively ineffective. Milton Friedman (1982) had long opposed CBI, partly on the grounds that central banks were wasteful bureaucracies. His monetary rule did not require an independent central bank, merely constitutional backing. Blinder (1998) was not convinced that central banks engaged in time inconsistent behaviour. Other economists called into question the methods used to measure CBI, and the robustness of the causal link from CBI to low inflation. There was often a discrepancy between what the law said about the independence of a central bank, and its level of independence in practice. Vicarelli (1988: 9) argued that central bank autonomy depended on the personality of the governor. A survey of central bankers and economists in the late 1990s suggested that a good track record was more important than CBI for establishing credibility (Blinder 2000). Many countries, including New Zealand, waited until *after* inflation had fallen to moderate levels before adopting CBI. Japan introduced legal CBI in the late 1990s, a period marked by alternating price stability and mild deflation. It was unclear whether the advocates of CBI preferred rules or discretion – they seemed to want a bit of both. Independent central banks were criticised for not being adequately accountable. The conservative central banker was accused of rigidity and indifference to the real economy (Forder 2005; Bibow 2004; Stiglitz 1998). Debate on these questions continues (de Haan, Masciandaro, and Quintyn 2008). For countries that have already reduced inflation, CBI may act as a barrier to the re-emergence of time-inconsistent behaviour.

Academic economists offered a rationale for CBI, but the critical decisions on central bank reform were made by governments and legislators. What justifications for CBI might appeal to politicians (King, Michael 2005: 99–100)? First, the adoption of CBI sends a signal to international capital markets that prudent, anti-inflationary policies will be followed. Consequently, it might become easier and cheaper to borrow externally (Maxfield 1997). This argument, which is of greatest relevance to developing and transitional countries, is equivalent to the claim that joining the gold standard reduced the cost of borrowing for peripheral economies in the early twentieth century. Second, the domestic financial sector could put pressure on the government to introduce CBI because high and variable inflation creates uncertainty and may be harmful for business (Posen 1995). Thirdly, politicians might find it convenient to delegate monetary policy to the central bank, irrespective of external pressure (Bernhard, Broz, and Clark 2002), especially if monetary management is a source of discord at the cabinet table. It might be useful to leave unpopular decisions, such as raising interest rates, to central bankers. Under CBI, moreover, politicians have greater scope to engage in central bank 'bashing'. At the same time, some politicians will find it hard to choose between a dependent central bank that can be manipulated, and an independent central bank that can be tormented (Havrilesky 1995). Fourthly, when granting autonomy to the central bank, the intention of the government might be to constrain the monetary policies of future regimes. This motive was a major consideration in New Zealand, as well as in Chile and Mexico (Boylan 2001).

The various political rationales for CBI are not mutually exclusive, nor are they necessarily at odds with the economic rationale for CBI. Many factors affected the decision to adopt CBI in the 1990s, just as many factors influenced the decision to set up central banks earlier in the twentieth century.

Reform of the RBNZ

New Zealand was the first country to take into account the new economic thinking on CBI when rewriting its central bank statutes. Because the 1989 RBNZ Act was so distinctive it stimulated a further round of debate on CBI and accountability among academics and central bankers (Singleton *et al.* 2006).

New Zealand's central bank ranked poorly in terms of legal and practical independence in the 1970s and 1980s. It operated under the terms of the 1964 amendment to the Reserve Bank Act, which stated that:

[T]he Minister [of Finance] may from time to time communicate to the bank the monetary policy of the Government, which shall be directed to the maintenance and promotion of economic and social welfare in New Zealand having regard to the desirability of promoting the highest degree of production, trade, and employment and of maintaining a stable internal price level. (Quoted in Singleton *et al.* 2006: 15)

In other words, the central bank was expected to follow the government's orders. New Zealand's macroeconomic performance became increasingly volatile in the mid-1970s. Inflation rates were high and variable. The banking sector was subject to tight regulation. Bank interest rates were controlled by the state until 1977–8. Monetary policy was implemented by varying the reserve asset ratio of the banks and through other regulations. Policy was accommodating much of the time, as the government sought to counteract the impact of the oil shocks and other disturbances on real incomes and employment. The most peculiar feature of the New Zealand scene was the dominant role of Robert Muldoon (Gustafson 2000), the prime minister *and* minister of finance from 1975 to 1984. An accountant by training, Muldoon was a populist and a bully. By the early 1980s, Muldoon was convinced that he understood the economy far better than did his official advisors, and he ceased to listen to them. One governor of the RBNZ decided not to seek a second term because he had had enough of Muldoon; his successor was instructed to retire early.

Frustrated by the economic situation, Muldoon lurched towards greater interventionism in the early 1980s. He reintroduced interest rate controls, imposed a compulsory wage–price freeze, and reverted from a crawling peg to a fixed exchange rate. The RBNZ and the Treasury advised against these policies, but Muldoon dismissed all criticism. During the wage–price-interest rate–exchange rate freeze of 1982–4, New Zealand was the most regulated 'first world' country (OECD 1983a).

A tipsy Muldoon announced a surprise election in June 1984. Muldoon's National Party was defeated and a Labour government was formed. Labour's economic policy was driven by Roger Douglas, a recent convert to free market ideas. Labour devalued in July 1984 and floated the currency in March 1985. Controls over interest rates, bank reserves, and international capital flows were abolished. Monetary conditions were now determined in the market. The central bank focused on controlling the monetary base, and on assisting the government to plan and manage debt sales to the public. Nominal interest rates were permitted to find their own level. With the abolition of wage, price, and credit controls, there was an initial surge in inflation, but high interest rates and an appreciating exchange rate began to take their toll, and by 1987 the inflation rate was in retreat (RBNZ 1986, 1993b).

The RBNZ welcomed the broad thrust of Labour's policy. Douglas was willing to take advice, and to discuss his plans with the central bank. The change in government had substituted a sympathetic minister for a contemptuous one, but the minister still called the shots. Douglas was uncomfortable with this situation, and in March 1986 he informed the RBNZ board that he had asked the governor (Spencer Russell) to consider new legislation to give the central bank more independence and more responsibility for policy formulation (RBNZ Archives 1986). Douglas later explained to Parliament that he wished 'to make certain that no future politician can interfere with the Bank's primary objective of ensuring price stability, or manipulate its operations for their own purposes, without facing the full force of public scrutiny' (quoted in Singleton et al. 2006: 138). In essence, Douglas wanted to 'Muldoon-proof' the RBNZ. He envisaged a price stability mandate for monetary policy, and the overhaul of the central bank's decision-making mechanisms and accountability.

Douglas's initiative coincided with a wave of public sector reform. Treasury contemplated turning the RBNZ into a state-owned enterprise, along the lines of the railways, Air New Zealand, and the power utilities. This was an alarming prospect for the central bank. In July 1986 Russell responded to Douglas, noting that price stability was essential for good economic performance, and suggesting that an agency with operational independence would be better placed to achieve this outcome than one subordinated to the needs of fiscal policy. The state-owned enterprise model was rejected by Russell, but no blueprint was advanced at this stage.

Battle was joined in November 1986 when the Treasury sent the central bank a proposal for converting it into a profit-maximising state-owned enterprise. This unpalatable scheme forced the RBNZ to think more deeply about what a central bank ought to do, and how its relationship with government should be structured. Senior RBNZ officials and economists were conversant with the literature on time inconsistency and credibility, and their insights influenced the central bank's response. At a joint meeting with the Treasury in 1987, the RBNZ suggested a two-pronged approach. The first prong involved monetary policy independence, with a primary goal of price stability, and perhaps a secondary goal of financial stability. The second prong involved greater accountability and incentives. Significantly, the RBNZ was anxious to retain an independent income stream, for how could a central bank that depended on the government for every cent claim to be independent?

Douglas encouraged a wide debate. He did not give the RBNZ carte blanche to determine its own future. At one meeting of officials, tempers flared and a central banker threatened to take a Treasury official outside and thump him. The RBNZ called for reinforcements, including Charles Goodhart of the London School of Economics, who argued that the New Zealand Treasury was mired in the controversies of the 1840s. Some of the Treasury's rhetoric about performance indicators and outputs sounded annoying and trivial to central bankers. (It also sounded annoying and trivial to other professional groups such as government engineers and doctors.) But the Treasury's insistence that new central bank legislation should incorporate criteria for measuring success or failure, and a mechanism for holding someone accountable for results, including the efficient use of resources, was fundamentally reasonable. Many matters were difficult to resolve. How many monetary policy objectives should there be? Should the central bank be answerable to Parliament or to the government? Should the board or the governor alone be held responsible? Should the government have the power to override policy decisions? Who should determine the central bank's budget? In 1987 Douglas delegated oversight of the central bank project to a more junior minister, Peter Neilson, who believed that the governor alone should be held to account for the central bank's performance. Neilson and the RBNZ agreed on a legislative proposal in 1988. Two years of debate, much of it conducted from first principles, ensured that the RBNZ Act 1989 was original. The new act came into force in February 1990.

According to the 1989 Act, the 'primary function of the [Reserve] Bank is to formulate and implement monetary policy directed to the economic objective of achieving and maintaining stability in the general level of prices'. There was no mandate to pursue additional objectives such as full employment or economic growth. As well as striving for stable prices, the RBNZ was required to promote the systemic stability and efficiency of the financial sector. Responsibility for monetary policy operations lay with the governor alone. The governor was appointed by the government for a five-year term, but could not take office until he or she had negotiated a Policy Targets Agreement (PTA) with the minister of finance. The PTA gave precision to the central bank's primary objective, and in practice was couched in terms of an inflation target. After signing the PTA, the governor was free to take whatever policy actions were necessary to attain the target. All operational decisions were made by the governor, who was advised by a staff monetary policy committee. The governor's performance vis-à-vis the PTA target was monitored by the RBNZ's directors in consultation with the minister of finance. Any breach of the target would have to be explained, and in the worst case the governor could be dismissed. The government could override the PTA in an emergency – a suggestion of Goodhart – but would have to do so openly and not in secret. The governor was obliged to report to the public on the Bank's activities and plans, for example through regular monetary policy statements and appearances before a Parliamentary committee (Dawe 1990). Under the 1989 Act the objectives of the RBNZ were much more transparent than before. There was no leeway for time inconsistent actions. As the 1989 Act was so radical, the increase in transparency helped to secure its legitimacy. The Act also addressed resource use by requiring the governor and the minister to negotiate a funding agreement, setting out the central bank's permitted expenditure. Excess expenditure would be scrutinised by the board and Parliament. Management became much more focused on operating efficiently (Singleton et al. 2006: ch. 8).

The changes to objective setting, accountability, and internal financial management were similar to those faced by state agencies in New Zealand. Several innovative features deserve comment. The 1989 Act distinguished between goal and operational independence in anticipation of Debelle and Fischer (1994). The contractual nature of the relationship between the governor and the minister helped to spark academic debate on central bank contracts (Walsh 1995b). New Zealand's solution to the problems of central bank accountability and incentives was praised by a leading academic (Walsh 1995a). Don Brash, who became governor in 1988, was at first surprised at the extent of his personal responsibility under the forthcoming legislation. The minister told him: 'We can't fire the whole Bank. Realistically, we can't even fire the whole Board. But we sure as hell can fire you' (Brash 2002: 66). However, when the RBNZ exceeded its inflation target several times in the mid 1990s, Brash was let off with a caution (Singleton *et al.* 2006: 184–92).

The RBNZ was one of the most independent central banks in the world in the 1990s (Siklos 2002: 68). Whilst the decision to reform the Reserve Bank Act had its origins in political economy considerations – the need to Muldoon-proof the central bank – the content of the new legislation was a product of engagement with the relevant literature on economics and public management. The RBNZ succeeded on the whole in controlling inflation under the new framework, and government interference at the operational level has not been detected.

Central bank reform in the 1990s

The 1990s brought sweeping institutional reforms in central banking. These reforms cannot be attributed to any single factor such as the influence of the New Zealand model. Indeed the Bundesbank continued to offer an alternative model of CBI – one with an impressive track record, despite major shortcomings in the realm of accountability. Several aspects of the 1989 RBNZ Act lacked widespread appeal, including the heavy reliance on a contract, and the concentration of power and responsibility in one individual. Of much greater interest, especially in countries struggling with high inflation, were the single-minded focus on price stability and the safeguards against government interference in operational matters.

States that intended to participate in European Economic and Monetary Union (EMU) were legally bound by the Treaty on European Union to grant their central banks more autonomy prior to the formation of the European Central Bank (ECB). For example, the Bank of Italy and the Banque de France achieved independence with respect to the conduct of monetary policy in 1992 and 1993 respectively (McNamara 2002: 65–6). The ECB, created in 1998, became the world's most independent central bank as a result of political deals in the 1980s and 1990s (EMU and the ECB are discussed in Chapter 15). The weak accountability of the ECB (Forder 2002) is reminiscent of the situation at the Bundesbank, which should be no surprise because the ECB's 'role model' was the West German central bank (Baltensperger 1999: 513).

CBI spread rapidly to other parts of the world, including Asia (after the financial crisis of 1997–8), Africa, and Latin America. The unravelling of the Soviet empire led to the establishment of new central banks as well as the modernisation of existing ones. East European and central Asian countries were anxious to signal their respectability to international investors by introducing CBI. But the commitment of some of these countries to this principle should not be taken at face value: new central bank laws often combined elements of window dressing and wishful thinking. One recent study finds the central bank of Kazakhstan to be more independent overall than the RBNZ. While scoring highly in some areas, however, the central bank of Kazakhstan does not shine in accountability and transparency (Ahsan, Skully, and Wickramanayake 2007: 15–16), casting doubt on the result.

Not all countries saw a need to alter their central banking laws. The Reserve Bank of Australia (RBA) continued to operate under existing legislation, which was reinterpreted to give more de facto autonomy to the central bank (Bell, S. 2004). Similarly, there was no significant change in US central banking legislation. Yet much was made of CBI in both countries. The ethos of CBI could be powerful even in the absence of confirmatory legislation. It was not necessary to resort to legislation unless there was a clear perception that existing arrangements were untenable, or there were special circumstances such as EMU in western Europe and the transition to capitalism in eastern Europe.

A makeover for the Old Lady

The Conservative governments of Margaret Thatcher and John Major between 1979 and 1997 were divided over CBI. It was not until the advent of a Labour government in 1997 that the autonomy of the Bank of England was given statutory recognition. But the Bank of England Act 1998 was not a crisis measure. Inflation was under control, and there were no irresistible pressures for reform from either domestic or foreign financial interests. Rather Tony Blair's Labour government was anxious to consolidate its electoral victory by demonstrating conservative credentials in the economic policy field (King, Michael 2005).

Thatcher had insisted that it would be a sign of weakness for her government to relinquish control of monetary policy before the inflationary dragon, which showed signs of new life in the late 1980s, was finally slain. She was not interested in tying the hands of future governments, for she could not imagine defeat. Thatcher's chancellor during the second half of the 1980s, Nigel Lawson, had different ideas, and he presented her with a scheme for an autonomous central bank with a mandate to protect the stability of the currency. After losing the debate with Thatcher, Lawson used his resignation speech in 1989 to bring the issue of CBI into the open (Lawson 1992: 867–73, 1059–64; Thatcher 1993: 706–8).

Following the 1992 sterling crisis, when the UK was forced to leave the European Exchange Rate Mechanism (ERM), the credibility of British monetary policy was in tatters. Norman Lamont, the chancellor, called for the adoption of CBI in order to restore confidence in British policy. Major rejected this suggestion because his government was split between pro and anti-European factions. Since CBI was a requirement for participation in EMU, the Eurosceptics might regard reform of the Bank of England as part a conspiracy to scrap the pound in favour of the proposed common currency. For tactical reasons, Major also wanted to retain the power to make interest rate decisions. In his resignation speech in 1993, Lamont called for the Bank of England to be made independent.

The mid 1990s witnessed two important studies of CBI. Lord Roll of SG Warburg, a merchant bank, chaired a City group that investigated CBI and the accountability of the Bank of England. A House of Commons committee also conducted a detailed study of the options for central bank reform. Alternative models of CBI were evaluated, including those of New Zealand, Germany, and the USA. Each model had pros and cons, and none provided a complete blueprint for the Bank of England (Roll 1993; Treasury and Civil Service Committee 1993–4). Both reports favoured an autonomous central bank, but a convincing proposal with strong cross-party support failed to emerge. The government made some concessions by increasing transparency, and delegating some additional powers to the Bank of England, but it did not endorse the call for CBI.

Meanwhile the opposition Labour Party was holding talks with foreign central bankers and academics. Labour was struggling to shake off its old image as the party of high inflation. If Labour intended to win consecutive elections it would have to appear competent, prudent, and disciplined. Ed Balls, a financial journalist and Labour advisor, introduced the prospective chancellor, Gordon Brown, to leading central bankers including Don Brash and Alan Greenspan. Labour was pledged to restructure the Bank of England, and to enhance its accountability and autonomy, but a decision on CBI was not made until shortly before the 1997 election. Brown did not reveal his plans for CBI to Eddie George, the governor, until after the election. According to Michael King (2005: 108), George was astonished by this development. The Bank of England had not lobbied for CBI, nor could it have done.

The new Bank of England Act came into force in June 1998 (Rodgers 1998). Priority was accorded to price stability, but the central bank was also required to strive for other macroeconomic objectives, including growth and employment, provided that the primary objective was not undermined. The Bank of England was stripped of the banking supervision function, which passed to the new Financial Services Authority, but it continued to be responsible for systemic stability. In 1998 responsibility for the management of government debt was transferred to the Treasury.

Bean (1998) found the British version of CBI to have more in common with the RBNZ than the Bundesbank model, since it entails operational but not goal independence. The chancellor sets the target (in practice a point inflation target) and this is handed down to the central bank. The Bank of England is then free to conduct monetary policy operations as it sees fit in order to fulfil the target. A high degree of transparency is ensured by regular reporting to the public and Parliament, for example through the release of minutes of the expert Monetary Policy Committee (MPC) after a six-week delay. This reporting also contributes to accountability. However, there are significant differences between the British and New Zealand frameworks. The governor is not as dominant or as exposed in the UK. Interest rate decisions are made collectively by the MPC, which is chaired by the governor. The governor is not held personally accountable for success or failure in attaining the target. Policy makers must render account to the Court (in effect the board), the chancellor, and the Treasury Select Committee of the House of Commons. Accountability is diluted when decisions are taken by a committee, but most economists now believe that policy is best made by a group rather than by an individual (Blinder 2007).

CBI in Asia

How did Asian countries respond to the new thinking emanating from North America, New Zealand, and western Europe? Not only was CBI fashionable, but it was relatively easy for government lawyers to draw up state of the art legislation. However, the extent to which support for CBI was genuine varied from case to case.

Language was used in a different way in Asia than in the west. In 1983 the People's Bank of China (PBC) became a genuine central bank when its commercial banking functions were spun off into new state-owned commercial banks. The PBC was separated from the Ministry of Finance in 1984. The PBC Law 1995 gave formal recognition to the central bank's responsibilities for monetary policy and banking supervision, and stated that central bank was to 'independently implement monetary policies' under the 'leadership of the State Council' (Chung and Tongzon 2004: 89). A monetary policy committee was created, supposedly along the lines of the FOMC. While the PBC Law was a step towards modernity, the references to independence were misleading (Goodfriend and Prasad 2006). Appointments to senior positions were still made on political grounds. The State Planning Commission and the Central Financial Work Committee, a Communist Party cell, continued to intervene in policy formulation. In addition, regional branches of the PBC, having fallen under the sway of local politicians, often ignored instructions on lending policy from headquarters (Chung and Tongzon 2004: 91–3).

Japan was the most advanced Asian economy, though its performance in the 1990s was blighted by stagnation, financial turmoil, and even a measure of deflation. Against this background of failure, the Bank of Japan was granted independence from the government in 1998. Relations between the Japanese central bank and the Ministry of Finance were ambiguous under the Bank of Japan Law 1942. Although the central bank often seemed to be under the thumb of the Ministry of Finance, it was capable of acting decisively from time to time. The central bank's comparative success in restraining inflation during the 1970s increased its authority within the policy-making community. Governor Mieno's pricking of the asset price bubble in the early 1990s involved a strong assertion of autonomy (Cargill, Hutchison, and Ito 2001). The Ministry of Finance, which was responsible for prudential supervision, came under heavy criticism when many financial institutions descended into crisis in the 1990s. Dissatisfaction with the Ministry of Finance intensified, not least in the Diet (Dwyer 2004). Since politicians were afraid to confront this powerful ministry, they embarked on a flanking movement, calling for the Bank of Japan to be granted independence. A more autonomous central bank implied a weaker finance ministry. The advocates of CBI looked to Europe for inspiration. Several European central banks had recently gained autonomy. If the Japanese financial system was to be revitalised, it would require an up-to-date central banking framework. Unwilling to offend the Ministry of Finance, the leadership of the central bank expressed no more than cautious support for CBI. According to Nakakita (2001: 58), CBI was therefore 'the result of divine grace', which was also the case in the UK and elsewhere.

The Bank of Japan Law 1997 came into force in 1998. The Policy Board (created in 1949) was given authority to determine monetary policy without government interference. Its members are appointed by the cabinet. Since 2000 the Policy Board has been chaired by the governor. The 1997 law tasks the central bank with achieving price stability and the stability of the payment and settlement system. Although the central bank consults with the government, it cannot be given specific orders. The Bank of Japan reports regularly to the Diet and to the public through press conferences. Minutes of monetary policy meetings are released after a short delay. This reform represents a substantial improvement in accountability and transparency within a traditionally secretive culture. Gerdesmeier, Mongelli, and Roffia (2007) stress the convergence of the central banking frameworks in Japan, Europe, and the USA at the end of the twentieth century.

Comparative analyses of central bank autonomy measure the rhetoric of CBI as well as the substance. One recent attempt suggests that the PBC was more autonomous than the Bank of Japan until 1998, but less autonomous than the Bank of Japan thereafter (Ahsan, Skully, and Wickramanayake 2007: 44). This study, which takes into account legal and political independence, the emphasis given to price stability, the control of exchange rate and monetary policy, and accountability and transparency, also places the Reserve Bank of India (RBI) and the PBC on a par. Admittedly the Indians were still wrestling with the notion of operational autonomy (Jadhav 2003: 64), but such results are hard to credit. Surely the Bank of Japan (both before and after 1998) and the RBI possessed more autonomy and more authority than the PBC.

New legislation in 1999 catapulted Bank Indonesia from abject subordination to a level of autonomy that surpassed that of the Bank of Japan and equaled that of the RBNZ, according to Ahsan, Skully, and Wickramanayake (2007: 42, 48). No country suffered more than Indonesia during the Asian financial crisis of 1997–8. Starting in Thailand, the crisis spread rapidly, bringing turmoil to currency and financial markets and banking systems, and causing a deep recession. President Suharto intervened personally in the management of the crisis in Indonesia, not least in the conduct of the lender of last resort function. Suharto attempted to sideline the central bank, and dismissed the governor, Soedradjad Djiwandono (who was related to him by marriage) and several directors. The Suharto government also made allegations of corruption against central bankers. The fact that Bank Indonesia received moral and technical support from the IMF further inflamed Suharto (Kenward 1999; Djiwandono 2000). After Suharto's fall in 1998, the new president, B. J. Habibie, agreed to tighten monetary policy, and promised to grant more autonomy to the central bank. The 1999 central bank law (which was refined in 2004) stated that Bank Indonesia must defy all political interference. In the monetary arena, the new legislation appeared to confer both operational and goal independence on the central bank, which was to maintain the 'stability' of the rupiah. Since the act did not specify whether this meant price stability or exchange rate stability the central bank could in principle choose its own goals. Indeed Bank Indonesia was permitted to set its own monetary policy targets. Accountability for monetary policy outcomes was loose (McLeod 2003).

While this sounds similar to the Bundesbank model, Indonesia is not at all like West Germany. The integrity and credibility of Bank Indonesia continued to be undermined. In 2002 the Governor, Sjahril Sabirin, was convicted of corruption for his part in the Bank Bali scandal in which funds were diverted to aid Habibie's 1999 election campaign. Sabirin's conviction was overturned on appeal (Galpin 2002). His successor as governor, Burhanuddin Abdullah, was sentenced to five years in prison in 2008. The court found that he had used central bank funds to bribe members of parliament and pay the legal fees of other central bankers facing graft charges (BBC 2008). In February 2009, President Yudhoyono demanded that the supposedly independent central bank intervene to stop further depreciation of the rupiah (Maulia 2009). Whether Bank Indonesia can cement its autonomy in the long run, especially in relation to banking supervision and the role of lender of last resort, remains to be seen. It will be difficult for politicians and their business cronies to resist compromising CBI whenever they get into trouble.

Central bank reform in Asia is difficult to interpret. It must be understood on several levels. First, moves to establish CBI are designed to impress foreigners including private financial institutions, the international agencies, and other central banks. Secondly, central bank reform has an aspirational component. New legislation cannot establish CBI overnight, but it can provide a framework within which the central bank can struggle for greater autonomy. Thirdly, CBI may be a rhetorical smokescreen behind which it is business as usual.

CBI without new legislation

Not all countries participated in the rush to enact legislation conferring independence on central banks. In some cases, including Germany and the USA, this was because the central bank was already commonly regarded as autonomous.

Despite possessing substantial legal autonomy, the Fed appears to have been amenable to political pressure, especially in the late 1960s and 1970s. But this charge is harder to sustain for the 1980s and 1990s when Volcker and Greenspan were at the helm. Under the Federal Reserve Act, as amended in 1977, the central bank has a dual mandate 'to promote effectively the goals of maximum employment [and] stable prices' (quoted in Blinder and Reis 2005: 23). This mandate was reinforced by the Humphrey Hawkins Act 1978. In practice, however, the dual mandate has not constrained the central bank's room for manoeuvre or discomforted its leaders. The Fed has been allowed to choose the weights to be given to the twin objectives of maximum employment and stable prices. According to Blinder and Reis (2005: 75), 'the Federal Reserve is a truly independent central bank. As long as it stays within its statutory authority, it has complete control over monetary policy. And it has been years since there was even a veiled threat to that independence, much less an overt one.' For some critics on the left and the right, the Fed was too independent and insufficiently accountable (Bartel 1995–96; Friedman, M. 1982).

The Fed did not seek new central bank legislation, partly because of fears that its detractors in Congress, including Henry Gonzales, would use the opportunity to undermine its existing autonomy. Though more open than some central banks, there was a perception in the early 1990s that the Fed was not transparent enough. Here was a point of vulnerability that could be exploited by critics such as Gonzales. Greenspan reacted by making pre-emptive concessions. In 1993 he reinstituted the lapsed practice of publishing FOMC minutes after a five-year delay; in 1994 he began to release statements following meetings at which policy actions were taken, and so on. Increased transparency helped to defuse attacks, thereby safeguarding the Fed's independence (Havrilesky 1995). Chairman Bernanke (2008) later stressed that transparency made it easier for everyone to understand what the Fed was trying to do, enabling monetary policy to be implemented more smoothly and effectively.

Canada and Australia responded to the new central banking philosophy by granting de facto autonomy to their own institutions, but not by passing new legislation. In Canada proposed new legislation was thwarted (King, Michael 2001), while in Australia there were deep political divisions over CBI (Bell, S. 2004). Nevertheless, Canada and Australia had governments in the 1990s that were prepared to pull back from direct involvement in the affairs of their central banks.

Some countries found alternatives to CBI when faced with serious monetary and banking disturbances. Argentina introduced a currency board in 1991, following repeated currency and banking crises and outbreaks of rampant inflation. With a currency board the scope for discretion in the conduct of monetary policy disappears, while lender of last resort intervention becomes much more difficult. The currency board, which was operated by the central bank, survived until a new crisis in 2002 (de la Torre et al. 2004; Wolf et al. 2008: 117–43). Ecuador abandoned its currency, the sucre, in 2000 in the wake of economic and financial turmoil, adopting the US dollar instead. The Ecuadorian central bank was not abolished, and continued to act as banker to the government and the commercial banks, and as issuer of small coins (Beckerman 2001). These were drastic solutions.

Conclusion

Central bank independence, credibility, accountability, and transparency were amongst the buzzwords of the 1990s. The legal side of CBI is only part of the story. CBI is always contingent, and can wax or wane regardless of the legislative position. The personality of the governor makes a difference. For example, Greenspan was better than Burns or Miller at asserting the Fed's autonomy. CBI did not cure inflation, but it did put an obstacle in the way of its resurgence. After the traumas of the 1970s and 1980s, governments were prepared to delegate the conduct of monetary policy to central bankers. It was not so much that governments were unable to resist the temptation to inflate – inflation had been reduced in many countries *before* CBI became popular – but rather that the temptation would always be there.

Central banks did not campaign for CBI, for that would have taken them into party politics, but there is no reason to doubt that they welcomed greater autonomy. CBI was often accompanied by new forms of accountability. Transparency was an increasingly valued component of central bank accountability. It was hard to deny that the public had a right to know what their central bankers were doing. But for the most part accountability remained toothless, and sanctions were not applied to central bankers who missed their inflation targets. Central bank accountability rarely extended to matters of internal efficiency. Most central banks, the RBNZ being the obvious exception, continued to be gold plated (Courtis and Nicholl 2005).

CBI was a safeguard against the resurgence of inflation in developed countries. In the developing world it was to some extent a pledge of good behaviour. The CBI debate focused on monetary policy, and effectively ignored other activities including the lender of last resort function and central bank's responsibility for systemic stability. Even so, the rise of CBI constitutes a revolution in the central banking world, equivalent to the earlier revolution in the mid twentieth century.

13 Reputations at stake: financial deregulation and instability

> Society supports banking regulation because it believes it will ensure a more stable banking system. It supports deregulation because of a belief that regulation leads to inefficient markets. The relative strength of these arguments is difficult to determine because the stability rationale is macro in scope while the efficiency argument is micro in scope.
>
> R. C. West, Federal Reserve Bank of Kansas City (1983: 362)

> If financial instability occurs, costs to society may be high. Damage to our reputation could be potentially high too.
>
> Sir Andrew Large, Bank of England, 2005
> (quoted in Kapstein 2008: 122)

Rapid financial innovation, sweeping changes in the mechanisms of financial regulation and supervision, growing competition between financial institutions, internationalisation, and a dramatic increase in the frequency and seriousness of financial crises were important features of the final third of the twentieth century. Perhaps the intensity of financial regulation exhibits a cyclical pattern, equivalent to the long swings in CBI identified by Goodhart, Capie, and Schnadt (1994: 48–9). Financial regulation was tightened after the depression. By the late 1960s, however, regulation was coming to be seen as a drag on efficiency. This re-evaluation led to more than thirty years of financial liberalisation. We might now be witnessing the beginnings of another reversal in the wake of the crisis of 2007–9. The degree of risk that society is prepared to tolerate in the financial system may be a function of time since the last disaster. Though it is tempting to judge financial liberalisation from the perspective of very recent events, the main purpose of this chapter is to examine the involvement of central banks in this process. Most central bankers supported deregulation, but few advocated a free for all. Instead they promoted improvements in the monitoring and supervision of banks, particularly of banks engaged in cross-border transactions. After outlining the causes and consequences of financial liberalisation and globalisation, we discuss the contribution of central banks to the maintenance of financial stability in a deregulated system.

Central banks (and other financial institutions) lacked experience of coping with banking instability, which was rare between 1945 and 1970. Besides, financial stability was also a more elusive concept than price stability. Even in the early twenty-first century central banks had no agreed definition of financial stability (Osterloo and de Haan 2004). At the broadest level, there is financial stability when the financial system is fulfilling its basic tasks of attracting savings and allocating capital, and has the capacity to withstand shocks. Central banks have a mission to defend the stability of the system as a whole, but there is no consensus as to whether they should supervise, or be the lender of last resort to, individual banks. Some countries assign prudential supervision to the central bank, and some to a different agency (or agencies), while elsewhere responsibility is shared. The central bank is not the *ultimate* source of funds for large-scale emergency interventions, this dubious privilege being reserved for the taxpayers. Convergence in monetary policy frameworks in the late twentieth century was only partially replicated in the regulatory and supervisory sphere, despite attempts to promote harmonisation through the Basel process. Financial stability proved more difficult to embed than monetary stability.

Liberalisation

Starting in West Germany, the USA, Canada, and the UK, financial liberalisation gradually spread through the developed, and then the developing, world. West Germany was a pioneer, allowing interest rate controls to lapse in 1967 (Franke 1999: 257). Liberalisation embraced the relaxation or abolition of controls over international capital flows, the domestic financial sector, and the stock market, as well as the lowering of barriers to entry. The role of technology was significant. Equipped with computers and improved telecommunications, banks and other financial institutions proved nimbler than their regulators. The pace of deregulation varied between market segments, countries, and regions. New Zealand (1984–5), though a late starter, acted with great speed once it began to deregulate. The USA was an early starter, but proceeded at a more sedate pace. US banks were not allowed to combine investment (merchant) and commercial banking until after the Gramm-Leach-Bliley Act 1999 (Barth, Brumbaugh, and Wilcox 2000). Every country retained at least some controls, often requiring the registration of banks and the maintenance of minimum levels of capital, and imposing limits on lending to single or related customers.

Liberalisation did not go smoothly, particularly in the developing world. In Latin America many defunct financial controls were resurrected in the early 1980s in response to the debt crisis, though a second round of liberalisation followed in the late 1980s and 1990s (Abiad, Detragiache, and Tressel 2008). The Asian financial crisis of 1997–8 prompted some economists and countries to rethink the costs and benefits of liberalisation, especially in relation to capital flows (Kaminsky and Schmukler 2003; Caprio, Honohan, and Stiglitz 2001; Henry 2007).

One early manifestation of the resurgence of international financial business was the rise of the euromarkets in the 1960s. The euromarkets were largely beyond the reach of regulators. As noted above (Chapter 9), their growth aroused mixed feelings in central banks. Sympathy for the competitive spirit was combined with apprehension, for innovation brought new threats to banking stability. The euromarkets had a powerful advocate in the Bank of England, which was anxious to drum up business for London. Deane and Pringle (1994: 154) suggest that neither central nor commercial banks fully understood these markets, but were 'clever enough' not to admit it.

Financial liberalisation was supported and opposed by shifting alliances of interests. Rosenbluth (1989) describes in great detail the many-sided nature of the debate over financial liberalisation in Japan in the 1980s (Takeda and Turner 1992). The Japanese were also under American pressure to liberalise access to their financial markets, though Rosenbluth does not regard this factor as decisive. Dynamic financial institutions in the USA, the UK, West Germany, Switzerland, and Japan demanded the right to compete in foreign markets. Many economists, central bankers, and officials of international agencies, such as the IMF, wished to encourage competition in the financial sector, and to reduce the compliance costs and allocative distortions associated with regulation. They looked forward to the gradual dismantling of controls over domestic and international banking and capital flows.

In 1971 the Bank of England unveiled a strategy entitled Competition and Credit Control (CCC). Leslie O'Brien, the governor, explained that CCC was intended 'to permit the price mechanism [i.e. interest rates] to function efficiently in the allocation of credit, and to free the banks from the rigidities and constraints which have for too long inhibited them' (quoted in Roberts, R. 1995: 180). CCC represented a major change of direction for the UK. In the USA, the Fed welcomed the landmark Depository Institutions Deregulation and Monetary Control Act 1980, noting that many of the scrapped regulations had been 'obsolete', and pointing out that the Federal Reserve Board had expressed 'strong support' for key aspects of the new legislation (Brewer 1980: 3). The old regulations had also made it costly for banks to retain membership of the Federal Reserve System, inducing many to quit. None of this is to say that central bankers were sanguine about the risks accompanying deregulation and the onset of genuine competition (West 1983). Steven Solomon (1995: 45) concluded that 'Central bankers were uncomfortable with the added ... technical challenges being thrust upon them'. Nor did central bankers present a united front, and the Swedish Riksbank actually resisted deregulation in the early 1980s (Englund 1999: 83).

Opponents of liberalisation included weaker banks and non–bank financial institutions (NBFIs), as well as those politicians and officials that profited from the manipulation of financial restrictions. Bankers realised that liberalisation had both pros and cons. On the one hand, they resented administrative constraints over their ability to offer attractive deposit rates and compete with NBFIs. On the other hand, regulation sustained an environment favourable to banking cartels (Cassis 2006; Rajan and Zingales 2003; Battilossi 2000; Helleiner 1994; Pauly 1988).

Liberalisation was not confined to the world's major economies. Some smaller jurisdictions, including Singapore and Hong Kong (Schenk 2002), welcomed the opportunity to participate in global financial markets. Others found it difficult to resist the pressures of financial liberalisation and globalisation. To have resisted indefinitely would have reduced their standing in the major financial centres. Abiad and Mody (2005) find that liberalisation commonly followed a shock, such as a change of government or an economic crisis, which tilted the balance of power towards the supporters of deregulation. Several shocks might be required to achieve full liberalisation. (Moreover, certain shocks could halt or reverse the process, albeit temporarily.) Another factor promoting liberalisation was learning. Successful reforms defused criticism and paved the way for further liberalisation. Deregulation in one part of the financial sector might cause new distortions, leading to demands for the extension of reform to other activities – the deregulatory snowball effect (Hammond and Knott 1988).

Crisis

Liberalisation was accompanied by the return of a phenomenon rarely, if ever, seen since the 1930s, namely the banking crisis. Most financial crises between 1945 and 1971 were a result of unsustainable exchange rate parities and did not involve the banking industry. After 1971, however, there were numerous banking crises and twin currency and banking crises, as well as more crises overall (Eichengreen and Bordo 2003). In fact there were 112 systemic banking crises in ninety-three countries between the late 1970s and late 1990s. The cost to the taxpayer could be severe when governments or central banks bailed out or recapitalised failing banks or had to meet generous guarantees to depositors. The fiscal cost of systemic banking crises was 13 per cent of GDP on average, but much higher in some cases, reaching 50 per cent of GDP in Argentina in the early 1980s and Indonesia in 1997–9. Such figures exclude other costs including losses of depositors and creditors not covered by the authorities, and the macroeconomic fall-out. Some interventions had the unintended effect of prolonging crises. Many interventions created moral hazard for the future (Honohan and Klingebiel 2000; Barth, Caprio, and Levine 2001: 60, 66, 71).

Banking crises were common in the first few years after deregulation. Credit explosions often followed domestic financial liberalisation, as pent-up demand was released, and banks and other financial institutions fought to gain or defend market share. The lifting of capital controls also encouraged cross-border financial flows. Sometimes these processes were linked – a credit boom might lead to a surge in equity and property prices, attracting capital from abroad. Rising interest rates after the lifting of financial repression also sucked in foreign capital, much of it 'hot' and capable of departing at short notice. Lacking experience of managing risk in a deregulated environment, banks and financial institutions often made unwise lending decisions to clients wishing to buy property and financial assets at inflated prices. Prudential policy was weak in this phase, as central banks and other supervisors struggled to develop and implement new procedures. When the asset price bubble burst, banks were left with non-performing loans on their balance sheets. Some banks failed and/or were bailed out. Short-term foreign investors might also take fright, bringing down the exchange rate. Notwithstanding important local variations, the same basic pattern fits a range of countries, from the UK in the mid 1970s, to the USA and New Zealand in the 1980s, to Scandinavia and Japan in the early 1990s, and Thailand, Indonesia, and South Korea in 1997–8. The boom-and-bust cycle was more dramatic in less developed countries (Reid 1982; Singleton et al. 2006: ch. 7; Honkapohja 2009; Noble and Ravenhill 2000). Kaminsky and Schmukler (2003) argue that after the initial period of instability, the incidence of crises recedes and the net benefits of deregulation become more evident. Approaches to the management and monitoring of risk and the supervision of financial institutions become more effective. However, as we all know, crises can still happen.

Explaining financial crises in general is extraordinarily difficult (Bordo *et al.* 2001: 75). Many factors are involved and they are not easily disentangled. It would be foolish to place all the blame on liberalisation. For example, the Savings and Loan (S&L) debacle in the USA in the 1980s had several causes, including tougher competition in the wake of deregulation, and a sharp rise in interest rates that eroded the market value of fixed interest securities held by thrifts, wrecking their balance sheets. Higher interest rates were in part a reflection of increased competition for deposits, but they were also due to the tightening of monetary policy in the Volcker era (Gilbert 1986; West 1983: 365). A global economic downswing contributed to the Nordic banking crisis of the early 1990s. Post-liberalisation cycles were affected by the financial accelerator mechanism. In the upswing, bank lending was given an additional boost by the rising market value of collateral in the form of property and other assets. In the downswing, borrowers were constrained by the falling value of collateral (Bernanke 2007).

Numerous crises had international ramifications. Most obviously, the 1997 financial crisis in Thailand spread rapidly to other countries in the region. The collapse of Bankhaus Herstatt in 1974 was also an event of lasting significance for the international banking industry. When Herstatt was closed by West German government supervisors (not the Bundesbank) after close of business on 26 June 1974, its New York correspondent bank immediately stopped making US dollar payments from its account. Banks that had irrecoverably sold DM to Herstatt received nothing in return. Settlement was not simultaneous for either domestic or international transactions. Even banks not directly involved became reluctant to make payments before receiving confirmation of the receipt of the countervalue, thereby disrupting the New York settlement system, which saw a 60 per cent drop in the gross value of funds handled over a three-day period (Galati 2002). This episode was a reminder of the interdependence of banking systems. Though the international transmission of banking problems was not unprecedented, the only bankers (or central bankers) with experience in this area were fossils from the 1930s. The Herstatt case prompted central banks to consider how the international aspects of financial failures could be contained.

Prudential supervision

Financial liberalisation was not meant to be a free for all for banks and other financial institutions. Some economists contend that a bank is just another firm, and that its collapse need be no more disruptive than the failure of a manufacturer of similar size (Benston and Kaufman

1995). But most economists believe that banks are particularly risky, and that many people and businesses are harmed when they collapse, providing grounds for some form of prudential supervision. Banks typically borrow short term and lend long term, creating a maturity mismatch. When a bank fails, its depositors could lose their shirts, while its customers might not easily find alternative sources of credit, with damaging repercussions. When a large bank (or banks) collapses, there might be a regional or national credit crunch. Furthermore, the payment and settlement system could break down if members cannot settle their obligations to one another. Almost by definition the emergency lender of last resort must make decisions in a hurry. Should distressed banks be propped up, should arrangements be made for their sale to other banks, or should they be abandoned? Should additional liquidity be injected into the system as a whole, through OMOs or rediscounting, in order to avert a widening crisis, and if so how much is enough? During the 2007–9 UK banking crisis, the authorities persuaded Lloyds TSB to take over the ailing HBOS bank, and effectively nationalised Northern Rock and Royal Bank of Scotland. The Bank of England injected many billions of pounds of liquidity into the system.

Economists could debate these issues at their leisure; politicians were inclined to side with the advocates of caution. If banks were no longer to be subjected to tight regulation, they would have to be monitored and inspected to ensure that management was behaving prudently. Imprudent banks would be admonished or punished until they mended their ways, or until a buyer could be found for them. Procedures were required for dealing with failing banks and their depositors, and for protecting the overall integrity of the financial system. The appropriate form and degree of prudential supervision continue to be debated. The looser the supervision, the lower the compliance costs, but the less well-informed the authorities. But the tighter the supervision, the more the authorities are implicated in any banking problems. Supervisors might look incompetent if they allow a supervised bank to collapse. These are tricky issues (Goodhart *et al.* 1998; Mishkin 2001; Brealey *et al.* 2001; Mayes, Halme, and Liuksila 2001; Sijben 2002a, 2002b; Barth, Caprio, and Levine 2006).

Prudential policy was a matter of secondary concern to central banks before the 1970s. Nevertheless, central banks did have *some* prudential role: they needed to monitor the status of domestic counterparties; they had a responsibility, albeit ill-defined, for overall financial stability; and as emergency lenders of last resort they needed as much information as possible about the members of the banking system. Institutional arrangements continued to vary (Hall 1993).

Though the Bundesbank and the Bank of Japan were not the primary supervisors of banks in West Germany and Japan respectively, they conducted bank examinations on behalf of the supervisory authorities (Bebenroth, Dietrich, and Vollmer 2007). The Federal Reserve System shared the supervisory function with other public agencies, and complex procedures were required to ensure coordination where their duties overlapped (Greenlee 2008). New Zealand had no system of prudential supervision until 1987 – several years *after* financial liberalisation – when this function was at last given to the central bank (Singleton *et al.* 2006: 206). The Bank of England allocated very few resources to banking supervision until the secondary banking crisis of the 1970s (Goodhart, Capie, and Schnadt 1994: 73; Blunden 1975). In 1979, the Bank of England received a legislative mandate to supervise banks, but this was withdrawn in 1997 when the Financial Services Authority (FSA) was created as a unified regulator of the financial services industry.

The fashion in the late 1980s and 1990s was for the separation of prudential supervision from the central bank. Even so, Barth, Caprio, and Levine (2006: 90–1) find that at the start of the 2000s the central bank was the sole banking supervisor in 46 per cent (of a sample of 151) countries; it had a share of supervisory responsibility in 14 per cent of countries; and it had no involvement in 40 per cent of countries. There were regional variations, with central banks being in charge in most Asia-Pacific countries, but having a limited role in the Americas. Grossman (2006) argues that younger central banks were more likely than older central banks to be given the prudential function, perhaps because they were perceived to be more flexible. He also identifies a tendency for central banks to act as supervisor in developing countries, and speculates that this might reflect their superior capabilities and prestige compared with alternative regulators. Grossman turns next to the unified supervisory agencies established in Norway (1986), Sweden (1991), the UK (1997), Austria (2002), and other countries. In none of these states was there a strong tradition of central bank involvement in prudential supervision, and they were unable to resist the withdrawal of this function. Equally intriguing are the results of a survey by Goodhart, Schoenmaker, and Dasgupta (2002), comparing the human capital devoted to prudential supervision by central banks and other supervisory agencies at the end of the twentieth century. Central banks hired more supervisors than did other agencies, and employed a higher ratio of economists to lawyers in this area. Economists might be more useful than lawyers when the macroeconomic aspects of banking stability are being considered.

The arguments for and against the allocation of the prudential function to the central bank are numerous (Goodhart and Schoenmaker 1995). Central banks already have a relationship with members of the banking industry, but this could cut either way, and raises the possibility of regulatory capture. Central banks require prudential information anyway in order to perform their other functions. Banks are their counterparties. The central bank needs to know what is happening in the major banks in order to ensure systemic financial stability. In small countries it might be wasteful to have several public agencies working in the banking sphere. On the other hand, an organisation that concentrates on supervision could develop specialised skills that a central bank might lack. In so far as financial conglomerates operate in related markets, including banking, funds management, and insurance, it could be more efficient to set up a unified financial regulator. The central bank might be reluctant to become embroiled in the supervision of insurance companies or funds managers. Having more than one agency involved in the supervision of each financial conglomerate is messy, especially if the supervisors do not trust one other, and the conglomerate is determined to exploit any confusion. Governments might prefer to have prudential supervision in their own hands as taxpayers are likely to bear the cost of salvaging troubled banks. Assigning prudential stability to the central bank might make it too powerful, though the same argument could be used in relation to a unified financial regulator. Arguably, a central bank with prudential responsibilities could be diverted from its primary responsibility of securing price stability. Faced with serious problems in the banking industry, the central bank might be tempted to inject large amounts of liquidity into the system, allowing the inflation target to slip out of sight. However, a central bank with reason to believe that macroprudential stability is in jeopardy has little alternative but to provide emergency liquidity, even if it is not the banking supervisor. Another solution – the twin peaks model – splits the responsibility for the supervision of financial services (including banking) into two spheres, namely systemic stability and consumer protection. According to Goodhart *et al.* (1998: 104, 173), there is no optimal answer to the question of where prudential supervision should be located, though they feel that the central bank is the best option for developing countries. Analysis of the appropriate institutional framework for prudential supervision lagged behind that of monetary policy institutions. Not until the second half of the 1990s was much thought given to the independence, accountability, and governance of prudential supervisors (Masciandaro and Quintyn 2007).

Prudential practice was not uniform. The standard approach in the 1980s and 1990s was labour intensive, involving detailed onsite inspections by supervisors. One country did things significantly differently. From 1996, prudential supervision in New Zealand was based on a system of disclosure and attestation that had been designed by the central bank. Instead of inspecting banks, the RBNZ required them to publish regular disclosure statements, containing information to enable depositors and other stakeholders to assess their financial position. Bank directors were obliged to attest to the accuracy of the disclosure statement, and faced prosecution if it was misleading. Other jurisdictions were interested in the New Zealand approach, but proved reluctant to copy it. Critics accused the RBNZ of free-riding on supervisors in Australia and the UK, since nearly all of the New Zealand banking sector was owned by groups from these countries (Singleton *et al.* 2006: 228; Turner 2000).

Many countries have schemes to insure the depositors of failed banks up to certain limits. Deposit insurance is normally provided by specialised agencies and not by the central bank. In countries without explicit deposit insurance, however, the central bank and government may provide implicit protection. Deposit insurance, while politically necessary in most jurisdictions, especially for the protection of small and unsophisticated depositors, creates problems for banking supervisors and central banks. Insured depositors have less incentive to monitor their banks. If managers become more reckless, extra resources might have to be devoted to prudential supervision, and the probability of bank failures might rise (Demirgüç-Kunt and Kane 2002; Demirgüç-Kunt, Kane, and Laeven 2008).

Buiter and Sibert (2008) suggest that 'monetary policy is easy; preventing or overcoming a financial crisis is hard'. Measuring the impact of monetary policy on inflation is not too difficult. Assessing the effectiveness of a prudential regime is not so straightforward, though we can all recognise a spectacular failure like the north Atlantic financial meltdown of 2007–9. Developments in supervision often stimulate financial innovation, which in turn leads to new headaches for central bankers and other supervisors. In the late twentieth century, banks made increasing use of securitisation, or the packaging and sale of bundles of loans in order to reduce their exposure to capital requirements. By this process they could move assets off their own balance sheets and onto those of 'special purpose' entities, or other banks, financial institutions, and benighted retail investors. In so far as loans disappeared from the balance sheet, banks reduced the amount of capital that they needed in order to satisfy the supervisors. In principle there was nothing wrong with securitisation. Due to the complexity of the packaging, however, the purchasers of securitised debt often did not know how much risk was being traded, and neither did the supervisors.

The Basel process

Central bank cooperation was extended into the prudential field after 1975. Central bankers were spurred into action by the failure of the Franklin National Bank in the USA and the Bankhaus Herstatt. The Herstatt collapse drew attention to the lack of communication and coordination amongst banking supervisors. How could the danger of international contagion be mitigated? Despite provoking some tensions, the central banking community had found another common interest (Kapstein 1992; 2008; Lastra 1996; Wood, D. 2005).

Gordon Richardson, the governor of the Bank of England, seized the initiative in 1974 (Goodhart 2004: 346). With the endorsement and support of the BIS, the Bank of England and the other G-10 central banks set up the Standing Committee on Banking Regulations and Supervisory Practices, known as the Basel Committee or the Cooke Committee. Previous discussion of prudential matters in the BIS had been desultory and intermittent (Toniolo 2005: 469–71). The Basel Committee's first achievement was the Basel Concordat, inaugurated in 1975, and revised in 1983 and the early 1990s. The Concordat was a non-binding agreement that called upon banking supervisors to cooperate in the supervision of all banks engaged in international activities, and the management of cross-border banking crises. Home and host supervisors of such banks were to work together and share information. The division of responsibilities between home and host country supervisors was refined in 1983 when the Concordat was revamped. Another revision in the early 1990s strengthened the emphasis on information sharing. This followed several breakdowns in cooperation, including the refusal of the Bank of England to pass on information about the criminal dealings of the Bank of Credit and Commerce International (BCCI), a rogue bank registered in Luxembourg and based in the UK (Wood, D. 2005: 52–67; Kapstein 1989: 329–30). Regardless of the aspirations enshrined in the Concordat, however, central banks and other supervisors had an incentive to behave strategically in some situations (Holthausen and Ronde 2004).

The debt crisis of the early 1980s posed a new challenge to the stability of the international financial system. In the second half of the 1970s, banks in OECD countries made large loans to developing countries, especially in Latin America. Many of these loans became non-performing in the 1980s when the borrowers were adversely affected by rising real interest rates in world financial markets, falling commodity prices, and the second oil shock. Fed chairman Paul Volcker was fishing in Wyoming in 1982 when he was told that Mexico was in dire straits: 'I headed back to Washington almost fishless' (Volcker and Gyohten 1992: 200). Since the onset of financial deregulation, competition had driven many banks to reduce their capital to asset ratio. This rendered the situation in the early 1980s even more dangerous. Without a strong capital base the capacity of a bank to absorb losses without becoming insolvent is limited. Sorting out these problems occupied governments and central banks for many years. A major report from the OECD (1983b: 85–96) highlighted the special risks associated with international banking, including sovereign risk and exchange rate risk, though this was hardly news after the Mexican default.

During the 1980s the thoughts of banking supervisors began to turn towards crisis prevention. The Americans in particular started to agitate for an international agreement on minimum capital to asset ratios, or capital adequacy standards. Not only would this initiative create a larger buffer against insolvency, but it would also remove a competitive disadvantage of US banks vis-à-vis some foreign banks. As matters stood, Japanese banks were permitted to hold less capital relative to assets than their US rivals. This enabled the Japanese to expand their international market share at American expense. Indeed some scholars argue that levelling the playing field was the primary objective of US policy makers (Oatley and Nabors 1998).

Volcker was prominent in the campaign for agreed capital adequacy standards (Kapstein 1989: 333). The Basel Committee shared his concerns about international financial stability, and with the help of the BIS investigated the underresearched question of capital adequacy. The BIS recommended that any capital adequacy regime should encompass off balance sheet as well as on balance sheet exposures, and take into account the fact that different asset classes were associated with different levels of risk – cash was perfectly safe, residential mortgages were reasonably safe, but a loan to a struggling football club was not. The UK had adopted a risk-adjusted approach to capital adequacy in 1980. Essentially, the riskier the assets held by a bank, the larger the capital it was required to hold (Committee on Banking Regulation and Supervisory Practices 1986; BIS 1986).

In 1986 the Federal Reserve brought a proposal for uniform capital adequacy standards to the Basel Committee. No consensus was reached at this stage, as a number of G-10 central banks were unwilling to give up their own national standards. West Germany's standards were stricter and Japan's more permissive than those envisaged. The Fed then invited the Bank of England to bilateral discussions. In January 1987 a common Anglo-American position emerged, involving a uniform definition of capital that included equity, retained earnings, minority interests in subsidiaries, and perpetual debt. Each type of asset – cash, mortgages, business loans, and so on – would be assigned to an appropriate category for the purpose of calculating the risk-based capital (RBC) to asset requirement. This scheme failed to satisfy the Japanese or some continental European members of the Basel Committee. But they were now faced with the prospect of the Americans and British going it alone. Would banks from countries that rejected an Anglo-American 'Accord' encounter discrimination in the world's key financial markets?

Bowing to American and British pressure, the Basel Committee agreed on a modified version of the Anglo-American scheme. Under the Basel Accord 1988 (or Basel I), internationally active banks from G-10 countries were to achieve a minimum RBC ratio of 8 per cent by 1992, at least 4 per cent of which had to come from 'tier 1' capital, with the remainder coming from 'tier 2'. In essence, tier 1 capital comprised shareholders' equity, but the makeup of tier 2 capital was partly at the discretion of the authorities in each country, which also had some leeway to modify the risk categories. In other words, the Federal Reserve did not have everything its own way. G-10 countries met their obligations under Basel I with time to spare (Wood, D. 2005: 68–99).

Basel I was adopted eventually by over 100 countries, including developing countries, and was applied to many domestic as well as internationally active banks. Less prominent states were under informal pressure to introduce the framework approved by the G-10 central banks (Simmons 2001: 604–5). However, the degree of commitment of some apparently compliant nations was questionable. In Indonesia, for example, the central bank had good intentions, and started to introduce capital adequacy requirements that looked strict on paper, but this process was incomplete when crisis struck in 1997–8. Moreover, there was a 'lack of effective enforcement of the [prudential] regulations'. Bank Indonesia 'supervisors were far from independent, with their actions constrained by the bankers and the government' (Baldwin *et al.* 2001: 64).

Basel I was not expected to be a panacea, but an interim step in the quest for improved supervision of internationally active banks. Unfortunately, the process of building up capital prior to the 1992 deadline constrained bank lending, and exacerbated the recession of the early 1990s (Goodhart, Hofmann, and Segoviano 2004). Ingenious bankers reduced their Basel I capital requirements by engaging in regulatory capital arbitrage. In other words, ways could still be found of transferring securitised assets to unregulated off-balance sheet entities (Jones, D. 2000). International financial turmoil persisted with crises in Latin America, Japan, and the communist transition countries. Consequently, the G-7 governments asked the Basel Committee to devise standards for banking supervision in developing countries. Working closely with supervisors from Chile, China, the Czech Republic, Hong Kong, Mexico, Russia, and Thailand, the Basel Committee responded in 1997 with a set of 'Core Principles for Effective Banking Supervision' (Wood, D. 2005: 103–8). The Basel Committee also engaged in other financial stability initiatives, and collaborated with regional groupings of supervisors.

In 1998 the Basel Committee decided to review and update the Accord. Oliver Page (2005: xvii), a member of the committee, recalls that the original intention was to make modest changes – 'at most Basel 1½' – but that in the end the committee decided on a more ambitious approach. Basel II would be based on the three pillars of capital requirements, supervisory review, and market discipline, and would be far more sophisticated than its predecessor. A 'standardised' approach would be offered to smaller and less experienced international banks. Their capital requirements would be calculated by external ratings agencies, on the basis of a more refined assessment of risks. Experienced international banks could opt for the 'internal ratings' option. They would be allowed to use their own financial models, where approved, to determine capital requirements. The debate on the Basel II proposals was protracted, with big countries and the banking industry exerting themselves, with mixed results, to manipulate the outcome. Agreement was at length reached in 2004, and implementation began in 2007 (Wood, D. 2005: 123–51). Ben Bernanke (2005) notes that the 'new Basel II international capital accord ... may well be the most economically sophisticated regulation scheme ever devised', though it does not necessarily follow that it will be effective.

The origins of the 2007–9 crash lay in the era of Basel I. It is by no means certain, however, that the earlier adoption of Basel II would have made much difference. Both versions of the Accord have attracted criticism. Whilst the methods commonly used to measure risk are adequate under normal market conditions, they are unable to predict or comprehend systemic failure (Daníelsson 2002). Fixed capital adequacy ratios also have procyclical implications, causing banks to reduce lending when the economy is weak and increase lending when it is already overheating, leading to exaggerated booms, busts, and troughs in financial markets and the macroeconomy (Caprio, Demirgüç-Kunt, and Kane 2008; Goodhart, Hofmann, and Segoviano 2004).

Central bankers and banking supervisors in the late 1990s did not anticipate the crisis of 2007–9. Whether the crash could have been averted whilst the international authorities were locked into a particular way of thinking about risk is debatable. Alan Greenspan, the most powerful central banker in the world, was an advocate of further deregulation on the familiar grounds that the market knows best (Calomiris 2006). Yet there was an ill-defined sense of unease in some quarters. Riles (2001: 5–6) captures the atmosphere in Tokyo on the brink of the new millennium: 'central bankers at the Bank of Japan … were both amazed at what they imagined as their own creation – a global market of seemingly infinite scale and complexity – and fearful of their own powerlessness vis a vis their creation'.

Reform of the payment and settlement system

Financial liberalisation raised questions about the resilience of existing payment and settlement networks. Users of these networks are exposed to operational, legal, credit, and liquidity risk. Payment systems process transactions and determine how much each bank must pay or receive from other banks. These obligations are fulfilled when funds arc transferred in or out of each bank's settlement account at the central bank (Summers 1994; Fry et al. 1999; Mayes 2006). A bank with insufficient funds in its settlement account (and no means of getting more funds) must cease payment, causing a ripple through the payment and settlement system. In extreme situations the system could break down unless the authorities step in to provide additional liquidity.

Payment systems can be linked to settlement accounts either directly or indirectly. Retail payment systems typically feed instructions into large value payment systems. In most cases requests to the central bank for transfers between settlement accounts are made on either a deferred net settlement (DNS) or a real-time gross settlement (RTGS) basis. Under DNS, payments are aggregated, and a single round of net settlements occurs at the end of the banking day. This arrangement is very convenient and DNS economises on liquidity, which may be costly to provide. But the damage caused by the failure of a participating bank to settle at the end of the day could be very large. By contrast, under RTGS a stream of gross payments is processed throughout the day. Although RTGS requires more liquidity, any problems with settlement come to light at an early stage, and the bank in difficulty will not be permitted to run up large debits with the rest of the system. The central bank can then decide whether to supply additional liquidity to the market or the illiquid bank or do nothing. If the difficulty is expected to be transitory, the unmet request for settlement may be shunted into a loop and presented again later in the day, by which time the bank concerned might have gained liquidity. RTGS protects banks and their customers as well as the financial system from some risks, but requires the central bank to be much more active in the supply of liquidity, often on an intra-day basis. Whereas DNS is a centuries-old approach, RTGS was first introduced in 1971 by Fedwire, a payment system owned by the Federal Reserve System. The Danish National Bank was the next to adopt RTGS in 1981. From the mid 1980s onwards there was a scramble to switch from DNS to RTGS, first in developed and then in developing countries (Bech and Hobijn 2006). The extent to which this migration was justified by the relative merits of the two methods continues to be discussed (Kahn, McAndrews, and Roberds 2003).

The degree of central bank involvement in the ownership of payment systems varies. Khiaonarong (2003: 20) found that 64 per cent of a sample of large value payment systems in Europe and the Asia-Pacific in the early 2000s were owned by central banks, whereas 13 per cent were in private ownership, and 24 per cent were in joint central bank and private ownership. Private ownership predominated in the sphere of retail payment systems. Some central banks followed a minimalist approach, owning the core RTGS system (and retaining ultimate control over access to settlement accounts) but leaving the rest of the payment system in private hands. The Bank of Finland and the RBA fell into this category, whereas the Bank of England did not even own the RTGS platform. By contrast the Bank of Thailand pursued a maximalist approach, owning the bulk of Thailand's large value payment system. The USA occupied an interim position. Fedwire, founded in 1918, was one of two principal large value payment systems, the other being a privately owned system called Clearing House Interbank Payments System (CHIPS). Fedwire tended to specialise in domestic transactions, CHIPs in international transactions. Central banks that owned payment systems commonly subsidised their users, sometimes lavishly. The efficiency of payment and settlement systems differed substantially, with costs tending to be lower under the minimalist approach (Khiaonarong 2003: 21–37).

If the private sector is able to operate payment systems relatively cheaply, why are central banks still involved in this area? For the Federal Reserve, ownership of Fedwire today is partly a matter of history. Central banks might be reluctant to shed major functions for reasons of prestige. Moreover, those central banks – and there are still many – that are not hampered by a tight budget constraint can easily bear their share of the costs of offering payment services. But there are other, less bureaucratic considerations. Large economies of scale attend the operation of many payment systems. Ought these mechanisms, which are crucial to financial stability and efficiency, to be entrusted to a private monopolist or banking cartel? The integrity of the payment and settlement system must be protected. Even if the central bank does not own payment systems it will have to regulate them. Many central banks are reluctant to give commercial banks or their agents control over access to settlement accounts. In any case, the banking industry might be slow to agree on a large new investment, such as the introduction of RTGS. The decision of the RBNZ to build and operate an RTGS system in New Zealand in the 1990s was influenced by these considerations (Singleton *et al.* 2006: 231–5).

Riles (2004) provides an unusual account of the adoption of RTGS by the Bank of Japan in 2001, which until then had relied on DNS. Bank of Japan officials regarded the introduction of RTGS as more than a practical matter. Their support for RTGS was a symbol of their commitment to modernisation, and their eagerness to participate at the highest levels of the international central banking community. Riles also interprets this episode in anthropological and psychological terms. By introducing RTGS, the Bank of Japan was forcing the members of the banking industry to enter into a more grown-up relationship with their 'mother', the central bank.

Illiquid banks are by no means the only threats to the payment and settlement system. Exogenous shocks, such as the 11 September 2001 attack on the World Trade Center, could be equally dangerous. On 11 September the offices of a number of large financial firms were put out of action, many employees were killed, and communications were disrupted. There was immediate confusion in the payment system – no one was sure who owed what to whom – and a significant threat to financial stability. The Federal Reserve reacted quickly by announcing that it was ready to provide the liquidity necessary to keep the system afloat. This intervention proved effective in averting a deeper crisis. In truth the Fed's routines meant that substantial additional liquidity would have been supplied automatically, but the announcement that everything possible was being done was a comfort and a source of confidence (Lacker 2004). Computer viruses, technical failures, human error, and fraud could also threaten the payment system. In New Zealand, the main worry was earthquakes, Wellington, the capital, being astride several fault lines (White, B. 1997).

There was relatively little international discussion of payment and settlement systems until the late 1980s, when the BIS began to take an interest. In 1990 the G-10 central banks established a Committee on

Payment and Settlement Systems (CPSS). Both the BIS and the CPSS announced standards for payment and settlement systems. They were well aware that the rapid growth in cross-border transactions was intensifying the risks borne by payment systems and their users. 'Herstatt risk', in which the seller, having handed over currency X, fails to receive payment in currency Y, had the potential to disrupt payment and settlement systems. The situation was not helped by the fact that each country had its own rules, laws, and infrastructure. A desire for greater consistency encouraged the spread of RTGS at the end of the twentieth century. Members of the EU were required by the Lamfalussy Standards, announced in 1993, to adopt RTGS if they had not already done so. A platform called TARGET, or the Trans-European Automated Real-time Gross settlement Express Transfer system, was developed to connect the settlement systems of the EU (Eisenbeis 1997).

In 2000 the daily value of foreign exchange transactions passing through the British payment and settlement system was equivalent to 47 per cent of GDP (Galati 2002: 56–7). Herstatt risk was a genuine worry for many countries. After the adoption of RTGS by the world's major financial powers, however, it became easier to synchronise each leg of the international payment and settlement processes. A group of large international banks established CLS Bank International, which opened for business in 2002. CLS stood for continuous linked settlement. This organisation arranges for the completion and settlement of transactions involving the major world currencies in real time, reducing but not eliminating risks. Though privately owned, CLS works closely with central banks (Galati 2002: 60–4).

Conclusion

Central banks were inclined to welcome financial liberalisation, but the ride proved to be bumpier than anticipated. The loosening or abolition of financial regulations created a more competitive environment, one for which many banks were unprepared. Central banks and other banking supervisors were equally unprepared. Banking crises became commonplace in the final quarter of the twentieth century. The story of prudential supervision, both at the national and Basel levels, revolves around desperate efforts by the authorities to keep up with developments in the private sector. As we know, these efforts were ultimately unsuccessful. From Bankhaus Herstatt through the BCCI scandal and the Asian economic crisis until today, the supervisors have been several steps behind. The removal of some central banks' mandate to conduct prudential supervision appears not to have helped. As members of a wider policy community, central bankers must share some of the blame for the inadequacy of measures to reduce financial instability. Perhaps central bankers spent too much time on monetary policy and too little on financial stability issues. Even if we agree with Kindleberger (1996) that panics and crashes will happen from time to time, because of human nature, there may still be room for improvement in prudential arrangements. Of course, Kindleberger was not very popular in the 1990s and early 2000s, when the dominant attitude was one of hubris.

14   Inflation targeting: the holy grail?

> It is always premature to declare that policy makers have found the Holy Grail in the current design of monetary policy ... Nevertheless, it should be noted that the inflation targeting regime will soon surpass in longevity all the other monetary policy regimes over the last half century or so of economic history.
>
> Pierre Siklos (2002: 308)

> By imposing a conceptual structure and its inherent discipline on the central bank, but without eliminating all flexibility, inflation targeting combines some of the advantages traditionally ascribed to rules with those ascribed to discretion.
>
> Bernanke *et al.* (1999: 6)

Inflation targeting was an important component, alongside CBI, accountability, and transparency, of the second revolution in central banking. A number of central banks began to target inflation directly in the 1990s, rather than indirectly through an intermediate target such as the growth rate of the money supply. By 2004, formal inflation-targeting regimes were in place in countries making up one-quarter of the world economy (Rose 2007: 664, 679), including both developed and developing countries. But this underestimates the influence of inflation targeting. In addition the ECB followed a policy that was in many respects akin to inflation targeting. The argument was sometimes made that the Fed already had an 'implicit' inflation target under Greenspan (Goodfriend 2007: 54). Ben Bernanke, his successor, was an advocate of inflation targeting, but did not make this into official policy.

Central banks appeared to be moving towards a consensus on the conduct of monetary policy that has been dubbed 'flexible rules cum constrained discretion' (Arestis and Mihailov 2009). Studies based on the Taylor rule suggest that in practice central banks tried to smooth deviations in both inflation and output, whether or not they subscribed formally to inflation targeting. This was a fudge, but then so was the brand of monetarism applied in the Volcker and Thatcher era.

241

Defining price stability

Central bankers have always been interested in price stability. In the 1990s this aspiration was given numerical precision, and a time-frame for its achievement was set out. Inflation targets were broadcast, enabling the success or failure of central bankers to be judged by the public. Although inflation targeting was not an academic creation, it inspired a vast theoretical and empirical literature. It emerged in order to meet the practical concerns of policy makers, including politicians as well as central bankers (Bernanke and Woodford 2005; Mahadeva and Sterne 2000; Siklos 2002; Goodfriend 2007).

Inflation targeting caught on after, not before, the start of the 'great moderation' in inflation and output volatility in many countries. Furthermore, it was no more of a cure all than CBI was. Central banks with inflation targets achieved additional reductions in inflation in the 1990s, but so too did many (though not all) non-inflation targeting central banks. The point was that inflation targeting signalled the determination of the central bank to stop inflation from taking off again. Inflation targeting may not have eased the pain of disinflation, as measured by lost output and jobs during the transition. Once price stability was attained, however, the new framework did not hinder strong economic growth.

There was widespread agreement by the mid 1990s that the main monetary policy tool should be some form of short-run interest rate (Borio 1997). After more than three decades of inflation, the developed world was reverting to very low rates of inflation. Greenspan (2001) defined 'price stability ... as an environment in which inflation is so low and stable over time that it does not materially enter into the decisions of households and firms', and thought that an inflation target would merely introduce a spurious precision.

The waning of inflation may have lulled some central bankers into a false sense of security. Other challenges were massing, largely unnoticed, in the distance. Inflation targeting focused on the control of a consumer price index (CPI), but did not take 'asset prices', which were set in the property and share markets, into account. The fallout from instability in asset markets led to financial crisis in the USA and western Europe in the 2000s, as it had done in Japan and East Asia in the 1990s. The generals (central bankers) had worked out how to win the previous war – the great inflation – but they were ill prepared for the next one.

Monetary policy in limbo

With the prominent exceptions of Bundesbank and the Swiss National Bank, the leading central banks sooner or later began to downplay or abandon monetary targeting during the 1980s. Rising instability in the demand for money function hampered attempts to exert control over spending through monetary targeting. However, there was a lag of some years between the abandonment of monetary targeting and the introduction of inflation targeting. The framework within which monetary policy was conducted for much of the 1980s and early 1990s was eclectic.

One of the most eclectic approaches to monetary policy was that of the Reserve Bank of Australia. Having discontinued a rather mild form of monetary targeting in January 1985, the RBA began to consider a 'checklist' of indicators when formulating monetary policy. This checklist comprised the monetary aggregates, interest rates, the exchange rate, the external accounts, and the current performance and outlook for the economy, including asset prices, inflation, and inflation expectations. In essence, there was a return to discretion, the traditional approach to decision making of central bankers (Johnston 1985; Macfarlane, I. J. 1998).

The Federal Reserve System's anti-inflationary framework after October 1982, when the targeting of non-borrowed reserves was abandoned, was tortuous in the extreme. Officially, the new policy was to target *borrowed* bank reserves. Unofficially, it was to target a short term interest rate, namely the federal funds rate (FFR). The FOMC took various factors into account when choosing the desired FFR. Not to put too fine a point on it, the Fed misled the public, Congress, and the financial markets about its monetary policy framework. It was still required by Congress to set monetary targets. Furthermore, any acknowledgement that it was reverting to a policy based on interest rates would have been seen as an admission of failure. This subterfuge was exposed in 1989. But the Fed did not admit that it had a short-term interest rate target until 1991; it declined to announce the direction of policy changes until 1994; and it did not admit to a precise target for the FFR until 1999 (Thornton 2006).

Many western European countries were committed to a fixed exchange rate, essentially against the DM, through participation in the Exchange Rate Mechanism (ERM) of the European Monetary System (EMS). An ERM member with a looser monetary policy than the Bundesbank's would struggle to maintain the exchange rate. After 'shadowing the DM' for several years, the British entered the ERM in October 1990. Robin Leigh-Pemberton (1990), the governor of the Bank of England, explained that the objective was to provide an additional anti-inflationary discipline. This was a bad mistake. German monetary policy tightened substantially in the early 1990s in response to the fiscal costs of national reunification. At the same time the UK economy slipped into recession, and the government came under pressure to save jobs. Financial market actors decided that the British commitment to the ERM was not credible under these circumstances, and in dramatic (though not unprecedented) fashion the UK and several other countries, including Italy, were forced to quit the ERM in 1992. Attempting to control inflation by fixing the exchange rate was as hit and miss as monetary targeting.

Exchange rate policy impinged on monetary policy proper in many other countries. New Zealand was the only country operating a 'pure' float with no policy-related intervention in the foreign exchange market. Many Asian countries fixed their exchange rate either formally or informally to the US dollar (Kawai 2002). Amongst the largest economies – the USA, Japan, and West Germany – there were demands for intervention when exchange rates reached politically unacceptable levels. This was a recurring theme in economic relations between the USA, West Germany, and Japan in the 1980s. During the first half of the 1980s the US dollar strengthened markedly against the DM and yen, creating dismay in the US manufacturing sector. Though the appreciation of the US dollar was in many respects a reflection of domestic economic policies, including Paul Volcker's tight monetary regime, and the heavy borrowing of the Reagan government, the Americans accused Japan and West Germany of manipulating their currencies to gain competitive advantage, and demanded corrective measures. Failure to concede ground to the USA would have led to repercussions, possibly in the trade or defence fields.

In 1985 the finance ministers and central bank governors of the G-5 countries met at the Plaza Hotel, New York, and agreed to take concerted action to weaken the USD relative to the other major currencies. For West Germany and Japan in particular, the Plaza Accord required large official sales of US dollar reserves, accompanied by interest rate hikes. By early 1987 the US dollar had returned to a more competitive level, and in another session at the Louvre in Paris the G-5 decided that relative exchange rates were now about right. Some commentators suspected a secret deal to establish exchange rate bands. Whatever the truth of this allegation, further large gyrations occurred in the key exchange rates in subsequent years. Japanese policy makers had in effect been required by the Americans to target the yen–US dollar exchange rate. After growing increasingly concerned about the impact of the yen's appreciation on Japanese industry, the government and the Bank of Japan loosened fiscal and monetary policy in 1987. Combined with financial liberalisation – another policy shift demanded by the Americans – these measures led to disastrous bubbles in the equity and property markets (Takagi 2007).

It might appear that central banks were drifting aimlessly after ter-
minating the monetarist experiment. They did not possess a coherent
intellectual framework that could guide to policy. On the other hand,
they had a much stronger mandate for combating inflation than they
had had in the 1970s, while a new approach to the formulation and
implementation of monetary policy would emerge at the end of the
1980s.

The pioneer of inflation targeting

New Zealand was the first country to introduce the direct targeting of
inflation. Between 1975 and 1984, when monetarism was at the height of
its influence elsewhere, monetary policy in New Zealand was controlled
by Robert Muldoon, a political leader whose inclination was to resort
to administrative controls in a crisis. When Muldoon fell from power in
1984, monetarism was already losing popularity internationally.

After 1984, monetary policy in New Zealand was tightened by allowing interest rates to rise to market levels. The exchange rate was floated
in 1985. Rising interest rates and exchange rate appreciation started to
exert downward pressure on inflation from 1986. For a while the RBNZ
used an Australian-style checklist when gauging the stance of monetary policy (Singleton *et al.* 2006: 99–120). The impression of many,
including some ministers, was that the RBNZ used the exchange rate
as an intermediate target: interest rates were raised in order to engineer a currency appreciation which in turn reduced import prices and
dampened the spending power of those involved in the tradeable goods
sector. The central bank denied having a rigid exchange rate target, but
admitted employing the exchange rate as a guide or calibration device
when setting monetary policy (Grimes and Wong 1994: 176–7, 181–2).
This distinction was too subtle for some critics.

Within the central bank there was growing support for the prop-
osition that price stability should be the overriding goal of monetary
policy, and for the fixing of a desired inflation time path, for either
public or in-house use. As with CBI, however, it was left to the minister of finance, Roger Douglas, to take the initiative. By early 1988
inflation had fallen significantly. Many New Zealanders, though not
Douglas, regarded an inflation rate of about 5 per cent per annum as
perfectly acceptable. On 31 March 1988, however, Douglas instructed
Treasury and RBNZ officials that inflationary expectations must be
squeezed further, and that inflation must be reduced to Swiss (i.e. very
low) levels. To the surprise of the RBNZ, Douglas appeared on television the next day to announce that annual inflation would be reduced

to a maximum of 1 per cent within a couple of years (Reddell 1999). Douglas did not unveil a formal inflation-targeting framework; this developed gradually as the RBNZ and the government sought to interpret and give effect to his aspirations. The initial response of the RBNZ was cautious. Economic projections suggested that price stability could be achieved by 1992–3 without any changes in policy settings. Any attempt to tighten monetary policy further in order to achieve price stability by 1990 would involve substantial additional losses of jobs and output. For Douglas, however, these costs were supportable. In the 1988 budget speech he looked forward to the achievement of a 'virtually inflation free economy' within two years.

After Douglas left the cabinet at the end of 1988, the Labour government seemed to be in flux. There were persistent, albeit groundless, rumours of a reversal of policy and a split between the RBNZ and David Caygill, the new minister of finance. In April 1989, the RBNZ advised Caygill that the lack of a precise deadline for price stability was fuelling uncertainty. Governor Brash sent Caygill a draft of his annual report, in which he suggested that price stability (0 to 2 per cent annual inflation) could be attained by March 1993. Caygill then asked whether this could be brought forward to December 1992, and Brash agreed. The RBNZ's *Annual Report* for 1989 expressed the price stability objective as a conditional forecast and not as a hard target. Provided that an increase in sales tax did not feed through into higher wages, and there were no unexpected events, annual CPI inflation should fall to 3.1 per cent in the year to March 1991, which was deemed 'consistent with a further decline into the 0–2 per cent range by December 1992' (RBNZ 1989: 6). The 1989 budget speech confirmed December 1992 as the deadline for price stability. Market sentiment was at first sceptical, and not without reason. Caygill told central bank officials that they would not be held to the target if it became too difficult (Reddell 1999: 69–70). In the event economic activity proved softer than expected. Global recession intensified the impact of tight monetary policy. Price stability was not too difficult to reach in this climate, though the extent of the transitional costs continued to be debated (Hutchison and Walsh 1998).

The inflation targeting regime was inaugurated when the first Policy Targets Agreement (PTA), negotiated by Brash and Caygill, came into force in March 1990. This specified a deadline of December 1992 for price stability, defined as annual CPI inflation of 0–2 per cent. The target was achieved by the end of 1991, and thereafter was couched in terms of the maintenance of 0–2 per cent annual inflation. Once the PTA was signed, the governor enjoyed complete operational independence in the conduct of monetary policy. Monetary conditions were tightened (loosened) by withdrawing (injecting) liquidity. This quantitative approach to policy implementation was superseded in 1999 by one based on the announcement of an official cash rate (OCR). The RBNZ undertook to lend to banks on collateral at 0.25 per cent above the OCR, and to borrow from them at 0.25 per cent below the OCR.

Inflation targeting was not as straightforward as it sounded. One complication was the possibility that 'underlying' inflation might deviate from 'headline' inflation or the official CPI index. Deviations could occur for several reasons, including the odd treatment of housing costs in the New Zealand CPI, and the impact of special situations or 'caveats'. In brief, headline inflation could be pushed off course by one-off events, such as a change in indirect tax rates, a swing in the terms of trade, or a natural disaster. The governor was expected to focus on underlying inflation when determining policy. If headline inflation breached the target range because of a 'caveatable' event, the circumstances had to be reported to the government. Provided there were plans to avert 'second round' effects on other prices and wages such a breach could be forgiven. The first measure of underlying inflation was called the Housing Adjusted Price Index. With a change in the calculation of the CPI in 1997, the distinction between headline and underlying inflation disappeared, but this did not remove the possibility that inflation rates could be distorted by special events.

The fact that monetary policy took at least several quarters, and perhaps up to two years, to affect the inflation rate meant that inflation targeting had to be forward-looking. When deciding whether to tighten or relax monetary discipline, the governor focused on anticipated changes in inflationary pressure. In other words policy reacted to changes in inflation forecasts. The RBNZ was the first central bank to grapple with these issues. In its pursuit of price stability in the early 1990s, the central bank devoted close attention to the exchange rate 'pass through'. Other things being equal, tighter monetary policy would cause an appreciation of the currency, which would affect the prices of traded goods, spending, and inflation. By the mid 1990s the RBNZ understood that monetary policy could also have a potent effect through the interest rate channel. Great store was set by the transparency of the new regime. The publication of forecasts and the announcement of policy intentions were designed to anchor expectations and reduce uncertainty and volatility (Singleton *et al.* 2006: 163–202).

The target band was widened to 0–3 per cent in 1996 and for the first time the price stability objective was justified in terms of laying the foundations for sustainable economic growth, employment, and development (Dalziel 1997). Brash and Michael Cullen, the incoming Labour treasurer, signed the sixth PTA in 1999, which incorporated the following significant statement: 'In pursuing its price stability objective, the Bank shall implement monetary policy in a sustainable, consistent and transparent manner and shall seek to avoid unnecessary instability in output, interest rates and the exchange rate' (RBNZ 1999). The timing of policy actions henceforth took these factors into account, in so far as this was possible without compromising the pursuit of price stability. Economic growth and inflationary pressure often moved together, so action to smooth fluctuations in inflation often helped to smooth fluctuations in output. Cullen and Alan Bollard, who succeeded Brash as governor, negotiated a seventh PTA in 2002. This required the central bank to keep *future* CPI inflation within a target band of 1–3 per cent on average over the medium term. But inflation targeting had always been forward looking in practice.

During the recession of the early 1990s inflation targeting and the 1989 RBNZ Act were unpopular. Jim Bolger, the prime minister between 1990 and 1996, who was unsympathetic towards the new framework, urged Brash to soften his policy stance. This pressure appears to have been resisted, but the survival of the framework was not guaranteed until the economy entered a strong recovery phase between 1992 and 1996. Inflation remained within the target band most of the time, except in 1995 and 1996, and even then the annual rate (according to the post-1997 definition of CPI) did not exceed 2.7 per cent. As this was an era of euphoria, it was not worth the government's effort to punish the governor.

The changes in the target range from 0–2 per cent (1990), to 0–3 per cent (1996), to 1–3 per cent on average over the medium term (2002), and the adoption of a clause requiring the central bank to endeavour to smooth output, employment and the exchange rate (1999), did not constitute backsliding. Inflation targeting was untried in 1990, and it is not surprising that the framework evolved as more was learned. Even in the early 1990s considerable attention was paid to the condition of the real economy when determining policy. However, the rhetoric of the RBNZ was harsh in the early days. At an international conference in 1995, David Archer (1997: 8), a senior RBNZ official, stated that the central bank's procedure was 'to ignore the short-run output and employment consequences' of monetary policy. It was this rhetoric, rather than practice, that was modified after 1995, not least in order to head off populist attacks.

After Labour returned to power in 1999, Lars Svensson, a prominent Swedish monetary economist, was commissioned by the government to review the performance of the RBNZ since 1990. Whilst visiting the RBNZ in 1997 he had produced a working paper on the distinction between strict and flexible inflation targeting (Svensson 1997). Svensson was an advocate of the latter, but he found relatively little to criticise in the conduct of monetary policy by the RBNZ in the 1990s. He was uncomfortable, however, with the concentration of responsibility for monetary policy in the hands of the governor. In general the Svensson report was complimentary. 'The Reserve Bank has been a pioneer in inflation targeting, without the possibility of learning from previous experience by other central banks ... During the 1990s the Reserve Bank achieved a remarkable stabilization of inflation at a low level' (Svensson 2001: 36). No compelling evidence was found to indicate that monetary policy had caused 'unnecessary variability' in output, interest rates, or the exchange rate, except for a brief period in 1997–9, which constituted the RBNZ's only 'substantial deviation from the best practice of inflation targeting' (Svensson 2001: 36).

The New Zealand case has been discussed in detail because it was so influential during the 1990s. The fact that the RBNZ was a comparatively small and nimble central bank helped it to be an innovator. A larger and more bureaucratic central bank, such as the Federal Reserve System, would have been less prepared to risk pioneering a new approach to monetary policy.

The spread of inflation targeting

Inflation targeting was contagious. One study found that at least fifty-four countries were applying inflation targets by 1998 (Mahadeva and Sterne 2000: 38). Bernanke and Mishkin (1997: 114) wondered 'whether inflation targeting will prove to be a fad or a trend'. There may have been an element of fashion in the rapid dissemination of inflation targeting in the late 1990s, but for pioneers such as New Zealand and Canada, the new framework had, by 2005, shown greater durability than the 1958–71 Bretton Woods adjustable peg system (Siklos 2008: 17), not to mention most forms of monetary targeting. Of course, there can be no guarantee of the continued popularity of inflation targeting, and in new circumstances other objectives could attain priority over price stability.

Inflation targeting was not completely unprecedented. Sweden adopted a price level target after leaving the gold standard in 1931. The objective of the Riksbank was to reverse deflation and not to counter inflation (Berg and Jonung 1999). According to the history of the Bundesbank (Richter 1999: 529), several German members of the

Economic Advisory Council of the American and British zones called in 1951 for the proposed West German 'central bank to be assigned – to put it in modern terms – a concrete, statutory inflation target, more precisely one of zero per cent'. A sort of inflation target was implicit in the monetary targeting apparatus of the Bundesbank and the Swiss National Bank from the mid 1970s. The Bundesbank employed a quantity theory equation to set the monetary target for the coming year. As part of this process an assumption had to be made about inflation. Until 1984 the Bundesbank assumed a low but positive rate of inflation on the grounds that a certain amount of inflation was unavoidable because of inertia in wage and price setting. After 1984 the assumed inflation rate was zero. The Swiss followed a similar procedure (Bernanke *et al.* 1999: 57–8, 63–4).

There were many practical details to work out when a central bank was converted to inflation targeting. How should inflation be measured? Should the target be specified in terms of the price level or a rate of inflation? What was the appropriate numerical value of the target, and should it be specified as a point or a range? What was the appropriate time horizon for meeting the target? What information should be used in decision-making? How should the central bank react to deviations from the target? When should the new framework come into force? For tactical reasons it was convenient to start when inflationary pressures were slack and the target was easily attainable. What information should be communicated to the public? How should the central bank be held to account for the accuracy of its strategy? Most of these were secondary issues, but they were not to be taken lightly (Bernanke *et al.* (1999: 26–38).

Canada was the second country to announce an inflation target. In a speech in January 1988, John Crow, the governor of the Bank of Canada, argued that price stability was the appropriate goal for monetary policy, but he did not define this term precisely (Crow 2002: 16, 160–1). In 1990 Crow decided to seek advice from New Zealand through central banking channels:

The Bank [of Canada] did not send anyone to New Zealand to check matters over, but at one point in our process Gordon Thiessen [a senior official] did go over some key points by telephone with the New Zealand Reserve Bank's senior deputy governor – taking care, as central bankers must, to be as vague as possible about why we wanted to know what we wanted to know. (Crow 2002: 171)

In the event, it was the finance minister, Michael Wilson, who proposed that Canada should adopt inflation targeting. Crow welcomed this suggestion. The central bank and the government announced a series of agreed inflation targets in February 1991. Annual inflation was to be reduced in stages, with a view to stabilising at 2 per cent (plus or minus 1 per cent) by December 1995 (Dodge 2002). This agreement was informal, and lacked the weight of the New Zealand PTA, yet it was no less successful.

Mervyn King (1994: 115) described the UK as one of several countries 'following the earlier lead of New Zealand and Canada' over inflation targeting. The UK introduced a target of 1 to 4 per cent for annual underlying inflation in October 1992. From 1995, the Bank of England was required to 'aim consistently to achieve an inflation rate of 2.5% or less some two years ahead' (King, Mervyn 1997: 91). Inflation targeting was intended to provide a new anchor for monetary policy after the forced departure of sterling from the ERM. King, then the chief economist at the Bank of England, told Don Brash that the British version of inflation targeting was modelled on New Zealand's. Instead of being announced jointly by the governor and the chancellor, however, the British inflation target was proclaimed unilaterally by the chancellor. The Bank of England reforms of 1997–8 left the determination of the inflation target in the hands of the government, whereas in New Zealand it was a matter for negotiation between the government and the central bank (Bean 1998). Elements of the policy making framework were different in the UK, but this did not prevent the achievement of satisfactory outcomes. Sweden also adopted inflation targeting in the wake of the ERM crisis (Andersson and Berg 1995).

Australia's route to inflation targeting was more cautious. During the early 1990s, the new monetary policy framework in New Zealand was a bone of contention between the Australian Labor government and the Liberal-led opposition. The RBA did not wish to be drawn into this rumpus. Moreover, Bernie Fraser, the governor of the RBA, was uncomfortable with the notion that price stability should be the sole objective of monetary policy. He believed that the RBA should continue to aim for high employment as well as low inflation, and regarded the RBNZ's approach as rigid. The RBA and the RBNZ were in frequent contact, though not always in agreement. In 1993, however, Fraser (1993: 2) acknowledged that there could be merit in a loose form of inflation target: 'if the rate of inflation in underlying terms could be held to an average of 2 to 3 per cent over a period of years, [then] that would be a good outcome'. This position evolved into a sort of 'target', which was then enshrined in the 1996 agreement on the conduct of monetary policy between the RBA and the new Liberal-led coalition. The RBA's dual mandate was retained, but the goal of high employment was subordinated to that of price stability. The Australian target became somewhat firmer in the late 1990s, but not as firm as its New Zealand counterpart (Bell, S. 2004: 80–90).

Within the emerging market and developing worlds, inflation targeting was embraced by a number of countries including Brazil (Barbosa-Filho 2008), Chile, Colombia, the Czech Republic, Hungary, Israel, South Korea, Mexico, Peru, the Philippines, Poland, South Africa, and Thailand. For example, South Africa adopted inflation targeting in 2000, after studying the examples of New Zealand, Canada, the UK, and other countries (Mbowemi 1999; Aron and Muellbauer 2007). Inflation targeting gained in popularity in east Asia after the 1997–8 financial crisis, not least as a means of signalling the commitment of governments to orthodox policies (Filardo and Genberg 2009). Each of the economies considered so far is either small or medium sized. What of the world's largest economies, the EU, the USA, Japan, and China? Evidently inflation targeting was not seen as the holy grail everywhere.

The unconvinced and the uncommitted

At the end of the twentieth century all central banks and the vast majority of governments acknowledged the desirability of price stability, but some were reluctant to commit themselves to formal inflation targets and/or to renounce monetary targeting, while others were either unwilling or unable to abandon some form of dual mandate. Failure to adopt a formal system of inflation targets did not necessarily involve repudiation of the underlying concept. With the softening of the early rhetoric and the advent of flexible inflation targeting, the distinction between inflation-targeting and non-inflation-targeting countries began to blur.

The case of the ECB is particularly tricky. Indeed, according to Bibow (2005: 9), it is difficult for minds trained in the 'Anglo-Saxon' tradition to comprehend the ECB's monetary policy regime and its relation to inflation targeting. Although the EU and the ECB were influenced by inflation targeting, official statements were rather coy about using this term. Under the Maastricht Treaty (the Treaty on European Union), price stability was declared to be the primary objective of the prospective ECB. The treaty did not define price stability, but to be fair neither did the 1989 RBNZ Act. The ECB's Governing Council determined in 1998 that price stability would mean 'a year-on-year increase in the Harmonised Index of Consumer Prices (perilously close to HICCUP) for the euro area of below 2%' (Scheller 2004: 81) over the medium term.

However, the ECB also decided to publish a 'reference value' for M3 growth, and this is where the fun begins. The reference value – supposedly not a target – was set at 4.5 per cent per annum, the rate deemed compatible with the maintenance of price stability over the medium term (Scheller 2004: 85). Clearly the reference value reflected the influence of the Bundesbank, but how seriously was it taken? Bernanke and Mihov (1997) argue that the Bundesbank was a closet inflation targeter in the 1990s. If their interpretation is correct, then the ECB's reference value can be dismissed as an embellishment imposed by the Germans to reassure domestic public opinion about the anti-inflationary credentials of the new central bank. Bibow contends that on the contrary the monetary 'pillar' was vital to the Bundesbank, and remains important to the ECB. He quotes Otmar Issing, the ECB's chief economist, who said at a press conference in 2003, 'we have confirmed our two-pillar approach. This is totally different from what is normally seen as inflation targeting' (quoted in Bibow 2005: 5). Issing (2004: 175) maintains that the ECB pays close attention to the monetary aggregates because of their relationship to the underlying as opposed to the proximate causes of inflation. The framers of the ECB's approach monetary policy seem to have courted ambiguity, creating a mechanism that contains elements of monetary targeting as well as inflation targeting.

The Federal Reserve System also appears to court ambiguity with respect to inflation targeting. The FOMC has never announced an inflation target, yet Mankiw (2001) portrays it as a covert inflation targeter. Blinder and Reis (2005: 5), however, look at the Fed from a very different angle:

For years now, U.S. monetary policy has been said to be on 'the Greenspan standard,' meaning that it is whatever Alan Greenspan thinks it should be. Similarly, the so-called nominal anchor for US monetary policy has been neither the money supply nor any sort of inflation target, but rather the Greenspan standard itself.

Later on they list a number of principles included in the Greenspan Standard, starting with 'keep your options open', and 'don't let yourself get trapped in doctrinal straightjackets' (Blinder and Reis 2005: 83–4). Of course, the possibility cannot be ruled out that the decisions of the FOMC or Greenspan were the same as, or similar to, those that would have been taken by an inflation targeting central banker, such as Brash, in the same situation. Hetzel argues that at root both Volcker (from 1982 onwards) and Greenspan aimed for 'nominal expectational stability' or in other words 'low, stable expected inflation' (Hetzel 2008: 7). An institutional preference for airy fairy business-speak over the more precise language of modern economics meant that neither chairman 'articu-lated the new monetary standard they had created' (Hetzel 2008: 263).

Though personally a supporter of inflation targeting, Bernanke did not impose this framework after becoming chairman of the Federal Reserve Board. The Fed's elaborate ambiguity has been described as a mechanism to thwart political attack (Hetzel 2008: 317). Despite these inadequacies in the eyes of the advocates of inflation targeting, the Fed's monetary policy in the 1990s was at least as successful as those of inflation targeting central banks. The ECB and the Federal Reserve System were occupants of a half-way house with respect to inflation targeting.

None of the three largest Asian countries adopted inflation target-ing. The People's Bank of China made targets for growth of the money supply rather than inflation targets the cornerstone of its monetary pol-icy (Burdekin and Siklos 2008). In 2000 Governor Jalan of the RBI expressed doubts about the suitability of inflation targeting for a coun-try such as India. Interest rates could not be determined by the needs of monetary policy alone, and had to be responsive to the government's debt management requirements. Given the patchy development of financial institutions and markets, the transmission channel for monet-ary policy was uncertain. There was insufficient data on which to base a western-style inflation-targeting regime. Moreover, large supply shocks originating in the agricultural sector have a major impact on inflation in India and other developing countries (Jadhav 2003: 35–9). Whether these objections are as serious as was claimed is a moot point. The RBI continued to embrace multiple objectives, including stable infla-tion, the encouragement of economic growth, the avoidance of severe exchange rate instability, and interest rate stability (Jha 2008: 264).

Conditions in Japan were different again. Here the problem was not the control of inflation, but the threat and reality of mild deflation. Some western economists and central bankers urged the Japanese author-ities to introduce a positive inflation target, so as to raise inflationary expectations, reduce the real interest rate, overcome the liquidity trap, and stimulate spending. Krugman (1998) suggested an inflation target of 4 per cent per annum over a period of fifteen years. The response of the Bank of Japan was prim. Not only was the central bank uncertain as to the level of inflation might be appropriate, but it had no idea how to go about achieving such a target. Failure to create inflation would undermine the central bank's credibility (Okina 1999). This was the opposite of the concerns of central bankers in most other countries.

Even after the great moderation, inflation was allowed to run out of control in some countries, the most famous example being Zimbabwe.

The government debauched the Reserve Bank of Zimbabwe in the 2000s, compelling it to expand the money supply in order to finance various fiscal programmes that were uncovered by taxation and borrowing. The central bank made huge losses, not least as a result of foreign exchange operations (Munoz 2007). More importantly, hyperinflation was unleashed. The problems in Zimbabwe were ultimately political, as they were in Germany in the 1920s and Indonesia in the 1960s.

Assessing inflation targeting

Inflation targeting was not a panacea. New Zealand, Canada, and the UK all achieved significant reductions in inflation *before* adopting a formal inflation target (Mishkin and Posen 1997: 94). Announcing an inflation target did not confer instant credibility on a central bank with a poor recent track record of fighting inflation. Nor did the introduction of an inflation target reduce the transitional loss of output (the sacrifice ratio) accompanying disinflation (Debelle 1996). A more modest claim might be that inflation targeting assisted countries and central banks that were committed to price stability to focus on the job at hand and avoid distractions.

Inflation targeting can be justified on the grounds that it improves transparency. The public has a right to know what their monetary policy makers are doing. A change in the objectives of the central bank might be more easily concealed in a jurisdiction that lacks the apparatus of inflation targeting.

Inflation targeting became the mainstream way of thinking about monetary policy, not least among US academics. Nevertheless, academic support for this framework was not universal, and criticism was voiced from both the Keynesian left and the monetarist right. Paul Davidson (2006: 700–1) thought inflation targeting was a euphemism for monetary brutalism: 'those who advocate "inflation targeting" monetary policy by the central bank are implicitly indorsing an incomes policy based on "fear" of loss of jobs and sales revenues for firms that produce goods and services domestically'. Yet in practice inflation targeting was not associated with persistently high unemployment, at least in the conditions prevailing in the second half of the 1990s and early 2000s. Rather less histrionically, Stiglitz (1998) argued that the dangers of inflation were exaggerated by the promoters of CBI and inflation targeting. Milton Friedman (2002) was sceptical about inflation targeting, which he feared would be a less reliable framework than monetary targeting. At the same time, Friedman was impressed by Greenspan's deft conduct of monetary policy in the 1990s, despite the fact that it appeared to be based on discretion rather than a monetary rule (Nelson, E. 2007a: 27–30). Oddly, Friedman had more confidence in the Greenspan standard that in inflation targeting.

Another common criticism of inflation targeting was that it ignored asset prices. It is worth noting that asset prices could also be neglected within other frameworks such as monetary targeting. Though central banks were adept at controlling some version of the CPI, low inflation did not necessarily prevent dramatic swings in share and property prices, swings that could be as destabilising as high and variable rates of inflation. Increases in money supply that were not allowed to cause CPI inflation might well flow into asset markets. Was it legitimate or feasible for central banks to target some level of asset prices? (Dodge 2008; Demirgüc-Kunt and Servén 2009). This question remains controversial. Surely, however, interest rates have enough to do without expecting them to regulate asset prices. Interfering with asset price movements could be as dangerous as ignoring them. After having contributed to the development of an asset price bubble, the Bank of Japan, fearing that the bubble would spill over into consumer spending and prices, tightened monetary policy at the end of the 1980s. The central bank hoped to restrain speculative excess, but the market response to the change in policy was disproportionate, and the bubble was popped so decisively that Japan entered a prolonged financial and economic crisis (Nakakita 2001: 53).

Conclusive proof that inflation targeting generates lower and less variable rates of inflation, and smoother output growth, has not been forthcoming for the developed world. Inflation targeting countries did achieve further reductions in inflation, and enjoyed better overall macroeconomic performance during the 1990s, but so too did other countries, including the USA, that did not target inflation explicitly (Ball and Sheridan 2003; Lin and Ye 2007). Several possible explanations present themselves. First, some other influence may have reduced inflationary pressure in both types of country. Globalisation is the obvious candidate. With increased international competition in the markets for many goods and services it became easier for the monetary authorities to contain inflation (Borio and Filardo 2007). Secondly, central banks may have adjusted interest rates in a similar way, irrespective of their position on inflation targeting.

Lin and Ye (2009) report quite different results for developing economies. On average the introduction of inflation targeting was accompanied by a 3 percentage point reduction in inflation in developing countries. However, they also find substantial variations between developing countries because of other factors, such as the fiscal stance.

For Mishkin (2008: 5), the success of inflation targeting in emerging and developing economies requires more than the announcement of a target. In addition there should be:

[A]n institutional commitment to price stability as a primary goal of monetary policy; an information-inclusive strategy in which many variables, not just monetary aggregates or the exchange rate, are used to decide the setting of policy instruments; increased transparency of monetary policy strategy through communication with the public and the markets about the plans, objectives, and decisions of the monetary authorities; and increased accountability of the central bank regarding attaining its inflation objectives.

The finding that inflation targeting and non-inflation targeting central banks conducted monetary policy in more or less the same way, at least in the developed world, stems from work on the 'Taylor rule'. In an influential paper, John Taylor (1993), a former research adviser to the Federal Reserve Bank of Philadelphia, argued that central banks should follow a simple rule when setting the policy interest rate. In the refined form of the Taylor rule, the policy interest rate reacts with equal force to percentage deviations of actual from potential output (the output gap) and percentage deviations of actual inflation from a point inflation target (Asso, Kahn, and Leeson 2007). The Taylor rule has the potential to appeal to Keynesians as well as advocates of inflation targeting because it explicitly takes into account the state of the real economy. Moreover, Taylor showed that an activist monetary policy was feasible, a claim that had been called into question in the 1970s and 1980s. This was comforting for central bankers who had never wanted to abandon discretion. Though the Taylor rule involved several doctrinal compromises, empirical research found that it was able to predict the past behaviour of the FOMC reasonably well. Some members of the FOMC as well as some Fed staff economists began to pay close attention to the Taylor rule. They saw it as a useful benchmark or rule of thumb. But the Taylor rule was not adopted formally either in the USA or elsewhere (Nelson, E. 2008; Taylor 1999; Svensson 2003).

The Taylor rule also appeared to shadow the monetary policy decisions of inflation targeting central banks, including the RBNZ. Plantier and Scrimgeour (2002: 9) found 'a broad similarity between the Taylor rule's interest rate profile for New Zealand and the interest rate profile that has resulted from policy decisions made by the [Reserve] Bank'. There were some periods, however, when the Taylor rule was not such a good fit. According to Plantier and Scrimgeour (2002: 8), it was one of 'a wide range of ... tools for assessing inflationary conditions, including a good measure of judgement' that were used in conjunction with the econometric model, but it had no formal status. The fact that the

Taylor rule aped what policy makers did most of the time provided further confirmation that inflation targeting was implemented in a flexible manner with an eye to smoothing real fluctuations. The Taylor rule downplays the practical differences between inflation targeting and non-inflation targeting central banks.

Conclusions

The rise of inflation targeting in the 1990s helped to embed the victory over inflation that had been achieved in the 1980s with a 'just do it' approach. Thus it was part of the second revolution in central banking which occurred in reaction to the problems of the 1970s and 1980s. In that sense inflation targeting was a backward-looking framework, concerned with the burning issues of the past. Inflation targeting was not designed to cope with situations such as the 2007–9 crash. Perhaps inflation targeting was also more of a rhetorical device than its early proponents would have been willing to admit. In practice inflation targeting central banks did not ignore the condition of the real economy when making monetary policy decisions. They sought to smooth output and interest rates whenever possible. Central banks, such as the Federal Reserve and the ECB, that did not seek membership of the inflation targeting club, often behaved in more or less the same way as members because they attached an equal weight to price stability. A new policy consensus extended to all central banks in the developed world and many in the developing world at the end of the twentieth century, but this was a consensus designed for a particular environment. When that environment was undermined in the mid 2000s, the inflation targeting framework began to look rather inadequate.

15 The long march to European monetary integration

> EU central bankers were strengthened as a 'professional' network by the negotiation of EMU [Economic and Monetary Union] ... The new institutional framework of the ESCB [European System of Central Banks] provides them with more than just a new formal role to play ... it is sociologically important in offering EU central bankers a new European identity within which that role is acted out.
>
> Kenneth Dyson (2000: 72)

> Together, national central banks have a powerful voice at the ECB – 11 of the 17 seats on its decision-making council – but the Bundesbank has just one, no more than the Irish. When the [Bundesbank's] board met last week, the press barely noticed. Contrast that with previous meetings, when journalists and economists pored over every comma.
>
> *The Economist* (1999: 86)

The seminal event in the central banking world at the close of the twentieth century was the creation of the European Central Bank (ECB) and the establishment of a new currency called the euro. While the ECB was not the first supranational central bank – the Austro-Hungarian central bank (1878–1919) and the central banks of the CFA Franc zone take precedence – it was from the outset an institution of far greater significance. Monetary union was not an aspiration of European central bankers until the late 1980s, when the European political and bureaucratic elite finally succeeded in harnessing them to the integrationist chariot. Ultimately, the formation of the ECB conferred enhanced power and prestige on some, though not all, European central bankers.

Whether there will be a more widespread disengagement from the national principle in money (and central banking), which proved so attractive to governments during the nineteenth and twentieth centuries, remains to be seen (Helleiner 2003a). The disintegration of the Soviet Union in the early 1990s, followed by the formation of new central banks in parts of eastern Europe and central Asia, demonstrated afresh the eagerness of many newly independent nations to control their own monetary destinies. However, in several new states, including

Latvia, this enthusiasm was balanced by the desire to join the European Union (EU) and adopt the euro.

Western Europe, the birthplace of central banking, returned to the forefront of developments in the late twentieth century. The legitimacy and sustainability of monetary union in the EU were debated vigorously in the 1990s. Monetary union was even more of a political than it was an economic project. The goal was to bind the member states of the EU closer together. Some western European nations and their central banks held aloof from these events. Switzerland and Norway were not EU members. The UK, Sweden, and Denmark were members of the EU, but their central banks remained independent of the ECB and the Eurosystem, there being insufficient public support in these countries for participation in the monetary union.

Most of this chapter deals with the road to monetary union in Europe, and stresses the contribution of central bankers to this journey. Consideration is given to the structure of the Eurosystem as well as to the governance and policies of the ECB. The ECB is compared with other federal central banks, including the Fed and the old Bundesbank. Questions of independence, transparency, and accountability are addressed. Thought is also given to the development of modern central banking in the former states of the Warsaw Pact and in the nations that separated from Russia in the 1990s. Great importance was attached to giving new central banks the veneer, if not always the reality, of independence.

The first faltering steps

How far back in time the story of European monetary union should be taken is a moot point. The Latin Monetary Union (LMU) and the Scandinavian Monetary Union (SMU) in the late nineteenth and early twentieth centuries appear to be the most obvious candidates for the mantle of precursors of the Eurosystem. However, Eichengreen (2008) shows that they were nothing of the sort. Rather they were agreements among groups of countries – France, Belgium, Italy, Switzerland, and later Greece in the first case, and Denmark, Sweden, and later Norway in the second – on the circulation and acceptance of certain types of coin, issued by each member state, within their respective areas. There was no attempt in either case to set up a common central bank, or to coordinate what might have passed for monetary policy. Neither the LMU nor the SMU was intended to pave the way for political union.

Another candidate is the Austro-Hungarian monetary union, which was presided over by the Austro-Hungarian Bank. Austro-Hungarian monetary politics were labyrinthine, as Flandreau (2006) demonstrates, but in other respects the parallels with contemporary Europe are limited. The Austro-Hungarian monetary union had but two full members, and operated within an imperial context that has little in common with the modern EU. The sterling area during the mid twentieth century was a monetary area but not a monetary union: not only did this group contain a number of central banks but exchange rates between member currencies were not irrevocably fixed (Bell, P. W. 1956).

The official EU account of monetary integration begins with the publication by the European Commission of the Marjolin Memorandum or Action Plan in 1962 (Scheller 2004: 16). The Treaty of Rome (1957), which set up the European Economic Community (EEC), comprising Belgium, France, Italy, Luxembourg, the Netherlands, and West Germany (the Six), was sketchy on macroeconomic issues. Trade and agriculture were the main concerns of the new community. However, the Marjolin Memorandum envisaged an economic and political union by the end of the 1960s. A 'monetary union' was proposed, but not a common currency or a European central bank. The goal was to achieve the permanent fixing of exchange rates between member currencies. Exchange rate adjustments within the EEC would affect relative competitiveness, and therefore might undermine support for intra-community free trade. The Bretton Woods system could not be relied on to maintain fixed pegs. Indeed West Germany and the Netherlands revalued in 1961. Although the Marjolin scheme was not implemented, it marked the assertion by the Commission of a stake in the monetary arena. EEC central bankers had not been impressed by the Marjolin scheme, and preferred to work for stability within the global framework based on Bretton Woods and the BIS. Even so, the grandly titled Committee of Governors of Central Banks of Member States of the European Economic Community (Committee of Governors for short) was established in 1964, with the encouragement of the Commission, partly with a view to involving central banks in the European project (Maes 2006).

In 1971 the Werner Report formulated proposals for an economic and monetary union in Europe by 1980. This scheme also proved too ambitious (Tsoukalis 1977). New challenges arose for EEC countries and their central banks in the early 1970s, as the Bretton Woods system unravelled and inflation accelerated. In 1972 the EEC introduced the 'snake', which was a regime to peg the value of member currencies closely to each other while allowing for flexibility against external currencies. The weaker EEC currencies drifted in and out of the snake, and periodic readjustments were made to exchange rates between member currencies. A European Monetary Cooperation Fund was unveiled in 1973 to support the snake. The snake was not a great success. Following negotiations between the French and West German governments, a revised scheme, the European Monetary System (EMS), came into operation in 1979. The Exchange Rate Mechanism (ERM) of the EMS was, like the snake, a kind of adjustable peg system for member currencies, the pegs now being against the 'ecu', a composite unit of account based on a basket of EEC currencies. In practice the ERM had many of the same problems as the snake. The DM was the strongest currency in the mechanism. To defend their pegs, other countries needed to run monetary policies that were at least as tight as the Bundesbank's. This discipline proved too onerous for many, leading to churning in the membership of the ERM and intermittent adjustments to exchange rates. National reunification in 1990 imposed a large fiscal burden on the German government, and German interest rates rose sharply. This raised the monetary bar for other members including the UK, and the result was the ERM crisis of 1992–3 (Bernholz 1999: 750–72).

Exchange rate strategy was ultimately a matter for decision by governments, even in West Germany. But EEC central banks were closely involved in the discussion of policy options, and the Committee of Governors was responsible for the overall management of the snake and the ERM. Relations between western European central banks were already close as a result of their participation in the BIS and the EPU. In order to emphasise their special status and their global interests, the members of the Committee of Governors held their meetings outside the EEC at the BIS in Switzerland (Andrews 2003: 958). Their relationship with the EEC's high command was semi-detached in the 1970s and early 1980s.

The Delors Committee and preparations for monetary union

A new and more vigorous drive towards Economic and Monetary Union (EMU) was initiated by the European Council at the Hanover Summit in 1988. This campaign, which extended beyond the monetary sphere, was spearheaded by Jacques Delors, the president of the European Commission. It is important to bear in mind the complexity of the debate over EMU, which had vital political as well as economic dimensions for each of the nations of the EEC. The motives of the main actors were not straightforward, and there was endless horse trading (Dyson and Featherstone 1999; Ungerer 1997). Strong disagreement was evident even within national policy-making circles. For example, whereas the Bundesbank was sceptical about EMU, the West German government regarded it as an important political goal. By contrast, the Bank of England was more open to the idea of monetary union than was the British government.

At the time of the Hanover Summit, many European central bankers, including Karl Otto Pöhl, president of the Bundesbank, were unconvinced of the merits of a monetary union (Andrews 2003: 964). From the perspective of the Bundesbank, there was a serious risk that monetary union with a single currency and a European central bank would fuel inflation in Germany, because the authorities in less inflation-averse countries might be given a say in monetary policy. Of course, this was also one of the reasons why monetary union might appeal in such countries. It rankled with some countries that in the EMS the Bundesbank set the monetary policy stance for the rest of the membership. The British government was expected to be troublesome, but the German attitude was regarded as crucial. EMU could not proceed without the support of the Bundesbank whose views carried enormous authority in West Germany.

If central bankers could be persuaded to endorse the EMU scheme, the prospects for its acceptance would be improved. The European Council proceeded to establish a Committee for the Study of Economic and Monetary Union. Chaired by Delors, this committee comprised all twelve EEC central bank governors and three independent experts. Commissioning this group was a clever manoeuvre. The Delors Committee, as it was known, was permitted to meet in the congenial surroundings of Basel. In short, the governors were invited to draw up a blueprint for monetary unification. Any governor who declined to participate in these discussions risked being portrayed as unreasonable. Pöhl considered boycotting the Delors Committee, but in the end took his seat (Maes 2004: 32).

The terms of reference of the Delors Committee assumed that EMU was a good idea. The governors did not seek to extend their remit in order to debate the pros and cons. Professor Niels Thygesen (1989: 638), one of the three independent experts on the committee, admitted that this could be regarded as the 'cowardly' option. The key figures on the Delors Committee were Delors himself and Pöhl. Of the major players, the French, Italian, and Spanish central banks were the most positive towards EMU (Ungerer 1997: 200), and the German and British central banks were the most sceptical. Delors was prepared to concede almost anything in order to obtain the Bundesbank's endorsement. Pöhl insisted that any European central bank must be at least as committed to price stability, and at least as independent from political control, as the Bundesbank. Only thus could West German interests, as perceived by the Bundesbank, be safeguarded. Monetary conservatism and institutional independence were principles that appealed to the other governors; moreover, these principles were in the ascendant in the academic literature on monetary policy. Pöhl's position was strengthened by the fact that most of his peers were under pressure from their own governments to keep him on board. The stance of the British government was very different. Margaret Thatcher was counting on Pöhl and Robin Leigh-Pemberton, governor of the Bank of England, to dilute or deflect the EMU proposals (Thatcher 1993: 707–8).

The German model triumphed. Delors would have preferred a European central bank that was more open to political pressure and less focused on a single objective, but he had given way in order to reach agreement (Apel 2003: 171). The Delors Report outlined EMU and the stages that would have to be passed through on the way to its achievement. The report was unanimous: even Leigh-Pemberton signed it, greatly to the displeasure of Thatcher. This is not to say that the signatories were equally enthusiastic, but rather that the doubters did not want to make trouble. Erik Hoffmeyer of the Danish National Bank, for example, remained sceptical of the prospects for EMU, and ambivalent about its desirability (Marcussen 2009).

The Delors Report envisaged that monetary union would involve free capital movements within the community and irrevocably fixed exchange rates. National currencies would be replaced by a single currency as soon as possible thereafter, but how soon was not specified. (Whether there should be a single European currency or a regime in which a new European currency coexisted with existing national currencies had been considered at length by the committee members.) Monetary union would be presided over by a European System of Central Banks (ESCB), consisting of a central institution and the incumbent national central banks. Price stability would be the primary goal of the system. Power would rest with the ESCB Council, composed of the EEC central bank governors and certain persons nominated by EEC governments. Decisions of the ESCB would be implemented by a Board. Neither the ESCB Council nor the Board would accept instructions from member governments or community bodies such as the Commission. The Report also made recommendations for economic union including the coordination of macroeconomic policy and the control of budget deficits. Union would be achieved in three stages. In the first stage efforts would be devoted to completing the internal market, harmonising the economic policies of member states, eliminating barriers to financial integration, and enhancing monetary cooperation.

In the second stage, the institutional structure of EMU would be put in place. In the third stage exchange rates would be locked and the agencies of EMU would come into full operation (Committee for the Study of Economic and Monetary Union 1989).

Having extracted a blueprint for monetary union from a group of central banking experts, the promoters of EMU were in a stronger position than before, though there were still some political hurdles to overcome. The collapse of communism in eastern Europe provided both an additional incentive and an opportunity to press ahead. Western Europe needed assurance that West Germany remained committed to the integration process, while the West German government required the political support of its partners for the absorption of East Germany. EMU would bind the enlarged Germany permanently to its western partners.

Under the Treaty on European Union 1992, commonly known as the Maastricht Treaty, EMU was to be implemented by stages. (Henceforth the community also became the European Union or EU.) The stages set out in the Maastricht Treaty were similar to those recommended by the Delors Report. However, several countries, led by the UK, decided to opt out of the project, and it was by no means inevitable that monetary union, which was scheduled for 1999, would be achieved on time, if at all. Aspiring participants in the monetary union were expected to meet certain minimum criteria, relating to inflation, the long-term interest rate, exchange rate stability, the ratio of public debt to GDP, and the ratio of the fiscal deficit to GDP. The Bundesbank insisted on strict entry conditions on the grounds, which were not universally accepted, that strains on the single currency could be alleviated if member countries had similar rates of inflation and fiscal positions (Wyplosz 1997: 7). At the institutional level, the Committee of Governors was transformed, in 1994, into the Council of the European Monetary Institute (EMI) (Andrews 2003). Based in Frankfurt rather than Basel, the EMI was a central bank in embryo.

Before examining the structure of the ECB and the monetary union in detail, it is worth stepping back and asking two questions. First, how should we assess the role of central bankers on the Delors Committee and during the run up to monetary union? Second, what were the economic pros and cons of the proposals for a single currency and central bank for the EU? So far, EMU has been treated as a political initiative, as part of a much wider process of European integration. Yet the advocates of EMU maintained that it would also have significant economic benefits.

EMU could be interpreted as a triumph for central bankers, and proof that they had become an influential epistemic community. Central bankers and not politicians or the European central bureaucracy drew up the plans for the ECB and monetary union, and they did so in accordance with the latest monetary orthodoxy. The ECB was to be 'independent' and not subject to interference from national governments. Seen from another angle, however, the governors were manipulated by Delors, who required them to reach conclusions that were favourable to the EMU project. Could the governors really be called an epistemic 'community' when one, Pöhl, was so dominant? As usual, the answer to such questions is not all or nothing. The European Council involved the central bankers because their support and advice were valuable. Delors' deft management of proceedings was a credit to his political skills. It is rare for the members of any group or community to be equally influential. The fact that Pöhl was first among equals among EEC central bankers does not mean that the other governors were irrelevant, or that there was no central banking community in western Europe (Verdun 1999; Marcussen 1998; Kaelberer 2003; Helleiner 1994: 19, 198–201). Dyson (2000: 72, 103) calls top EEC central bankers a 'professional network' rather than an epistemic community, adding that they developed a common interpretation of how EMU was achieved or 'socially constructed'. They became members of a 'discourse coalition', talking about EMU in agreed terms. Perhaps they came to see themselves as campaign veterans.

A plausible, but far from compelling, economic rationale can be offered for monetary union. One of the earliest attempts to list the economic benefits of a single European currency was provided by Gros and Thygesen (1990). Exchange rate transaction costs would disappear within the union, saving between 0.25 per cent and 0.5 per cent of community GDP. Savings of up to 2 per cent of GDP might also follow from easier price comparisons between countries, simpler accounts, and reduced price discrimination between national markets. Other benefits were more conjectural. Dynamic gains would be created by a better allocation of capital, and because it would no longer be necessary to take exchange rate risk into account when appraising investment proposals. Financial integration would accelerate once the single currency was in place. At the macroeconomic level there would be savings in the quantity of international reserves required within the community. The European currency could become a partial alternative to the US dollar as a medium for transactions and a store of value, leading to modest seigniorage gains and shifts in portfolios away from the dollar. Great emphasis was given to the prospect of a more effective control over inflation across member countries.

The potential Achilles heel of the project stemmed from the rather obvious fact that western Europe did not resemble an optimum currency area (OCA). In an OCA each region has a similar economic structure, and macroeconomic shocks affect them simultaneously and in the same way. But the economies of Germany or Belgium were very different from those of Ireland or Portugal. One of the commonly stated British objections to monetary union was that the business cycle in the UK was out of kilter with its counterpart on the continent. How would the ECB manage monetary policy when, for example, the southern half of the EU was in danger of overheating but the northern half was stagnating? Adjusting the exchange rate between these regions would not be an option. Should monetary policy be tightened to prevent inflation in the south or loosened to avert recession in the north?

The larger the economic entity, the less likely it is to be an OCA. There is considerable regional diversity in the USA and other large countries. But in the USA there are ameliorating factors such as high internal labour mobility and an elaborate system of fiscal transfers. US workers have a high propensity to shift from areas facing a downturn to those that are growing. Labour is not as mobile in the EU on account of language and cultural differences. Moreover, fiscal policy remains in the hands of national governments, and there is only a limited capacity for the EU to compensate struggling regions. Critics of the EMU project emphasised that there would be losers as well as winners amongst the membership, depending on the geographical incidence of shocks and the reaction of monetary policy makers. The ECB would be lobbied to ameliorate conditions for the losers. At some point, the losers might decide to quit the monetary union in order to reclaim control over exchange rate and monetary policy. Supporters of EMU hoped that any tensions would prove mild, and that they would diminish over time as the community became more homogeneous and integrated (Eichengreen 1997, 1998; Kenen 1995; De Grauwe 1992; Bean 1992).

Despite numerous attempts to read the entrails, nobody knew for certain how things would turn out. Monetary union would be a great experiment. 'It is a bold step into the unknown. Not unlike Alice [in Wonderland]'s leap down the rabbit hole', said Willem Buiter (1999: 182), a member of the Bank of England's Monetary Policy Committee. The strongest arguments for (and against) monetary union transcended economics. Tommaso Padoa-Schioppa (1994), an Italian central banker who had been one of the experts on the Delors Committee, argued that the process of political and economic integration had to move forward or risk failure, raising the spectre of a return to inward-looking, nationalistic policies. The choice was ultimately about whether one was a supporter or an opponent of the federalist dream, as British eurosceptics (Connolly 1995), including the United Kingdom Independence Party and some Conservatives, realised.

The ECB and the inception of monetary union

After many vicissitudes, monetary union was achieved in 1999. The currencies of the initial member states were transformed into the euro at agreed rates on 1 January 1999 (Scheller 2004: 26), but national notes and coins continued to circulate until the start of 2002. The ECB, based in Frankfurt, became the sole author of monetary policy in the euro area from 1999. Eleven aspirants for membership of the union were deemed to have met the entry requirements, but this had not been a foregone conclusion. 'As late as 1997 ... there was widespread scepticism about whether European Monetary Union ... would begin on schedule as a broad union and, in some quarters, whether it would happen at all' (Cecchetti and Schoenholtz 2008: 1). Established in 1998, the ECB grew out of the EMI. The UK, Denmark, and Sweden opted out, preferring to retain their own currencies and monetary policy autonomy. However, the Danes fixed their currency to the euro (De Grauwe 2007).

In 2004, Jean-Claude Trichet (2004: 9), the president of the ECB, described his institution as the 'captain of the European monetary team, namely the Eurosystem'. But he understated the ECB's authority, which was more like that of the captain of a ship than that of a sports team. EU terminology requires a little explanation. The ECB is the central bank of the euro area. The ECB plus the national central banks of countries within the monetary union constitute the Eurosystem. The Eurosystem plus the national central banks of EU countries outside the monetary union, such as the Bank of England and the Swedish Riksbank, make up the European System of Central Banks. The ECB rules the Eurosystem: thus in the monetary policy arena, the Bundesbank and the Banque de France are merely agents of the ECB in the German and French money markets. It must be stressed, however, that the ECB does not control the other functions of Eurosystem central banks. The Delors Report had not contemplated that some members of the ESCB would remain outside the monetary union, and the ECB has no authority over the central banks of the UK, Sweden, and Denmark.

As explained in Chapter 14 above, price stability is the paramount goal of the ECB's monetary policy. In pursuit of this objective the ECB employs a number of policy tools. It announces three short term interest rates (the rate on main refinancing operations, the rate on the deposit facility, and the rate on the marginal lending facility) at which the system is prepared to transact with banks; it determines the scope and direction of OMOs; finally, it requires banks to hold certain minimum levels of reserves. Policy is implemented in national financial markets by the national central banks. The decentralisation of monetary policy implementation within the Eurosystem goes beyond the practice in the Federal Reserve System where OMOs are conducted by just one reserve bank, the FRBNY.

Setting monetary policy for the Eurosystem was at first a daunting challenge (Dornbusch, Favero, and Giavazzi 1998). Institutional arrangements, including the transmission mechanism, differed considerably from country to country. ECB modellers and policy makers could not be as confident about the response of the private sector to policy actions as were their counterparts in the USA or the UK. Otmar Issing, a founder member of the Executive Board of the ECB, regarded this as alarming: 'What really shocked me [when I arrived] was the lack of any reasonable information (data, etc.). We were preparing monetary policy for totally uncharted waters' (quoted in Cecchetti and Schoenholtz 2008: 6). That monetary policy was implemented reasonably smoothly may be attributed to a combination of good judgement, cooperation, and good fortune, and the introduction in January 1999 of TARGET, the Eurosystem's real-time gross settlement system. TARGET, which is owned and operated by Eurosystem central banks, integrates the market for overnight liquidity within the Eurosystem (Rosati and Secola 2006).

It was difficult, and in some cases humiliating, for national central bankers to cede control over monetary policy to the ECB. For the Bundesbank in particular the creation of the ECB was a bittersweet moment. German demands for an independent central bank with tough membership criteria had been met, but giving up the DM was a huge wrench. Issing exchanged a place on the board of the Bundesbank for one on the Executive Board of the ECB. For many others at the Bundesbank the prospects were not as attractive. *The Economist* (1999: 86) reported that two Bundesbank Board members had quit, upset over their loss of status, and drew an unkind comparison between the ECB's 'glitzy tower' and the 'drab concrete' of the Bundesbank on the other side of Frankfurt. Bundesbank staff feared restructuring; a few applied for and were appointed to jobs at the ECB. Publicly, however, there was a determination to put on a brave face.

As a federal central banking system, the Eurosystem was often compared to the Federal Reserve System. Comparisons were also made between the Eurosystem and the Bundesbank, which was composed of a central directorate and regional Landeszentralbanken, and the Bank of Japan, which exhibited some features of decentralisation without being a federal central bank (Apel 2003; Pollard 2003; Eijffinger 2003). One analysis, written by three ECB economists, argued that despite various institutional differences between the ECB, the Fed, and the Bank of Japan, they approached monetary policy in very similar ways (Gerdesmeier, Mongelli, and Roffia 2007). Fontana (2006) preferred the Fed's dual mandate to the narrower mandate of the ECB, while Cecchetti and O'Sullivan (2003) made the rather obvious point that the ECB and the Fed should learn from each other.

Given the magnitude of the ECB's responsibilities, it was at first a small organisation. In 1999 the ECB had a mere 732 employees. The Board of Governors of the Federal Reserve System had 1,700 employees in 1996. Both the ECB and the Board of Governors presided over empires: the Eurosystem's payroll was 48,000 in 1999, whereas employment in the Federal Reserve System was 25,000 in 1996. It is worth noting that the Bundesbank's central directorate employed 2,579 in 1998, comfortably outnumbering the staff of the Board of Governors of the Fed. The German style of central bank independence had served German central bank employees well between 1957 and 1999. By the end of 2008 the ECB had more than doubled its workforce to 1,536 full-time equivalent employees (European Central Bank 2009: 208). There are prima facie grounds for thinking that there is considerable duplication and redundancy within the Eurosystem and the Fed.

In the early years of the Federal Reserve System, the authority of the Board in Washington over the Reserve Banks was uncertain (Eichengreen 1991). This problem does not arise in the Eurosystem, at least with respect to monetary policy, as the power of decision-making rests firmly with the Governing Council and Governing Board of the ECB. The Governing Council of the ECB formulates monetary policy. Membership of this body comprises the governors of the national central banks of the Eurosystem plus the members of the Executive Board of the ECB. The Executive Board consists of the president (the governor) and the vice-president of the ECB and four other monetary and banking experts. Board members are appointed for a single term of at least eight years by common agreement of Eurosystem heads of state or government, on the recommendation of the EU Council after consulting the European Parliament. The functions of the Executive Board are to ensure the implementation of monetary policy decisions, and to manage the ECB on a day-to-day basis. Instructions are sent by the Board to the national central banks (Scheller 2004: 51–61).

Members of the Governing Council are supposed to put aside national interests and approach policy making from a European perspective. Policy is decided by a voting process, but the voting record of individual members is not published, partly in order to insulate them from domestic pressures. When the ECB was created it seemed doubtful that central bank governors would be able to transcend national allegiances. But ECB insiders, interviewed in 2007–8 by Cecchetti and Schoenholtz (2008: 14–15), felt that on questions of monetary policy the members of the Governing Council did adopt a European point of view. On other issues, such as the rationalisation of note-printing facilities, they were more likely to defend national positions.

The ECB is not goal independent, for it is required to aim for price stability, but it does enjoy strong operational independence. Article 108 of the European Communities Treaty, as amended by the Maastricht Treaty, prohibits the ECB from seeking or taking 'instructions' from any external body, including the governments of member states and other EU institutions. The ECB is also prohibited from making loans to the public sector. The ECB is owned by national central banks and not by the EU or national governments, and has its own budget. Operational independence is not absolute, however, for the EU Council has reserve powers to determine 'general orientations for exchange rate policy', though at the time of writing it had not made use of this authority (Gerdesmeier, Mongelli, and Roffia 2007: 1795). According to Pollard (2003: 24), 'Even the nonrenewable term of office of the members of the Executive Board was designed to protect them from political interference.' Even so, the French government made a political issue of the appointment of the first ECB president (Buiter 1999: 185).

To what extent is the ECB accountable for its actions? Compared with the RBNZ, where the governor can in principle be sacked for missing the agreed monetary policy target, decision makers at the ECB are sitting pretty. No-one can dismiss them for failure. Critics have lambasted the weak accountability of the ECB. Buiter (1999: 187) expressed concerns about the legitimacy of the ECB, which in his view was not answerable to anybody in particular: 'In a democratic society … decision-making by technocrats is acceptable and viable only if the institution to which these decisions are delegated is accountable to the public at large and to its elected representatives'.

Resuscitating the economics of bureaucracy literature, Forder (2002) argued that the ECB was in essence free to pursue its own interests, which might well include empire building and the evasion of any responsibility for errors. ECB statements could not be taken at face value. According to Forder, the bureaucracy literature had been swept aside in the 1980s and 1990s in the surge of enthusiasm for the doctrine of central bank independence. In addition, we have seen how Delors made a conscious decision to let central bankers design the monetary union and define the independence of the ECB. He did not do so because he was naïve, but because he was constructing a political alliance in favour of EMU.

Issing (1999: 505) rose to the defence of the ECB against Buiter, contending that it was already 'the most transparent and accountable central bank in the world'. The ECB was accountable for its performance in relation to the price stability mandate. There were statutory reporting requirements to the European Parliament, the Council of Ministers and the Commission. The ECB president presented these reports and answered questions on them. The European Parliament could summon other Board members for questioning. Issing maintained that the EU was transparent about its policy decisions, which were explained by senior officials, but he was against publishing the minutes of the Governing Council or the votes of its members. Forder (2002) was unimpressed by Issing's rearguard action. There is more to accountability than explaining oneself and answering a few questions. De Haan and Eijffinger (2000: 405), who saw merits on both sides of the debate, did not accept that the ECB was one of the most accountable and transparent central banks in the world. A universally accepted combination of CBI and accountability may always be elusive, not least because both concepts are hard to define. Yet there can be no denying that in the case of the ECB the balance is tilted towards independence.

The ECB's jurisdiction did not extend to banking supervision – it was not a 'full service' central bank like the RBNZ or the pre-1999 Bank of Italy. The Bundesbank had not wanted the ECB to be drawn too far into the prudential arena, lest monetary control be compromised by lending to problem banks (Dyson 2000: 34–5). But this position was not shared by some prominent ECB figures. In a speech at the London School of Economics in 1999, Padoa-Schioppa, who was now a member of the ECB's Executive Board, expressed lukewarm support for the separation of the monetary policy and prudential functions within the Eurosystem. He noted that it was fashionable to separate them – even the UK and Australia had done so – but pointed out that there were arguments on both sides (Padoa-Schioppa 1999). In most Eurosystem countries, the main exceptions being Italy and the Netherlands, prudential supervision was the responsibility primarily of separate agencies, and this approach persisted.

Under previous EU policy and the Basel Concordat and Accord, a measure of harmonisation had been achieved in the area of prudential supervision. Importance was attached to the mutual recognition of supervisory regimes within the EU, the responsibilities of the home-country supervisor, and cooperation between agencies. There was a Groupe de Contact for European financial supervisors and a Banking Supervisory Group, the latter having been established by the Committee of Governors. The ECB hosted a Banking Supervisory Committee, membership of which extended to the central banks and supervisory agencies of all EU member states (Scheller 2004: 111–14). That such arrangements were somewhat messy was acknowledged, and in 2004 the Lamfalussy framework for cooperation in EU financial regulation was extended to banking, but even this did not constitute a unified regime. With the onset of global financial crisis in 2007, senior ECB figures became increasingly worried about the baroque nature of the supervisory framework. The ECB was responsible for the liquidity of the European banking system, but matters relating to the solvency of individual banks were dealt with at the national level. Some banks were so large that as well as being too big to fail, they were too big for their home jurisdictions unaided to save (Cecchetti and Schoenholtz 2008: 31–6).

It was fortunate that monetary union occurred during a long upswing in the world and European economies. The ECB proved adept at controlling inflation in the early 2000s without generating politically unsustainable divergences in prosperity. Whether monetary union will survive more troubled times remains to be seen.

Eastern Europe

After the collapse of the communist system the transition economies scrambled to adopt a western-style economic framework, including central bank independence. There were parallels between the 1990s and the 1920s, when a previous cohort of independent central banks was established in central and eastern Europe.

Many countries turned to the west for advice and reassurance. As Michel Camdessus, the managing director of the IMF between 1987 and 2000, explained in relation to Russia: 'we were confronted with the dismantling of the party and of the state. So we had to help reconstruct everything: a central bank, a ministry of finance, a treasury' (Camdessus and Naim 2000: 41). Western central banks offered training and support to their east European counterparts, who were struggling to come to terms with the operation of a market economy. The

Bank of England created a Centre for Central Banking Studies in 1999 with such work in mind (Davies, H. 1997: 228).

German monetary, economic, and social reunification took place in July 1990. The East German currency was replaced by the DM at negotiated exchange rates. The Staatsbank, the East German central bank was stripped of its central banking responsibilities, becoming the Staatsbank Berlin. The Bundesbank stepped into its place. As was the case with the EMU project, the Bundesbank was unenthusiastic about economic and monetary union with East Germany, fearing that monetary control would be compromised by the need to supply currency to the east, and that re-absorption of the east would impose a crippling fiscal burden on the German government. Though somewhat exaggerated, these concerns were not groundless. The Bundesbank tightened monetary policy in the early 1990s in order to maintain low inflation in the new environment, a decision that had awkward consequences for Germany's partners in the ERM (Frowen and Hölscher 1997; Streit 1999).

Western advisers played a part in the reform of monetary institutions in eastern Europe, and nowhere more so than in Bosnia-Herzegovina, a country devastated by inter-ethnic violence after the disintegration of communist Yugoslavia. The Central Bank of Bosnia-Herzegovina (CBBH), established in 1997 under the terms of the Dayton Treaty, was designed by the IMF in conjunction with US officials. The first two governors were appointed by the IMF: the first was French, and the second a New Zealander. For the initial six years of its existence the CBBH was required to operate as a currency board without interference from the Bosnian parliament (Coats, W. 1999).

Elsewhere the influence of western practices was less direct. Price (1998) observed a tendency for central banks in east central Europe to take on the function of prudential supervision, despite the fact that some western central banks were losing this function. Perhaps it made sense to combine monetary policy and prudential supervision in countries where financial skills were scarce. Other aspects of the western central banking model, including CBI and inflation targeting, proved more popular. Hillman (1999: 81) wondered why so many former socialist countries opted for CBI in the 1990s, and offered several possible answers: they were free to design their central banks from scratch, they responded to pressure from international agencies, and they wished to emulate western success, and in particular that of the Bundesbank. Other possibilities are that CBI was regarded as a prerequisite for the control of inflation, and that it was a precondition for participation in EMU. A number of eastern European countries aspired to membership of the EU and the Eurosystem (Cukierman, Miller, and Neyapati 2002: 254). Words and deeds did not always tally. Belarus set up an 'independent' central bank, but then jailed the governor, apparently for disagreeing with the government's economic policy. The unfortunate governor was thus said to be 'independent but not free' (quoted in Hillman 1999: 81).

Central banks in transition economies discovered that inflation was almost impossible to contain during the early stages of liberalisation. The prices of many goods and services – not least those of basic foodstuffs and fuel – had been controlled by the communist authorities. Access to goods and services had been rationed by quantity rather than price. With the lifting of many of these controls, prices shot up. The exposure of inefficient businesses to competition was followed by deep recession. Governments responded by running large fiscal deficits. Central banks were required to monetise these deficits. Balino, Hoelscher, and Horder (1997) show how the Russian central bank was caught in this maelstrom in the early 1990s. Corruption, banking instability, the inadequate development of financial markets, and political interference hindered the efforts of central banks to exert monetary control during the early years of liberalisation, regardless of whether they had been granted 'independence'. These constraints were shared by many developing countries. A second round of legislation was often needed in order to confirm CBI. In any case, a western-style monetary policy could not be pursued until a measure of economic normality was restored (Cukierman, Miller, and Neyapati 2002).

The Czech Republic was one of the most economically and institutionally advanced of the transition economies. After the dismantling of communism in the early 1990s the Czechs pegged their currency, the crown, to a basket dominated by the DM and the US dollar for several years. When this approach came unstuck, the Czechs looked for an alternative nominal anchor, adopting an inflation targeting regime in January 1998. (This is what the British had done a few years earlier after the ERM crisis. Whereas the Czech National Bank became independent in 1991, however, the Bank of England did not achieve this status until 1997–8.) The Czech Republic was the first former communist country to introduce inflation targeting. Although the inflation target was undershot on several occasions because of strong exchange rate appreciations (Holub and Hurnik 2008), the new framework proved reasonably successful. Poland adopted inflation targeting in 1999, followed by Hungary in 2001 (Yilmazkuday 2008).

In 2004 and 2007 a number of eastern European countries were admitted to the EU, most with aspirations to enter the Eurosystem and adopt the euro. The pros and cons of their plans to join the monetary union are beyond the scope of this book, but in the interim some have been inclined to choose their exchange rate and monetary policies with this objective in mind.

Conclusion

Nowhere has the institutional framework within which central bankers work changed more rapidly since the late 1980s than in Europe. Monetary union was not on the agenda of most EEC central bankers in 1985, yet it was a reality by 1999. Few imagined that the Soviet empire would disintegrate and that independent central banks – several of them genuinely independent – would be established in eastern Europe. Few believed that within a few years the Bundesbank would be subordinated to an even more independent supranational central bank. (But no one would have been surprised that the British chose to watch developments from the sidelines.)

These were exciting times for central bankers. The governors of the EEC central banks were invited by the European Council, and encouraged by Jacques Delors, to draw up the blueprint for Economic and Monetary Union and the creation of a supranational central bank. Central bankers' involvement in this project strengthened the bonds between them – they were an epistemic community with common values, perceptions, and objectives. The ECB offered a grand stage for the performances of Europe's leading central bankers. After the fall of communism, eastern European central bankers attained a new status. They aspired to the technical skills of their western counterparts, and sought to become part of the European central banking club.

For the Bundesbank, however, European monetary union was hard to accept, but so many concessions were made to accommodate the Germans that it was impossible to reject. Having 'replaced the Wehrmacht as Germany's best-known and best-feared institution' in the second half of the twentieth century (Marsh 1993: 10), the Bundesbank was reduced almost to powerlessness by 2000. The resilience of the new central banking framework was not seriously tested in the early 2000s. Only time will tell whether it has the resilience to persist in less benign conditions.

16   A world with half a million central bankers

> This has been a central-banking century ... the number of central
> banks has risen from 18 in 1900 to 172 in 1998. The world now has
> almost half a million central bankers.
>
> The Economist (1998: 162)

> There seems to be a widespread perception that the global economy
> now stands on the brink, but the brink of what remains the question.
>
> Bank for International Settlements (2000: 142)

For the world of central banking, the twentieth century ended with the
retirement of Alan Greenspan from the chairmanship of the Federal
Reserve Board on 31 January 2006. At the time, Greenspan was widely
believed to have been one of the most successful central bankers ever.
Even Milton Friedman, a long-standing critic both of the Fed and of
discretionary monetary policy, extolled Greenspan's deft monetary
management in the 1990s (Nelson, E. 2007b). The Greenspan years
witnessed several close misses with financial meltdown, including
the 1987 stock market crash, emerging market crises in Asia, Latin
America, and Russia, the Long-Term Capital Management (LTCM)
fiasco in 1998, the dotcom implosion in the early 2000s, and the attacks
on 11 September. Greenspan, the great helmsman, was credited with
steering the ship away from the rocks each time. The praise heaped on
him by many commentators, including academics (Kahn 2005), was
also an endorsement of the central banking profession, which seemed
to have triumphed over inflation, and appeared to be on the verge of
implementing more effective techniques for averting and containing
financial crises through Basel II.

With the onset of the first major financial and economic crisis of the
twenty-first century in 2007–9 (Bordo 2008), the standard interpretation of recent financial history was brought into question. Not only
did Greenspan's reputation suffer, so did that of the central banking
profession as a whole. Central bankers had not seen disaster loom-
ing. The banking crisis of 2007–9 led to the resurgence of government

intervention and ownership in the banking industry in some countries, turning back the clock to a previous era. Though central bankers could point out that there is no reliable method of predicting crashes, they might still face a backlash. The late twentieth-century orthodoxy, based on central bank independence (CBI) and inflation targeting, might not last forever (Singleton 2009).

Central bankers were not oblivious to the fact that banks were taking on more risk in the early years of the twenty-first century, especially in the area of housing-related lending. By and large, however, they continued to feel that underlying conditions were benign. In its April 2007 *Financial Stability Report*, the Bank of England warned banks to pay more attention to risk, but added reassuringly that the probability of systemic instability was very low:

The UK financial system remains highly resilient. But strong and stable macro-economic and financial conditions have encouraged financial institutions to expand further their business activities and to extend their risk-taking ... That has increased the vulnerability of the system as a whole to an abrupt change in conditions ... [Nevertheless the] operating environment for UK banks and global financial institutions has remained stable over much of the period since the July 2006 [*Financial Stability*] *Report*. Conditions are likely to remain favourable. (Bank of England 2007: 5)

This point was reinforced by a diagram showing a normal distribution of events with a small 'tail' of seriously adverse outcomes. Within two years, the British government had, in the face of mounting panic, become the outright owner of two troubled medium-sized banks, Northern Rock and Bradford and Bingley, and a major shareholder of two of the country's largest banks, the Royal Bank of Scotland (RBS) and Lloyds Banking Group. Lloyds had earlier been encouraged by the authorities to acquire the troubled Halifax Bank of Scotland.

Despite the problems in the UK with Northern Rock and RBS, and those in the USA with Bear Stearns, Lehman Brothers, and others, Iceland was hit the hardest in relative terms. The Icelandic banking system and currency collapsed in 2008. The 2007 financial stability report of the Central Bank of Iceland expressed some concern about credit risk, but was apparently blissfully unaware of the extent of the challenge facing the financial sector:

On the whole, the Central Bank's finding is that the financial system is broadly sound. It is equipped to withstand shocks to the economy and financial markets, to mediate credit and payments, and to redistribute risks appropriately. In other words, it is capable of performing its function in an orderly and efficient way. Iceland's banking system meets the demands made of it and performs well on stress tests conducted by the Central Bank and FME [the Financial Supervisory Authority]. (Central Bank of Iceland 2007: 7)

The BIS was somewhat less sanguine about global prospects in its 2006–7 annual report, released in June 2007. While the consensus forecast was for continued growth in the world economy, there were many uncertainties, including several related to credit risk. Prior to the collapse of LTCM in 1998, noted the BIS, this hedge fund was commonly believed to be appropriately diversified, highly liquid, and well capitalised, but in fact it was none of these.

Economics is not an exact science … economic forecasts are often widely off the mark, particularly at cyclical turning points … Indeed … we face a fundamentally uncertain world – one in which probabilities cannot be calculated – rather than simply a risky one … [V]irtually no one foresaw the Great Depression of the 1930s, or the crises which affected Japan and Southeast Asia in the early and late 1990s, respectively. In fact, each downturn was preceded by a period of non-inflationary growth exuberant enough to lead many commentators to suggest that a 'new era' had arrived. (Bank for International Settlements 2007: 139)

While the BIS did not foresee the impending disaster, it did at least emphasise the dangers of assuming that recent trends could be projected into the future. Later on there was a lot of explaining to do: 'A spokesman for Buckingham Palace said the Queen has displayed a particular interest in the causes of the recession, summoning Bank of England governor Mervyn King to a private audience earlier this year to explain what he was doing to tackle it' (Stewart 2009).

Were central banks ready for the crisis?

Work on this book started in 2006, before the onset of the crisis, and this final chapter does not attempt to address that episode in any detail. None the less, historians of central banking can make some useful observations on recent events. In particular, we might enquire what had exercised the minds of central bankers at the start of the new millennium.

Most central banks were rather pleased with themselves following their gains in autonomy and their success on the monetary policy front in the late twentieth century. The smooth transition to monetary union in Europe was also a reason for celebration in part of the central banking world. Fears that payment systems could be disrupted by computer failure at the start of the year 2000 (the Y2K problem) proved totally unfounded. It would be unfair to suggest that central bankers were complacent about the threats to financial stability. The fact that some central banks started to publish financial stability reports in the 1990s attests to their growing interest in macroprudential issues, as well as to their newfound commitment to the principle of transparency. Banks and banking systems were subjected to stress tests by computer models, and were constantly urged to improve their risk management procedures. Basel II was inspired by concerns about financial instability, though the inordinate amount of time spent in haggling over the terms of the new accord suggests a lack of urgency in some quarters.

In October 2000, Otmar Issing of the ECB delivered the 'Millennium Year Lecture' at St Edmund's College, Cambridge. He had been commissioned to discuss 'Faith and finance in the new millennium', but found this a rather daunting task, and one has some sympathy for him. Instead he asked: 'Should we have faith in central banks?' Issing said that people could have confidence in central banks (especially the ECB) because under the new dispensation of CBI, transparency, accountability, and credibility, they were more likely to deliver price stability than in the past. But he did not address the role of central banks in the maintenance of financial stability (Issing 2000). Was there nothing to fear on that score?

Addressing the Federal Reserve Bank of Kansas City's annual symposium at Jackson Hole, Wyoming in 1999, Mervyn King (1999: 11) endeavoured to 'assess the role of central banks in the modern world'. During the twentieth century central banks had spread across the face of the globe. In recent years they had achieved a 'position of power and responsibility unrivalled in their history'. But, he wondered, 'How many will there be one hundred years from now? Will central banks survive at all? This was 'no time for hubris':

There is a widespread intellectual consensus – almost a conventional wisdom about the objectives that central banks should pursue, and the means by which they should pursue them. This is a very dangerous position. Could it be that 1999 is the apogee of the power of central banks? I believe that if central banks are to retain their central position in economic policy making, they must face up to the intellectual and technological challenges that lie ahead. Unless they do so, popularity will turn to disillusion. (King 1999: 14)

King devoted most of his paper to the problems of designing and embedding a monetary policy regime that would continue to deliver price stability in changing circumstances, and thus preserve the legitimacy of the CBI and inflation targeting framework. Towards the end of the paper, he touched on two other issues. First, there would be fewer national central banks if monetary unions became more popular. Secondly, if the private sector developed effective means of making final settlement without the assistance of central banks, they would struggle to implement monetary policy and could become redundant.

The rapid growth of electronic money could produce such a situation. 'Societies have managed without central banks in the past. They may well do so again in the future' (King 1999: 50). But the main threats to the status quo evidently did not include widespread financial turmoil.

This is not to suggest that financial instability was ignored. After all, central bankers were busy negotiating Basel II. Though the annual report of the BIS for 2000 found the world economy in good shape, attention was drawn to the growing danger of 'excess', and the emergence of major 'imbalances'. Perhaps the most alarming of these imbalances was the US current account deficit, which was funded by capital inflows, especially from Asia. It was uncertain how long foreigners would be willing to accommodate the US deficit (BIS 2000: 31, 33). If they ceased, then the US economy would be in serious trouble and repercussions would be felt throughout the world. Some unease was expressed about the mechanisms for the avoidance, management, and resolution of financial crises: 'With respect to each, the actual progress made has been substantial, but is dwarfed by what remains to be done' (BIS 2000: 148). Devising appropriate policies was difficult enough, but implementing them would be an even bigger challenge. The incidence of crises had risen in recent decades and the future was unknowable, points that the BIS reiterated in June 2007. Ultimately it was reckless US sub-prime mortgage lending, combined with opaque loan securitisation, and facilitated by capital inflows, that precipitated panic in the global financial system, something that no one, including the BIS, had foreseen clearly in 1999–2000.

The response of central banks and governments once the alarm was sounded was relatively swift, which indicates that many of the lessons of 1929–33 had been digested. It helped that the new chairman of the Federal Reserve Board was an expert on the economic history of the depression, but in any case enough was known about the failures of the 1930s to prevent any repetition of the inaction and perversity shown then by policy makers. It is not suggested that the management of the crisis was optimal – many clumsy errors were made and future historians will pick over them at their leisure – but at least the measures taken were largely expansionary rather than deflationary or neutral, unlike in the early 1930s. Furthermore, it was beneficial that exchange rates, other than within the Eurosystem, were flexible in 2007–9.

Regardless of how much central banks are genuinely to blame for the current financial turmoil, they will be criticised, and there will be calls for the scrapping or modification of the existing framework. An accommodating monetary policy after the dotcom crash of the early

2000s, when there were fears of deflation (Taylor 2009: 2–4), reinforced by perceptions that the Fed would always come to the rescue (the 'Greenspan put'), encouraged risk taking. The distress or failure of so many banks is prima facie evidence of the failure of banking supervision and 'macroprudential' oversight of the system. Although the responsibility of central banks for supervising individual banks varies, their responsibility for upholding systemic stability is unambiguous. Perhaps there were shortcomings in coordination between central banks and other supervisors. At any rate central banks have now become a potential target for politicians, as they were in the 1930s and 1940s.

The depression was followed by the nationalisation of many central banks, and to a greater or lesser extent the incorporation of others into a government-managed economic policy complex. The dominant economic doctrines also changed in the mid twentieth century, resulting in a growing emphasis on planning, regulation, and fiscal policy. Central banks were unable to oppose the policy revolution of the 1930s and 1940s because they could not afford to take sides in party politics. Government-imposed changes in senior personnel, and the advent of a new generation of central bankers who were not committed to the gold standard, also ensured the gradual assimilation of new ways of thinking about policy.

Central bank independence and inflation targeting, the dominant paradigm of the 1990s and 2000s, might prove to be no less vulnerable than the gold standard paradigm in the 1930s (Singleton 2009). In the USA, the 'Ron Paul revolution', which involves demands for greater public scrutiny of the Fed, with a view to its eventual abolition, could be the first stage of the assault on orthodoxy. Paul demonstrates that attacks may come from the populist right as well as the left (Paul 2009a).

The current crisis has brought politics back into the domain of central banking (Demirgüc-Kunt and Servén 2009; Reinhart and Felton 2008; Felton and Reinhart 2009). Politicians were involved alongside central bankers and banking supervisors in deciding when to rescue ailing banks (and when not to in the case of Lehman Brothers), and sooner or later taxpayers and/or savers must foot the bill. Central bankers appeared in the company of senior government officials and ministers to announce and defend rescue packages. The need for heavy government borrowing to finance the bail out and recapitalisation of the banking system, and to meet the routine fiscal costs of recession at a time of falling tax revenues, will tempt some politicians to turn on the printing presses. Before inflating away increased debt, politicians will have to withdraw the autonomy of the central bank, or at least coerce the central bank into compliance. The massive injection of liquidity by the authorities in order to preserve systemic stability also creates the potential for inflation in the future. Willem Buiter (2009) speculates that the current financial crisis has 'signalled the beginning of the end' for central bank independence. Another leading monetary economist, Guido Tabellini (2008), suggests that even though governments may delegate monetary policy to central banks when the objectives are clear and success is easily measured, when 'larger and more uncertain questions open up, politicians will be tempted to break central bank independence and take back decision-making'.

Unless the world economy and banking systems enjoy full and speedy recoveries, central banks could be 'on the brink' of yet another new era. A third central banking revolution cannot be ruled out, potentially undoing or at least compromising some of the changes introduced in the 1980s and 1990s. The only area in which it would be impracticable to turn back the clock is transparency. Once transparency has been granted, a return to secrecy would be hard to justify.

Unresolved problems

In an influential analysis of the development of central banking in the second half of the twentieth century, Pierre Siklos (2002: 204–18, 306–8) argued that after decades of experimentation there was a growing consensus on the most appropriate monetary policy framework in the 1990s. But one result of the crisis of 2007–9 may be that the central banking conundrums that appeared to have been solved in the 1990s will be revisited.

The relationship between central banks and the societies in which they operate will always be subject to renegotiation, as Mervyn King (2004: 1), the governor of the Bank of England, explained to a meeting of the American Economic Association:

[T]he core of the monetary-policy problem is uncertainty about future social decisions resulting from the impossibility and the undesirability of committing our successors to any given monetary-policy strategy. The impossibility stems from the observation that collective decisions cannot be enforced, so that it is impossible to commit to future collective decisions; the undesirability reflects the fact that we cannot articulate all possible future states of the world.

The same principle applies to other public policy agencies such as banking supervisors (including central banks where they have this role), state audit offices, the police, and the armed forces. Ultimately, there is nearly always 'joint central bank–government responsibility for monetary policy' and governments nearly always have the power to override central banks (Siklos 2002: 303). The exception to this rule may be the ECB which operates under a law that cannot be changed without altering an EU treaty. The question of how best to structure the relationship between the government and the central bank is a recurring one. Different answers have been found in different eras and contexts. How much power should the state delegate to technocrats in the central bank, and how and to whom should they be held accountable? The state has set the goals of the central bank from the days of gold convertibility onwards, through the period of multiple objectives after the Second World War, and into the modern era of inflation targeting. Sometimes central banks have been left to get on with implementation, and sometimes governments have intervened in, or sought to direct, operations. Whilst the distinction between goal and operational independence is often assumed to be a product of the 1990s, it was implicit in the approach of earlier economists such as Keynes (Bibow 2002), and was grappled with throughout the twentieth century.

There is nothing to stop a government (except in the Eurosystem for reasons indicated above) from once again assigning multiple goals – say price stability, a zero output gap, and stable asset prices – to the central bank, whilst retaining the principle of operational independence. This might not be a sensible thing to do, but it is a conceivable policy option. In countries such as the UK, Japan, and New Zealand, further legislation would be required to change the goals of the central bank, but in others such as Australia, Canada, or the USA it would be sufficient to twist a few arms and agree on the reinterpretation of old legislation. Governments might also decide that a return to macroeconomic policy coordination was desirable, and seek to reduce the operational autonomy of central banks. Since there is no consensus as to the proper location of banking supervision, there could be further changes in this area. In 2009 the British Conservative Party proposed returning this function to the Bank of England, an approach confirmed by the new government in 2010.

Different forms of accountability are associated with different central banking frameworks. The weaker the autonomy of the central bank, the stronger will be the lines of accountability to the executive branch of the state. The more independent the central bank, the greater is the likelihood that accountability will take the form of having to explain its actions to the legislature and the public. In some cases accountability could amount to little more than transparency plus a willingness to listen to (but not necessarily heed) criticism. Of course it is important to know for what the central bank is held accountable. When there is a single and fairly clear goal, such as gold convertibility or price stability, it is relatively easy to judge the performance of the central bank, and if desired impose penalties for failure. But even the RBNZ has multiple goals, namely price stability and financial stability, because it has several functions. When there are multiple goals the central bank always has a plausible excuse for failure, and the potential to avoid being held accountable. This state of affairs is unlikely to change.

Whilst the current preference is for a mixture of rules and discretion (or constrained discretion) there have been so many changes of thinking on this issue that it would be reckless to predict the future. Nothing is fixed. Even the advocates of free banking continue to come forward with intellectually plausible proposals, including one for the use of inflation targeting by individual banks in a free banking system (Ferris and Galbraith 2006), though we can at least be fairly confident that this idea will not be implemented in the foreseeable future.

Central banking revolutions

According to Steven Solomon (1995: 13), 'Central bankers' fingerprints are everywhere behind the daily financial headlines.' This would not have been the case in 1900, when there were fewer central banks and central bankers, and their sphere of operations was more limited. The twentieth century saw the spread of central banks across the world. The reasons for their foundation were many and varied. In developed countries central banks have always been concerned with monetary and financial stability, but these concerns were expressed in very different ways at different times. In developing countries they have also been agencies and symbols of economic modernisation. Sometimes under duress from governments, their developmental role was allowed to usurp their responsibilities for the promotion of monetary and financial stability. In communist nations central banks were agents of the plan, though even this state of affairs began to change, in China in particular in the 1980s. Towards the end of the twentieth century, there was a large measure of convergence around the world towards a model of central banking based on operational autonomy (whether formal or informal) and a determined approach to the control of inflation, whether or not this extended to a formal inflation targeting framework. However, in some countries official statements of support for this model were belied by continued government manipulation behind the scenes.

Central banks began as small organisations, but grew into monsters in the mid to late twentieth century. This was partly a reflection of the acquisition of new functions, especially in the regulatory arena after the Second World War. But it was also a product of loose budget

constraints. Employment did not expand only in relatively autonomous central banks such as the Bundesbank and the Federal Reserve
System. Indeed this growth was a global phenomenon until the 1990s,
when English-speaking and Scandinavian central banks in particular
began to pay more attention to questions of internal efficiency, partly in
response to pressure from governments. At the same time, some central
banking functions were becoming redundant. Cheque processing, one
of the activities of the US Federal Reserve Banks, has been contracting
in recent years because fewer cheques are being written. Rationalisation
of cheque processing facilities is leading the Reserve Banks to shed substantial amounts of labour (Federal Reserve Financial Service Policy
Committee 2008). In future there may not be a great deal for the
Reserve Banks, other than the FRBNY, to do except conduct economic
research ... but don't tell anyone.

As central banks in the developed world have withdrawn from
some routine operational activities, they have closed many branches
and reduced staff numbers. The Bank of Spain, for example, closed
30 branches between 2000 and 2004. Central banks are concentrating
increasingly on their core policy functions, which employ more highly
skilled and expensive staff (Galan Camacho and Sarmiento Paipilla
2007). Research in the early twenty-first century indicated the presence of large variations in efficiency levels amongst central banks, as
might be expected given their lack of competitors, and differences in
the laxity of their budget constraints, functional scope, and access to
human capital. Ironically, the Icelandic central bank was identified as
one of the least inefficient (McKinley and Banaian 2005).

There were two revolutions in central banking during the twentieth century. The first occurred in the 1930s and 1940s. Appalled by
recent policy disasters, and influenced by Keynesian, corporatist,
and socialist doctrines, political leaders in many countries rewrote
their central banking laws. Even in those countries, such as the USA,
where legislative change was more modest, governments became much
more involved in the management of monetary and exchange rate policy. Many central banks were allocated new functions including the
administration of exchange controls and banking regulations. As well
as contributing to monetary policy, banking regulation substituted for
prudential supervision.

The second revolution in the late twentieth century was in a sense
part of a wider programme of public sector restructuring. This wave of
reform addressed problems arising from high inflation, the discredit-
ing of Keynesianism (and later of monetarism), and perceptions of time
inconsistent behaviour by policy makers. Central bank independence

and inflation targeting became the new orthodoxy in the 1990s. Many countries passed legislation to grant autonomy to their central banks, often reversing the decisions of the mid twentieth century; others (including the USA and Australia) reinterpreted existing legislation either to reinforce or establish autonomy. With respect to CBI, the pendulum moved in both directions in the twentieth century (Goodhart, Capie, and Schnadt 1994: 48–9), an analogy suggesting that it could swing again.

Central bankers changed over the course of the century. At the outset they were specialised bankers with a limited public policy role. Knowledge of the markets made up for ignorance of economic theory. With the outbreak of war in 1914, central bankers started to enter more closely into the public policy arena; by the 1940s they were public or civil servants as well as bankers, though most would not have welcomed this description. From the Second World War onwards the influence of economics and of economists began to grow, albeit at a different pace in each country, with the Fed taking the lead. By the close of the twentieth century the economists had in many cases taken over: their culture was grafted on to the earlier banking and civil service cultures. The development and transformation of the central banking profession was accomplished by generational change.

International contacts between central bankers emerged in the 1920s, as Montagu Norman and his peers attempted to salvage the gold standard. They were united by a gold standard *mentalité*, though this did not prevent them from pursuing national interests as well. Another surge in central bank cooperation occurred in the second half of the twentieth century. Central bankers came to form an epistemic community with common principles, attitudes, and intellectual positions, though these positions changed as intellectual fashion evolved. This epistemic community played a role in the unsuccessful defence of the Bretton Woods system, the Basel project for the coordination of prudential supervision, and the design and implementation of European monetary union.

Central bankers proved adept at protecting their turf, a term used in this context by Havrilesky (1995). Each of the functions commonly assigned to central banks could have been performed by another agency. Monetary policy could have been taken under the umbrella of the Treasury, while commercial banks could have settled with one another on the books of a trusted private institution. Yet central banks held their ground. They had expertise and skills that would have been expensive to recreate, and they benefited from the fact that governments often found it convenient to delegate responsibility for unpopular monetary policy decisions to them. They also made themselves useful by offering governments an alternative source of economic advice, one that was frequently as well informed as the Treasury. Central banks could be entrepreneurial, searching for answers to some of the pressing international economic problems of the day, such as how to cope with the enhanced risk of banking crises in a globalised and deregulated financial marketplace. Unlike other nationalised industries, central banks rarely had to ask their governments for hand outs. Wherever possible, they strove to enhance their credibility and status by achieving their policy goals. Yet central bankers were also pragmatists who were prepared to sacrifice their autonomy if this was necessary to guarantee their survival. When things were not going well, moreover, they attempted to shift blame on to others. They could play off different external groups, such as the government, academics, and the banking system, against one another. Over many decades, central bankers cultivated an aura of mystery and secret knowledge. With the advent of transparency they had to become more open, but their use of the language of economics (or econometrics) allowed them to retain a body of knowledge that was impenetrable to outsiders whilst confirming their scientific status.

The late twentieth century was the golden age of central banking when everything seemed to fall into place. Governments were eager to proclaim the independence of their central banks. Inflation – the bugbear of the 1970s and 1980s – had been overcome. Central bankers seemed to know what they were doing. They were widely respected, and one or two were even the focus of adulation. True, financial stability was a nagging concern, but the Basel Committee was working on a solution. Other threats such as the spread of electronic money were in the distant future. What could go wrong?

References

Abiad, A., Detragiache, E., and Tressel, T. 2008. 'A new database of financial reforms', IMF Working Paper WP/08/266

Abiad, A. and Mody, A. 2005. 'Financial liberalization: what shakes it? what shapes it?', *American Economic Review* **95**, 1: 66–88

Abrams, B. A. 2006. 'How Richard Nixon pressured Arthur Burns: evidence from the Nixon tapes', *Journal of Economic Perspectives* **20**, 4: 177–88

Acheson, K. and Chant, J. F. 1986. 'Bureaucratic theory and the choice of central bank goals: the case of the Bank of Canada', in Toma and Toma (eds.), pp. 129–50

Adams, E. S. 1957. 'The impact of monetary management on commercial banks in the United States', in Bundesverband des Privaten Bankgewerbes, *Relations between the central banks and commercial banks*. Frankfurt am Main: Fritz Knapp, pp. 129–41

Aghevli, B. B., Khan, M. S., Narvekar, P. R., and Short, B. K. 1979. 'Monetary policy in selected Asian countries', *IMF Staff Papers* **26**, 4: 775–824

Ahamed, L. 2009. *Lords of finance: the bankers who broke the world*. New York: Penguin

Ahrensdorf, J. 1959. 'Central bank policies and inflation: a case study of four less developed economies, 1949–57', *IMF Staff Papers* **7**, 2: 274–301

Ahsan, A., Skully, M., and Wickramanayake, J. 2007. 'Does central bank independence and governance matter in Asia Pacific?' Bocconi University, "Paolo Baffi" Centre Research Paper Series No. 2008–27

Aldcroft, D. H. 2007. 'The fatal inversion: the African growth disaster', in M. J. Oliver, and D. H. Aldcroft (eds.), *Economic disasters of the twentieth century*. Cheltenham: Edward Elgar, pp. 312–54

Aldcroft, D. H. and Oliver M. J. 2001. *Exchange rate regimes in the twentieth century*. Cheltenham: Edward Elgar

Alhadeff, D. A. 1968. *Competition and controls in banking; a study of the regulation of bank competition in Italy, France, and England*. Berkeley: University of California Press

Amsden, A. H. 1989. *Asia's next giant*. New York: Oxford University Press

Andersson, K. and Berg, C. 1995. 'The inflation target in Sweden', in A. G. Haldane (ed.), *Targeting inflation*. London: Bank of England, pp. 207–25

Andrews, D. M. 2003. 'The Committee of Central Bank Governors as a source of rules', *Journal of European Public Policy* **10**, 6: 956–73

Anon. 1975. 'From racism to genocide: extracts from Report of the International Commission of Jurists', *Transition* 49: 8–19

Anon.2001. 'Women in central banks', *Central Banking* **XI**, 3: 59–66

Apel, E. 2003. *Central banking systems compared: the ECB, the pre-euro Bundesbank, and the Federal Reserve System.* New York: Routledge

Archer, D. 1997. 'The New Zealand approach to rules and discretion in monetary policy', *Journal of Monetary Economics* 39: 3–15

Arestis, P. and Mihailov A. 2009. 'Flexible rules cum constrained discretion: a new consensus in monetary policy', *Economic Issues* **14**, 2: 27–54

Aron, J. and Muellbauer, J. 2007. 'Review of monetary policy in South Africa since 1994', *Journal of African Economies* **16**, 5: 705–44

Asso, P. F., Kahn, G. A., and Leeson, R. 2007. 'The Taylor rule and the transformation of monetary policy', Federal Reserve Bank of Kansas City Research Working Paper No. 07–11

Baer, G. D. 1999. 'Sixty-five years of central bank cooperation at the Bank for International Settlements', in Holtfrerich, Reis, and Toniolo (eds.), pp. 341–61

Bagehot, W. 1873. *Lombard Street.* London: King

Baker, B. and Singer, Z. 2006. 'Interview: Jean-Pierre Roth', *Central Banking* **17**, 1: 35–41

Balachandran, G. 1994. 'Towards a "Hindoo Marriage": Anglo-Indian monetary relations in interwar India, 1917–35', *Modern Asian Studies* **28**, 3: 615–47

1998. *The Reserve Bank of India, 1951–1967.* Delhi: Oxford University Press

Balasubramanyam, V. N. 2001. *Conversations with Indian economists.* Basingstoke: Palgrave

Balderston, T. 1989. 'War finance and inflation in Britain and Germany, 1914–1918', *Economic History Review* 42: 222–44

1991. 'German banking between the wars: the crisis of the credit banks', *Business History Review* **65**: 554–605

2002. *Economics and politics in the Weimar Republic.* Cambridge University Press

Baldwin, B. E., Enoch, C., Frecault, O., and Kovanen, A. 2001. 'Indonesia: anatomy of a banking crisis', IMF Working Papers No. 01/52

Balino, T. J. T., Hoelscher, D. S., and Horder, J. 1997. 'Evolution of monetary policy instruments in Russia', IMF Working Paper No. WP/97/180

Ball, L. and Sheridan, N. 2005. 'Does inflation targeting matter?', in B. S. Bernanke and M. Woodford (eds.), *The inflation-targeting debate.* University of Chicago Press, pp. 249–76

Baltensperger, E. 1999. 'Monetary policy under conditions of increasing integration (1979–96)', in Deutsche Bundesbank (ed.), pp. 439–523

Bank for International Settlements 1963. *Eight European central banks.* London: George Allen & Unwin

1986. *Recent innovations in international banking.* Basel: BIS

2000. *70th Annual Report.* Basel: BIS

2007. *77th Annual Report.* Basel: BIS

Bank of Canada 2001. 'Fact sheet: seigniorage revenue', www.bankofcanada.ca/en/backgrounders/bg-m3.html (accessed 6 August 2009)

Bank of England 1976. 'The work of the Economic Intelligence Department', *Bank of England Quarterly Bulletin* **16**, 4: 436–46

2007. *Financial stability report April 2007*. London: Bank of England

2008. '*The Wind in the Willows* display', www.bankofengland.co.uk/education/museum/exhibitions/thewindinthewillows.htm (accessed 13 October 2008)

Bank of Thailand 1992. *50 years of the Bank of Thailand 1942–1992*. Bangkok: Bank of Thailand

Barbosa-Filho, N. H. 2008. 'Inflation targeting in Brazil: 1999–2006', *International Review of Applied Economics* **22**, 2: 187–200

Barro, R. and Gordon, D. 1983a. 'A positive theory of monetary policy in a natural rate model', *Journal of Political Economy* **91**, 4: 589–610

1983b. 'Rules, discretion and reputation in a model of monetary policy', *Journal of Monetary Economics* **12**, 1: 101–21

Bartel, R. D. 1995–6. 'Federal Reserve independence and the people's quest for full employment and price stability', *Journal of Post-Keynesian Economics* **18**, 2: 231–49

Barth, J., Brumbaugh, D., and Wilcox, J. 2000. 'Glass-Steagall repealed: market forces compel a new bank legal structure', *Journal of Economic Perspectives* **14**, 2: 191–204

Barth, J., Caprio, G., and Levine, R. 2001. 'Banking systems around the world: do regulations and ownership affect performance and stability?', in Mishkin (ed.), pp. 31–88

2006. *Rethinking banking regulation: till angels govern*. Cambridge University Press

Batra, R. 2005. *Greenspan's fraud: how two decades of his policies have undermined the global economy*. New York: Palgrave Macmillan

Battilossi, S. 2000. 'Financial innovation and the golden ages of international banking: 1890–1931 and 1958–81', *Financial History Review* 7: 141–75

Bayoumi, T., Eichengreen, B., and Taylor, M. P. (eds.) 1996. *Modern perspectives on the gold standard*. Cambridge University Press

BBC 2008. 'Indonesia banker jailed for graft', http://news.bbc.co.uk/go/pr/fr/-/1/hi/world/asia-pacific/7697244.stm (accessed 13 February 2009)

Bean, C. 1992. 'Economic and Monetary Union in Europe', *Journal of Economic Perspectives* **6**, 4: 31–52

1998. 'The new UK monetary arrangements: a view from the literature', *Economic Journal* **108**, 451: 1795–809

1999. 'Australasian monetary policy: a comparative approach', *Australian Economic Review* **32**: 64–7

Bebenroth, R., Dietrich, D., and Vollmer, U. 2007. 'Bank regulation and supervision in Japan and Germany: a comparison', Kobe University Department of Economics Working Paper No. 211

Bech, M. L. and Hobijn, B. 2006. 'Technology diffusion within central banking: the case of real-time gross settlement', *Federal Reserve Bank of New York Staff Reports*, No. 260

Beckerman, P. 2001. 'Dollarization and semi-dollarization in Ecuador', World Bank Policy Research Working Paper No. 2643

Beckhart, B. H. 1972. *Federal Reserve System*. New York: Columbia University Press

Beenstock, M. 2007. 'The rise, fall and rise again of OPEC', in M. J. Oliver and D. H. Aldcroft (eds.), *Economic disasters of the twentieth century*. Cheltenham: Edward Elgar, pp. 133–61

Bell, P. W. 1956. *The sterling area in the post-war world*. Oxford University Press

Bell, S. 2004. *Australia's money mandarins: the Reserve Bank and the politics of money*. Cambridge University Press

Benston, G. J. and Kaufman, G. G. 1995, 'Is the banking and payments system fragile?', *Journal of Financial Services Research* 9: 209–40

Berg, C. and Jonung, L. 1999. 'Pioneering price level targeting: the Swedish experience 1931–1937', *Journal of Monetary Economics* 43: 525–51

Berger, H. 1997. 'The Bundesbank's path to independence: evidence from the 1950s', *Public Choice* 93: 427–53

Bergh, T. 1981. 'Norway: the powerful servants', in Coats (ed.), pp. 133–74

Bernanke, B. S. 1983. 'Nonmonetary effects of the financial crisis in the propagation of the great depression', *American Economic Review* 73, 3: 257–76

    1995. 'The macroeconomics of the great depression: a comparative approach', *Journal of Money, Credit, and Banking* 27, 1: 1–28

    2000. *Essays on the great depression*. Princeton University Press

    2005 'Panel discussion – the transition from academic to policymaker: remarks by Mr Ben S. Bernanke, Member of the Board of Governors of the US Federal Reserve System, at the Annual Meeting of the American Economic Association, Philadelphia, 7 January 2005', *BIS Review* 1: 1–3

    2007. 'The financial accelerator and the credit channel'. Speech at the Credit Channel of Monetary Policy in the Twenty-first Century Conference, Federal Reserve Bank of Atlanta, Atlanta, Georgia, June 15. www.federalreserve.gov/newsevents/speech/bernanke20070615a.htm (accessed 1 October 2009)

    2008. 'The Fed's road toward greater transparency', *Cato Journal* 28, 2: 175–86

Bernanke, B. S., Laubach, T., Mishkin, F. S., and Posen, A. S. 1999. *Inflation targeting: lessons from the international experience*. Princeton University Press

Bernanke, B. S. and Mihov, I. 1997. 'What does the Bundesbank target?', *European Economic Review* 41: 1025–53

Bernanke, B. S. and Mishkin, F. S. 1997. 'Inflation targeting: a new framework for monetary policy?', *Journal of Economic Perspectives* 11, 2: 97–116

Bernanke, B. S. and Woodford, M. (eds.) 2005. *The inflation targeting debate*. University of Chicago Press

Bernhard, W., Broz, J. L., and Clark, W. R. 2002. 'The political economy of monetary institutions', *International Organization* 56, 4: 693–723

Bernholz, P. 1999. 'The Bundesbank and the process of European monetary integration', in Deutsche Bundesbank (eds.), pp. 731–89

Beyen, J. W. 1949. *Money in a maelstrom*. London: Macmillan

Bhagwati, J. 1993. *India in transition*. Oxford: Clarendon Press

Bhatt, V. V. 1974. 'Some aspects of financial policies and central banking in developing countries', *World Development* 2, 10–12: 59–67

Bibow, J. 2002. 'Keynes on central banking and the structure of monetary policy', *History of Political Economy* 34, 4: 749–87

2004. 'Reflections on the current fashion for central bank independence', *Cambridge Journal of Economics* 28, 4: 549–76

2005. 'Refocussing the ECB on output stabilization and growth through inflation targeting?', Levy Economics Institute, Economics Working Paper Archive No. 425

2009. 'On the origin and rise of central bank independence in West Germany', *European Journal of the History of Economic Thought* 16, 1: 155–90

Bindseil, U. 2004. *Monetary policy implementation: theory, past, and present.* Oxford University Press

Blaazer, D. 2005. 'Finance and the end of appeasement: the Bank of England, the National Government and the Czech gold', *Journal of Contemporary History* 40, 1: 25–39

Blinder, A. S. 1998. *Central banking in theory and practice.* Cambridge, MA: MIT Press

2000. 'Central-bank credibility: why do we care? How do we build it?', *American Economic Review* 90, 5: 1421–31

2007. 'Monetary policy by committee: why and how?' *European Journal of Political Economy* 23: 106–23

Blinder, A. S. and Reis, R. 2005. 'Understanding the Greenspan standard', Princeton University Center for Economic Policy Studies Working Paper No. 114

Bloomfield, A. I. 1957. 'Some problems of central banking in underdeveloped countries', *Journal of Finance* 12, 2: 190–204

Blunden, G. 1975. 'The supervision of the UK banking system', *Bank of England Quarterly Bulletin* 15, 2: 188–94

Board of Governors of the Federal Reserve System 1994. *The Federal Reserve System: purposes and functions,* 8th edn. Washington, DC: Board of Governors of the Federal Reserve System

Bonin, H. 1992. 'The political influence of bankers and financiers in France in the Years 1850–1914', in Y. Cassis (ed.), *Finance and financiers in European history 1880–1960.* Cambridge University Press, pp. 219–42

2000. 'The emergence of the central banking functions at Banque de France', *Bankhistorisches Archiv* 26, 2: 97–116

Bopp, K. R. 1944. 'Central banking at the crossroads', *American Economic Review* 34, 1, part 2: 260–77

1952. 'Bank of France: brief survey of instruments, 1800–1914', *American Journal of Economics and Sociology* 11, 3: 229–44

1954. 'Central banking objectives, guides, and measures', *Journal of Finance* 9, 1: 12–22

Bordo, M. D. 2002. 'The lender of last resort: alternative views and historical experience', in C. Goodhart and G., Illing (eds.), *Financial crises, contagion, and the lender of last resort.* Oxford University Press, pp. 109–25

2007. 'Growing up to financial stability', NBER Working Paper No. 12993

2008. 'An historical perspective on the crisis of 2007–2008', NBER Working Paper No. 14569

Bordo, M. D., Edelstein, M., and Rockoff, H. 1999. 'Was adherence to the gold standard a "good housekeeping seal of approval" during the interwar period?', NBER Working Paper No. 7186

Bordo, M. and Eichengreen, B. (eds.) 1993. *A retrospective on the Bretton Woods system*. University of Chicago Press

Bordo, M., Eichengreen, B., Klingebiel, D., and Martinez-Peria, M. S. 2001. 'Financial crises: lessons from the last 120 years', *Economic Policy* **32**: 51–82

Bordo, M. D., Humpage, O., and Schwartz, A. J. 2007. 'The historical origins of U.S. exchange market intervention policy', *International Journal of Finance and Economics* **12**, 2: 109–32

Bordo, M. D. and Redish, A. 1987. 'Why did the Bank of Canada emerge in 1935?', *Journal of Economic History* **47**: 405–17

Bordo, M. D. and Schwartz, A. J. (eds.) 1984. *A retrospective on the classical gold standard, 1821–1931*. University of Chicago Press

Bordo, M. D. and Schwartz, A. J. 1996. 'Why clashes between internal and external stability goals end in currency crises, 1797–1994', *Open Economies Review* **7**: 437–68

2006. 'David Laidler on monetarism', NBER Working Papers, No. 12593

Borio, C. 1997. 'The implementation of monetary policy in industrial countries: a survey.' BIS Economic Papers, No. 47

Borio, C. and Filardo, A. 2007. 'Globalisation and inflation', BIS Working Papers, No. 227

Borio, C. and McCauley, R. N. 2002. 'Comparing monetary policy operating procedures in Indonesia, Korea, Malaysia and Thailand', in G. de Brouwer (ed.), *Financial markets and policies in East Asia*. London: Routledge, pp. 253–85

Borio, C., Toniolo, G., and Clement, P. (eds.) 2008. *Past and future of central bank cooperation*. Cambridge University Press

Borio, C. and Toniolo, G. 2008. 'One hundred and thirty years of central bank cooperation: a BIS perspective', in Borio, Toniolo, and Clement (eds.), pp. 16–75

Boughton, J. M. 2003. 'On the origins of the Fleming-Mundell model', *IMF Staff Papers* **50**, 1: 1–9

Bouvier, J. 1988. 'The Banque de France and the state from 1850 to the present day', in Toniolo (ed.), pp. 73–104

Boylan, D. M. 2001. *Defusing democracy: central bank autonomy and the transition from authoritarian rule*. Ann Arbor: University of Michigan Press

Boyle, A. 1967. *Montagu Norman*. London: Cassell

Bradsher, G. 1999. 'Nazi gold: the Merkers mine treasure', *Prologue: Quarterly Review of the National Archives and Records Administration* **31**, 1: 6–21

Brash, D. T. 1994. 'Discussion', in Capie, Goodhart, Fischer, and Schnadt, pp. 208–15

2002. 'Inflation targeting 14 years on', *RBNZ Bulletin* **65**, 1: 58–70

Brealey, R. A. *et al.* 2001. *Financial stability and central banks: a global perspective*. London: Routledge

Bremner, R. P. 2004. *Chairman of the Fed: William McChesney Martin Jr and the creation of the American financial system.* New Haven, CT: Yale University Press

Breton, A. and Wintrobe, R. 1978. 'A theory of "moral suasion"', *Canadian Journal of Economics* 11, 2: 210–19

Brewer, E. 1980. 'The Depository Institutions Deregulation and Monetary Control Act of 1980', *Federal Reserve Bank of Chicago Economic Perspectives* 4, 5: 3–23

Brimmer, A. F. 1971. 'Central banking and economic development: the record of innovation', *Journal of Money, Credit and Banking* 3, 4: 780–92

Brittan, S. and Lilley, P. 1977. *The delusion of incomes policy.* London: Temple Smith

Britton, A. 1994. *Macroeconomic policy in Britain, 1974–1997.* Cambridge University Press

Broadberry, S. and Harrison, M. (eds.) 2005. *The economics of World War I.* Cambridge University Press

Brown, C. V. 1966. *The Nigerian banking system.* London: George Allen & Unwin

Broz, J. L. 1998. 'The origins of central banking: solutions to the free-rider problem', *International Organisation* 52, 2: 231–68

1999. 'Origins of the Federal Reserve System: international incentives and the domestic free-rider problem', *International Organization* 53, 1: 39–70

Broz, J. L. and Grossman, R. S. 2004. 'Paying for the privilege: the political economy of Bank of England charters, 1694–1844', *Explorations in Economic History* 41: 48–72

Bruni, F. 2001. 'Financial stability, regulation, supervision, and modern central banking', in A. M. Santomero, S. Viotti, and A. Vredin (eds.), *Challenges for central banking.* Boston, MA: Kluwer, pp. 19–37

Buiter, W. 1999. 'Alice in Euroland', *Journal of Common Market Studies* 37, 2: 181–209

2009. 'What's left of central bank independence?', blogs.ft.com/maverecon/2009/05/whats-left-of-central-bank-independence/ (accessed 7 July 2009)

Buiter, W. and Sibert, A. 2008. 'The central bank as the market maker of last resort: from lender of last resort to market maker of last resort', in C. Reinhart and A. Felton (eds.), 'The first global financial crisis of the 21st century', MPRA No. 11862, pp. 168–75

Burdekin, R. C. K. and Siklos, P. L. 2008. 'What has driven Chinese monetary policy since 1990? Investigating the People's Bank's policy rule', *Journal of International Money and Finance* 27: 847–59

Burk, K. 2004. 'Cunliffe, Walter, first Baron Cunliffe (1855–1920)', in *Oxford Dictionary of National Biography.* Oxford University Press. www.oxforddnb.com/view/article/37332 (accessed 12 June 2007)

Burk, K. and Cairncross, A. 1992. *Goodbye, Great Britain: the 1976 IMF crisis.* New Haven, CT: Yale University Press

Burn, G. 1999. 'The state, the City and the Euromarkets', *Review of International Political Economy* 6, 2: 225–61

Burns, A. F. 1979 'The anguish of central banking', in P. Ciocca (ed.), *Money and the economy: central bankers' views*. Basingstoke: Macmillan, pp. 147–66

Buyst, E. and Maes, I. 2008a. 'Central banking in nineteenth-century Belgium: was the NBB a lender of last resort?', *Financial History Review* **15**, 2: 153–73

2008b. 'The regulation and supervision of the Belgian financial system (1830–2005)', Bank of Greece Working Paper No. 77

Cain, P. J. 1996. 'Gentlemanly imperialism at work: the Bank of England, Canada, and the Sterling Area, 1932–1936', *Economic History Review* **49**, 2: 336–57

Cain, P. J. and Hopkins, A. G. 1993a. *British imperialism: innovation and expansion, 1688–1914*. London: Longman

1993b. *British imperialism: crisis and deconstruction, 1914–1990*. London: Longman

Cairncross, A. 1985. *The years of recovery: British economic policy, 1945–51*. London: Methuen

1988. 'The Bank of England: relationships with the government, the civil service, and Parliament', in Toniolo (ed.), pp. 39–72

1998. *Living with the century*. Fife: Iynx

Calomiris, C. W. 2006. 'The regulatory record of the Greenspan Fed', *American Economic Review* **96**, 2: 170–3

Calvo, G. 1978. 'On the time consistency of optimal policy in a monetary economy', *Econometrica* **46**: 1411–28

Camdessus, M. and Naim, M. 2000. 'A talk with Michel Camdessus about God, globalization, and his years running the IMF', *Foreign Policy* **120**, September – October: 32–45

Capie, F. H. 1990. 'The evolving regulatory framework in British banking', in M. Chick (ed.), *Governments, industries and markets*. Aldershot: Edward Elgar, pp. 127–41

2007. 'Inflation in the twentieth century', in M. J. Oliver and D. H. Aldcroft (eds.), *Economic disasters of the twentieth century*. Cheltenham: Edward Elgar, pp. 162–81

2010. *The Bank of England, 1950s to 1979*. Cambridge University Press

Capie, F. H., Goodhart, C., Fischer, S., and Schnadt, N. 1994. *The future of central banking: the tercentenary symposium of the Bank of England*. Cambridge University Press

Capie, F. H. and Wood, G. E. 1991. *Unregulated banking: chaos or order?* New York: St. Martin's Press

Caporale, B. 2003. 'The influence of economists on the Federal Reserve Act', *Scottish Journal of Political Economy* **50**, 3: 311–25

Caprio, G., Demirgüç-Kunt, A., and Kane, E. 2008. 'The 2007 meltdown in structured securitization: searching for lessons not scapegoats', World Bank Working Paper No. 4756

Caprio, G., Honohan, P., and Stiglitz, J. E. (eds.) 2001. *Financial liberalization: how far, how fast?* Cambridge University Press

Cargill, T. F., Hutchison, M. M., and Ito, T. 1997. *The political economy of Japanese monetary policy*. Cambridge, MA: MIT Press

2001. *Financial policy and central banking in Japan*. Cambridge, MA: MIT Press

Carli, G., 1993. 'Concluding remarks to the Annual Reports of the Bank of Italy 1960–1974', *Banca Nazionale del Lavoro Quarterly Review*, Special Issue, December, pp. 1–520.

Cassis, Y. 2006. *Capitals of capital: a history of international financial centres, 1780–2005*. Cambridge University Press

Castillo, A. V. 1948. 'Central banking in the Philippines', *Pacific Affairs* 21, 4: 360–71

Cecchetti, S. G. and O'Sullivan, R. 2003. 'The European Central Bank and the Federal Reserve', *Oxford Review of Economic Policy* 19, 1: 30–43

Cecchetti, S. G. and Schoenholtz, K. L. 2008. 'How central bankers see it: the first decade of ECB policy and beyond', NBER Working Papers No. 14489

Central Bank of Iceland 2007. *Financial Stability 2007*. Rejkjavik: Sedlabank

Central Bank of the Philippines 1970. *Central Bank of the Philippines January 3, 1949 – January 3, 1974*. Manila: Central Bank of the Philippines

1974. *Lectures: eighth SEANZA central banking course*. Manila: Central Bank of the Philippines

Cesarano, F. 2006. *Monetary theory and Bretton Woods*. Cambridge University Press

Chakrabarty, T. K. 2003. 'Rural income: some evidence of effect of rural credit during last three decades', *Reserve Bank of India Occasional Papers* 24, 3: 225–39

Champ, B. 2007. 'The National Banking System: a brief history', Federal Reserve Bank of Cleveland Working Paper 07/23

Chandavarkar, A. 1992. 'Of finance and development: neglected and unsettled questions', *World Development* 20, 1: 133–42

Chandler, A. D. 1990. *Scale and scope: the dynamics of industrial capitalism*. Cambridge, MA: Belknap Press

Chandler, L. V. 1958. *Benjamin Strong*. Washington, DC: Brookings Institution

Chant, J. F. and Acheson, K. 1986. 'The choice of monetary instruments and the theory of bureaucracy (1)', in Toma and Toma (eds.), pp. 107–28

Chung, C. W.-W. and Tongzon, J. L. 2004. 'A paradigm shift for China's central banking system', *Journal of Post Keynesian Economics* 27, 1: 87–103

Chung, M.-C. (ed.) 2000. *The Bank of Korea*. Seoul: Bank of Korea

Clapham, J. 1944. *The Bank of England*, 2 vols. Cambridge University Press

Clark, H. A. 2006. *When there was no money: building ACLEDA Bank in Cambodia's evolving financial sector*. Berlin: Springer

Clarke, S. V. O. 1967. *Central bank cooperation, 1924–31*. New York: Federal Reserve Bank of New York

Clavin, P. 1992. ' "The fetishes of so-called international bankers": central bank co-operation for the World Economic Conference, 1932–3', *Contemporary European History* 1, 3: 281–311

2003. ' "Money talks": competition and cooperation with the League of Nations, 1929–30', in Flandreau (ed.), pp. 219–48

Clay, H. 1957. *Lord Norman*. London: Macmillan

Clifford, A. J. 1965. *The independence of the Federal Reserve System*. Philadelphia: University of Pennsylvania Press

Coats, A. W. (ed.) 1981. *Economists in government*. Durham, NC: Duke University Press

Coats, W. 1999. 'The Central Bank of Bosnia-Herzegovina: its history and its issues', in M. I. Blejer and M. Škreb (eds), *Central banking, monetary policies, and the implications for transition economies*. Boston, MA: Kluwer, pp. 367–99

Collins, M. (ed.) 1993. *Central banking in history*, 3 vols. Aldershot: Edward Elgar

Collins, M. and Baker, M. 1999. 'Bank of England autonomy: a retrospective', in Holtfrerich, Reis, and Toniolo (eds.), pp. 13–33

Collins, R. M. 1996. 'The economic crisis of 1968 and the waning of the "American Century" ', *American Historical Review* **101**, 2: 396–422

Committee for the Study of Economic and Monetary Union 1989. *Report on Economic and Monetary Union in the European Community*. Luxembourg: Office for Official Publications of the EC

Committee on Banking Regulations and Supervisory Practices 1986. *The management of banks' off-balance sheet exposures*. Basel: BIS

Committee on the Working of the Monetary System 1959. *Report*. Cmnd 827. London: HMSO

Conant, C. A. 1896. *A history of modern banks of issue*. New York: G. P. Putnam's Sons

Congdon, T. 2007. *Keynes, the Keynesians and monetarism*. Cheltenham: Edward Elgar

Connolly, B. 1995. *The rotten heart of Europe*. London: Faber & Faber

Coombs, C. 1976. *The arena of international finance*. London: Wiley

Coombs, H. C. 1981. *Trial balance*. South Melbourne: Macmillan

Cooper, R. N. 2008. 'Almost a century of central bank cooperation', in Borio, Toniolo, and Clement (eds.), pp. 76–112

Copland, D. B. 1949. 'Balance of production in the Australian post-war economy', *Economic Record* **25**, 2: 1–6

Cornish, S. 1993. 'Sir Leslie Melville: an interview', *Economic Record* **69**: 437–57

Cottrell, P. L. 1997. 'Norman, Strakosch and the development of central banking: from conception to practice, 1919–1924', in P. L. Cottrell (ed.), *Rebuilding the financial system in central and eastern Europe, 1918–1994*. Aldershot: Scolar, pp. 29–73

  2003. 'The financial system of the United Kingdom in the twentieth century', in De Rosa (ed.), pp. 43–71

Courtis, N. and Nicholl, P. (eds.) 2005. *Central bank modernisation*. London: Central Banking Publications

Cross, R. and Laidler, D. 1976. 'Inflation, excess demand and expectations in fixed exchange rate open economies: some preliminary empirical results', in M. Parkin and G. Zis (eds.), *Inflation in the world economy*. Manchester University Press, pp. 221–54

Crow, J. 2002. *Making money: an insider's perspective on finance, politics, and Canada's central bank*. Etobicoke, ON: John Wiley

Cukierman, A. 1992. *Central bank strategy, credibility and independence.* Cambridge, MA: MIT Press

Cukierman, A., Miller, G. P., and Neyapati, B. 2002. 'Central bank reform, liberalization and inflation in transition economies – an international perspective', *Journal of Monetary Economics* 49: 237–64

Cukierman, A. and Webb, S. B. 1995. 'Political influence on the central bank: international evidence', *World Bank Economic Review* 9, 3: 397–423

Dalziel, P. 1997. 'Setting the Reserve Bank's inflation target: the New Zealand debate', *Agenda* 4, 3: 285–96

Danielsson, J. 2002. 'The emperor has no clothes: limits to risk modelling', *Journal of Banking & Finance* 26: 1273–96

Daunton, M. J. 1992. 'Financial elites and British society, 1880–1950', in Y. Cassis (ed.), *Finance and financiers in European history, 1880–1960.* Cambridge University Press, pp. 121–46

Davidson, P. 2006. 'Can, or should, a central bank inflation target?', *Journal of Post Keynesian Economics* 28, 4: 689–703

Davies, H. 1997. 'European central banking – east and west: where next', *Bank of England Quarterly Bulletin* 37, 2: 228–35

Davies, S. G. 1960. 'Introduction', in S. G. Davies (ed.), *Central banking in South and East Asia.* Hong Kong University Press, pp. vii–xi

Davis, J. S. 1920. 'World currency and banking: the first Brussels financial conference', *Review of Economic Statistics* 2, 12: 349–60

Dawe, S. 1990. 'Reserve Bank of New Zealand Act 1989', *RBNZ Bulletin* 53, 1: 29–36

Deane, M. and Pringle, R. 1994. *The central banks.* London: Viking

Debelle, G. 1996. 'The ends of three small inflations: Australia, New Zealand, and Canada', *Canadian Public Policy* 22: 56–78

Debelle, G. and Fischer, S. 1994, 'How independent should a central bank be?', in J. Fuhrer (ed.), *Goals, guidelines and constraints facing monetary policymakers.* Boston, MA: Federal Reserve Bank of Boston, pp. 195–221

de Fraine, H. G. 1960. *Servant of this house: life in the old Bank of England.* London: Constable

De Grauwe, P. 1992. *The economics of monetary integration,* 1st edn. Oxford University Press

  2007. *The economics of monetary integration,* 7th edn. Oxford University Press

De Haan, J. and Eijffinger, S. C. W. 2000. 'The democratic accountability of the European Central Bank: a comment on two fairy tales', *Journal of Common Market Studies* 38, 3: 393–407

De Haan, J., Masciandaro, D., and Quintyn, M. 2008. 'Does central bank independence still matter?', *European Journal of Political Economy* 24: 717–21

De Kock, G. 1954. *A history of the South African Reserve Bank (1920–52).* Pretoria: J. L. Van Schaik

De Kock, M. H. 1949. *Central banking,* 2nd edn. London: Staples Press

  1974. *Central banking,* 4th edn. London: Crosby Lockwood Staples

De la Torre, A., Levy Yeyati, E., and Schmukler, S. L. 2004. 'Living and dying with hard pegs: the rise and fall of Argentina's currency board', World Bank Policy Research Working Paper No. 2980

DeLong, J. B. 1997. 'America's peacetime inflation: the 1970s', in C. D. Romer and D. H. Romer (eds.), *Reducing inflation: motivation and strategy.* University of Chicago Press, pp. 247–76

De Rosa, L. (ed.) 2003. *International banking and financial systems.* Aldershot: Ashgate

de Vries, M. G. 1987. *Balance of payments adjustment, 1945–1986: the IMF experience.* Washington, DC: IMF

Demirgüç-Kunt, A. and Kane, E. 2002. 'Deposit insurance around the globe: where does it work?', *Journal of Economic Perspectives* **16**, 2: 175–95

Demirgüç-Kunt, A., Kane, E., and Laeven, L. (eds.) 2008. *Deposit insurance around the world.* Cambridge, MA: MIT Press

Demirgüc-Kunt, A. and Servén, L. 2009. 'Are all the sacred cows dead? Implications of the financial crisis for macro and financial policies', World Bank Policy Research Working Paper No. 4807

Deutsche Bundesbank (ed.) 1999. *Fifty years of the Deutsche Mark.* Oxford University Press

Dickhaus, M. 1998. 'The West German central bank and the construction of an international monetary system in the 1950s', *Financial History Review* **5**, 2: 159–78

Djiwandono, J. S. 2000. 'Bank Indonesia and the recent crisis', *Bulletin of Indonesian Economic Studies* **36**, 1: 47–72

Dodge, D. A. 2002. 'Inflation targeting in Canada: experience and lessons', *North American Journal of Economics and Finance* **13**: 113–24

2008. 'Central banking at a time of crisis and beyond: a practitioner's perspective', C. D. Howe Institute, Benefactor's Lecture

Dornbusch, R. 1987. 'Lessons from the German inflation experience of the 1920s', in R. Dornbusch, S. Fischer and J. Bossons (eds.), *Macroeconomics and finance.* Cambridge, MA: MIT Press, pp. 337–66

Dornbusch, R., Favero, C., and Giavazzi, F. 1998. 'Immediate challenges for the European Central Bank', *Economic Policy* **13**, 26: 17–52

Dorrance, G. S. 1965. 'The instruments of monetary policy in countries without highly developed capital markets', *IMF Staff Papers* **12**, 2: 272–81

Dow, J. C. R. 1970. *The management of the British economy, 1945–60.* Cambridge University Press

Dowd, K. (ed.) 1992. *The experience of free banking.* London: Routledge

Drake, P. J. 1977. 'Securities markets in less-developed countries', *Journal of Development Studies* **13**, 2: 73–91

Drake, P. W. 1989. *The money doctor in the Andes.* Durham, NC: Duke University Press

Dwyer, J. H. 2004. 'Explaining central bank reform in Japan', *Social Science Japan Journal* **7**, 2: 245–62

Dykes, S. E. 1989. 'The establishment and evolution of the Federal Reserve Board: 1913–23', *Federal Reserve Bulletin* **75**, 4: 227–43

Dyson, K. 2000. *The politics of the euro-zone: stability or breakdown?* Oxford University Press

Dyson, K. and Featherstone, K. 1999. *The road to Maastricht: negotiating Economic and Monetary Union.* Oxford University Press

Eckes, A. E. 1975. *A search for solvency: Bretton Woods and the international monetary system, 1941–1971*. Austin: University of Texas Press

Economist, The 1998. 'Central bankers', 28 November, p. 162

1999. 'The Bundesbank: in search of a role', 23 January, p. 86

Eichengreen, B. 1984. 'Central bank cooperation under the interwar gold standard', *Explorations in Economic History* **21**, 1: 64–87

Eichengreen, B. (ed.) 1985. *The gold standard in theory and history*. London: Methuen

Eichengreen, B. 1991. 'Designing a central bank for Europe: a cautionary tale from the early years of the Federal Reserve System', NBER Working Paper No. 3840

1992a. *Golden fetters: the gold standard and the Great Depression, 1919–1939*. New York: Oxford University Press

1992b. 'The origins and nature of the Great Slump revisited', *Economic History Review* **45**, 2: 213–39

1993. *Reconstructing Europe's trade and payments*. Manchester University Press

1995. 'Central bank co-operation and exchange rate commitments: the classical and interwar gold standards compared', *Financial History Review* **2**: 99–117

1996. *Globalizing capital: a history of the international monetary system*. Princeton University Press

1997. *European monetary unification: theory, practice and analysis*. Cambridge, MA: MIT Press

1998. 'European monetary integration: a tour d'horizon', *Oxford Review of Economic Policy* **14**, 3: 24–40

2007. *Global imbalances and the lessons of Bretton Woods*. Cambridge, MA: MIT Press

2008. 'Sui generis EMU', CEPR Discussion Paper Series, No. 6642

Eichengreen, B. and Bordo, M. D. 2003. 'Crises then and now: what lessons from the last era of financial globalization?', in P. Mizen (ed.), *Monetary history, exchange rates and financial markets*, vol. II. Cheltenham: Edward Elgar, pp. 52–91

Eichengreen, B. and Simmons, B. 1995. 'International economics and domestic politics: notes on the 1920s', in C. H. Feinstein (ed.), *Banking, currency, and finance in Europe between the wars*. Oxford: Clarendon Press, pp. 131–47

Eichengreen, B. and Temin, P. 2000. 'The gold standard and the Great Depression', *Contemporary European History* **9**, 2: 183–207

Eijffinger, S. C. W. 2003. 'The federal design of a central bank in a monetary union: the case of the European System of Central Banks', *International Journal of Finance and Economics* **8**: 365–80

Einzig, P. 1931. *Behind the scenes of international finance*. London: Macmillan

1932. *Montagu Norman*. London: Kegan Paul, Trench, Trubner

1960. *In the centre of things*. London: Hutchinson

Eisenbeis, R. A. 1997. 'International settlements: a new source of systemic risk', *Federal Reserve Bank of Atlanta Economic Review* **82**, 2: 44–50

Ellerton, C. 1957. 'Relations between the Bank of England and the commercial banks of the United Kingdom', in Bundesverband des Privaten

Bankgewerbes, *Relations between the central banks and commercial banks.* Frankfurt am Main: Fritz Knapp, pp. 107–28

Englund, P. 1999. 'The Swedish banking crisis: roots and consequences', *Oxford Review of Economic Policy* 15, 3: 80–97

Epstein, G. 2005. 'Central banks as agents of economic development', Political Economy Research Institute, University of Massachusetts, Amherst, Working Paper No. 104

European Central Bank 2009. *Annual Report 2008.* Frankfurt am Main: ECB

Fay, S. 1988. *Portrait of an Old Lady: turmoil at the Bank of England.* Harmondsworth: Penguin

Federal Reserve Financial Service Policy Committee 2008. Press Release: Federal Reserve Banks announce reduced number of check processing sites and accelerated restructuring schedule, November 6. www.federalreserve.gov/newsevents/press/other/20081106a.htm (accessed 25 July 2009)

Feinman, J. N. 1993. 'Reserve requirements: history, current practice, and potential reform', *Federal Reserve Bulletin* 79, 6: 569–89

Feldman, G. D. 1997. *The great disorder: politics, economics, and society in the German inflation, 1914–1924.* New York: Oxford University Press

Felton, A. and Reinhart, C. (eds.) 2009. *The first global financial crisis of the 21st century, Part II, June – December 2008.* London: VoxEU Publications

Ferguson, N. 1996. 'Constraints and room for manoeuvre in the German inflation of the early 1920s', *Economic History Review* 46, 4: 635–66
    2001. *The cash nexus: money and power in the modern world, 1700–2000.* London: Allen Lane

Ferris, J. S. and Galbraith, J. A. 2006. 'On Hayek's denationalization of money, free banking and inflation targeting', *European Journal of the History of Economic Thought* 13, 2: 231–31

Fforde, J. S. 1992. *The Bank of England and public policy, 1941–1958.* Cambridge University Press

Fielding, D. 2002. *The macroeconomics of monetary union: an analysis of the CFA franc zone.* London: Routledge

Filardo, A. and Genberg, H. 2009. 'Targeting inflation in Asia and the Pacific: lessons from the recent past', BIS Representative Office for Asia and the Pacific Working Paper

Fink, C. 1984. *The Genoa Conference.* Chapel Hill, NC: University of North Carolina Press

Fischer, S. (ed.) 1980. *Rational expectations and economic policy.* University of Chicago Press

Fischer, S. 1994. 'Modern central banking', in Capie, Goodhart, Fischer, and Schnadt, pp. 262–308

Fischer, S., Sahay, R., and Vegh, C. A. 2002. 'Modern hyper- and high inflations', *Journal of Economic Literature* 40, 3: 837–80

Flandreau, M. 1997. 'Central bank cooperation in historical perspective: a sceptical view', *Economic History Review* 50, 4: 735–63

Flandreau, M. (ed.) 2003. *Money doctors: the experience of international financial advising, 1850–2000.* London: Routledge

Flandreau, M. 2006. 'The logic of compromise: monetary bargaining in Austria-Hungary, 1867–1913', *European Review of Economic History* **10**: 3–33

2007. 'Pillars of globalization: a history of monetary policy targets, 1797–1997', CEPR Discussion Paper No. 6252.

Flandreau, M., Le Cacheux, J., Zumer, F. Dornbusch, R., and Honohan, P. 1998. 'Stability without a pact? Lessons from the European gold standard, 1880–1914', *Economic Policy* **13**, 26: 115–62

Fontana, G. 2006. 'The Federal Reserve and the European Central Bank: a theoretical comparison of their legislative mandates', *Journal of Post Keynesian Economics* **28**, 3: 433–50

Forder, J. 2002. 'Interests and "independence": the European Central Bank and the theory of bureaucracy', *International Review of Applied Economics* **16**, 1: 51–69

2003. '"Independence" and the founding of the Federal Reserve', *Scottish Journal of Political Economy* **50**, 3: 297–10

2005. 'Why is central bank independence so widely approved?', *Journal of Economic Issues* **39**, 4: 843–65

Franke, G. 1999. 'The Bundesbank and financial markets', in Deutsche Bundesbank (ed.), pp. 221–66

Frankman, M. J. 1974. 'Sectoral policy preferences of the Peruvian government, 1946–1968', *Journal of Latin American Studies* **6**, 2: 289–300

Fraser, B. W. 1993. 'Some aspects of monetary policy', *Reserve Bank of Australia Bulletin* April: 1–7

Fratianni, M. U. and Salvatore, D. (eds.) 1993. *Monetary policy in developed economies*. Westport, CT: Greenwood

Frenkel, J. 1994. 'Contribution to discussion', in Capie, Goodhart, Fischer, and Schnadt, pp. 327–8

Frenkel, J. A. and Johnson, H. G. (eds.) 1976. *The monetary approach to the balance of payments*. London: Allen & Unwin; University of Toronto Press

Friedman, B. M. 2006. 'The Greenspan era: discretion rather than rules', *American Economic Review* **96**, 2: 174–7

Friedman, M. 1953. 'The case for floating exchange rates', in M. Friedman (ed.), *Essays in positive economics*. University of Chicago Press, pp. 157–203

Friedman, M. (ed.) 1956. *Studies in the quantity theory of money*. University of Chicago Press

Friedman, M. 1960. *A program for monetary stability*. New York: Fordham University Press

1962. 'Should there be an independent monetary authority?', in L. B. Yeager (ed.), *In search of a monetary constitution*. Cambridge, MA: Harvard University Press, pp. 219–43

1968. 'The role of monetary policy', *American Economic Review* **58**, 1: 1–17

1982. 'Monetary policy: theory and practice', *Journal of Money, Credit and Banking* **14**, 1: 98–118

1985. 'Monetarism in rhetoric and in practice', in A. Ando, H. Eguchi, R. Farmer, and Y. Suzuki (eds.), *Monetary policy in our times*. Cambridge, MA: MIT Press, pp. 15–28

1986. 'Monetary policy: theory and practice', in Toma and Toma (eds.), pp. 11–35

2002. 'Interview: Milton Friedman', *Central Banking* 13, 1: 15–23

Friedman, M. and Schwartz, A. J. 1963. *A monetary history of the USA, 1870–1960*. Princeton University Press

Frowen, S. F. and Hölscher, J. (eds.) 1997. *The German currency union of 1990: a critical assessment*. Basingstoke: Macmillan

Fry, M. J., Goodhart, C. A. E., and Almeida, A. (eds.) 1996. *Central banking in developing countries*. London: Routledge

Fry, M. J., Kilato, I. R., Senderowicz, S., Sheppard, D., Solis, F., and Trundle, J. 1999. *Payment systems in global perspective*. London: Routledge

Galan Camacho, J. E. and Sarmiento Paipilla, M. 2007. 'Staff, functions, and staff costs at central banks: an international comparison with a labor-demand model', *Money Affairs* 20, 2: 131–79

Galati, G. 2002. 'Settlement risk in foreign exchange markets and CLS Bank', *BIS Quarterly Review* December: 55–65

Gallarotti, G. M. 1995. *The anatomy of an international monetary regime: the classical gold standard, 1880–1914*. New York: Oxford University Press

2005. 'Hegemons of a lesser god: the Bank of France and monetary leadership under the classical gold standard', *Review of International Political Economy* 12, 4: 624–46

Galpin, R. 2002. 'Court acquits Indonesian banker', http://news.bbc.co.uk/1/hi/world/asia-pacific/2224620.stm (accessed 13 February 2009)

Gardner, R. 1980. *Sterling-dollar diplomacy in current perspective*. New York: Columbia University Press

Garside, W. R. and Greaves, J. I. 1996. 'The Bank of England and industrial intervention in interwar Britain', *Financial History Review* 3, 1: 69–86

Gavin, F. J. 2004. *Gold, dollars, and power: the politics of international monetary relations, 1958–1971*. Chapel Hill: University of North Carolina Press

Gelsomino, C. O. 1999. 'The Bank of Italy from its foundation to the 1950s: institutional aspects', in Holtfrerich, Reis, and Toniolo (eds.), pp. 161–85

George, E. 1996. 'Foreword', in Fry, Goodhart, and Almeida (eds.), pp. x–xi

Geraats, P. M. 2002. 'Central bank transparency', *Economic Journal* 112, 483: F532–F565

Gerdesmeier, D., Mongelli, F. P., and Roffia, B. 2007. 'The Eurosystem, the U.S. Federal Reserve, and the Bank of Japan: similarities and differences', *Journal of Money, Credit, and Banking* 39, 7: 1785–819

Giblin, L. F. 1951. *The growth of a central bank: the development of the Commonwealth Bank of Australia, 1924–1945*. Melbourne University Press

Gilbert, R. A. 1986. 'Requiem for Regulation Q: what it did and why it passed away', *Federal Reserve Bank of St. Louis Review* 68, 2: 22–37

2000. 'The advent of the Federal Reserve and the efficiency of the payments system: the collection of checks, 1915–1930', *Explorations in Economic History* 37: 121–48

Gilbert, R. A. and Trebbing, M. E. 1981. 'The FOMC in 1980: a year of reserve targeting', *Federal Reserve Bank of St. Louis Review* August/September: 8–22

Giovannini, A. 1986. ' "Rules of the game" during the international gold standard: England and Germany', *Journal of International Money and Finance* **5**: 467–83

Glentworth, G. and Hancock, I. 1973. 'Obote and Amin: change and continuity in modern Uganda politics', *African Affairs* **72**, 288: 237–55

Gollan, R. 1968. *The Commonwealth Bank of Australia: origins and early history.* Canberra: ANU Press

Goodfriend, M. 1986. 'Monetary mystique: secrecy and central banking', *Journal of Monetary Economics* **17**, 1: 63–92

2007. 'How the world achieved consensus on monetary policy', *Journal of Economic Perspectives* **21**, 4: 47–68

Goodfriend, M. and Hargreaves, M. 1983. 'A historical assessment of the rationales and functions of reserve requirements', *Federal Reserve Bank of Richmond Economic Review* **69**: 3–21

Goodfriend, M. and King, R. 2005. 'The incredible Volcker disinflation', *Journal of Monetary Economics* **52**, 5: 981–1015

Goodfriend, M. and Prasad, E. 2006. 'A framework for independent monetary policy in China', IMF Working Paper WP/06/111

Goodhart, C. 1984. *Monetary theory and practice: the UK experience.* London: Macmillan

1988. *The evolution of central banks.* Cambridge, MA: MIT Press

1989. *Money, information and uncertainty,* 2nd edn. Basingstoke: Macmillan

2004. 'The Bank of England 1970–2000', in R. Michie and P. Williamson (eds.), *The British government and the City of London in the twentieth century.* Cambridge University Press, pp. 340–71

Goodhart, C., Capie, F., and Schnadt, N. 1994. 'The development of central banking', in F. Capie, C. Goodhart, S. Fischer, and N. Schnadt (eds.), *The future of central banking: the tercentenary symposium of the Bank of England.* Cambridge University Press, pp. 1–112

Goodhart, C., Hartmann, P., Llewellyn, D., Rojas-Suárez, L., and Weisbrod, S. 1998. *Financial regulation: why, how and where now?* London: Routledge

Goodhart, C., Hofmann, B., and Segoviano, M. 2004. 'Bank regulation and macroeconomic fluctuations', *Oxford Review of Economic Policy* **20**, 4: 591–615

Goodhart, C. and Schoenmaker, D. 1995. 'Should the functions of monetary policy and banking supervision be separated?', *Oxford Economic Papers* **47**, 4: 539–60

Goodhart, C., Schoenmaker, D., and Dasgupta, P. 2002. 'The skill profile of central bankers and supervisors', *European Finance Review* **6**, 3: 397–427

Green, D. and Singleton, J. 2009. *The watchdog: New Zealand's audit office, 1840–2008.* Dunedin: University of Otago Press

Green, E. H. H. 1992. 'The influence of the City over British economic policy, c. 1880–1960', in Y. Cassis (ed.), *Finance and financiers in European history, 1880–1960.* Cambridge University Press, pp. 193–218

Greenlee, M. B. 2008. 'Historical review of "umbrella supervision" by the Board of Governors of the Federal Reserve System', Federal Reserve Bank of Cleveland Working Paper (Financial Stability) No. 08–07

Greenspan, A. 2001. 'Remarks by Chairman Alan Greenspan on transparency in monetary policy at the Federal Reserve Bank of St. Louis, Economic Policy Conference, St. Louis, Missouri (via videoconference), October 11', www.federalreserve.gov/boarddocs/speeches/2001/20011011/default. htm (accessed 15 July 2009)

2008 *The age of turbulence*. London: Penguin

Greider, W. 1987. *Secrets of the temple: how the Federal Reserve runs the country*. New York: Simon & Schuster

Griffiths, B. and Wood, G. E. (eds.) 1981. *Monetary targets*. London: Macmillan

Grimes, A. and Wong, J. 1994. 'The role of the exchange rate in New Zealand monetary policy', in R. Glick and M. M. Hutchison (eds.), *Exchange rate policy and interdependence: perspectives from the Pacific Basin*. Cambridge University Press, pp. 176–97

Gros, D. and Thygesen, N. 1990. 'The institutional approach to monetary union in Europe', *Economic Journal* **100**, 402: 925–35

Grossman, R. S. 1994. 'The shoe that didn't drop: explaining banking instability during the Great Depression', *Journal of Economic History* **54**, 3: 654–82

2001. 'Charters, corporations and codes: entry restriction in modern banking law', *Financial History Review* **8**, 2: 107–21

2006. 'The emergence of central banks and banking regulation in comparative perspective', Wesleyan Economics Working Papers No. 2006–21

Gunasekera, H. A. de S. 1962. *From dependent currency to central banking in Ceylon*. London: G. Bell and Sons

Gurley, J. G. 1960. 'The Radcliffe Report and evidence', *American Economic Review* **50**, 4: 672–700

Gustafson, B. 2000. *His way: a biography of Sir Robert Muldoon*. Auckland University Press

Guttmann, S. 2005. *The rise and fall of monetary targeting in Australia*. Melbourne: Australian Scholarly Press

Haas, P. 1992. 'Introduction: epistemic communities and international policy coordination', *International Organization* **46**: 1–35

Hafer, R. W. and Wheelock, D. H. 2001. 'The rise and fall of a policy rule: monetarism at the St. Louis Fed, 1968–1986', *Federal Reserve Bank of St. Louis Review* **83**, 1: 1–24

Hall, M. J. B. 1993. *Banking regulation and supervision: a comparative study of the UK, USA and Japan*. Cheltenham: Edward Elgar

Hamada, K. and Hayashi, F. 1985. 'Monetary policy in postwar Japan', in A. Ando, H. Eguchi, R. Farmer, and Y. Suzuki (eds.), *Monetary policy in our times*. Cambridge, MA: MIT Press, pp. 83–121

Hamilton-Hart, N. 2002. *Asian states, Asian bankers: central banking in Southeast Asia*. Ithaca, NY: Cornell University Press

Hammond, T. H. and Knott, J. H. 1988. 'The deregulatory snowball: explaining deregulation in the financial industry', *Journal of Politics* **50**, 1: 3–30

Hartcher, P. 2006. *Bubble man: Alan Greenspan and the missing 7 trillion dollars*. New York: Norton

Havrilesky, T. 1995. 'Restructuring the Fed', *Journal of Economics and Business* 47, 2: 95–111

Hawke, G. R. 1973. *Between governments and banks: a history of the Reserve Bank of New Zealand*. Wellington: Government Printer

1985. *The making of New Zealand*. Cambridge University Press

Hawtrey, R. G. 1922a. 'The Federal Reserve System of the United States', *Journal of the Royal Statistical Society* **85**, 2: 224–69

1922b. 'The Genoa resolutions on currency', *Economic Journal* **32**: 290–304

1932. *The art of central banking*. London: Longmans, Green

Helleiner, E. 1994. *States and the reemergence of global finance*. Ithaca, NY: Cornell University Press

2003a. *The making of national money: territorial currencies in historical perspective*. Ithaca, NY: Cornell University Press

2003b. 'The Southern side of "embedded liberalism": America's unorthodox money doctoring during the early post-1945 years', in Flandreau (ed.), pp. 249–75

Helliwell, J. F. 2005–2006. 'From flapper to bluestocking: what happened to the young woman of Wellington Street?' *Bank of Canada Review* Winter: 31–9

Hennessy, E. 1992. *A domestic history of the Bank of England, 1930–1960*. Cambridge University Press

1995. 'The governors, directors and management of the Bank of England', in R. Roberts and D. Kynaston (eds.), *The Bank of England: money, power and influence 1694–1994*. Oxford: Clarendon Press, pp. 185–216

Henry, P. B. 2007. 'Capital account liberalization: theory, evidence, and speculation', *Journal of Economic Literature* **45**, 4: 887–935

Hetzel, R. L. 2008. *The monetary policy of the Federal Reserve: a history*. Cambridge University Press

Hetzel, R. L. and Leach, R. F. 2001a. 'The Treasury-Fed Accord: a new narrative account', *Federal Reserve Bank of Richmond Economic Quarterly* **87**, 1: 33–55

2001b. 'After the Accord: reminiscences of the birth of the modern Fed', *Federal Reserve Bank of Richmond Economic Quarterly* **87**, 1: 57–64

Hickey, D. and Mortlock, G. 2002. 'Managing human resources – a central bank perspective', *RBNZ Bulletin* 65, 1: 34–42

Hillman, A. L. 1999. 'Political culture and the political-economy of central-bank independence', in M. I. Blejer and Š. Marko (eds.), *Central banking, monetary policies, and the implications for transition economies*. Boston, MA: Kluwer, pp. 73–86

Hodd, M. 1987. 'Africa, the IMF and the World Bank', *African Affairs* **86**: 331–42

Hogan, M. J. 1987. *The Marshall Plan: America, the UK and the reconstruction of western Europe, 1947–52*. Cambridge University Press

Holbik, K. (ed.) 1973. *Monetary policy in twelve industrial countries*. Boston, MA: Federal Reserve Bank of Boston

Holder, R. F. 1965. 'Australia', in W. F. Crick (ed.), *Commonwealth banking systems*. Oxford: Clarendon Press, pp. 54–110

Holmes, F. W. 1999. *Thoroughbred among banks in New Zealand, 1945–1984*, vol. II. Wellington: National Bank of New Zealand

Holtfrerich, C.-L. 1988. 'Relations between monetary authorities and governmental institutions: the case of Germany from the 19th century to the present', in Toniolo (ed.), pp. 105–60

1999. 'Monetary policy under fixed exchange rates', in Deutsche Bundesbank (ed.), pp. 307–401

Holtfrerich, C.-L. and Iwami, T. 1999. 'Post-war central banking reform: a German-Japanese comparison', in Holtfrerich, Reis, and Toniolo (eds.), pp. 69–110

Holtfrerich, C.-L. and Reis, J. 1999. 'Introduction', in Holtfrerich, Reis, and Toniolo (eds.), pp. 1–10

Holtfrerich, C.-L., Reis, J., and Toniolo, G. (eds.) 1999. *The emergence of modern central banking from 1918 to the present*. Aldershot: Ashgate

Holthausen, C. and Ronde, T. 2004. 'Cooperation in international banking supervision', ECB Working Paper Series No. 316

Holub, T. and Hurník, J. 2008. 'Ten years of Czech inflation targeting: missed targets and anchored expectations', *Emerging Markets Finance & Trade* 44, 6: 67–86

Honkapohja, S. 2009. 'The 1990's financial crises in Nordic countries', Bank of Finland Research Discussion Papers No. 5/2009

Honohan, P. and Klingebiel, D. 2000. 'Controlling the fiscal costs of banking crises', World Bank Policy Research Working Paper No. 2441

Hood, C. 1995. 'The "New Public Management" in the 1980s: variations on a theme', *Accounting, Organizations & Society* 20, 2/3: 93–109

Horiuchi, A. and Shimizu, K. 2001. 'Did amakudari undermine the effectiveness of regulator monitoring in Japan?', *Journal of Banking and Finance* 25, 3: 573–96

Howe, A. 1994. 'From "old corruption" to "new probity": the Bank of England and its directors in the age of reform', *Financial History Review* 1: 23–41

Howitt, P. W. 1993. 'Canada', in Fratianni and Salvatore (eds.), pp. 459–508

Howson, S. 1993. *British monetary policy, 1945–51*. Oxford: Clarendon Press

1994. 'Money and monetary policy in Britain, 1945–1990', in R. Floud and D. McCloskey (eds.), *The Cambridge economic history of modern Britain*, vol. III. Cambridge University Press, pp. 136–166

Hsieh, C.-T. and Romer, C. D. 2006. 'Was the Federal Reserve constrained by the gold standard during the great depression? Evidence from the 1932 open market purchase program', *Journal of Economic History* 66, 1: 140–76

Husain, S. A. (ed.) 1992. *History of the State Bank of Pakistan (1948–1960)*. Karachi: State Bank of Pakistan

Hutchison, M. M. and Walsh, C. E. 1998. 'The output-inflation tradeoff and central bank reform: evidence from New Zealand', *Economic Journal* 108: 703–25

International Monetary Fund 2004. 'Monetary policy implementation at different stages of market development', Washington, DC: IMF

Israelsen, L. D. 1985. 'Marriner S. Eccles, Chairman of the Federal Reserve Board', *American Economic Review* 75, 2: 357–62

References309

Issing, O. 1997. 'Monetary targeting in Germany: the stability of monetary policy and of the monetary system', *Journal of Monetary Economics* **39**, 1: 67–79

1999. 'The Eurosystem: transparent and accountable or "Willem in Euroland"', *Journal of Common Market Studies* **37**, 3: 503–19

2000. 'Should we have faith in central banks?', Speech by Professor Otmar Issing, Member of the Executive Board of the European Central Bank, St Edmund's College Millennium Year Lecture, Cambridge, 26 October 2000. www.ecb.int/press/key/date/2000/html/sp001026_2.en.html (accessed 11 July 2009)

2004. 'Inflation targeting: a view from the ECB', *Federal Reserve Bank of St. Louis Review* **86**, 4: 169–79

2005. 'Why did the great inflation not happen in Germany?' *Federal Reserve Bank of St. Louis Review* **87**, 2, part 2: 329–35

Jackson, R. H. 1946. 'Closing address before the International Military Tribunal', http://avalon.law.yale.edu/imt/07-26-46.asp (accessed 13 August 2009)

Jacobsson, E. E. 1979. *A life for sound money: Per Jacobsson his biography.* Oxford: Clarendon Press

Jadhav, N. 2003. 'Central bank strategies, credibility and independence: global evolution and the Indian experience', *Reserve Bank of India Occasional Papers* **24**, 1 & 2: 1–104

James, H. 1986. *The German slump: politics and economics, 1924–1936.* Oxford: Clarendon Press

1996. *International monetary cooperation since Bretton Woods.* Oxford University Press

1999a. 'The International Monetary Fund and central banking', in Holtfrerich, Reis, and Toniolo (eds.), pp. 323–40

1999b. 'The Reichsbank, 1876–1945', in Deutsche Bundesbank (ed.), pp. 3–53

2001. *The end of globalization: lessons from the Great Depression.* Cambridge, MA: Harvard University Press

2002. 'Central banks and the process of financial internationalization: a secular view', in S. Battilossi and Y. Cassis (eds.), *European banks and the American challenge.* Oxford University Press, pp. 200–18

Japanese Bankers Association 2001. *The banking system in Japan.* Tokyo: Japanese Bankers Association

Jha, R. 2008. 'Inflation targeting in India: issues and prospects', *International Review of Applied Economics*, **22**, 2: 259–70

Johnston, R. A. 1985. 'Monetary policy – the changing environment', *Reserve Bank of Australia Bulletin*, June, 807–14

Jones, D. 2000. 'Emerging problems with the Basel Capital Accord: regulatory capital arbitrage and related issues', *Journal of Banking & Finance* **24**: 35–58

Kaelberer, M. 2003. 'Knowledge, power and monetary bargaining: central bankers and the creation of monetary union in Europe', *Journal of European Public Policy* **10**, 3: 365–79

Kahler, M. 2002. 'Bretton Woods and its competitors: the political economy of institutional choice', in D. M. Andrews, C. R. Henning, and L. W. Pauly (eds.), *Governing the world's money*. Ithaca, NY: Cornell University Press, pp. 38–59

Kahn, C. M., McAndrews, J., and Roberds, W. 2003. 'Settlement risk under gross and net settlement', *Journal of Money, Credit and Banking* **35**, 4: 591–608

Kahn, G. A. 2005. 'The Greenspan era: lessons for the future – a summary of the Bank's 2005 economic symposium', *Federal Reserve Bank of Kansas City Economic Review* **90**, 4: 35–45

Kaminsky, G. L. and Schmukler, S. L. 2003. 'Short-run pain, long-run gain: the effects of financial liberalization', IMF Working Paper WP/03/34

Kaldor, N. 1960. 'The Radcliffe Report', *Review of Economics and Statistics* **42**, 1: 14–19

Kaplan, J. J. and Schleiminger, G. 1989. *The European Payments Union*. Oxford: Clarendon Press

Kapstein, E. B. 1989. 'Resolving the regulator's dilemma: international coord-ination of banking regulations', *International Organization* **43**, 2: 323–47

1992. 'Between power and purpose: central bankers and the politics of regu-latory convergence', *International Organization* **46**, 1: 265–87

2008. 'Architects of stability? International cooperation among financial supervisors', in Borio, Toniolo, and Clement (eds.), pp. 113–52

Karunatilake, H. N. S. 1973. *Central banking and monetary policy in Sri Lanka*. Colombo: Lake House

Kawai, M. 2002. 'Exchange rate arrangements in East Asia: lessons from the 1997–98 currency crisis', *Monetary and Economic Studies* **20**, S-1: 167–204

Kemmerer, E. W. 1918. *The ABC of the Federal Reserve System*. Princeton University Press

1927. 'Economic advisory work for governments', *American Economic Review* **17**, 1: 1–12

Kenen, P. B. 1995. *Economic and monetary union in Europe: moving beyond Maastricht*. New York: Cambridge

Kenward, L. R. 1999. 'What has been happening at Bank Indonesia?' *Bulletin of Indonesian Economic Studies* **35**, 1: 121–7

Kettl, D. F. 1986. *Leadership at the Fed*. New Haven, CT: Yale University Press

Keynes, J. M. 1923. *A tract on monetary reform*. London: Macmillan

1936. *The general theory of employment, interest, and money*. London: Macmillan

Khatkhate, D. 1977. 'Evolving open market operations in a developing economy: the Taiwan experience', *Journal of Development Studies* **13**, 2: 92–101

1991. 'The central bank's role in financial sector development', in P. Downes and R. Vaez-Zadeh (eds.), *The evolving role of central banks*. Washington, DC: IMF, pp. 16–29

Khiaonarong, T. 2003. 'Payment systems efficiency, policy approaches, and the role of the central bank', Bank of Finland Discussion Papers 1/2003

Killick, T. (ed.) 1984. *The IMF and stabilisation*. London: Heinemann

Killick, T. and Mwega, F. M. 1993. 'Kenya, 1967–88', in Page (ed.), pp. 39–77

Kindleberger, C. P. 1986. 'International public goods without international government', *American Economic Review* **76**, 1: 1–13

1987. *The world in depression, 1929–1939*. London: Pelican

1996. *Manias, panics, and crashes: a history of financial crashes*, 3rd edn. New York: Wiley

King, Mervyn 1994. 'Monetary policy in the UK', *Fiscal Studies* **15**: 109–28

1997. 'Changes in UK monetary policy: rules and discretion in practice', *Journal of Monetary Economics* **39**: 81–97

1999. 'Challenges for monetary policy: new and old', in New challenges for monetary policy: a symposium sponsored by the Federal Reserve Bank of Kansas City, Jackson Hole, Wyoming, 26–28 August, 1999, pp. 1–57

2004. 'The institutions of monetary policy', *American Economic Review* **94**, 2: 1–13

King, Michael 2001. 'The Bank of Canada's pursuit of price stability: reputation as an alternative to independence', *Central Banking* **12**: 68–78

2005. 'Epistemic communities and the diffusion of ideas: central bank reform in the United Kingdom', *West European Politics* **28**, 1: 94–123

Kisch, C. H. and Elkin, W. A. 1932. *Central banks*, 2nd edn. London: Macmillan

Klasen, K. 1957. 'Relations between the German central banking system and the commercial banks', in Bundesverband des Privaten Bankgewerbes, *Relations between the central banks and commercial banks*. Frankfurt am Main: Fritz Knapp, pp. 19–43

Komiya, R. and Yamamoto, K. 1981. 'Japan: the officer in charge of economic affairs', in A. W. Coats (ed.), pp. 262–90

Kriz, M. A. 1948. 'Central banks and the state today', *American Economic Review* **38**, 4: 565–80

Krozewski, G. 2001. *Money and the end of empire*. Basingstoke: Macmillan

Krugman, P. R. 1998. 'It's baaack: Japan's slump and the return of the liquidity trap', *Brookings Papers on Economic Activity* 2: 137–87

Kunz, D. B. 1987. *The battle for Britain's gold standard in 1931*. London: Croom Helm

Kydland, F., and Prescott, E. S. 1977. 'Rules rather than discretion: the inconsistency of optimal plans', *Journal of Political Economy* **85**, 3: 473–92

Kynaston, D. 1995. 'The Bank of England and the government', in R. Roberts and D. Kynaston (eds.) *The Bank of England: money, power and influence, 1694–1994*. Oxford: Clarendon Press, pp. 19–55

La Porta, R., Shleifer, A., and Lopez-de-Silanes, F. 2002. 'Government ownership of banks', *Journal of Finance* **57**, 1: 265–301

Lacker, J. M. 2004. 'Payment system disruptions and the federal reserve following September 11, 2001', *Journal of Monetary Economics* **51**: 935–65

Laidler, D. 1969. *The demand for money*. New York: Harper & Row

Lastra, R. M. 1996. *Central banking and banking regulation*. London: LSE Financial Markets Group

Laurens, B. (ed.) 2005. 'Monetary policy implementation at different stages of market development'. IMF Occasional Paper No. 244

Lawson, N. 1992. *The view from No. 11*. London: Bantam

League of Nations 1945. *The League of Nations reconstruction schemes in the inter-war period.* Geneva: League of Nations

Leeson, R. (ed.) 2000. *A. W. H. Phillips: collected works in contemporary perspective.* Cambridge University Press

Leigh-Pemberton, R. 1990. 'Some remarks on exchange rate regimes', *Bank of England Quarterly Review* **30**, 4: 482–4

Leone, A. 1991. 'Effectiveness and implications of limits on central bank credit to the government', in P. Downes and R. Vaez-Zadeh (eds.), *The evolving role of central banks.* Washington, DC: IMF, pp. 363–413

Levine, R. 1997. 'Financial development and economic growth: views and agenda', *Journal of Economic Literature* **35**, 2: 688–726

Lexis, W. 1910. 'The German bank commission, 1908–9', *Economic Journal* **20**, 78: 211–21

Lin, S. and Ye, H. 2007. 'Does inflation targeting make a difference? Evaluating the treatment effect of inflation targeting in seven industrial countries', *Journal of Monetary Economics* **54**: 2521–33

2009. 'Does inflation targeting make a difference in developing countries?', *Journal of Development Economics* **89**: 118–23

Lohmann, S. 1992. 'Optimal commitment in monetary policy: credibility versus flexibility', *American Economic Review* **82**, 1: 273–86

1998. 'Federalism and central bank independence: the politics of German monetary policy 1957–92', *World Politics* **50**, 3: 401–46

Lombra, R. E. and Moran, M. 1980. 'Policy advice and policymaking at the Federal Reserve', *Carnegie-Rochester Conference Series on Public Policy* **13**: 9–68

Lucas, R. E. 1973. 'Some international evidence on output-inflation tradeoffs', *American Economic Review* **63**, 3: 326–34

1976. 'Econometric policy evaluation: a critique', *Carnegie-Rochester Conference Series on Public Policy* **1**: 19–46

MacDougall, D. 1957. *The world dollar problem.* London: Macmillan

Macfarlane, D. 2008. 'The value of a "Coyne": the Diefenbaker government and the 1961 Coyne affair', *Past Imperfect* **16**: 120–42

Macfarlane, I. J. 1998. 'Australian monetary policy in the last quarter of the twentieth century', *Reserve Bank of Australia Bulletin*, October, pp. 6–19

Mackie, J. A. C. 1967. *Problems of the Indonesian inflation.* Ithaca, NY: Cornell University Modern Indonesia Project

Maddison, A. 1991. *Dynamic forces in capitalist development.* Oxford University Press

1995. *Monitoring the world economy, 1820–1992.* Paris: OECD

Maes, I. 2004. 'On the origins of the Franco-German EMU controversies', *European Journal of Law and Economics* **17**: 21–39

2006. 'The ascent of the European Commission as an actor in the monetary integration process in the 1960s', *Scottish Journal of Political Economy* **53**, 2: 222–41

Mahadeva, L. and Sterne, G. (eds.) 2000. *Monetary policy frameworks in a global context.* London: Routledge

Maier, C. S. 1975. *Recasting bourgeois Europe.* Princeton University Press

Mankiw, N. G. 2001. 'U.S. monetary policy during the 1990s', NBER Working Paper No. 8471
2006. 'A letter to Ben Bernanke', *American Economic Review* **96**, 2: 182–4
Marcussen, M. 1998. 'Central bankers, the ideational life-cycle and the social construction of EMU', European University Institute, Robert Schuman Centre, Paper No. 98/33
2009. 'The Danish central bank: consistent search for stability, but reluctance regarding international integration', University of Copenhagen
Marichal, C. and Díaz Funtes, D. 1999. 'The emergence of central banks in Latin America: are evolutionary models applicable?', in Holtfrerich, Reis, and Toniolo (eds.), pp. 279–319
Marsh, D. 1993. *The Bundesbank: the bank that rules Europe.* London: Mandarin
Martin, W. M. 1970. 'Toward a world central bank?' *Atlantic Community Quarterly* **8**, 4: 503–15
Mas, I. 1995. 'Central bank independence: a critical view from a developing country perspective', *World Development* **23**, 10: 1639–52
Masciandaro, D. and Quintyn, M. (eds.) 2007. *Designing financial supervision institutions.* Cheltenham: Edward Elgar
Masera, F., Fazio, A., and Padoa-Schioppa, T. (eds.), 1975. *Econometric research in European central banks.* Rome: Banca d'Italia
Maulia, E. 2009. 'Indonesia's central bank ordered to protect rupiah', *Jakarta Post*, 6 February
Maxfield, S. 1994. 'Financial incentives and central bank authority in industrializing nations', *World Politics* **46**, 4: 556–88
1997. *Gatekeepers of growth: the international political economy of central banking in developing countries.* Princeton University Press
Mayer, M. 2001. *The Fed: the inside story of how the world's most powerful financial institution drives the market.* New York: Free Press
Mayer, T. 1999. *Monetary policy and the great inflation in the United States.* Cheltenham: Edward Elgar
Mayes, D. G. 2006. *The future of financial markets.* Basingstoke: Palgrave Macmillan
Mayes, D. G., Halme, L., and Liuksila, A. 2001. *Improving banking supervision.* Basingstoke: Palgrave
Mbowemi, T. T. 1999. 'Inflation targeting in South Africa', *South African Journal of Economics* **67**, 4: 400–9
McCallum, B. T. 1995. 'Two fallacies concerning central bank independence', *American Economic Review* **85**, 2: 207–11
McClam, W. D. 1978. 'Targets and techniques of monetary policy in Western Europe', *Banca Nazionale del Lavoro Quarterly Review* **124**: 3–27
McKenna, C. D. 2006. *The world's newest profession: management consulting in the twentieth century.* Cambridge University Press
McKinley, V. and Banaian, K. 2005. 'Central bank operational efficiency: meaning and measurement', in Courtis and Nicholl (eds.), pp. 167–82
McLeod, R. H. 2003. 'Towards improved monetary policy in Indonesia', *Bulletin of Indonesian Economic Studies* **39**, 3: 303–24

314   References

McNamara, K. 2002. 'Rational fictions: central bank independence and the social logic of delegation', *West European Politics* 25, 1: 47–76

Meek, P. (ed.) 1983. *Central bank views on monetary targeting.* New York: Federal Reserve Bank of New York

Mehrling, P. 2002. 'Retrospectives: economists and the Fed: beginnings', *Journal of Economic Perspectives* 16, 4: 207–18

Meltzer, A. H. 2003. *A history of the Federal Reserve*, vol. I, *1913–1951*. University of Chicago Press

   2005. 'Origins of the great inflation', *Federal Reserve Bank of St. Louis Review* 87, 2, part 2: 145–75

Mendzela, J. 2005. 'Why change?', in Courtis and Nicholl (eds.), pp. 15–27

Merrett, D. T. 1998. 'Capital markets and capital formation in Australia, 1945–1990', *Australian Economic History Review* 39, 2: 135–54

Meyer, R. H. 1970. *Bankers' diplomacy: monetary stabilization in the twenties.* New York: Columbia University Press

Mikesell, R. F. 1954. *Foreign exchange in the postwar world.* New York: Twentieth Century Fund

Miller, M. B. 2003. 'The business trip: maritime networks in the twentieth century', *Business History Review* 77, 1: 1–32

Milward, A. S. 1984. *The reconstruction of Western Europe.* London: Methuen

Mishkin, F. S. 1995. *Financial markets, institutions, and money.* New York: HarperCollins

   (ed.) 2001. *Prudential supervision: what works and what doesn't.* University of Chicago Press

   2008. 'Challenges for inflation targeting in emerging market countries', *Emerging Markets Finance & Trade* 44, 6: 5–16

Mishkin, F. S. and Posen, A. S. 1997. 'Inflation targeting: lessons from four countries', *Federal Reserve Bank of New York Economic Policy Review* 3, 3: 1–110

Mitchell, W. C. 1911. 'The publications of the National Monetary Commission', *Quarterly Journal of Economics* 25, 2: 563–93

Mitchener, K. J., Shizume, M., and Weidenmier, M. D. 2009. 'Why did countries adopt the gold standard? Lessons from Japan', NBER Working Paper No. 15195

Moggridge, D. E. 1969. *The return to gold, 1925: the formulation of economic policy and its critics.* London: Cambridge University Press

   1992. *Maynard Keynes: an economist's biography.* London: Routledge

Moggridge, D. E. and Howson, S. 1974. 'Keynes on monetary policy, 1910–1914', *Oxford Economic Papers* 26, 2: 226–47

Mooij, J. 2005. 'Corporate culture of central banks: lessons from the past', *Journal of European Economic History* 34, 1: 11–42

Morrell, K. G. 1979. 'Non-bank financial institutions, II: the market for long-term funds', in R. S. Deane and P. W. E. Nicholl (eds.), *Monetary policy and the New Zealand financial system.* Wellington: Reserve Bank of New Zealand, pp. 99–116

Mouré, K. 1992. 'The limits to central bank cooperation, 1916–36', *Contemporary European History* 1, 3: 259–79

   2002. *The gold standard illusion: France, the Bank of France, and the international gold standard, 1914–1939.* Oxford University Press

Muirhead, B. 1999. *Against the odds: the public life and times of Louis Rasminsky*. University of Toronto Press

Mundell, R. A. 2000. 'A reconsideration of the twentieth century', *American Economic Review* **90**, 3: 327–40

Munoz, S. 2007. 'Central bank quasi-fiscal losses and high inflation in Zimbabwe: a note', IMF Working Paper WP/07/98

Nakakita, T. 2001. 'Restructuring the Ministry of Finance and revising the Bank of Japan Law', *The Japanese Economy* **29**, 1: 48–86

Nash, G. D. 1959. 'Herbert Hoover and the origins of the Reconstruction Finance Corporation', *Mississippi Valley Historical Review* **46**, 3: 455–68

Nelson, E. 2005a. 'The great inflation of the 1970s: what really happened?' *Advances in Macroeconomics* **5**, 1, Article 3

  2005b. 'Monetary policy neglect and the great inflation in Canada, Australia, and New Zealand', *International Journal of Central Banking* **1**, 1: 133–79

  2007a. 'The great inflation and early disinflation in Japan and Germany', *International Journal of Central Banking* **3**, 4: 23–76

  2007b. 'Milton Friedman and U.S. monetary history: 1961–2006', *Federal Reserve Bank of St. Louis Review* **89**, 3: 153–82

  2008. 'Friedman and Taylor on monetary policy rules: a comparison', *Federal Reserve Bank of St. Louis Review* **90**, 2: 95–116

Nelson, R. H. 1987. 'The economics profession and the making of public policy', *Journal of Economic Literature* **25**, 1: 49–91

Neumann, M. J. M. 1999. 'Monetary stability: threat and proven response', in Deutsche Bundesbank (ed.), pp. 269–306

New York Times 1922. 'Four swam ashore in river of flame', 12 September

Nicholls, G. 2001. 'Central banking in the context of a currency union: a case study of the ECCB', *Social and Economic Studies* **50**, 3–4: 75–107

Niemeyer, O. 1931. *Banking and currency in New Zealand*. Wellington: Government Printer

Noble, G. W. and Ravenhill, J. (eds.) 2000. *The Asian financial crisis*. Cambridge University Press

Norman, M. 1932. 'Foreword', in Kisch and Elkin, pp. v–vi

Nurkse, R. 1944. *International currency experience*. Geneva: League of Nations

Oatley, T. and Nabors, R. 1998. 'Redistributive cooperation: market failure, wealth transfers, and the Basle Accord', *International Organization* **52**, 1: 35–54

Obstfeld, M., Shambaugh, J. C., and Taylor, A. M. 2004. 'Monetary sovereignty, exchange rates, and capital controls: the trilemma in the interwar period', *IMF Staff Papers* **51**: 75–108

Officer, L. 2001. 'Gold standard', EH.Net Encyclopedia, ed. R. Whaples, http://eh.net/encyclopedia/article/officer.gold.standard (accessed 22 August 2009)

Ohnuki, M. 2007. 'The Bank of Japan network and financial market integration: from the establishment of the Bank of Japan to the early 20th century', *Monetary and Economic Studies* **25**, 1: 95–127

Okazaki, T. 1995. 'The evolution of the financial system in post-war Japan', *Business History* **37**, 2: 90–106

Okina, K. 1999. 'Monetary policy under zero inflation: a response to criticisms and questions regarding monetary policy', *Monetary and Economic Studies* **17**, 3: 157–82

Oliver, M. J. 2007. 'Financial crises', in M. J. Oliver and D. H. Aldcroft (eds.), *Economic disasters of the twentieth century* Cheltenham: Edward Elgar, pp. 182–235

Olsson, U. and Jörnmark, J. 2007. 'The political economy of commercial banking in Sweden: a bird's eye view of the relations between industry and banking over 150 years', in P. L. Cottrell, E. Lange, and U. Olsson (eds.), *Centres and peripheries in banking*. Ashgate: Aldershot, pp. 197–210

Onado, M. 2003. 'Financial regulation in Europe and in Italy', in De Rosa (ed.), pp. 165–83

Orbell, J. 2004. 'Baring, (George) Rowland Stanley, third earl of Cromer (1918–1991)', in *Oxford dictionary of national biography*. Oxford University Press; online edn, January 2008, www.oxforddnb.com/view/article/49616 (accessed 17 April 2008)

Organisation for Economic Cooperation and Development 1974. *Monetary policy in the United States*. Paris: OECD

1983a. *Economic survey: New Zealand*. Paris: OECD

1983b. *The internationalisation of banking*. Paris: OECD

O'Rourke, K. H. and Williamson, J. G. 1999. *Globalization and history*. Cambridge, MA: MIT Press

Orphanides, A. 2002. 'Monetary policy rules and the great inflation', *American Economic Review* **92**, 2: 115–20

2003. 'Historical monetary policy analysis and the Taylor rule', *Journal of Monetary Economics* **50**, 5: 983–1022

2004. 'Monetary policy rules, macroeconomic stability and inflation: a view from the trenches', *Journal of Money, Credit and Banking* **36**, 2: 151–75

Osterloo, S. and de Haan, J. 2004. 'Central banks and financial stability: a survey', *Journal of Financial Stability* **1**: 257–73

Padoa-Schioppa, T. 1994. *The road to monetary union in Europe: the emperor, the kings and the genies*. Oxford: Clarendon Press

1999. 'EMU and banking supervision: lecture by Tommaso Padoa-Schioppa, Member of the Executive Board of the European Central Bank, at the London School of Economics, Financial Markets Group on 24 February 1999', www.ecb.int/press/key/date/1999/html/sp990224.en.html# (accessed 1 July 2009)

Page, O. 2005. 'Foreword', in J. Tattersall and R. Smith (eds.), *A practitioner's guide to the Basel Accord*. Old Woking: City & Financial Publishing, pp. xvii–xxii

Page, S. (ed.) 1993. *Monetary policy in developing countries*. London: Routledge

Palgrave, R. H. I. 1894. *Dictionary of political economy*, vol. I. London: Macmillan,

1903. *Bank rate and the money market*. London: John Murray

Parker, R. E. (ed.) 2002. *Reflections on the Great Depression*. Cheltenham: Edward Elgar

2007. *The economics of the Great Depression: a twenty-first century look back at the economics of the interwar period*. Cheltenham: Edward Elgar

Patrick, H. T. 1965. 'External equilibrium and internal convertibility: financial policy in Meiji Japan', *Journal of Economic History* **25**, 2: 187–213
Paul, R. 2009a. *End the Fed*. New York: Grand Central
2009b. 'Fed audit will show what they're hiding', www.ronpaul.com/2009–
08–01/fed-audit-will-show-what-theyre-hiding/ (accessed 6 August
2009)
Pauly, L. W. 1988. *Opening financial markets: banking politics on the Pacific Rim.*
Ithaca, NY: Cornell University Press
1997. *Who elected the bankers? Surveillance and control in the world economy.*
Ithaca, NY: Cornell University Press
Pazos, F. 1972. *Chronic inflation in Latin America*. New York: Praeger
Peden, G. C. 2000. *The Treasury and British public policy, 1906–1959*. Oxford
University Press
Persson, T. and Tabellini, G. 1993. 'Designing institutions for monetary sta-
bility', *Carnegie-Rochester Conference Series on Public Policy* **39**: 53–84
Péteri, G. 1992. 'Central bank diplomacy: Montagu Norman and central
Europe's monetary reconstruction after World War I', *Contemporary
European History* **1**, 3: 233–58
Phelps, E. S. 1967. 'Phillips curves, expectations of inflation, and optimal
unemployment over time', *Economica* **34**, 3: 254–81
Pigou, A.C. 1921. *The political economy of war*. London: Macmillan
Plantier, C. and Scrimgeour, D. 2002. 'The Taylor rule and its relevance to
New Zealand monetary policy', *RBNZ Bulletin* **65**, 1: 5–13
Plessis, A. 1992. 'Bankers in French society, 1860s–1960s', in Y. Cassis (ed.),
Finance and financiers in European history 1880–1960. Cambridge University
Press, pp. 147–60
2007. 'The Banque de France and the emergence of a national financial mar-
ket in France during the nineteenth century', in P. L. Cottrell, E. Lange,
and U. Olsson (eds.), *Centres and peripheries in banking*. Aldershot: Ashgate,
pp. 143–60
Plumptre, A. F. W. 1940. *Central banking in the British dominions*. University of
Toronto Press
Pollard, P. S. 2003. 'A look inside two central banks: the European Central
Bank and the Federal Reserve', *Federal Reserve Bank of St. Louis Review*
85, 2: 11–30
Posen, A. S. 1995. 'Declarations are not enough: financial sector sources of cen-
tral bank independence', in B. Bernanke and J. Rotemberg (eds.), *NBER
Macroeconomics Annual 1995*. Cambridge, MA: MIT Press, pp. 253–74
Prast, H. M. 2003. 'Financial stability and efficiency in the twentieth cen-
tury: the Netherlands', in De Rosa (ed.), pp. 185–204
Price, L. 1998. 'The responsibilities of central banks in the transition economies', *Journal of International Development* **10**: 643–57
Rajan, R. G. and Zingales, L. 2003. 'The great reversals: the politics of financial development in the twentieth century', *Journal of Financial Economics*
69: 5–50
Rasminsky, L. 1987. 'The role of the central banker today', in P. Ciocca (ed.),
Money and the economy: central bankers' views. Basingstoke: Macmillan,
pp. 57–78

Reddell, M. 1999. 'Origins and early development of the inflation target', *RBNZ Bulletin* **62**, 3: 63–71

Reid, M. 1982. *The secondary banking crisis, 1973–75.* London: Macmillan

Reinhart, C. and Felton, A. (eds.) 2008. *The first global financial crisis of the 21st century.* London: VoxEU Publications

Reinhart, C. and Savastano, M. A. 2003. 'The realities of modern hyperinflation', *Finance and Development* **40**, 2: 20–3

Reis, J. 2007. 'An "art", not a "science"? Central bank management in Portugal under the gold standard, 1863–1871', *Economic History Review* **60**, 4: 712–41

Reserve Bank of New Zealand 1963. *Money and banking in New Zealand.* Wellington: RBNZ

1986. *Financial policy reform.* Wellington: RBNZ

1989. *Annual report 1989.* Wellington: RBNZ

1993a. 'Interview with Don Brash', *RBNZ Bulletin* **56**, 3: 284–90

1993b. *Monetary policy and the New Zealand financial system,* 3rd edn. Wellington: RBNZ

1994. 'The way we were', *Bank Notes* 44, 4 August

1999. 'New Policy Targets Agreement', www.rbnz.govt.nz/news/1999/0092613.html (accessed 8 October 2009)

RBNZ Archives 1972. Box A0071: 'Inflation in New Zealand', 6 November 1972

1986. 'Board minutes', 13 March

Rhodes, J. R. and Yoshino, N. 1999. 'Window guidance by the Bank of Japan', *Contemporary Economic Policy* **17**, 2: 166–76

Rich, G. 2003. 'Swiss monetary targeting 1974–1996: the role of internal policy analysis', ECB Working Paper No. 236

Richter, R. 1999. 'German monetary policy as reflected in the academic debate', in Deutsche Bundesbank (ed.), pp. 525–71

Riefler, W. R. 1936. 'The dilemma of central banking as illustrated in recent literature', *Quarterly Journal of Economics* **50**, 4: 706–18

Riles, A. 2001. 'Real time: governing the market after the failure of knowledge', *Northwestern Law Legal Working Paper Series. Law and Economics Papers.* Working Paper No. 41, law.bepress.com/nwwps/lep/art41 (accessed 1 October 2009)

2004. 'Real time: unwinding technocratic and anthropological knowledge', *American Ethnologist* **31**, 3: 392–405

Ritter, L. S. 1980. 'Allan Sproul 1896–1978: a tower of strength', in L. S. Ritter (ed.), *Selected papers of Allan Sproul.* New York: Federal Reserve Bank of New York, pp. 1–21

Roberts, P. 1998. ' "Quis custodiet ipsos custodes?" The Federal Reserve System's founding fathers and allied finances in the First World War', *Business History Review* **72**, 4: 585–620

2000. 'Benjamin Strong, the Federal Reserve, and the limits to interwar American nationalism: Part I: Intellectual profile of a central banker', *Federal Reserve Bank of Richmond Economic Quarterly* **86**, 1: 61–76

Roberts, R. 1995. 'The Bank of England and the City', in R. Roberts and D. Kynaston (eds.), *The Bank of England: money, power and influence, 1694–1994.* Oxford: Clarendon Press, pp. 152–84

References

Robertson, P. L. and Singleton, J. 2001. 'The Commonwealth as an economic network', *Australian Economic History Review* **41**, 3: 241–66

Robertson, R. R. 1968. *The Comptroller and bank supervision*. Washington, DC: Office of the Comptroller of the Currency

Rockwood, C. E. 1969. *National incomes policy for inflation control*. Tallahassee: Florida State University Press

Rodgers, P. 1998. 'The Bank of England Act', *Bank of England Quarterly Bulletin* **38**, 2: 93–6

Rogoff, K. 1985. 'The optimal degree of commitment to an intermediate monetary target', *Quarterly Journal of Economics* **100**, 4: 1169–89

Roll, E. 1993. *Independent and accountable: a new mandate for the Bank of England*. London: Centre for Economic Policy Research

Romer, C. D. 1992. 'What ended the Great Depression?', *Journal of Economic History* **52**, 4: 757–84

Romer, C. D. and Romer, D. H. 2002a. 'The evolution of economic understanding and postwar stabilization policy', NBER Working Paper No. 9274

2002b. 'A rehabilitation of monetary policy in the 1950s', *American Economic Review* **92**, 2: 121–27

2004. 'Choosing the Federal Reserve chair: lessons from history', *Journal of Economic Perspectives* **18**, 1: 129–61

Rosati, S. and Secola, S. 2006. 'Explaining cross-border large-value payment flows: evidence from TARGET and EURO1 data', *Journal of Banking and Finance* **30**, 6: 1753–82

Rose, A. 2007. 'A stable international monetary system emerges: inflation targeting is Bretton Woods, reversed', *Journal of International Money and Finance* **26**, 5: 663–81

Rosenberg, E. S. 1998. 'Revisiting dollar diplomacy: narratives of money and manliness', *Diplomatic History* **22**, 2: 177–98

Rosenbluth, F. M. 1989. *Financial politics in contemporary Japan*. Ithaca, NY: Cornell University Press

Ross, D. M. 2004. 'Domestic monetary policy and the banking system in the UK 1945–1971', in R. Michie and P. Williamson (eds.), *The British government and the City of London in the twentieth century*. Cambridge University Press, pp. 298–321

Rowse, T. 2002. *Nugget Coombs: a reforming life*. Cambridge University Press

Sacerdoti, E. 1991. 'Central bank operations and independence in a monetary union: BCEAO and BEAC', in P. Downes and R. Vaez-Zadeh (eds.), *The evolving role of central banks*. Washington, DC: IMF, pp. 147–66

Sachs, J. D. 1986. 'The Bolivian hyperinflation and stabilization', NBER Working Paper 2073

Sanchez-Arroyo, A. 1996. 'The Mexican payment and settlement system: the quality and quantity leaps ahead', *North American Journal of Economics and Finance* **7**, 2: 171–9

Santaella, J. A. 1993. 'Stabilization programs and external enforcement: experience from the 1920s', *IMF Staff Papers* **40**, 3: 584–21

Sayers, R. S. 1957. *Central banking after Bagehot*. Oxford: Clarendon Press

1958. *Modern banking*, 4th edn. Oxford: Clarendon Press

1961. 'Alternative views of central banking', *Economica* **28**, 110: 111–24

1968. *Gilletts in the London money market, 1867–1967.* Oxford: Clarendon Press

1976. *The Bank of England, 1891–1944,* 3 vols. Cambridge University Press

Schacht, H. 1955. *My first seventy-six years.* London: Allan Wingate

Schedvin, C. B. 1992. *In reserve: central banking in Australia, 1945–75.* St Leonards NSW: Allen & Unwin

Scheller, H. K. 2004. *The European Central Bank: history, role and functions.* Frankfurt am Main: ECB

Schenk, C. R. 1992. 'The sterling area and British policy alternatives in the 1950s', *Contemporary Record* **6**, 2: 266–86

1993. 'The origins of a central bank in Malaya and the transition to independence, 1954–59', *Journal of Imperial and Commonwealth History* **21**, 2: 409–31

1994. *Britain and the sterling area.* London: Routledge

1997. 'Monetary institutions in newly independent countries: the experience of Malaya, Ghana and Nigeria in the 1950s', *Financial History Review* **4**, 2: 181–98

2002. 'Banks and the emergence of Hong Kong as an international financial centre', *Journal of International Financial Markets, Institutions and Money* **12**, 4–5: 321–40

2004. 'The new City and the state in the 1960s', in R, Michie and Philip Williamson (eds), *The British government and the City of London in the twentieth century.* Cambridge University Press, pp. 322–39

2008. 'Malaysia and the end of the Bretton Woods system 1965–72: disentangling from sterling', *Journal of Imperial and Commonwealth History* **36**, 2: 197–220

2010. *The decline of sterling: managing the retreat of an international currency, 1945–1992.* Cambridge University Press.

Schiltz, M. 2006. 'An "ideal bank of issue": the Banque Nationale de Belgique as a model for the Bank of Japan', *Financial History Review* **13**, 2: 179–96

Schloss, H. H. 1958. *The Bank for International Settlements: an experiment in central bank cooperation.* Amsterdam: North-Holland

Schnabel. I. 2004. 'The German twin crisis of 1931', *Journal of Economic History* **64**, 3: 822–71

Schubert, A. 1992. *The Credit Anstalt crisis of 1931.* New York: Cambridge University Press

1999. 'The emergence of national central banks in central Europe after the break-up of the Austro-Hungarian monarchy', in Holtfrerich, Reis, and Toniolo (eds.), pp. 186–230

Schultz, F. H. 2005. 'The changing role of the Federal Reserve', *Federal Reserve Bank of St. Louis Review* **87**, 2, part 2: 343–8

Schwartz, A. J. 1993. 'Currency boards: their past, present and possible future role', *Carnegie-Rochester Conference Series on Public Policy* **39**: 147–87

Scott, W. A. 1914. 'Banking reserves under the Federal Reserve Act', *Journal of Political Economy* **22**, 4: 332–44

Seidel, R. N. 1972. 'American reformers abroad: the Kemmerer Missions in South America', *Journal of Economic History* **32**, 2: 520–45

Shih, V. C. 2008. *Factions and finance in China.* Cambridge University Press

Shughart, W. F. and Tollison, R. D. 1986. 'Preliminary evidence on the use of inputs by the Federal Reserve System', in Toma and Toma (eds.), pp. 67–90

Sijben, J. J. 2002a 'Regulation and market discipline in banking supervision: an overview – part 1', *Journal of International Banking Regulation* 3, 4: 363–80

2002b 'Regulation and market discipline in banking supervision: an overview – part 2', *Journal of International Banking Regulation* 4, 1: 55–71

Siklos, P. L. 2002. *The changing face of central banking*. Cambridge University Press

2008. 'Inflation targeting around the world', *Emerging Markets Finance & Trade* 44, 6: 17–37

Simha, S. L. N. 1970. *History of the Reserve Bank of India (1935–51)*. Bombay: Reserve Bank of India

Simmons, B. 1993. 'Why innovate? Founding the Bank for International Settlements', *World Politics* 45, 3: 361–405

2001. 'The international politics of harmonization: the case of capital market regulation', *International Organization* 55, 3: 589–620

2008. 'The future of central bank cooperation', in Borio, Toniolo, and Clement (eds.), pp. 174–210

Simons, H. C. 1936. 'Rules versus authorities in monetary policy', *Journal of Political Economy* 44, 1: 1–30

Singleton, J. 1995. 'Labour, the Conservatives and nationalisation', in R. Millward and J. Singleton (eds.), *The political economy of nationalisation in Britain 1920–50*. Cambridge University Press, pp. 13–33

1998. 'Anglo-New Zealand financial relations, 1945–61', *Financial History Review* 5: 139–57

2006. 'The central bank and government partnership in Australia and New Zealand since the 1930s', in G. Boyce, S. Mcintyre, and S. Ville (eds.), *How organisations connect*. Melbourne University Press, pp. 100–22

2007. 'Destruction and misery … the First World War', in M. J. Oliver and D. H. Aldcroft (eds.), *Economic disasters of the twentieth century*. Cheltenham: Edward Elgar, pp. 9–50

2009. 'The winds of change for central banks? The impact of economic crises on the central banking world'. Paper presented at the workshop on the global financial crisis: historical perspectives and implications for New Zealand, Reserve Bank of New Zealand, June

Singleton, J., with Grimes, A., Hawke, G., and Holmes, F. 2006. *Innovation and independence: the Reserve Bank of New Zealand, 1973–2002*. Auckland University Press

Singleton, J. and P. L. Robertson 2002. *Economic relations between Britain and Australasia 1945–1970*. Basingstoke: Palgrave

Skidelsky, R. 1994. *John Maynard Keynes: the economist as saviour 1920–1937*. London: Papermac

Small, D. H. and Clouse, J. A. 2004. 'The scope of monetary policy actions authorized under the Federal Reserve Act', Board of Governors of the Federal Reserve System Research Paper Series – FEDS Papers 2004–40

Smith, V. C. 1936. *The rationale of central banking*. London: P. S. King

Snowdon, B. 2002. *Conversations on growth, stability and trade*. Cheltenham: Edward Elgar

Solomon, R. 1982. *The international monetary system, 1945–1981*. New York: Harper & Row

Solomon, S. 1995. *The confidence game: how unelected central bankers are governing the changed global economy*. New York: Simon & Schuster

Sommariva, A. and Tullio, G. 1987. *German macroeconomic history 1880–1979*. New York: St Martin's Press

Spence, J. D. 1981. *The gate of heavenly peace: the Chinese and their revolution 1895–1980*. New York: Viking

Sprague, O. M. W. 1914. 'The Federal Reserve Act of 1913', *Quarterly Journal of Economics* **28**, 2: 213–54

Sproul, A. 1967. 'Coordination of economic policy', *Journal of Finance* **22**, 2: 137–46

   1980. 'The "Accord" – a landmark in the first fifty years of the Federal Reserve System', in L. S. Ritter (ed.) *Selected papers of Allan Sproul*. New York: Federal Reserve Bank of New York, pp. 51–73

St-Amant, P., Tkacz, G., Guérard-Langlois, A., and Morel, L. 2005. 'Quantity, quality, and relevance: central bank research, 1990–2003', Bank of Canada Working Paper 2005-37

Stern, K. 1999. 'The note-issuing bank within the state structure', in Deutsche Bundesbank (ed.), pp. 103–64

Stewart, H. 2009. 'This is how we let the credit crunch happen, Ma'am', *The Observer*, 26 July, www.guardian.co.uk/uk/2009/jul/26/monarchy-credit-crunch (accessed 26 July 2009)

Stiglitz, J. E. 1998. 'Central banking in a democratic society', *De Economist* **146**, 2: 199–226

Stiglitz, J. E. and Uy, M. 1996. 'Financial markets, public policy, and the East Asian miracle', *World Bank Research Observer* **11**, 2: 249–76

Stockwell, E. (ed.) 1989. *Working at the Board, 1920–1970*. Washington, DC: Board of Governors of the Federal Reserve

Stockwell, S. E. 1998. 'Instilling the "Sterling Tradition": decolonization and the creation of a central bank in Ghana', *Journal of Imperial and Commonwealth History* **26**, 2: 100–19

Strakosch, H. 1921. 'The South African Reserve Bank', *Economic Journal* **31**, 122: 172–8

Streit, M. E. 1999. 'German monetary union', in Deutsche Bundesbank (ed.), pp. 639–81

Summers, B. J. (ed.) 1994. *The payment system: design, management, and supervision*. Washington, DC: International Monetary Fund

Sutton, M. 1984. 'Indonesia, 1966–70', in Killick (ed.), pp. 68–114

Svensson, L. E. O. 1997. 'Inflation targeting in an open economy: strict or flexible inflation targeting?', RBNZ Discussion Paper G97/8

   2001. *Independent review of the operation of monetary policy in New Zealand: report to the Minister of Finance*. Wellington: New Zealand Treasury

   2003. 'What is wrong with Taylor rules? Using judgment in monetary policy through targeting rules', *Journal of Economic Literature* **41**, 2: 426–77

Sylla, R. 1988. 'The autonomy of monetary authorities: the case of the U.S. Federal Reserve System', in Toniolo (ed.), pp. 17–38

Tabellini, G. 2008. 'Why central banking is no longer boring', http://voxeu. org/index.php?q=node/1259 (accessed 2 July 2009)

Takagi, S. 2007. 'Managing flexibility: Japanese exchange rate policy, 1971–2007', *Singapore Economic Review* **52**, 3: 335–61

Takeda, M. and Turner, P. 1992. 'The liberalization of Japan's financial markets: some major themes', *BIS Economic Papers* 34

Tamaki, N. 1995. *Japanese banking: a history, 1859–1959*. Cambridge University Press

Taylor, J. B. 1993. 'Discretion versus policy rules in practice', *Carnegie-Rochester Series on Public Policy* **39**: 195–214

2009. 'The financial crisis and the policy responses: an empirical analysis of what went wrong', NBER Working Paper No. 14631

Taylor, J. B. (ed.) 1999. *Monetary policy rules*. University of Chicago Press

Temin, P. 1989. *Lessons from the Great Depression*. Cambridge, MA: MIT Press

Thatcher, M. 1993. *The Downing Street years*. London: HarperCollins

Thirlwall, A. P. 1980. *Balance of payments theory and the United Kingdom experience*. London: Macmillan

Thornton, D. L. 2006. 'When did the Fed begin targeting the Federal Funds Rate? What the verbatim transcripts tell us', *Journal of Money, Credit and Banking* **38**, 8: 2039–71

Thygesen, N. 1989. 'The Delors Report and European Economic and Monetary Union', *International Affairs* **65**, 4: 637–52

Times, The 1903. 'Shooting outrage at the Bank of England', 25 November, p. 11

Toma, E. F. and Toma, M. (eds.) 1986. *Central bankers, bureaucratic incentives and monetary policy*. Dordrecht: Kluwer

Tomasson, G. 1970. 'Indonesia: economic stabilization, 1966–69', *Finance & Development* **7**, 4: 46–53

Toniolo, G. (ed.) 1988. *Central bank independence in historical perspective*. Berlin: Walter de Gruyter

Toniolo, G. 2005. *Central bank cooperation at the Bank for International Settlements, 1930–1973*. Cambridge University Press

Treasury and Civil Service Committee 1993–4. *First report on the role of the Bank of England*, vol. I. London: HMSO

Trescott, P. B. 1995. 'The money doctor in China: Edwin Kemmerer's commission of financial experts, 1929', in W. J. Samuels and J. E. Biddle (eds.), *Research in the history of economic thought and methodology*, vol. XIII, Greenwich, CT: JAI Press, pp. 125–58

2007. *Jingji Xue: the history of the introduction of western economic ideas into China, 1850–1950*. Hong Kong: Chinese University Press

Trichet, J.-C. 2004. 'Foreword', in H. K. Scheller, *The European Central Bank: history, role and functions*. Frankfurt am Main: ECB, pp. 9–10

Tsoukalis, L. 1977. *The politics and economics of European monetary integration*. London: George Allen & Unwin

Turner, J. D. 2000, 'The Hayekian approach to banking supervision in New Zealand', *Annals of Public and Cooperative Economics* **71**, 1: 105–25

Uche, C. U. 1997. 'Bank of England vs the IBRD: did the Nigerian colony deserve a central bank?', *Explorations in Economic History* 34: 220–41

Ungerer, H. 1997. *A concise history of European monetary integration: from EPU to EMU*. Westport, CT: Greenwood

Van Dormael, A. 1978. *Bretton Woods: birth of a monetary system*. London: Macmillan

Vaubel, R. 1997. 'The bureaucratic and partisan behaviour of independent central banks: German and international evidence', *European Journal of Political Economy* 13, 2: 201–24

Végh, C. A. 1992. 'Stopping high inflation: an analytical overview', *IMF Staff Papers* 39, 6: 26–95

Verdun, A. 1999. 'The role of the Delors Committee in the creation of EMU: an epistemic community?', *Journal of European Public Policy* 6, 2: 308–28

Vicarelli, F. 1988. 'Central bank autonomy: a historical perspective', in Toniolo (ed.), pp. 1–16

Vittas, D. and Wang, B. 1991. 'Credit policies in Japan and Korea', World Bank Policy Research Working Paper Series No. 747

Volcker, P. A. 1978. 'The role of monetary targets in an age of inflation', *Journal of Monetary Economics* 4, 2: 329–39

  2000, 'Commanding heights PBS interview with Paul Volcker', www.pbs.org/wgbh/commandingheights/shared/minitextlo/int_paulvolcker.html (accessed 4 April 2008)

Volcker, P. A. and Gyohten, T. 1992. *Changing fortunes: the world's money and the threat to American leadership*. New York: Times Books

von Furstenberg, G. M. and Ulan, M. K. 1998. *Learning from the world's best central bankers*. Boston, MA: Kluwer

von Hagen, J. 1999. 'A new approach to monetary policy (1971–8)', in Deutsche Bundesbank (ed.), pp. 403–38

Walsh, C. 1995a. 'Is New Zealand's Reserve Bank Act of 1989 an optimal central bank contract?', *Journal of Money, Credit and Banking* 27, 4: 1179–91

  1995b. 'Optimal contracts for central bankers', *American Economic Review* 85, 1: 150–67

Walters, A. A. 1986. *Britain's economic renaissance*. Oxford University Press

Watts, G. S. 1972. 'Government of Canada Treasury bills', *Bank of Canada Review* May: 3–13

  1993. *The Bank of Canada: origins and early history*, ed. T. K. Rymes. Ottawa: Carleton University Press

Wei, H. 1992. 'China's central banking system, 1949–1990: a historical analysis with comparisons with Indian central banking', Ph.D. thesis, University of Tennessee.

Weise, C. L. 2008. 'Political constraints on monetary policy during the great inflation', MPRA Paper No. 8694

Weitz, J. 1997. *Hitler's banker: Hjalmar Horace Greeley Schacht*. New York: Little, Brown

Weller, P. 1989. *Malcolm Fraser PM: a study in prime ministerial power in Australia*. Ringwood, Vic.: Penguin

Werner, R. A. 2002. 'Aspects of career development and information manage-
ment policies at the Bank of Japan', *The Japanese Economy* **30**, 6: 38–60
    2003. *Princes of the yen: Japan's central bankers and the transformation of the
    economy.* Armonk, NY: M. E. Sharpe
West, R. C. 1983. 'The evolution and devolution of bank regulation in the
United States', *Journal of Economic Issues* **17**, 2: 361–7
Wetterberg, G. 2009. *Money and power: from Stockholms Banco 1656 to Sveriges
Riksbank today.* Stockholm: Sveriges Riksbank/Atlantis
White, B. 1997. 'Preparing for natural disasters – where does the Reserve Bank
fit in?', *RBNZ Bulletin* **60**, 4: 332–41
White, L. H. 1989. *Competition and currency: essays on free banking and money.*
New York University Press
    1991. 'Banking without a central bank: Scotland before 1844 as a "free bank-
    ing" system', in F. Capie and G. E. Wood (eds.), *Unregulated banking: chaos
    or order?* New York: St Martin's Press, pp. 37–62
Whittlesey, C. R. 1963. 'Power and influence in the Federal Reserve System',
Economica **30**, 117: 33–44
Wicker, E. 1966. 'Federal Reserve monetary policy, 1922–33: a reinterpret-
ation', *Journal of Political Economy* **73**, 4: 325–43
    2005. *The great debate on banking reform: Nelson Aldrich and the origins of the
    Fed.* Columbus: Ohio State University Press
Willett, T. D. 1990. 'Studying the Fed: towards a broader public choice per-
spective', in T. Mayer (ed.), *The political economy of American monetary pol-
icy.* Cambridge University Press, pp. 13–25
Williams, J. H. 1978. *Postwar monetary plans and other essays.* New York:
Arno
Williamson, P. 2004. 'The City of London and government in modern
Britain: debates and politics', in R. Michie and P. Williamson (eds.), *The
British government and the City of London in the twentieth century.* Cambridge
University Press, pp. 5–30
Wolf, H. C., Ghosh, A. R., Berger, H., and Gulde, A.-M. 2008. *Currency boards
in retrospect and prospect.* Cambridge, MA: MIT Press
Wood, D. 2005. *Governing global banking: the Basel Committee and the politics of
financial globalization.* Aldershot: Ashgate
Wood, G. E. 2000. 'The lender of last resort reconsidered', *Journal of Financial
Services Research* **18**, 2/3: 203–27
Wood, J. H. 2005. *A history of central banking in Great Britain and the United
States.* Cambridge University Press
Woodward, B. 2000. *Maestro: Greenspan's Fed and the American boom.* New
York: Simon & Schuster
Woolley, J. T. 1984. *Monetary politics: the Federal Reserve and the politics of mon-
etary policy.* Cambridge University Press
World Bank 1993. *The East Asian miracle.* Washington, DC: World Bank
Wright, M. 2006. 'The policy origins of the Reserve Bank of New Zealand',
Reserve Bank of New Zealand Bulletin **69**, 3: 5–22
Wyplosz, C. 1997. 'EMU: why and how it might happen', *Journal of Economic
Perspectives* **11**, 4: 3–21

Yaffe, H. 2009. *Che Guevara: the economics of revolution*. Basingstoke: Palgrave Macmillan

Yilmazkuday, H. 2008. 'Structural breaks in monetary policy rules: evidence from transition countries', *Emerging Markets Finance & Trade* **44**, 6: 87–97

Yohe, W. P. 1990. 'The intellectual milieu at the Federal Reserve Board in the 1920s', *History of Political Economy* **22**, 3, 465–88

Zhang, X. 2005. 'The changing politics of central banking in Taiwan and Thailand', *Pacific Affairs* **78**, 3: 377–401

Zijlstra, J. 1985. *Jelle Zijsltra, a central banker's view*. Hingham, MA: Kluwer

Index

Abdullah, Burhanuddin, 219
Abrams, Burton, 21
accountability, 2, 11, 14, 48, 125, 171,
    205, 206, 207, 208, 221, 284
Addis, Sir Charles, 95
Adenauer, Konrad, 124
Aldrich, Nelson, 52, 53, 54
Aldrich Vreeland Act 1908, 52
amakaduri, 139
Amin, Idi, 173
Archer, David, 248
Arkell Smith, Sir Osborne, 67
Asfura, Victoria, 20
Asian Development Bank, 182
Asian financial crisis, 218, 224, 227, 252
Austrian National Bank, 59, 83, 105, 123
Austro-Hungarian central bank, 59, 259,
    260

Bagehot, Walter, 41
Balasubramanyam, V. N., 31
Ball, George, 163
Balls, Ed, 215
Banco de la República (Colombia), 60
Banco do Brasil, 169
Bank Bali scandal, 219
Bank deutscher Lander, 123, 124
Bank for International Settlements, 9, 30,
    92, 96, 105, 106, 147
  alleged collaboration with Nazis, 107,
    147, 149
  debate over liquidation 1940s, 153
  establishment, 103-4
  ethos and principles, 95
  exclusion of developing countries, 182
  expands membership and role 1960s,
    161
  rehabilitation after Second World War,
    155-8
  relations with IMF, World Bank,
    FRBNY, 155
  search for new role after 1931, 107

Second World War, 147-9
  services to EPU, 156-7
  support for Basel Committee, 232, 233
  warns of heightened risk early twenty-
    first century, 279, 281
Bank Indonesia, 172, 180, 218-19, 234
Bank Negara Malaysia, 168, 182
Bank of Canada, 65, 134, 142, 145, 152,
    159, 220, 250, 251
  Coyne affair, 29-30
Bank of Chosun, 176
Bank of Credit and Commerce
    International, 232
Bank of Danzig, 105
Bank of England, 19, 31, 34, 57, 74, 99,
    102, 284
  accountability, 216
  at 1900, 38-41
  attitude to economists, 80, 145
  Bank Act 1844, 39
  Bank of England Act 1998, 214, 215
  Bank Rate, 40, 42, 84, 86, 118
  bank regulation by consent, 133
  Basel Committee, 232, 234
  BCCI, 232
  Che Guevara, assessment of, 17
  Competition and Credit Control 1971,
    224
  conductor of the orchestra, 99
  convertibility episode 1947, 154
  Czech gold, 107
  departure from gold 1931, 84-5
  Empire letters, 96
  EMU, 263, 264, 268
  establishment of central banks in British
    dominions, 61-5
  establishment of central banks in central
    Europe after 1918, 59
  establishment of central banks in
    developing countries, 166-9
  euromarkets, 120, 160, 224
  European Monetary System, 243

327

Printed in the United States
By Bookmasters